Cultural Analysis, Cultural Studies, and the Law

D1621844

Contents

III Reading Legal Events

Cultural Analysis, Cultural Studies, and the Law

Cultural Analysis, Cultural Studies, and the Situation of Legal Scholarship

Austin Sarat and Jonathan Simon

E verywhere, it seems, culture is in ascendance. More and more social groups are claiming to have distinctive cultures and are demanding recognition of their cultural distinctiveness. Identity politics has merged with cultural politics so that to have an identity one must now also have a culture.[1] As a result, it sometimes seems as if almost every ethnic, religious, or social group seeks to have its "culture" recognized, and for precisely this reason the cultural itself has become a subject of political life to a greater extent than in the past.

The Death of the Social and the Turn to Culture

The backlash against the proliferation of cultures and identities, and what is called the "politics of recognition,"[2] has been vehement. Politicians proclaim "culture wars" in an effort to reassert both the meaning and centrality of certain allegedly transcendent human values.[3] Debates about the meaning and significance of culture become arguments about "civilization" itself, in which acknowledgment of cultural pluralism and its accompanying decanonization of the "sacred" texts of the Western tradition is treated as undermining national unity, national purpose, and the meaning of being "American."[4] Political contests are increasingly fought over values and symbols, with different parties advancing different cultural programs.[5]

With the decline of ideology as an organizing force in international relations, culture seems to provide another vantage point from which to understand new polarities.[6] In addition, the cache of the cultural is increasingly resonant in public policy where traditional goals like reducing crime and poverty are giving way to cultural goals like reducing fear of crime and eliminating the culture of dependency. The cultural is the implicit and explicit space of intervention for popular new strategies like "community policing"[7] and "workfare"[8] that promise to improve objective problems by altering the attitudes and experiences of the subjects of policing and welfare. Government and other formal organizations believe that it is essential to have cultural strategies in order to more effectively govern their employees and customers and to influence their broader popular image. The twentieth century familiarized us with the idea of propaganda and the fact that political forces had to utilize mass communications to realize their power. Today, however, the cultural has become more than a supplement or a delivery vehicle; it is quite literally where the action is.[9]

In the academy, sociologists, political scientists, and lawyers today find themselves invoking "culture" more often at the expense of, and in response to, a sense of emergent crisis, with their own master references like "the social," "public opinion," and "law." The cultural, in short, comes as a stand-in for interpretive grids that can no longer be effectively utilized. It is also emerging in the current retail boom in the United States, where the commodity nature of goods is increasingly acknowledged and marketed as such.[10] Indeed, Etienne Balibar has suggested that "culturalism" is a central logic of late capitalism.[11]

This turn to culture is but one sign of the decline of the social as central to the logic of governance throughout societies of the West. By "the social," we mean to invoke the conviction, so widely held in the West since the Renaissance, that the collective character of human populations determines history in ways not reducible to external factors like religion, sovereignty, or climate; we also mean to invoke the incredibly diverse range of discourses and forms of expertise that have occupied this field ever since. Some scholars now speak of the "death of the social."[12] One need not endorse so dramatic a view to acknowledge that the social in this historically specific sense faces increasing competition and challenges to its legitimacy. This decline comes after the end of a period that reached its peak in 1960s and 1970s, when governments in the advanced industrial societies sought to self-consciously govern through the social, a strategy sometimes described as "the social welfare state" or the "social activist state." During that period, the liberal rationality of government associated with laissez-faire and methodological individualism was generally reordered around the social as a terrain of positive knowledge and for effective governmental intervention. Thus social liberalism produced a powerful fusion of law, social science, and government.

However, after decades in which social problems, poverty, labor exploitation, and crime, for example, set the agenda of government, the social itself has come to be defined as a problem to be solved by reconfiguring government.[13] The general decline in confidence in virtually every institution and program of reform, or knowledge gathering, attached to the social is one of the most striking features of our present situation. Social work, social insurance, social policy, and social justice, once expected to be engines of building a more rational and modern society, are today seen as ineffectual and incoherent. Socialism, once taken to be a very real competitor with liberalism as a program of modern governance, has virtually disappeared from the field of contemporary politics. Whereas the social sciences—and especially sociology (the most social)—had become court sciences at the highest levels in the 1960s and 1970s, they are today largely absent from national government and are experiencing their own internal drift and discontent.

The United States, where both authors live and work, clearly represents the extreme case of the problematization of the social. The most florid forms of the social, such as social insurance, public transportation and housing, public health and social medicine, as well as socialism, were never as actively embraced by American state or federal governments as they were in comparably industrialized societies in Europe, Japan, Australia, and the Americas. Moreover, in no society was the political critique of the social as successful as it was in the United States under presidents like Ronald Reagan, George Bush I, and Bill Clinton. It is clear, however, that the crisis of the social is being experienced globally today, not only in the formerly welfarist Western nations but also in those states now industrializing. Where the social survives more intact than in the United States, one might expect to find the intellectual trends we describe here less well entrenched and more resisted.

Traditionally, law has had an important set of relationships to the state through the complex mechanisms of sovereignty, but in the twentieth century law became not just an expertise about sovereignty but also an expertise about governance, a currency that brought law into competition and collaboration with the social sciences. The social sciences likewise established themselves as important adjuncts to governance in part through the mediation of law (and to a lesser degree medicine), including criminology, social work, and public health, and later every aspect of economic and general policy.[14] Legal studies[15] never collapsed into pure policy studies, whatever the ambitions of some may have been, but to a great extent its critical efficacy came from its relationships with governance.[16]

In making these claims, we do not mean to raise anxieties about the closeness of knowledge and power; indeed, in the tradition of Foucault, we want to call attention to precisely how productive this relationship has often been.[17] Regardless of whether legal scholars imagine themselves as allies or critics of the policy apparatus, the practices of governance help set the agenda for legal scholarship.[18] Indeed, for legal scholarship to do its job, it must respond to changes in practices of governance by realigning its scholarly practices and knowledge paradigms. Thus one thing that is at stake in the movement from society to culture as a way of organizing social relations is the need for a realignment of scholarly practices, making way for a more prominent and productive engagement among cultural analysis, cultural studies, and law.[19]

Although it would take a book of its own to describe transformations in the field of legal studies associated with the decline of the social as a nexus of governing, evidence abounds that the shifting engagement between legal studies and government has altered the formation and deployment of legal knowledge at all levels. Consider how much of modern constitutional theory and jurisprudence has been a response to the expansion of the social liberal state. Likewise, the prestige of empirical research has been tied up with the access that social and legal scholars obtained as experimenters and expert consultants helping to administer a state engaged in interventions in problems like crime, gangs, and urban poverty. Even those discourses that have offered a more critical view of the enterprise of social policy and social research have often promoted both policy and research by exposing the gaps in action and imagination created by racism, patriarchy, and class privilege.[20]

Our interest here is to explore the implication of changing logics of governance for interdisciplinary legal scholarship.[21] Our claim is quite simple: namely, that as the logics of governance in the late modern era turn from society to culture, legal scholarship itself should turn to culture and more fully embrace cultural analysis and cultural studies. We see cultural analysis and cultural studies more as valuable supplements for the altered environment of the present than as competitors to the multitude of intellectual programs that already operate in what might be called the postrealist legal landscape, including varieties of realism, its moderate legal-process critics, as well as the more radical recent critical discourses including law and economics, critical legal studies, feminism, and critical race theory. Rather than as another interdisciplinary project to be added to the array of such projects, we view cultural studies as a kind of epistemological corrective to the plethora of problems posed for postrealist legal studies by the crises of the social liberal state and its allied forms of knowledge.[22]

It should be noted that these problems are not predominantly those of methodology. There has been, of late, a fair amount of worrying about the state of methodologies within legal studies. Such worrying is unsurprising. In their original attack on doctrinalism, legal studies scholars often raised the weapon of the superiority of their methodology. The rise of legal studies methodologies rooted in the humanities inevitably raises questions of turf and rights to speak. In our view, however, the methodological wars between doctrinalists and empiricists throughout the twentieth century reflected the enormous stakes for law, lawyers, and scholars in the social as a rationality of governance. The social, as such, has no methodology. The battle over methodology is more an effect than a cause of the rise of the social. Likewise, the renewed anxiety about methodology in legal studies since the 1980s reflects the destabilization of status and role within legal studies brought on by the breakdown of the social as a rationality of governance.

We also see legal studies as providing a crucial site of engagement for the broader movement of cultural analysis and cultural studies. Much of the analytic power of cultural studies in fields like literature and film studies has been to treat these discourses as law-like in being constitutive of the social relations they might otherwise seem only to simply represent. In looking beyond the narrowly juridical to show how novels, newspapers, and soap operas help create the nation as an imaginary community,[23] cultural studies often reads back into these narratives a model of law that is more rule-like, more coherent, and more functional than that described by legal studies.[24]

The emergent "cultural turn" in legal studies is one we welcome and have sought to participate in.[25] The cultural that is turned up naturally varies greatly with the knowledge practices of the analysts. Under the banner of privileging the cultural, research strategies have been employed that emphasize listening to the way ordinary people construct the law in their narratives about themselves,[26] listening to the way judges and law professors construct law in their narratives,[27] and reading the implicit norms that govern personal choices and behavior, just to name some of the ways it has been invoked.[28]

Looking for ways to build common links among the diverse knowledge strategies associated with the cultural is an important task that needs to continue now that some of the most polemical assumptions about the opposition between rigorous empirical work and the cultural turn have passed. It is time to explore the terrain of possibilities that might be opened up by a greater engagement between cultural analysis, cultural studies, and law. A good place to start is with the relationship between cultural analysis as a competitor to social analysis and cultural studies. There is one sense in which cultural studies is itself an example of the ubiquity of cultural analysis, representing as it were the opening up of a specific discipline with the cultural as its subject. In that sense, it might play the part that "sociology" played in the rise of the social, namely, that of being the discipline that articulates the most ambitious scope for knowledge of the social and that simultaneously expresses the vulnerabilities of government founded on the social. Cultural studies is a self-conscious reflection on the conditions of producing knowledge in a postsocial environment—that is, at a time when the forms of knowledge and power that have invested the social with power, truth, and significance are being decomposed and dismantled.

While suspicious of the social, cultural studies is far from being a promoter of cultural knowledge. It has flourished in disciplines like anthropology and literature that have dealt with "culture" as a key term for a long time, and in these disciplines cultural studies has been the banner waved by many of those most concerned with the power effects of cultural knowledge.

Before introducing the essays that make up this volume, we will briefly flesh out our claims about the value of engagement between cultural studies and law. If cultural studies is both a new sociology in the breadth of its claims and an engagement with the conditions of living in a time when the social is waning as a model of governance, it provides a compelling interlocutor for legal studies. We explore this claim by a brief comparison with the project of legal realism, a movement that reflected early on the power of the social for governance and thus the need for a law engaged with the social. The coming together of cultural studies and legal studies has parallels with the rise of legal realism, even as it represents the first true step away from it.

Unpacking the Cultural Baggage of Legal Realism

With the ascendancy of legal realism during the last two-thirds of the twentieth century, both law and social science found themselves engaged in the practical arts of governing to an extent barely imagined in the preceding century.[29] As the state came to reconfigure its approach to governing around problems of the social, both law and social science were invested with new resources and roles. Social and legal reform reached a peak in the 1960s and 1970s, not coincidentally as law and social science were reaching their own peaks of prestige. In the years since, there has been a great deal of internal criticism of the reform effort within both law and social science.[30] Moreover, the current generation of legal scholars must contend with a cultural programming that is increasingly constraining.[31] This programming limits the horizons of scholarly inquiry by emphasizing units and forms of analysis that may not be adequate in the face of contemporary social and political developments.

Among the most significant features of this programming are the imaginary boundaries of the social body within which the realist paradigm in both law and social science has been bound. Realist legal studies almost always operates within a political body, usually the nation, although this fact is not usually itself an object of analysis.[32] The boundaries and exclusions wrapped up in this national frame are made up not just of political borders but also of the racial, cultural, and linguistic embodiments. When a U.S. citizen of Hispanic origin is stopped by customs agents near the Mexican border of California, Arizona, or Texas, there is an evident surplus to their political identity that is neither identical with nor protected by citizenship in the political sense.[33] A similar emphasis on cultural citizenship seems to apply far from the border, or from direct questions of nationality, when African American drivers are pulled over by police almost anywhere along infamous Interstate 95.

Today, scholarship and politics increasingly confront an array of breaches in this imaginary order in the form of globalization, the Internet, identity politics, and the risk society, for which the realist paradigm seems inappropriate. New scholarship has taken up race, space, and the nation as an imaginary community within legal studies;[34] but so long as this scholarship is treated largely as a new mode of realist discourse, it may continue to have little effect on the great mass of legal thought.[35] Even when mainstream legal scholarship self-consciously looks beyond the national, the priority remains on those topics and actors of greatest concern to the Western nations, such as copyright protection and trade in goods and services, while the transnational flows of labor, black market profits, and refugees that concern much of the Third World tend to be ignored.

A second of its continuing constraints is the realism of legal realism, that is, its epistemological assumptions about the interpretive value of certain kinds of observations, such as those regarding the behavior of formal legal actors, social forces, and institutions. The first wave of realists entered into an alliance with practitioners of the fledgling social sciences, absorbing a positivist epistemology with its emphasis on counting and statistical analysis,[36] and this epistemological link has remained remarkably enduring.[37] Despite its academic success, the realist frame is being strained by transformations in the construction of subjectivity.

Postrealist legal studies, like much of the dominant social science discourse of the post–World War II era, has largely ignored the problem of the subject.[38] This has profound implications for our understandings of power since its exercise always has subjective effects on its targets and observers. These include terror, sexual arousal, admiration, and guilt. Often these are precisely the intended effects, but not infrequently they are also of a sort inconvenient for long-term domination.[39]

Moreover, the absence of interest in subjectivity does not guarantee the absence of an implicit model of the subject that constrains legal analysis; indeed, it practically guarantees that such constraints will show up. The breadth of subjective interest represented in most legal studies extends little beyond the rational actor of law and economics.[40] Little success has been achieved in making the gendering of this subject visible despite two decades of powerful feminist critiques. Other efforts to describe the "unthought" or "unconscious" parameters of legal studies have hardly begun. In addition, the new economy taking shape around the high technology sector in the United States reflects the tremendously successful cultural revolutions of the 1960s and 1970s with their emphasis on personal satisfaction (paradigmatically sexual), intense experiences (once drugs, now expensive trips to Nepal), and forms of interpersonal transcendence (sexual, religious, group process). For legal studies to address these revolutions, and to effectively unpack the place of culture in new logics of governance, it is incumbent on us to consider not only different sites of analysis (poems, novels, letters) but wholly different strategies of relating to different kinds of data.

As we shall detail in the next section, cultural analysis and cultural studies are well suited to aid postrealist legal discourses in accomplishing this task and to foreground the constraints of forms of knowledge production and engagement with governance that have shaped the disciplinary space in which those discourses operate. Since its beginnings in 1950s British Marxism, cultural studies, in particular, has long been concerned with the unthought or unconscious mechanisms that underlie the central solidarities of modern societies (nation, race, class position, gender).[41] Many of the techniques used by cultural studies to pursue this uncovering, including deconstruction, genealogy, psychoanalysis, Marxist dialectics, and feminism, are already widely familiar in legal studies. Less familiar, however, is the commitment to engage with the cultural imaginary and the unconscious as a factor in law.

Cultural studies has also long been attentive to both the role of subjectivity in history and to the complex interpenetrations of power and subjectivity,[42] or what Richard Johnson calls "the subjective side of social relations."[43] Indeed, much of the corpus of cultural studies consists of tools for tracking the production of subject positions as well as of a growing set of "case studies" in the subjective history of power in modern liberal democracies. Beyond methodological innovation, cultural studies can promote change in legal studies by widening the moments of subjectivity that are even considered in the analysis of law and legality. In addition, while there is a growing interest in popular culture in legal studies, it remains occasional and episodic.[44] Thus while legal scholars writing, for example, on rape or capital punishment regularly turn to Supreme Court opinions on those topics to tease out their cultural logic, few examine the leading contemporary films that have imagined and portrayed these experiences.[45] Cultural analysis and cultural studies encourage them to do so.

High Risk Contacts

For many inside legal studies, the crises we have ascribed to the social liberal state and its effects on the production of legal knowledge are experienced as a serious methodological weakening. A perceived decline in original empirical research, for example, is sometime ascribed to hostility toward science and social reform by younger scholars, yet it may be just as much a result of declining social reform activity and its attendant reduction in opportunities for classic empirical "gap" research. Given that sense of malaise, the entreaty to engage further with cultural analysis, let alone cultural studies, will strike many as a dangerous, high risk endeavor. Indeed, because cultural analysis and cultural studies often are identified with a particularly intense form of boundary breaking, a challenge to givens that regularly invokes the transgressive, one might rightly be skeptical about whether a legal studies field that experiences itself as vulnerable in a highly competitive academic universe would welcome the destabilizing agendas and strategies associated with them. To many, taking on cultural analysis and cultural studies seems like accepting an invitation to enter into the intellectual equivalent of a cocktail lounge where they will be exposed to second-hand smoke and perhaps worse.[46]

Various answers can be suggested. As Carol Weisbrod has recently noted, "One relates to the point that law creates the conditions of culture to some degree. Another notes that law, as a cultural product, may have something in common with other cultural products. Still another focuses on the point that while law is to some extent a mandarin text, it is itself a subject of popular culture."[47] As these suggestions indicate, a cultural analysis/cultural studies of law not only helps in challenging traditional ideas of culture, it also may help advance new conceptions of law. Among these conceptions are those that call us to attend to the possibility that the proliferation of law in film, on television, and in mass market publications has altered and expanded the sphere of legal life itself and to consider law as a world of images whose power is not located primarily in their representation of something exterior to the image, but is found in the image itself.[48] Just as almost a century ago legal realists helped put the study of law in action on the agenda of legal scholars, so today perhaps a cultural analysis/cultural studies of law will help expand the terrain of learning about law, open up new arenas for the exploration of law's power, for the pursuit of justice around, and perhaps through, law, and for the development of new understandings of the self's relation to the social. But just as the emergence of realism provoked intense anxiety, so too the emergence of cultural analysis and cultural studies arouses its own distinctive concerns.

In understanding those concerns and how to respond to them, it may be helpful to deepen this comparison with legal realism. Like cultural analysis and cultural studies, legal realism is not a single strand of work; rather, it describes several strands with a family resemblance rather than a deep conceptual unity.[49] And, like cultural analysis and cultural studies, legal realism has been both assimilated and criticized as a moral danger. Both are relatively easy to carica-ture. The canard about predicting the law by what judges eat for lunch con-tinues to make legal realism seem both extremist and silly decades after most of legal studies adopted the important realist innovations. Likewise such cultural studies icons as Judith Butler, Homi Bhabha, and Andrew Ross are sometimes dismissed as self-inflating dilettantes who use a forceful rhetoric to replace substantive analysis even as new generations of scholars put their insights to productive use.[50]

When we compare the anxieties associated with the cultural turn with those aroused by legal realism, we have in mind those provoked by innovations in the forms of knowledge acknowledged in legal discourse and the place of lawyers in practicing the arts of government.[51] From this perspective, the main contribution of legal realism was not to introduce a particular body of legal theory into the discursive universe of legal scholars (although it gave rise to multiple and conflicting theoretical expressions) but rather to position legal analysis with respect to new technologies of knowledge (the behavioral sci-ences) and to new forms of governing (the progressive and later New Deal state). The old legal science not only excluded the new knowledge from the high church of legal analysis (postrealism would do that as well) but purported to ignore its existence as well as the burgeoning administrative law created by the new modes of state power.[52] Realism as an academic revolution swept away these positions even if the establishment that replaced legal science was far more conservative than we associate with realism's vanguards. Cultural analysis and cultural studies may not prove as threatening to the established order as realism was, but their significance lies in the same direction, that is, in positioning legal studies in relation to new technologies of knowledge and power operating in the aftermath of the social liberal state.

Culturalism, Law, and Late Modernity

If Etienne Balibar is right that the cultural is all over the place, as a privileged source of knowledge, as a crucial level on which to govern effectively, as a commodity in the market, and that culturalism is a dominant logic of late capitalism (and one might easily add to or replace that with late modernity), we should not be surprised that the cultural is already emergent in legal studies. The question under these circumstances is whether in the midst of this cultural turn legal studies can make the status of the cultural a theoretical problem for itself, and whether such an enterprise is critical to gaining an "empirical" understanding of the legal life of late modernity.

As we take on these questions, it is important to recognize that the ascendance of the cultural comes paradoxically at a time when scholars increasingly have begun to contest the concept of culture and recognize its troubling vagueness. Talking about culture at the start of the twenty-first century means venturing into a field where there are almost as many definitions of the term as there are discussions of it,[53] with arguments about it raging inside as well as outside the academy.[54] In recent years, as we noted above, these arguments have come to play a progressively more visible role in our national life, and culture wars are also being fought within universities.[55] There the history, meaning, and utility of culture as a category of analysis in the humanities and social sciences are all up for grabs.[56] Where once the analysis of culture could neatly be assigned to the disciplines of anthropology or literature, today the study of culture refuses disciplinary cabining and forges new interdisciplinary connections.[57] Thus we should resist the temptation to treat battles like the "culture wars" over academic curricula and federal arts and museum programming as penumbras of some deeper social conflict: they represent their own very real conflict.

Traditionally, the study of culture was the study of "that complex whole which includes knowledge, belief, art, morals, law, custom, and any other capabilities and habits acquired by man as a member of society."[58] This definition, in addition to being hopelessly vague and inclusive, treats culture as a thing existing outside ongoing local practices and social relations. In addition, by treating it in terms of "capabilities and habits acquired" by members of society, culture was made into a set of timeless resources to be internalized in the "civilizing" process through which persons were made social. Finally, culture was identified as containing a kind of inclusive integrity, its parts combining into a "whole." This conception of culture still has its defenders and may even be on the rise as a political knowledge.[59]

Today, however, critiques of the traditional, unified, reified, civilizing idea of culture abound within the academy.[60] It is now indeed almost imperative to write, to quote Lila Abu-Lughod's influential essay, "against culture"[61] or, in the face of these critiques, to "forget culture."[62] Thus during the course of a suit filed by the Mashpee Indians of Cape Cod in 1977, James Clifford examined the way culture stood up in a context where the very idea of cultural authenticity was on trial. Culture, he said,

> was too closely tied to assumptions of organic form and development. In the eighteenth century culture meant simply "a tending toward natural growth." By the end of the nineteenth century the word could be applied not only to gardens and well-developed individuals but to whole societies. . . . [T]he term culture retained its bias toward wholeness, continuity, and growth. Indian culture in Mashpee might be made of unexpected everyday elements, but it had in the last analysis to cohere, its elements fitting together like parts of a body. The culture concept accommodates internal diversity and an "organic" division of roles but not sharp contradictions, mutations, or emergences. . . . This cornerstone of the anthropological discipline proved to be vulnerable under cross-examination.[63]

Culture, Clifford concluded, is "a deeply compromised idea. . . . Twentieth-century identities no longer presuppose continuous cultures or traditions."[64] Or, as T. M. Luhrmann has observed, the concept of culture is "more unsettled than it has been for forty years."[65]

In this unsettled moment in the life of the concept of culture, efforts are under way to rehabilitate and reform it. In this effort, contemporary cultural studies has played an especially important role.[66] Cultural studies has had a bracing impact in giving new energy and life to the study of culture, freeing it from its homogenizing and reifying tendencies. It has done so by radically extending what counts in the analysis of culture beyond the realm of "high culture."[67] It invites study of the quotidian world. Film, advertising, pop art, contemporary music, and other products of "popular culture" have been legitimized as objects of study.[68]

But, in addition to this liberating expansion in the objects of study, cultural studies has also linked the study of culture to questions of social stratification, power, and social conflict. "[C]ultural processes are," as Johnson notes, "intimately linked with social relations, especially with class relations and class formations, with sexual division, with the racial structuring of social relations. . . . [C]ulture involves power and helps produce asymmetries in the abilities of individuals and social groups to define and realize their needs. And . . . culture is neither an autonomous nor [an] externally determined field, but a site of social differences and struggles."[69] Thus culture, Johnson continues, can be understood as "historical forms of consciousness or subjectivity, or the subjective forms we live by."[70]

Law and legal studies are relative latecomers to cultural analysis and cultural studies.[71] As Robert Post explains,

> We have long been accustomed to think of law as something apart. The grand ideals of justice, of impartiality and fairness, have seemed to remove law from the ordinary, disordered paths of life. For this reason efforts to unearth connections between law and culture have appeared vaguely tinged with expose, as though the idol were revealed to have merely human feet. In recent years, with a firmer sense of the encompassing inevitability of culture, the scandal has diminished, and the enterprise of actually tracing the uneasy relationship of law to culture has begun in earnest.[72]

In the last thirty years, however, first with the development of critical legal studies, then with the growth of the law and literature movement, and finally with the growing attention to legal consciousness and legal ideology in sociolegal studies, legal scholars have come to attend to the cultural lives of law.[73] Fueled in part by Clifford Geertz's description of law as "a distinctive manner of imagining the real,"[74] they have begun to be attentive to the imaginative life of the law and the way law lives in our imagination. Law, as Geertz suggested, is not "a mere technical add-on to a morally (or immorally) finished society, it is, along of course with a whole range of other *cultural realities,* . . . an active part of it."[75] Treating law as a cultural reality means looking at the material structure of law to see it in play and at play, as signs and symbols, fantasies, and phantasms.[76]

In the tradition of cultural studies, the cultural analysis of law rejects "the dichotomy between agency and structure. . . . Treating consciousness as historical and situational, cultural analyses also shifts attention to the constitution and operation of social structure in historically specific situations."[77] It insists on examining the ways that the cultural lives of law contribute to what Johnson calls "asymmetries in the abilities of individuals and social groups to define and realize their needs."[78] The cultural study of law connects the symbolic and the material by resisting their dichotomization. As Silbey puts it, "[L]aw does more than reflect or encode what is otherwise normatively constructed; . . . law is part of the cultural processes that actively contribute in the composition of social relations."[79] Law is part of the everyday world, contributing powerfully to the apparently "stable, taken-for-granted quality of that world and to the generally shared sense that as things *are*, so *must* they be."[80]

Cultural analysis and cultural studies suggest that law operates largely by influencing modes of thought rather than by determining conduct in any specific case. It enters social practices and is, indeed, "imbricated" in them, by shaping consciousness, by making law's concepts and commands seem, if not invisible, perfectly natural and benign. Law is, in this sense, constitutive of culture, and it is "a part of the cultural processes that actively contribute in the composition of social relations."[81]

Cultural analysis insists, however, on the significance of agency. We are not merely the inert recipients of law's external pressures, but law's "demands" tend to seem natural and necessary, hardly like demands at all. In this way the cultural lives of law, Peter Fitzpatrick contends, have been central "in the scaffolding of the modern nation-state" with its construction of the rights-bearing subject, imagined social contract, and insistence on boundary and boundedness.[82] Nonetheless, legal meanings are not invented and communicated in a unidirectional process. Litigants, clients, consumers of culture, and others bring their own understandings to bear;[83] they deploy and use meanings strategically to advance interests and goals. They press their understandings in and on law and, in so doing, invite adaptation and change in the practices of law. Law thus exists, in the words of Raymond Williams, as a "moving hegemony."[84]

The priority of the cultural in late modern societies also raises the salience of law and legal studies. Most social relations are permeated with law. Long before we ever think about going to a courtroom, we encounter landlords and tenants, husbands and wives, barkeeps and hotel guests, roles that already embed a variety of juridical notions. The hypermediated quality of communities established under the conditions of late modern life embeds law at an even more molecular level because the very flesh of community, the bandwidths of the broadcast world, the networks of cable and phone lines known as the Internet, are more abstracted from everyday life and come to us already legally processed to a far greater degree.[85]

Law has played, and continues to play, a large role in regulating the terms and conditions of cultural production.[86] Cultural analysis and cultural studies call on scholars to attend to this role. The regime of copyright, to take a prominent example, has protected and promoted certain kinds of expression and discouraged others; it has tethered the life of signs to the fortunes of capital, and contributed importantly to the linkage of artistic value with ideas of originality, authenticity, and "ownership of the image."[87] Through doctrines of "personality rights," law "authors the celebrity" and, in so doing, gives a particular shape to the practices of "popular culture."[88] In such a setting, cultural analysis and cultural studies anchored in literature, cinema, or music must move beyond treating them as metaphors of legality. Novels and newspapers are not only analogous to legal acts; their operation and the way they circulate, with what kinds of limits are placed on them, are questions of law.

The cultural study of law is then important as a way of unpacking what Rosemary Coombe calls "the signifying power of law and law's power over signification."[89] It invites us to acknowledge that legal meaning is found and invented in the variety of locations and practices that comprise culture and that those locations and practices are themselves encapsulated, though always incompletely, in legal forms, regulations, and legal symbols. Thus the interpretive task for the cultural analyst is quite challenging as she seeks to read everyday cultural forms.

Moreover, the boundaries between cultural analysis/cultural studies as a distinct perspective and the cultural study of law are neither fixed nor clear. The essays collected in this book take on the concept of culture in spite of its vagueness and bring together work from within cultural studies and the broader movement to foster a cultural study of law. The book is, however, neither a comprehensive overview of the ways law shapes culture and culture shapes law nor a survey of cultural approaches to law. Instead, it provides a sampling of significant theoretical issues in the cultural analysis of law and illustrates some of those issues in provocative examples of that genre. It is designed as an encouragement in the still tentative efforts to forge a new interdisciplinary synthesis, a cultural studies of law.

What would legal study look like if it were to take on cultural analysis and/or cultural studies as one of its guiding paradigms? How does a cultural study of law enlarge and alter our conception of the way law lives in and through our identities, interpretations, and imaginings? Can the intellectual strategies of cultural analysis and cultural studies be disciplined and made serviceable as a vehicle for the analysis of legal phenomena? Can cultural studies be put into productive dialogue with other forms of cultural analysis, or will such dialogue diminish the significance of both as forces in legal scholarship? These are the questions that this collection of essays addresses. Doing so at this point in the development of cultural study and legal study is indeed daunting when the richness and plurality of the former is as great as it has ever been and when legal scholarship is as open as it has ever been to interdisciplinary interests. But, as we have tried to show, the separation of legal study and cultural analysis, in all its variety, is, at this time in the history of the rationalities of governance, increasingly costly. Maintaining it means missing altogether the surfaces to which empirical methods need to be applied for any hope of getting a purchase on the role of law in contemporary society.

This volume seeks to overcome that separation and to elaborate a cultural analysis of legal life. Yet the essays collected here march under no single programmatic banner. Each speaks in its own voice; each brings its own perspective to bear in talking about, or performing, a cultural analysis of law. Together, they exemplify the kinds of contributions that cultural analysis and cultural studies make to interdisciplinary legal study even as they highlight points of contrast between cultural studies and its allied forms of scholarship. Together, they help reposition legal study in response to the death of the social and the rise of culture in the governance of late modern societies.

Approaches to the Cultural Study of Law

The first section contains four essays that exemplify particular approaches to the cultural study of law. The juxtaposition of their perspectives maps the terrain that cultural analysis/cultural studies might traverse. This section begins with Naomi Mezey's effort to identify the contribution of cultural analysis to legal studies at a time when, as she notes, "culture is everywhere invoked and virtually nowhere explained." She describes the pervasive invocation of culture as a fact of late modern life, calling our attention to the explanations of the shootings at Columbine High School that made reference to a culture of violence or to the fact that the Juvenile Justice Bill debated in a recent Congress would have allowed schools to post copies of the Ten Commandments as a way of combating youth crime. Mezey quotes the critic Adam Gopnik as saying, "Every age has a term to explain things that resist explanation. The Elizabethans had Fate; the Victorians had History; we have Culture."

In light of the pervasiveness of culture as an explanation for social problems and a strategy of governance, Mezey argues that we need, even at a time in which we recognize its problematic status, to pursue a "cultural interpretation of law." What, Mezey asks, would such an interpretation do? First, it would give culture some definition, however provisional. Culture, in Mezey's view, is any set of signifying practices, shared practices by which "meaning is produced, performed, contested, or transformed." Second, a cultural interpretation requires that we attend to the way law orders meanings as well as to the "slippage" that almost inevitably accompanies its effort to do so. Mezey calls attention to such quotidian practices as the way gay men in California try to "pick up" other gay men by paying their highway tolls or the way wearing Oakland Raider football jackets signifies gang affiliation and to the ways their significations change in the face of legal regulations. Third, a cultural interpretation of law requires what Mezey calls "thick explanation." This involves analysis of the particularized ways cultural practices coincide or collide with law so as to alter the meaning of either or both.

The work of cultural interpretation, Mezey argues, will never have the parsimony of law and economics and will, as a result, struggle to find a place in the legal academy. Yet its complexity is precisely its virtue. And to neglect cultural interpretation in favor of other kinds of scholarship is to shirk our responsibility as scholars to make sense of the pervasiveness of culture as a category through which events in our world are now so frequently described and explained.

A similar sense of the ethical and political imperative of cultural analysis of law informs the next contribution. This essay claims that cultural studies is a preferred style or type of cultural analysis precisely because of its engagement with, and attentiveness to, the political struggles of our era. Toby Miller provides a definition and overview of cultural studies as well as an example of the kind of work Mezey advocates. His example is drawn from a real world struggle in which he was involved, namely, the effort of graduate students to unionize at New York University. Miller uses that example to highlight what happens at the intersection between legal institutions (in this case the National Labor Relations Board) and cultural practices (in this case what he sees as the exploitation of graduate students by research universities). That example, he says, also reminds us that cultural studies itself signifies an academic "commitment to progressive social change."

Miller's essay contains a genealogy of cultural studies that calls attention to its multigenerational, multinational origins and lays out a series of understandings of culture, some of which serve the needs of social reproduction and others of which, he claims, promote contestation and social transformation. At the heart of the difference in these uses of cultural analysis, Miller contends, is a commitment to "historical materialism." He argues that in facing new rationalities of governance scholars now need to bring together cultural studies and what he calls "critical political economy." The object is to politicize theory and theorize politics. The cultural analysis of law should contribute to an understanding of "the reproduction of culture through structural determinations on subjects versus their own agency, and the method is historical materialism."

Miller shows what such an analysis might look like in his description of the struggles of graduate students at NYU. In a dramatic shift in style, the second part of Miller's essay is both more personal and more "political." It is more personal in detailing his own engagement in the unionization effort. Here, Miller notes the contradictory position of university officials who in the name of maintaining a democratic university oppose the effort to democratically determine whether graduate students wish to collectively bargain under the auspices of a union. He also explores the difficulty of speaking to and through law, in this case the National Labor Relations Board. Throughout, Miller exposes the complicity of the politics of discursive practices and the political economy of university life.

Miller's genealogical and critical narrative, while it exemplifies the kind of work that Mezey seeks to encourage, becomes an (unnamed) object of critique in the essay by Paul Berman. Miller's style of work relies on what Berman, borrowing from Paul Ricoeur, calls the "hermeneutics of suspicion." Such an approach to cultural study seeks to "unmask, demystify, and expose the real from the apparent." It is relentlessly critical, seeing power and domination everywhere. Berman faults such an approach on two grounds. First, it situates the analyst in a superior position to her objects of study. By unmasking ideologies and power dynamics, "the writer may imply that he or she is able to get beyond the mystification and see the situation more accurately than those caught 'within' the system." Second, and more importantly, the hermeneutics of suspicion has, in Berman's view, a "corrosive effect both on our psyches and on society as a whole," leading us to despair of the prospect of social change through law.

Berman advocates "sympathetic reading" that identifies "what is worthwhile in the efforts of people to construct ideas, systems, or principles." He would fault Miller for not being more empathetic toward the university administrators he describes and would also fault the kind of cultural studies Miller practices for not telling stories of "beauty, of optimism, and of hope." Moreover, echoing Habermas and the tradition of American constitutional theory since John Hart Ely, Berman makes the case for law as a powerful institutional home for a view of culture that is both dynamic and tolerant. He urges scholars not to turn away from projects of reform and to tell stories that envision law "not merely as an instantiation of embedded power, but as an activity that might have true intellectual, imaginative, ethical, and political value."

Paul Kahn's work is directly critical of Berman's embrace of reform as a touchstone for, or object of, the cultural analysis of law. Such an approach, Kahn contends, treats the study of law as if it were the same as doing law. It exemplifies the powerful pull of law schools on the way law is studied. Law schools, Kahn argues, hold all scholarship to a pragmatic test, evaluating it in terms of its utility for policy. "The modern law school," he says, "lives with this burden of establishing the form of knowledge appropriate to law." Kahn wishes to distance himself from such a conception of what a cultural analysis of law must be.

He also wishes to distance himself from cultural studies as described by Miller, with its emphasis on the popular, on resistant practices, and so forth, and its view of law as a "set of sites of social conflict, and of resources . . . for those involved in such conflict." In contrast, he urges a focus on the top of the legal hierarchy, on the beliefs and self-conceptions of those who produce law. Studying that group reveals, Kahn argues, that the language of law's rule is our dominant language of political legitimacy. The task of cultural analysis should be to offer a "phenomenology of this distinctive American political culture of the rule of law." What is the world that is imagined in that culture? How is that world contested by other symbolic forms?

A cultural analysis of law should depend, Kahn argues, on distanced, disinterested analysis, just as it seeks to promote a conception of freedom in which understanding of the cultural presuppositions that guide our practices is treated as a precondition of informed action. Rather than pursuing projects of reform, cultural analysis should be turned on one's own beliefs. "Bringing cultural study into the heartland of the legal academy is," Kahn concludes, "a way of putting the self at risk" and of making self rather than other the subject of inquiry.

Deploying Law and Legal Ideas in Culture and Society

The three essays that make up the next section identify moments of coincidence and conflict between legal and cultural practices and chart the significance of these moments when law comes to culture and when culture comes to law. They show that while law may be part of a larger "culture," the latter is not a "system" in which law plays a consistent role across all contexts. Nobody in our culture would mistake a poem for a court's judgment, but neither would a jurisdictional hierarchy place law above or below poetry. Indeed, much of the work involved in producing culture and law lies in managing the boundaries between them, a game played with often ruthless seriousness by judges and lawyers. But, at the same time, law is always already thoroughly and irreversibly infected by the (often dated) cultural content of its own objects. This puts all of the authors in this section in the difficult position of explicating some of the connections between law and culture while working from some other point of contact between the two.

Carol Greenhouse uses the encounter between cultural studies and legal studies to confront the deep cultural connections between law, social science, and post–World War II American liberalism. That type of liberalism is now canonized in the landmark civil rights and civil liberties victories of the 1950s and 1960s. According to Greenhouse, the social movements of that period, especially the civil rights movement, produced both a "pragmatics" of reform that animated public discourse and a "poetics" of citizenship that helped shape and define a way of imagining America.

What remains of that era are deep but often hidden connections between the reform agenda of postwar liberalism, on the one hand, and ethnography and literature, on the other. These connections were welded together by the force of the civil rights movement. During the 1980s and 1990s, as the public influence of civil rights waned, and the U.S. Congress and the courts turned hostile to the civil rights agenda, the liberal project became more associated with literature, the arts generally, popular culture, and the academy. This new relationship constitutes, for Greenhouse, the cultural conditions of neoliberalism.

Literature and ethnography remain influential ways of imagining the United States as a national community paradoxically made up of autonomous local communities. Novels by African American women shaped directly by participation in the civil rights movement, like Alice Walker and Toni Morrison, have been best-sellers, even as the electorate has unashamedly rejected many of the legislative victories of the civil rights movement. While ethnography is read by a much smaller audience, there is a lively discourse of "community studies" focused very much on the legacy of the civil rights movement, including the fate of the inner city "ghettos" and their successor communities of the very poor and the ethnically or racially marginalized. Both literature and ethnography operate in the thrall of the now absent civil rights movement. Thus while many critics of the cultural turn in the American academy see it as an abandonment of engagement with power, Greenhouse shows that it is the unexamined relationship to liberalism, a regime of governmental power now in crisis, that haunts the academy.

Greenhouse offers an internal critique of American ethnography aimed at reestablishing its dialogue with the fading liberalism of the mid-twentieth century and the emerging neoliberalism at the turn of the twenty-first century. At the core of both post–civil rights literature and American ethnography, she contends, is the relationship of the national community, embodied in the federal government and its agencies, and sometimes in the narrators of the texts, to a local community defined as singular and yet quintessentially American. Ethnographic discourse came to be produced in part to make local communities available to the gaze of a federal government whose claims to power presumed direct access to the local.[90] Ethnography has continued in this mode since the 1970s despite the dismantling of much of the liberal governmental project. In its current form, it constitutes a kind of nostalgic program. Greenhouse suggests that if social-legal studies and ethnography more generally are to have a more critical role in the shaping of neoliberal governance, they must revisit their cultural background, reposition themselves with respect to those movements now shaping the cultural life of law, and pursue a new ethnography of American communities, one attentive to postcolonialism, globalization, and transnationalism.

The next essay in this section operates on a similar terrain, exploring law's relationship to its narrative others. Here, the other is science in the late nineteenth century and the first half of the twentieth. While the social sciences taken up in Greenhouse's essay directly competed and cooperated with law in a visible struggle to shape governance, the traces of science that Wai Chee Dimock explores are those of the natural sciences, as they operated in the imaginary of legal academics seeking to define their own status as producers of expertise (academic law). It is this expertise, in part, that helped form the civil rights coalition Greenhouse describes.

Since the nineteenth century (at the latest), those seeking to recast law as a practice and body of knowledge have repeatedly invoked the model of science. Christopher Langdell, dean of Harvard Law School and inventor of the influential "case method," described his goal as moving law from a craft to a science, for which the law library with its collection of judicial opinions would play the same role that the laboratory, the museum of natural history, and the botanical garden played for other disciplines in the university setting. Early in the twentieth century, Roscoe Pound, another Harvard dean and promoter of what he called "sociological jurisprudence," and, a bit later, the legal realists at Columbia and Yale rejected Langdell's approach as a form of mysticism and promoted their own empirical vision of legal studies as a scientific approach to law. As Dimock carefully shows, these invocations of science have often been strikingly distant from the actual practice of the sciences. Thus Langdell invoked the logical analysis of written texts as the model of science at a time when the physical and life sciences were increasingly experimental. Even the realists, who were closer to the empirical social sciences that were emerging in the same period, ignored real differences between the normative objectives of legal argument and the descriptive practice of social science.

The exploration of the discourse of science and its appropriation in law and legal scholarship that Dimock's essay provides is crucial to the project of understanding the rise and decline of the social that we described at the beginning of this essay. Those who endeavored to provide social knowledge of law and to use law to construct and respond to social problems did so in the name of a science of society that thought it could ape the procedures and methods of the natural sciences. In turn, the movement from the social to the cultural is, in part, premised on a new imagining of science of the kind that Dimock describes, an imagining with its own misreadings of the scientific enterprise. The kind of direct, if metaphoric, traffic between legal studies and the natural sciences that Dimock engages in is justified by the need to navigate around the problematic space of the social and its claim to a scientifically knowable objectivity all its own.

It is not only law and legal scholarship, however, that has engaged in a systematic misrecognition of its relationship to science. Science also has a metaphorical relationship to law, especially in the notion of a "law of science." The standard self-description of science emphasizes the discovery of "universal laws," that is, generalizations that apply across time and place. Dimock shows that the notion of the universe as "law-abiding" is itself a highly selective gloss of the sciences. Some sciences like physics do seem to move from empirically observed regularities to the discovery of law-like rules that apply everywhere and always. Yet most scientific work may ironically be far closer to the contingent predictions that lawyers give. The life sciences especially deal with phenomena in which so many factors, including contingency, come to bear that universal laws are rarely if ever described.

What law and most of the sciences actually share is a vulnerability to diachronic processes, history and time, that the metaphorical conception of law in both jurisprudence and science rarely acknowledges. This may be most critical in those areas where law and science interact in practice rather than speak about each other through metaphor. Dimock develops an important example in the field of intellectual property, a field that has drawn a great deal of interest in the emergent cultural studies of law. The legal enforcement of "patents," authorized in the U.S. Constitution itself, permits successful investigators to limit access to their inventions and discoveries in a manner that can slow or even halt scientific development subject to the demands of the patent holder. Yet the idea of patentable discovery held by framers of the Constitution was far more limited than the discoveries regularly recognized by courts today.

Dimock's analysis shows what cultural studies might look like if it sought to describe and interpret the cultural exchange between practices like law and science. This would mean being attentive to the diachronic stories often implicit in the constellations of discourse and practice that students of cultural studies produce. Most scholarship, according to Dimock, attends solely to structural patterns that link developments at any time among different institutional fields. The hard work of history carried out in terrains not preordained by political categories (nation, language) is all too often left undone.

Peter Brooks looks at one particular point of contact between law and a form of scientific expertise: therapy, and especially the production of knowledge from recovered memory. Recovered memory is only the most recent of a series of flashpoints between law and what Nikolas Rose calls the "psy" experts, that go back well into the nineteenth century if not earlier.[91] Indeed, it emerges at a time when, quite unlike the turn of the last century, the role of knowledge of the human psyche in the courtroom has been in general retreat. Few today would share Roscoe Pound's expectations that modern law would inevitably become a branch of human science.[92]

In Brooks's view, the recent trend of producing cultural analysis of law runs into the power of law to both exclude and domesticate other narratives and other forms of expertise. The recovered memory cases should be particularly troubling to law since the very facts underlying the cause of action, as in the incestuous sexual abuse of someone as a child, are produced through the work of therapy. Courts follow what Brooks considers a familiar pattern, admitting the claims while keeping out the therapeutic experts. Recovered memory gets in because it's a memory, but the only voice that should speak that memory is the subject to whom belongs, not the therapeutic discourse that produced it.

Under the banner of "common sense," psychological truth has become part of modern legal truth. The Supreme Court's confession jurisprudence, which

Brooks has made the subject of a recent book,[93] includes many psychological presumptions about what motivates subjects to confess but almost no serious discussion of the status of those theories in psychology or its fellow psy discourses. In place of critical dialogue between legal and psy expertise, there has been a series of largely metaphorical appropriations akin to those made by Dimock's academic legal theorists. This leaves law peculiarly vulnerable to cultural infection by discourses that it is not capable of recognizing as distinctive and potentially invasive. While Brooks does not provide the kind of historical examination suggested by Dimock, his discussion of confessions registers the receding role of the empirical social sciences that Greenhouse invoked with her "pragmatics" of reform. Brooks's warning that producers of cultural analysis of law should attend to how law appropriates outside analysis recalls Greenhouse's appeal for a critical engagement of social science and law with neoliberalism.

Reading Legal Events

Each of the essays in the last section of this book focuses on moments of judgment, moments in which law is asked to understand the world beyond its boundaries. Each shows law's dependence on a series of unacknowledged aesthetic, psychological, historical, and cultural assumptions. Each also reveals the power of law to produce forms of subjectivity and moments of truth, and each uses the techniques of cultural analysis and cultural studies to decode and critique the assumptions and pathways of power.

Shoshana Felman revisits one of the most contested moments of post–World War II legality, the 1957 trial of Holocaust administrator Adolf Eichmann. Turning to a trial as a crucial moment in the cultural production of law is by now a familiar mode of analysis among practitioners of cultural studies. Trials galvanize attention, call forth competing narratives, and shape meanings of basic legal categories. However, unlike many who turn to trials, Felman is explicit in her deployment of theory to read Eichmann's trial, and the theory on which she draws, psychoanalysis, is itself a source of great controversy within cultural studies of law.

Her essay focuses on a particularly searing moment of that trial (which was one of the first to be televised) to draw out its psychoanalytic resonance: the collapse—while on the stand—of a prosecution witness, Auschwitz survivor and author Yehiel Dinoor, better known as K-Zetnik (a slang term meaning "concentration camp inmate"). K-Zetnik was only one of many survivors to take the stand and describe the Holocaust directly from the perspective of the victims; but, as Felman points out, he was also one of the few survivors whose testimony was directly relevant to Eichmann's relationship to Auschwitz. His testimony had only barely begun when in response to a set of preliminary questions about his name, K-Zetnik went into a trancelike state, fainted, and had a paralytic stroke that kept him near death in a hospital for more than two weeks.

On one level, Felman raises a question similar to the one Brooks's essay discusses: namely, how does the law respond to the trauma of violence and of recovered memory? Here, the trauma is on a scale beyond comprehension, and the problem of recovery is less one of personal recall than the capacity to communicate the truth of a historical event. Felman shows us a different face of law's relationship to trauma. Whereas Brooks's judges were mainly concerned with normalizing the testimony of recovered memory and reducing it to a legally managed fact, the Eichmann trial was meant, by the prosecutors and the judge, to produce the emotional truth of the Holocaust through its survivors. At the same time, law's demand for tight control of other discourses set real limits on the terms by which the emotion of trauma may speak. Felman ultimately reads K-Zetnik's collapse as evidence both of these limits and of the kinds of sacrifice it takes to transcend them.

While in Brooks's account the battle is primarily between the law of evidence and the knowledge that therapy produces about recovered memory, the response to the Holocaust demonstrates multiple ways that law can relate to the production of such memories. The Eichmann trial, with its deliberate invocation of the voices of the survivors, was a striking contrast to the approach taken at the earlier trial of Nazi officers conducted by the Allies in the German city of Nuremberg. The Nuremberg prosecutors, led by the American lawyers, chose to put on a documentary case that would leave the voices of the survivors out of the evidence. The Eichmann trial was quite explicitly aimed at producing survivor testimony of the Holocaust. That strategy carried real risks of failure and of delegitimizing the trial.

From this perspective, K-Zetnik's collapse marks a moment where the narrative needs of law, especially the temporality that requires locating an event in the past, ran up against the explosive presentness of trauma to the victims.[94] Trials like Eichmann's are about the production of memories and the conversion of personal suffering into national memory. While legal theory has prioritized the difficulties of the judgments made at both the Nuremberg and the Eichmann trials, Felman's account reminds us that behind judgment come moments of memory that place law in far more jeopardy than somewhat abstract "legitimation crisis" judgments are said to entail. K-Zetnik's collapse, broadcast repeatedly over the years, produced its own cultural truth. In the end, Felman argues, the Eichmann trial succeeded as a work of legal art in allowing the muteness at the center of the Holocaust's horror to be represented in law but also as art.

Like Felman, Anthony Paul Farley draws on psychoanalysis to talk about haunting absences in legal events. Here, he explores the representations that haunt the Supreme Court's recent efforts to define the role of racial identity in the construction of constitutionally adequate voting districts. In striking down a number of black majority districts, the Court has emphasized seemingly neutral concerns like compactness but has inched precariously close to articulating a notion of whiteness underlying the body politic of the United States. Drawing on the work of Jacques Lacan, Farley probes the cultural penumbra of the implicit legal question at issue in most of these challenges: how are white people harmed by being represented by blacks? The answer lies not in the legal position of the parties but in the enduring threat that the black body poses to the imaginary coherence and power of the white body politic.

What Farley uncovers is a powerful cultural investment in black bodies as the negated bond holding white communities together. While notions of racial community are denigrated by official discourse of all sorts, and especially Supreme Court opinions, Farley finds explosive and unmistakable symbolic links between the Court's metaphysical reasoning on the shape of voting districts and the physical torture and dismemberment of blacks in the rituals of lynching. The Court's repugnance at oddly shaped districts reflects a displacement of the white community's enthusiasm for the hideous shapes produced by lynching, while their judgment reaffirms the central role of race in defining political community in the United States.

Farley's text is highly theorized and makes no claim to immediate intervention in legal struggle of the sort that Toby Miller engaged in during the NYU labor conflict; but, like Miller, Farley places relationships of power at the center of cultural studies work. Like Greenhouse and Felman, among others, he shows the great promise of the kind of interdisciplinary opening that cultural studies of law makes available. His essay provides provocative tools with which to read the law and to connect the way law is read to pervasive cultural anxieties about race and racial categories.

The final essay, by Alison Young, continues Farley's interest in the nature of legal judgment, its absences, and its haunting specters and in reading culture's anxieties. Young takes HIV and the legal cases and artistic images it generates to interrogate the meaning of legal judgment. Young first shows how, in a variety of cases arising from attacks on gay men or efforts to expel them from the military, law depends on what she calls an "aesthetics of appearance." In these cases, law relies on the visual force of phantasy—sometimes phantasies of abuse that are used to make sense of a violent attack on a gay man, sometimes phantasies of blood uncontrollably spilling forth to justify removal of an HIV-positive soldier from military service. Through these imaginings, gay men are subject to community values in such a way as to deny them a place in the community or to devalue the place that they occupy.

Young turns to art and film to explore the "aesthetics of disappearance." These cultural artifacts refigure the image, turning it from a device used to sever relations into a bridge, connecting viewers to the bodies of gay men with HIV. She reads various works of Felix Gonzalez-Torres, an artist who died of AIDS in 1996. These works—piles of paper, spills of candy, fabric blowing in the wind—suggest motion, disappearance, loss in the process of happening. Viewers, Young argues, are invited to both witness and participate in these moments. We are connected to, not severed from, the suffering of embodied, but disappearing beings. We are brought to respect alterity through a framework of judgment that brings self and other into a proximate relationship.

In Derek Jarman's film *Blue,* the image does not move. The camera stays fixed on a cobalt blue background as viewers hear voices, sounds, bells, poems. Jarman, who at the time he made this film was losing his eyesight to AIDS, captures and makes literal the difficulty of representing HIV, a difficulty never acknowledged in the legal cases that Young describes. In those cases, visual realism leads to a failure in legal judgment at both the aesthetic and the moral levels. "The written texts of law," Young suggests, "reconstruct the event (the 'real') of HIV in the order of vision, where judgment is governed by the desire to see, and in 'seeing,' to have done with HIV." For Young, cultural studies speaks to this failure by providing a different way of reading images and a different scene of judgment, one that can take account of the fragmented, suffering, fleshy body and help "the eye of the law . . . to flicker from the mark to the pain of the other in law" by subjecting "the legal and the living to the horizon of deathbound subjectivity."

In the readings of legal events and of the flow of legal ideas into and through culture, we encounter accounts, sometimes explicit, sometimes implicit, of the power and possibilities of cultural analysis/cultural studies described in the first section of this book. These readings do not fall prey to the type of reduction of the social to the cultural that marks the politics of our era even as they insistently attend to the cultural basis and operation of law. They call us to attend to the cultural not for its recuperative or redemptive potential but instead to expose the layers of power that the turn to culture in the political realm often seeks to mask. They call us to the cultural as a point of departure for a critique of the epistemology and ethics that today hold out culture as the explanation and cure for problems that cannot in truth be addressed through culture itself. In the end, they remind us, like the legal realism of the past, that legal scholarship can be both critical and transformative.

Notes

1 "[Q]uestions of culture . . . quickly become anguished questions of identity." See Joan Scott, "Multiculturalism and the Politics of Identity," in *The Identity Question* 3 (John Rajchman ed., 1995).

2 Charles Taylor, *Multiculturalism: Examining the Politics of Recognition* (1994).

3 See *Culture Wars: Opposing Viewpoints* (Fred Whitehead ed., 1994).

4 For a discussion of these debates see James Hunter, *Culture Wars: The Struggle to Define America* (1991).

5 Theodore Caplow and Jonathan Simon, "Understanding Prison Policy and Population Trends," in 26 *Crime and Justice: A Review of Research* 63–120 (Michael Tonry and Joan Petersilia eds., 1999); Ben J. Wattenberg, *Values Matter Most* (1995).

6 See Samuel Huntington, "The Clash of Civilizations," 36 *International Politics* (1999).

7 William Lyons, *The Politics of Community Policing: Rearranging the Power to Punish* (1999).

8 Nancy Ellen Rose, *Workfare or Fair Work: Workfare, Welfare, and Government Work Programs* (1995).

9 The recent advertising campaign for the new dollar coin is a noteworthy example of this. Who would have thought that you would need to advertise money? But, in recognizing that even currency must be given "currency," the Treasury Department discovered how much the cultural has become embedded in the economic and the political.

10 Consider the product designs and marketing of chains like Urban Outfitters and Old Navy.

11 Etienne Balibar, "Is There a 'Neo-Racism'?" in Etienne Balibar and Immanuel Wallerstein, *Race, Nation, Class* (1993).

12 Jean Baudrillard, *In the Shadow of the Silent Majorities, or "The Death of the Social"* (1983); but see Nikolas Rose, "The Death of the Social?: Re-figuring the Territory of Government," 25 *Econ. and Soc.* 327–56 (1996).

13 This movement is most widely associated with right-wing neoliberal thinking, for which the social is held to be virtually a simulacrum of government, and in which social problems are shown to disappear along with government (in theory mostly). Yet as the success of governments like those of President Clinton in the United States and Prime Minister Tony Blair in the United Kingdom has shown, the right has no monopoly on this shift. Nikolas Rose has usefully described this emerging paradigm as advanced liberalism. See Nikolas

Rose, *The Powers of Freedom* (1999); Jonathan Simon, "Law After Society," 24 *Law and Soc. Inquiry* 143–94 (2000).

14 Ronen Shamir, *Managing Legal Uncertainty: Elite Lawyers in the New Deal* (1995); Robyn Stryker, "Rules, Resources, and Legitimacy Processes: Some Implications for Social Conflict, Order, and Change," 99 *Am. J. of Sociology* 847–910 (1994).

15 We use the term *legal studies* inclusively to cover scholarly research on law and legal institutions from a variety of disciplinary perspectives, including those traditionally found in academic law schools, those associated with the social sciences—that is, political science, sociology, criminology, psychology, economics, history, and anthropology—and those rooted in the humanities—such as philosophy, rhetoric, and literature. We use the term in part because its ownership is ambiguous, sometimes being associated with particular disciplinary approaches (for example, the *Journal of Legal Studies* is widely associated with economic analysis of law) and sometimes with interdisciplinarity itself (a number of undergraduate majors or concentrations are titled "legal studies"). Since we include scholarship of the most diverse sorts in this term, it may fairly be decried as doing little analytic work; yet we want to highlight the fact that all of the discourses we incorporate now share a basic anxiety about their status and thus a reflexivity about how they produce truth.

16 Austin Sarat and Susan Silbey, "The Pull of the Policy Audience," 10 *Law and Policy* 98 (1988).

17 A striking example is the tradition of post–World War II empirical studies of criminal justice, much of which was funded by large corporately funded foundations and later by the government itself but which operated to expose the manifold failures of the existing institutions of justice in America. As late as the late 1960s, a government commission would employ legal sociologist Jerome Skolnick to study the causes of campus and urban civil disorders, producing a volume highly critical of American institutions and government.

18 Patricia Ewick, Robert Kagan, and Austin Sarat, "Legacies of Legal Realism: Social Science, Social Policy, and the Law," in *Social Science, Social Policy, and the Law* 1 (Patricia Ewick et al. eds., 1999).

19 Susan Silbey, "Making a Place for a Cultural Analysis of Law," 17 *Law and Soc. Inquiry* 39 (1992).

20 Austin Sarat, "Legal Effectiveness and Social Studies of Law: On the Unfortunate Persistence of a Research Tradition," 9 *Legal Stud. Forum* 23 (1985).

21 As we use them, "interdisciplinary legal scholarship" and "legal studies" are meant to be inclusive terms covering work on law from a variety of disciplinary perspectives, including political science, sociology, criminology, psychology, economics, history, anthropology, and literature. At the same time, however, the turn to the cultural and the associated shift in logics of governance has not had a uniform impact. As a result, we attend most particularly to research in political science, sociology, criminology, and law.

22 Or to try another kind of metaphor, a software upgrade (in Jack Balkin's sense of software) to the operating system of legal studies, largely set in place during the 1960s in response to the last phase of the social liberal state and its constitutional realization in the Warren Court. J. M. Balkin, *Cultural Software: A Theory of Ideology* (1998).

23 See Lauren Berlant, *The Queen of America Goes to Washington City: Essays on Sex and Citizenship* (1997).

24 For an interesting example of this tendency, see Marjorie Garber, "Cinema Scopes: Evolu-tion, Media, and the Law," in *Law in the Domains of Culture* (Austin Sarat and Thomas R. Kearns eds., 1998).

25 *Law in the Domains of Culture,* supra note 24.

26 Patricia Ewick and Susan Silbey, *The Common Place of Law: Stories from Everyday Life* (1998).

27 Paul Kahn, *The Cultural Study of Law* (1999). For a discussion of Kahn's contribution to the cultural analysis of law, see Austin Sarat, "Redirecting Legal Scholarship in Law Schools," 12 *Yale J.L. and Human.* 129 (2000).

28 Balkin, supra note 22.

29 See, for example, Larry Lessig, "The Regulation of Social Meaning," 62 *U. Chi. L. Rev.* 943–1045 (1995); Robert D. Putnam, *Making Democracy Work* (1993).

30 Bryant Garth and Joyce Sterling, "From Legal Realism to Law and Society: Reshaping Law for the Last Stages of the Social Activist State," 32 *Law and Soc'y Rev.* 709–72 (1998); Simon, supra note 13.

31 By cultural programming, we mean the logics of inquiry and imagination made available within a culture at any historical juncture.

32 Critical to twentieth-century projects of governance was the control of populations both in the United States and abroad. There were (and are) clear linkages between domestic policy development and the position of the United States in the international arena. Policy and reform were geared to the production and maintenance of American power abroad.

33 On the nature of this surplus, see Margaret Montoya, "Border/ed Identities: Narrative and the Social Construction of Legal and Personal Identities," in *Crossing Boundaries: Traditions and Transformations in Law and Society Research* 129 (Austin Sarat et al. eds., 1998).

34 For example, Ian Haney Lopez, *White by Law: The Legal Construction of Race* (1996), and David Delaney, *Race, Place, and the Law, 1836–1948* (1998).

35 A notable example is the hostility of the U.S. Supreme Court to the discussion of global legal norms. The United States is increasingly alone among liberal systems in ignoring the force of arguments from other legal systems.

36 See John Henry Schlegel, "American Legal Realism and Empirical Social Science-I: From the Yale Experience," 28 *Buff. L. Rev.* 459 (1979).

37 Today, some six or seven decades later, the elite law schools remain heavily invested in this model of interaction with the social sciences despite the fact that the social sciences themselves have evolved a far more complex set of research strategies.

38 When it inevitably has to explore the space of the subject in order to address the social-psychological motivations that underlie realist assumptions about social action, the results are far less persuasive or rigorous than the rest of the analysis. To take an influential example of a study that raises the problem of motivation and causation in legal and social change, see Gerald Rosenberg, *The Hollow Hope: Can Courts Make Social Change?* (1989). For an argument that this is the Achilles' heel of the project, see Jonathan Simon, "The Long Walk Home to Politics," 26 *Law and Soc'y Rev.* 923–42 (1992).

39 To take a well-known example that has sparked a good deal of research over the last two decades, the deployment of a new medicalized approach to defining and regulating homo-sexual conduct in the twentieth century, with its emphasis on deviant subjects rather than

abhorrent acts, invested great social significance in the distinctive subjectivity of the "homosexual." See Les Moran, *The Homosexual(ity) of Law* (1996). The highly successful movement to protect the civil rights of gay and lesbian people grew from this investment and its certainly unintended effect of making homosexual conduct a more powerful anchor for identity. On this phenomenon, see Lisa Keen and Suzanne B. Goldberg, *Strangers to the Law: Gay People on Trial* (1998).

40   See, for example, Robert Ellickson, *Order without Law: How Neighbors Settle Disputes* (1991).

41   Stuart Hall, "Cultural Studies: Two Paradigms," in *Culture/Power/History: A Reader in Contemporary Social Theory* 520–38 (Nicholas B. Dirks et al. eds., 1993).

42   Id.

43   Richard Johnson, "What Is Cultural Studies Anyway?" 16 *Soc. Text* 38 (1986).

44   Examples of this interest are found in Alison Young, "Murder in the Eyes of the Law," 17 *Stud. in Law, Politics, and Soc'y* 31 (1997); Les Moran, "From Part-Time Hero to Bent Buddy: The Male Homosexual as Lawyer in Popular Culture," 18 *Stud. in Law, Politics, and Soc'y* 3 (1998); and *Legal Reelism: Movies as Legal Texts* (John Denvir ed., 1996).

45   For an exception, see Austin Sarat, "The Cultural Life of Capital Punishment: Responsibility and Representation in *Dead Man Walking* and *Last Dance*," 11 *Yale J.L. and Human.* (1999), 153.

46   For another analogy, see Peter Brooks, "A Slightly Polemical Comment on Austin Sarat," 10 *Yale J.L. and Human.* 409 (1998). "In the humanities, we have seen cultural studies become a kind of hotel lobby where all disciplines can hang out, brought together by a self-satisfied discourse on the implication of knowledge with power, on the marginal and the hegemonic."

47   Carol Weisbrod, *Emblems of Pluralism* (2002).

48   This claim is made by Austin Sarat, "Imagining the Law of the Father: Loss, Dread, and Mourning in *The Sweet Hereafter*," 34 *Law and Soc'y Rev.* (2000) 3–46.

49   The diversity of legal realism is described by Gary Peller, "The Metaphysics of American Law," 73 *Cal. L. Rev.* 1152 (1985).

50   An example is the pillorying of Butler and Bhabha by a right-wing philosophy journal that awarded them a prize for unintelligibility, a story that was picked up uncritically by the news media, including NPR. See also John Leo, "Tower of Pomobabble," *U.S. News and World Report*, 15 March 1999, at 16.

51   The renewal of interest in realism and its meaning is itself evidence of the larger shift we discuss here. See John Henry Schlegel, *American Legal Realism and Empirical Social Science* (1995); *American Legal Realism* (William W. Fisher III et al. eds., 1993).

52   Herbert Wechsler makes this point in explaining that the Columbia of his law student days in the late 1920s was transformed by realism even though its new dean, Young B. Smith, was the candidate of the conservatives and many of the most ardent realists had left Columbia for Yale and the new program at Johns Hopkins. See Norman Silber and Geoffrey Miller, "Toward 'Neutral Principles' in the Law: Selections from the Oral History of Herbert Wechsler," 93 *Colum. L. Rev.* 854, 861 (1993).

53   An earlier version of the following pages appeared in Austin Sarat and Thomas R. Kearns, "The Cultural Lives of Law," in *Law in the Domains of Culture*, supra note 24. While we

acknowledge the difficulty of disciplining the concept of culture, we do not agree with those who believe it to be analytically useless. Exemplifying such claims is the following statement from Greenblatt: "Like 'ideology' (to which, as a concept, it is closely allied) 'culture' is a term that is repeatedly used without meaning much of anything at all, a vague gesture toward a dimly perceived ethos." Stephen Greenblatt, "Culture," in *Critical Terms for Literary Study* 225 (Frank Lentricchia and Thomas McLaughlin eds., 1995). Or, as Mary Douglas has said about the concept of culture, "[N]ever was such a fluffy notion at large . . . since singing angels blew the planets across the medieval sky or ether filled in the gaps of Newton's universe." Mary Douglas, "The Self-Completing Animal," *Times Literary Supplement*, 8 August 1975, 886.

54 As Rosaldo puts it, "These days questions of culture seem to touch a nerve." See Renato Rosaldo, *Culture and Truth: The Remaking of Social Analysis* ix (1989).

55 See Gerald Graff, *Professing Literature: An Institutional History* (1987).

56 "The recent critics of culture in no respect comprise an internally homogeneous block, and the objections currently in play represent a complex skein of partially discrete, partially convergent influences from political economy, modernist and postmodernist anthropologies, varieties of feminist writing, cultural studies, and diverse other sources." See Robert Brightman, "Forget Culture: Replacement, Transcendence, Reflexification," 10 *Cultural Anthropology* 509 (1995).

57 Annette Weiner notes about the discipline of anthropology and its relation to the idea of culture that "[t]oday . . . 'culture' is increasingly a prized intellectual commodity, aggressively appropriated by other disciplines as an organizing principle." Annette Weiner, "Culture and Our Discontents," 97 *Am. Anthropologist* 15 (1995).

58 Edward Tylor, cited by Greenblatt, supra note 53, at 225.

59 The fashionableness in recent years of speculating about the cultural deficits of the poor and the role of liberalism in worsening them speaks to this.

60 For a particularly useful summary of these critiques, see Brightman, supra note 56, at 509.

61 Lila Abu-Lughod, "Writing against Culture," in *Recapturing Anthropology: Working in the Present* 137 (Richard G. Fox ed., 1991).

62 See Brightman, supra note 56, at 509.

63 James Clifford, *The Predicament of Culture: Twentieth-Century Ethnography, Literature, and Art* 338 and 323 (1988).

64 Id., 10 and 14.

65 T. M. Luhrmann, "Review of Hermes' Dilemma and Hamlet's Desire: On the Epistemology of Interpretation," 95 *American Anthropologist* 1058 (1993).

66 See *Cultural Studies* (Lawrence Grossberg, Cary Nelson, and Paula Treichler eds. 1992).

67 Herbert Gans, *Popular Culture and High Culture: An Analysis and Evaluation of Taste* (1974).

68 See Steve Redhead, *Unpopular Cultures: The Birth of Law and Popular Culture* (1995).

69 Johnson, supra note 43, at 39.

70 Id., 43.

71 But see Stuart Hall, Chas Critcher, Tony Jefferson, John Clarke, and Brian Robert, *Policing the Crisis: Mugging, the State, and Law and Order* (1978).

72 *Law and the Order of Culture*, at vii (Robert Post ed., 1991).

73 See Silbey, supra note 19. See also Stewart Macaulay, "Images of Law in Everyday Life: The Lessons of School, Entertainment, and Spectator Sports," 21 *Law and Soc'y Rev.* 185 (1987); Anthony Chase, "Toward a Legal Theory of Popular Culture," 1986 *Wis. L. Rev.* 527; Anthony Chase, "Historical Reconstruction in Popular Legal and Political Culture," 24 *Seton Hall L. Rev.* 1969 (1994); "Symposium: Popular Legal Culture," 98 *Yale L.J.* 1545 (1989).

74 Clifford Geertz, *Local Knowledge: Further Essays in Interpretive Anthropology* 184 (1983).

75 Id., 218.

76 For a general discussion of the materiality of cultural life, see Raymond Williams, *Problems in Materialism and Culture: Selected Essays* (1980).

77 Silbey, supra note 19, at 47.

78 Johnson, supra note 43, at 39.

79 Silbey, supra note 19, at 41.

80 Austin Sarat and Thomas R. Kearns, "Across the Great Divide: Forms of Legal Scholarship and Everyday Life," in *Law in Everyday Life* 30 (Austin Sarat and Thomas R. Kearns eds., 1993).

81 Silbey, supra note 19, at 41.

82 Peter Fitzpatrick, *The Mythology of Modern Law* 202 (1992).

83 Austin Sarat, "'. . . the Law Is All Over': Power, Resistance, and the Legal Consciousness of the Welfare Poor," 2 *Yale J.L. and Human.* 343 (1990); Michel de Certeau, *The Practice of Everyday Life* 37 (Steven Rendell trans., University of California Press 1984); Jon Cruz and Justin Lewis, *Viewing, Reading, Listening: Audiences and Cultural Reception* (1994).

84 Williams defines hegemony as "a complex interlocking of political, social, and cultural forces" that sustains particular forms of inequality and domination. See Raymond Williams, *Marxism and Literature* 112 (1977). This concept, Barbara Yngvesson explains, allows us to recognize the "coexistence of discipline and struggle, of subjection and subversion, and directs attention toward a dynamic analysis of what it means to be caught up in power." Barbara Yngvesson, "Inventing Law in Local Settings: Rethinking Popular Legal Culture," 98 *Yale L.J.* 1693 (1989).

85 Rosemary Coombe, "Contingent Articulations: A Critical Cultural Studies of Law," in *Law in the Domains of Culture,* supra note 24, at 38.

86 See Jane Gaines, *Contested Culture: The Image, the Voice, and the Law* (1991).

87 See Melville Nimmer and David Nimmer, *Nimmer on Copyright: A Treatise on the Law of Literary, Musical, and Artistic Property and the Protection of Ideas* (4 vols., 8th ed., 1989); Bernard Edelman, *Ownership of the Image: Elements for a Marxist Theory of Law* (Elizabeth Kingdom trans., Routledge and Kegan Paul 1979). See also Peter Jaszi, "Toward a Theory of Copyright: The Metamorphoses of 'Authorship'" 1991 *Duke L.J.* 455.

88 Rosemary Coombe, "Author/izing the Celebrity: Publicity Rights, Postmodern Politics, and Unauthorized Genders," in *The Construction of Authorship: Textual Appropriation in Law and Literature* 101 (Martha Woodmansee and Peter Jaszi eds., 1994). See also Harold Gordon, "Right of Property in Name, Likeness, Personality, and History," 55 *Northwestern U.L. Rev.* 553 (1960); Joan Gross, "The Right of Publicity Revisited: Reconciling Fame, Fortune, and Constitutional Rights," 62 *B.U. L. Review* 986 (1982).

89 See Rosemary Coombe, supra note 85, at 61.

90 The famous "maximum feasible participation" formula of the 1960s "war on poverty" was

only one instance of this pattern of federal power from the 1930s on. See Daniel Moynihan, *Maximum Feasible Misunderstanding: Community Action in the War on Poverty* (1969).

91 Nikolas Rose, *Inventing Ourselves: Psychology, Power, and Personhood* (1996).

92 Thomas Green, "Freedom and Criminal Responsibility in the Age of Pound: An Essay on Criminal Justice," 93 *Mich. L. Rev.* 1915–2053 (1995).

93 Peter Brooks, *Troubling Confessions* (2000).

94 As it happens, Felman's reading of K-Zetnik's collapse and its legal meaning clashes directly with a portion of Hannah Arendt's legendary critique of the Eichmann trial, *Eichmann in Jerusalem* (1964). Felman takes the opportunity to read the event through the genealogy of that earlier effort to use the trials as a window into the relationship between law and evil. Arendt was highly critical of the prosecution's whole approach in the Eichmann case, which she regarded as in many respects a "show trial." Arendt pays specific attention to K-Zetnik's collapse, which she turns into a metaphor for the wages of producing the truth of the Holocaust through its victims.

  Reading Arendt psychoanalytically, Felman traces her harsh repression of the voice of the victim to Arendt's own grief for her friend Walter Benjamin's suicide while in custody at the Spanish border. Benjamin really was a victim of the banality of evil. The custody that Benjamin despaired of escaping was little more than bureaucratic bad luck at the border. By insisting that only law govern the meaning of the Holocaust, and that law avoid the risks of inviting the remembrance of violence, Arendt was excluding from the interpretation of the Holocaust what her friend Benjamin had prophetically described as "expressionless." Benjamin thought that the ability to give voice to a sense of trauma depended on a context shared between speaker and listener broad enough to encompass the trauma. Felman's analysis of Arendt reminds us that the power of law to transform the cultural meaning of events and memories, including its ability to demythologize evil, can be a political choice and not simply an inevitable expansionism in law or simply a strategy of those with the most power.

I   Approaches to the Cultural Study of Law

Law as Culture

Naomi Mezey

The notion of culture is everywhere invoked and virtually nowhere explained. Culture can mean so many things: collective identity, nation, race,
corporate policy, civilization, arts and letters, lifestyle, mass-produced popular
artifacts, ritual. Law, at first glance, appears easier to grasp if considered in
opposition to culture—as the articulated rules and rights set forth in constitutions, statutes, judicial opinions, the formality of dispute resolution, and the
foundation of social order. In most conceptions of culture, law is occasionally a
component, but it is most often peripheral or irrelevant. Most visions of law
include culture, if they include it at all, as the unavoidable social context of an
otherwise legal question—the element of irrationality or the basis of policy
conflicts. When law and culture are thought of together, they are conceptualized as distinct realms of action and only marginally related to one another. For
example, we tend to think of playing baseball or going to a baseball game as
cultural acts with no significant legal implications. We also assume that a lawsuit challenging baseball's exemption from antitrust laws is a legal act with few
cultural implications.[1] I think that both of these assumptions are profoundly
wrong. Our understandings of the game and the lawsuit are impoverished when
we fail to account for the ways in which the game is a product of law and the
lawsuit a product of culture—how the meaning of each is bound up in the other
and in the complex entanglement of law and culture.

If we are to make headway in understanding legal studies as cultural studies
and legal practice as cultural practice, then a contingent clarification of the
vague concept of culture is an important threshold consideration. The goal of

this interdisciplinary project is to understand law not in relationship to culture, as if they were two discrete realms of action and discourse, but to make sense of law as culture and culture as law—and to begin to think about how to talk about and interpret law in cultural terms.

This essay participates in an increasingly lively discussion within law and sociolegal studies about what we ought to mean by culture and what culture can mean for law. These questions have gained urgency of late thanks to recent efforts to investigate the relationship of culture to law, and vice versa, and to make a place in legal studies for a cultural analysis of law.[2] The engine of this investigation has been the popularity and usefulness of the interdisciplinary methods of cultural studies, which have been particularly keen to invade those disciplines, like law, which have traditionally insisted on their own formal integrity. Yet cultural studies suffers from the same definitional distress as culture itself: no one is exactly sure what it means to others, and everyone is loath to offer their own working definitions.

Another motivation for the academic pairing of law and culture emerges from the fact that political "culture wars" are being waged ever more explicitly on legal terrain. Congress, for instance, is increasingly confident that it can change culture through legislative initiative.[3] Take, for example, Congress's reaction to the shootings at Columbine High School and youth violence more generally. The rhetoric of the mostly partisan debate, as well as the substance of the proposed legislation,[4] focused more on regulating youth culture (in the form of movies, video games, and overly secularized public schools) than on regulating guns.[5] Like Congress, the Supreme Court is increasingly divided over whether the issues before them are issues of law or culture.[6] Congress is right that legislation can change culture, but it is right for all the wrong reasons. It is more likely that culture will be influenced by law in ways never intended or antici- pated by Congress. This common slippage between the purposes and meanings that appear to animate a particular legal rule (or even the absence of a rule) and the actual effects of a rule as it circulates through cultural practice is the object of inquiry in a cultural interpretation of law. Slippage, a concept on which I will elaborate later, identifies the dislocation between the production of legal mean- ing and its reception and rearticulation, all of which are mutually informed and always cultural. This dislocation in turn locates the inevitable intersection of law and culture.

This essay is an attempt to theorize the relationship of law to culture and culture to law beyond the intuitive, commonplace sense that law partakes of culture—by reflecting it as well as by reacting against it—and that culture refracts law. It proposes a theory of law as culture that, in detailing the mutually constitutive nature of the relationship, distinguishes itself from the way law and culture have been conceived of by realist and critical legal scholars, as well as by social norms writers. The essay concludes by speculating about one possible method by which this theorizing might be analytically employed in a cultural interpretation of law.

As an overture toward the goal of understanding law as culture, I offer in the first part of the essay what I hope is a clarification and rehabilitation of the concept of culture. After canvassing some of the best that has been thought and said about the concept, I offer a provisional way to think about culture as a set of shared signifying practices that are always in the making and always up for grabs.

The second part of the essay elaborates on what law as culture and culture as law can mean by showing the ways in which law is one of the signifying practices that constitute culture and vice versa. I give examples of three different ways in which we might understand law as culture: one that borrows from the realist and critical approaches by emphasizing the power of law over culture; another that shares some sympathies with a social norms approach by emphasizing the power of culture over law; and a third that envisions an unstable synthesis between the two, formed by a continuous recycling and rearticulation of legal and cultural meanings.

In the third part of the essay, I speculate about where this theory might lead by suggesting a very provisional structure for thinking about the work we ask culture to do, particularly with respect to law. What I propose is an investigation into the movement and moments of collision between the dependent discourses of law and culture. I suggest an approach that borrows from the ethnographic method: employing thick description in our accounts of law and culture in an effort to locate the slippage and elision between the two, directing us not so much to a singular explanation as to neglected questions and revealing juxtapositions. This sketch of a method does not aspire to the anthropological goal of making the foreign familiar; instead, it hopes to make the familiar foreign by giving further content to the proposition that law is culture. To this end, a cultural study of law envisions a robust interpretation of how conventionally understood legal and cultural meanings inform each other such that they are no longer intelligible as strictly legal or cultural. In a sense, the method presupposes the object of inquiry. As Sarat and Kearns aptly put it, to focus "on the production, interpretation, consumption, and circulation of legal meaning suggests that law is inseparable from the interests, goals, and understandings that deeply shape or comprise social life."[7]

What We Talk about When We Talk about Culture

Culture is a deeply compromised idea I cannot yet do without.—James Clifford, *The Predicament of Culture*

There are many ways to talk about culture and many ways to put it to work.[8] The contemporary work that culture is asked to do is most often explanatory; it is the product of a transformation in the concept of culture from "something to be described, interpreted, even perhaps explained . . . [to] a source of explanation in itself."[9] Adam Gopnik, an insightful culture critic for the *New Yorker*, made this point by reflecting on the pervasive use of the word "culture" in all the attempted explanations of the shootings at Columbine High School, and the ultimate misuse and even meaninglessness of the term in its constant invocations:

> But most often by "culture" we pop sociologists don't even mean violence in movies and TV and video games. We just mean—well, nothing, really. It's just decor. The only difference between saying that America is a violent country and saying that it has a "culture of violence" is that the second has a comforting, classy tone, and gives the illusion of depth. By appending the word "culture" to an observation, you somehow promote it from a description to an explanation. . . . Every age has a term to explain things that resist explanation. The Elizabethans had Fate; the Victorians had History; we have Culture.[10]

Of course, he is right, and he is not right. Gopnik is right in the sense that the word has become a kind of political expedient that we use to mean many different things and sometimes to mean nothing at all, and that this practice tends to erode the usefulness of the word. However, this problem may have as much to do with our "culture of confusion" as it does with our ubiquitous use of the word itself. Gopnik is wrong in the sense that the way he thinks we use culture is not the only way we might use it. As Gopnik suggests, when culture is deployed as political device, it is effective precisely because it has no analytical content, and it is popular because it sounds as if it did. But it only sounds as if it had analytic bite because the concept of culture belongs to a rich and contested intellectual history in which it has functioned frequently and effectively as an analytical device.[11] It is in this sense that I use the word. Culture as analytical device has not been drained of all interpretive and explanatory power simply because as a concept it resists explanation, or because we hope that its invocation alone explains more than it does. Culture is one way of explaining things.

When we make the effort to clarify what we mean by the term and are cautious about the sort of work we ask it to do, the concept may still prove to have teeth.

To talk about law and culture, or to suppose that law *is* culture, is to presume that we understand the concepts that provide the basis of our inquiry. At their most complex, these concepts undoubtedly resist the closure of definition. Culture especially is a "deeply compromised" concept.[12] Among anthropologists, there has been much hand-wringing, some of it very useful, about what it means to write culture.[13] Rosemary Coombe insists that "[t]he relationship between law and culture should not be defined" because both law and culture developed conceptually in the eighteenth and nineteenth centuries into categories that were understood as organic and discrete and were used to naturalize and legitimate European colonial power.[14] "An exploration of the nexus between law and culture will not be fruitful," she contends, "unless it can transcend and transform its initial categories."[15] I would argue that our understandings and uses of both law and culture are plastic—they cannot help but change and evolve—and that their evolution is mutually informed. Admittedly, while they have moved well beyond their initial categories, they also cannot help but bear that influence. "[E]ven if they are expressed in novel idioms, discourses on culture are not freely invented; they refer back to particular intellectual traditions that have persisted for generations. . . . New formulations can be set in a long genealogy, even if they are related to the needs of the moment."[16] I now turn to a brief summary of that genealogy.

Raymond Williams, that spectacular genealogist of culture, called "culture" "one of the two or three most complicated words in the English language."[17] Williams chronicles the meanings of the word beginning in the fifteenth century, following its association in English with the process of cultivation, first in husbandry and then in manners, to the German use of the word *Kultur* to mean civilization.[18] Williams locates an important innovation in the understanding of culture in the late eighteenth century, when it is first used in the plural, to mean "the specific and variable cultures of different nations and periods, but also the specific and variable cultures of social and economic groups within a nation."[19] This important move marks a rejection of the idea of culture as the universal progress of humanity and a shift toward something like "a particular way of life."[20] This conception of culture stands in contrast to the still popular use of the term to mean intellectual and artistic production,[21] "the best that has been thought and known in the world," in Matthew Arnold's words.[22] Finally, Williams distinguishes between culture as primarily material production, which he associates with archaeology and cultural anthropology, and culture as "signifying or symbolic systems," which he associates with history and cultural studies.[23] It is mainly in this latter sense, inspired by both cultural studies and sociology, that I use the term "culture."

Cultural studies has tended to favor, among the various definitions of culture that Williams has sketched elsewhere,[24] some form of what he calls the social definition, "in which culture is a description of a particular way of life, which expresses certain meanings and values not only in art and learning but also in institutions and ordinary behavior. The analysis of culture, from such a definition, is the clarification of the meanings and values implicit and explicit in a particular way of life, a particular culture."[25]

Williams himself was interested in reconciling the different views of culture that he canvassed, and he cautioned against accepting any singular approach to culture because the "variations of meaning" capture the complexity of the term.[26] As Williams realized, the concept of culture will always bear the imprint of the interests and ideologies that influenced its development. And this may not be such a bad thing; it certainly does not justify abandoning the term or adopting the convolutions of theoretical shorthand in order to speak of it only obliquely. It means that as we venture to name and give shape, no matter how provisionally, to our subjects, we must remain attentive to the ways in which they defy us, meaning at once more and less than we may wish.

Drawing from Williams's rather generalized social definition of culture, and emphasizing the importance of signifying systems that have been the focus of cultural studies, critical anthropology, and sociology, I will provisionally call culture any set of shared, signifying practices—practices by which meaning is produced, performed, contested, or transformed. As the sociologist William Sewell has put it, culture is *both* a semiotic system with its own logic and coherence *and* the practices that reproduce and contest that system—practices that are contradictory and always in flux.[27] Bearing in mind Williams's claim that the emergence of the modern concept of culture is "a process, not a conclusion,"[28] I want to emphasize the process of cultural practice as one of making, reproducing, and contesting meaning.

I want to distinguish here between a couple of different ways in which this version of culture might be read. Culture can be conceived as the almost unconscious meaning-systems that people inhabit and enact without choice. It can also be thought of as the more self-conscious deployment of certain symbols whose meaning becomes temporarily salient. It is at this slightly more conscious level of cultural practice that meanings are contested. Stuart Hall identifies a similar version of this distinction in cultural studies, which has used culture to mean "*both* the meanings and values which arise amongst distinctive social groups and classes . . . through which they 'handle' and respond to the conditions of existence; *and* as the lived traditions and practices through which those 'understandings' are expressed and in which they are embodied."[29] Culture as any set of shared, signifying practices can refer to both of these meanings.

The contradictions within and contestations over cultural meanings cannot be overemphasized. That contradictions exist within and between cultures is a point that can be missed by using terms—like "structure," "system," or "shared meaning"—that suggest an elegant coherence. Renato Rosaldo provides an important corrective when he argues for attention to the "internal inconsistencies, conflicts and contradictions" of cultures.[30]

In contrast with the classic view, which posits culture as a self-contained whole made up of coherent patterns, I use the term "culture" to mean a more porous array of intersecting practices and processes that emerge from within and beyond its borders. Such heterogeneous workings of culture often derive from differences of age, gender, class, race, and sexual orientation.[31]

Differences, conflicts, and confusion among people who otherwise share many signifying practices help explain why cultures are never neat, bounded, or complete.[32] It is also in the very construction of difference that we see the cultural integration of law, as law partly "generates the signs and symbols—the signifying forms—with which difference is constituted and given meaning."[33] Rosaldo, among others, emphasizes not just the differences and contradictions within cultures, but also the increasing hybridity among cultures and the fluidity of cultural boundaries that must be part of any cultural analysis.[34]

While it is critical to acknowledge that misunderstanding, conflict, and change occur within cultures and are sometimes due to differences in, say, age or race, it is equally important not to assume that the familiar categories popularized by identity politics are generally coterminous with a fixed cultural group. Whereas culture, in the sense of art, learning, and civilization, was once associated with Western superiority and whiteness, the inverse association is still true: certain practices deemed troubling or offensive are often attributed to a racialized culture.[35] The trajectory of the concept of culture has been such that culture might now be experienced as transparent for white Americans, who are sometimes thought not to "have culture," while "culture for communities of color is a fixed, monolithic essence that directs the actions of community members."[36]

Although in some cases cultures may be contiguous with communities of color or class, in most cases they cut across familiar categories because they are generally more complex than any one characteristic of a group can account for. Given the always incomplete and increasingly intersecting qualities of culture, it may sometimes make more sense to speak of specific subcultures. Yet to employ the term "subcultures" is not to imply that there is always a coherent and larger constellation known as culture that encompasses them, nor is it to equalize the power or substance among cultures. Some groups have more opportunities to make rules and organize meanings;[37] some cohere fleetingly, while others endure over generations. Culture, in the sense I am using it, can operate both horizontally across populations and vertically through generations. American urban professionals, young Goths, and Hasidic Jews constitute very different types of subcultures, but they all articulate and reproduce their respective identities through signifying practices specific to their respective cultures. The forms those practices take and the objects around which they evolve often reflect the relative power of different subcultures.

Dick Hebdige, in his well-known study of subculture, locates many of these signifying practices in the potent gestures of style: "[T]he tensions between dominant and subordinate groups can be found reflected in the surfaces of subculture—in the styles made up of mundane objects which have a double meaning."[38] The double meaning emerges when the symbols employed by a subculture (the sports utility vehicle, the trench coat, the tallis) draw ridicule or rage from others but are signs of identity and hence "sources of value" for those who use them.[39] Style, then, can be deployed as a partly self-conscious aspect of cultural practice. Sewell writes: "[T]o engage in cultural practice means to utilize the existing cultural symbols to accomplish some end. The employment of a symbol can be expected to accomplish some goal only because the symbols have more or less determinate meanings."[40] But, as Hebdige makes clear, the meaning of particular acts or symbols can change as they are referenced in new contexts or for new purposes.

For example, among some gay men in the Bay Area, paying a bridge toll for someone does not signify altruism, but sexual interest. The practice of picking up cute guys on the freeway is accomplished through a shared symbolic system that has other meanings in other contexts. The same potential for multiple or changing meanings of cultural symbols is also present in the symbolic power of clothing and the practice of dress: a trench coat can signify an affection for staying dry in the rain; it can allude to the tough but sympathetic figure cut by the 1940s private detective; or it can be worn to convey an affiliation with a subculture of disaffected middle-class youth.

Law as Culture

> [L]aw, rather than a mere technical add-on to a morally (or immorally) finished society, is, along of course with a whole range of other cultural realities from the symbolics of faith to the means of production, an active part of it.—Clifford Geertz, *Local Knowledge*

The view of culture sketched in the first part of this essay necessarily implicates law because law is one of the most potent signifying practices. As Paul Kahn puts it, the "rule of law is a social practice; it is a way of being in the world."[41] Law can be seen as one (albeit very powerful) institutional cultural actor whose diverse agents (legislators, judges, civil servants, citizens) order and reorder meanings.[42] For example, using the pick-up scenario I just mentioned, law might change the semiotic code operative in some segments of the gay population if the San Francisco city council decided to prohibit drivers from paying more than one toll or if undercover police used the code in order to identify and harass gay men. Or, more concretely, the trend toward statutory regulation of dress in schools has altered the meaning of the symbols at issue and the cultural practices of dress.[43]

As Geertz has said, law is one way in which we make sense of the world, one way of organizing meaning, one "distinctive manner of imagining the real."[44] Law is simply one of the signifying practices that constitute culture, and, despite its best efforts, it cannot be divorced from culture. Nor, for that matter, can culture be divorced from law. "To recognize that law has meaning-making power, then, is to see that social practices are not logically separable from the laws that shape them and that social practices are unintelligible apart from the legal norms that give rise to them."[45] Therefore, if one were to talk about the relationship between culture and law, it would certainly be right to say that it is always dynamic, interactive, and dialectical—law is both a producer of culture and an object of culture. Put generally, law shapes individual and group identity, social practices, and the meaning of cultural symbols, but all of these things (culture in its myriad manifestations) also shape law by changing what is socially desirable, politically feasible, legally legitimate. As Pierre Bourdieu puts it, "law is the quintessential form of 'active' discourse, able by its own operation to produce effects. It would not be excessive to say that it creates the social world, but only if we remember that it is this world which first creates the law."[46]

But perhaps we should not speak of the "relationship" between law and culture at all, as this tends to reinforce the distinction between the concepts that my description here seeks to deny. What I am after is to make sense of law *as* culture, not law *and* culture. This dynamic understanding of law as culture is influenced directly by Patricia Ewick and Susan Silbey's important book *The Common Place of Law*, in which they "conceiv[e] of law not so much operating to shape social action but *as* social action."[47] This conceptualization is related more generally to what many in sociolegal studies call a constitutive theory of law,[48] in which law is recognized as both constituting and being constituted by social relations and cultural practices.[49] In other words, law's power is discursive and productive as well as coercive. Law participates in the production of meanings within the shared semiotic system of a culture, but it is also a product of that culture and the practices that reproduce it. A constitutive theory of law rejects law's claim to autonomy and its tendency toward self-referentiality.[50] As Alan Hunt explains, "It serves to focus attention on the way in which law is implicated in social practices, as an always potentially present dimension of social relations, while at the same time reminding us that law is itself the product of the play and struggle of social relations."[51] Whether called constitutive theory or legal consciousness,[52] this understanding of the mutual constructedness of local cultural practices and larger legal institutions provides a way of thinking about law as culture and culture as law. At their most radical, these theories question the common conviction that law "is still recognizably, and usefully, distinguishable from that which is not law."[53]

While I agree that law and culture do not exist independently of each other, I disagree that their necessary interconnections make them indistinguishable from one another. Even acknowledging that the negotiation of legal meaning is always a cultural act, I believe that we still can, and should, distinguish between the way power is assigned to the law and legal actors and the way power and resistance are exercised among the least powerful. To talk about the making and contestation of meaning is necessarily to talk about power. According to Sarat and Felstiner, "Power is seen in the effort to negotiate shared understandings, and in the evasions, resistances, and inventions that inevitably accompany such negotiations."[54] It is partly in the different forms that power takes that law and culture are still recognizably distinct. Their differences are greatest when legal power manifests itself as state-sanctioned physical force or ideological influence. Indeed, most critical theorists of law think that law's hegemonic, ideological character is more effective than its violence.[55] While the differences between legal and cultural exercises of power are significant,[56] I think they are also too often exaggerated.[57] For example, law's hegemonic power depends deeply on culture to be effective, and much of the violence evident in culture likewise depends on inequalities directly and indirectly attributable to law.

Law as culture might be understood in a number of different ways. I want to suggest three possibilities. First, one might analyze the relationship between law and culture by articulating the unspoken power of law in the realm of culture. Second, one might think about the relationship by emphasizing the enduring power of culture over legal institutions and decision-making. Lastly, one might reject the distinctions suggested by a "relationship" between the two and seek to synthesize law and culture, by pointing to the ways in which they are one and the same. None of these understandings is wrong, and many of the examples that I give of each one could be recharacterized as belonging to the other two. Yet even though the distinctions are fragile, they enable us to appreciate what law as culture can mean.

The Power of Law

First, law as culture might mean emphasizing the pervasive power of law and excluding the possibility that there is an autonomous cultural realm that could be articulated without recourse to law. Here, culture is a colony in law's empire. "We live," as Ronald Dworkin puts it, "in and by the law. It makes us what we are: citizens and employees and doctors and spouses and people who own things."[58] This version of law as culture is best exemplified by the realist insight, elaborated by critical legal scholars, that law operates even when it appears not to, that legal permissions and prohibitions are in force in the most intimate and nonlegal relationships—indeed, that legal rules structure the very baseline from which we negotiate our lives and form our identities. Furthermore, these legal ground rules are all the more effective because they are not visible as law. Rather than think of legal permission as law, we tend to think of it as individual freedom, the market, or culture.

The realist insight was epitomized by the critique of the state's powerful role in determining the background rules for social action and maintaining an unequal distribution of wealth, particularly through the use of contract and property law.[59] Realists rejected the claims of classical theorists that contracts and property rights were part of a private law system based on individual autonomy rather than legal coercion.[60] Realists argued that contracts are public, rather than private, because individuals ask the state to enforce them by using law to aid one party against the other.[61] Likewise, they claimed that property is not a natural right protected by the state only in the rare event of a threat of dispossession; it is a right created by the state to exclude others generally. Thus the "law of property helps me directly only to exclude others from using the things which it assigns to me."[62] The law, then, does not merely protect owners in their possessions but also creates both owners and possessions, by creating and enforcing a right called property.

Property and contract rights together have powerful state-sanctioned distributional effects.[63] Property rights affect the relative bargaining power of the parties and hence the contract terms that can be bargained for; the terms of the contract in turn affect the ability of the parties to increase their power and possessions.[64] "The distribution of market power is thus only partly a function of private decisions of market actors; to a substantial extent, it is determined by the legal definition and allocation of property rights."[65] Thus the realists showed that conditions and relationships that were popularly thought to be nonlegal, like class or employment, were largely determined by law.[66]

The realist reconceptualization of law is captured in their view of the employer-employee relationship, a relationship they saw not as defined by two autonomous agents, whose actions were dictated by culture, but as a relationship determined by legal coercion. Law, by creating owners, also transforms nonowners into laborers, who need certain possessions to survive. As Robert Hale puts it: "Unless, then, the non-owner can produce his own food, the law compels him to starve if he has no wages, and compels him to go without wages unless he obeys the behests of some employer. It is the law that coerces him into wage-work under penalty of starvation—unless he can produce food. . . . [B]ut in every settled country there is a law which forbids him to cultivate any particular piece of ground unless he happens to be an owner."[67] Where we still tend to think of law as guiding employment relationships only at the margins, putting a floor on wages, a ceiling on hours, or governing the rules of a strike, the realists saw law as creating both employers and employees, and structuring that relationship in its most mundane and intimate aspects.

As the realists revealed, law reaches into our lives in its absence as much as in its presence. Affirmative laws create the rights of property owners. But the absence of law also creates rights of a sort. In the employment context, the absence of a federal law prohibiting employers from discriminating against people on the basis of sexual orientation means that where no local or state law dictates otherwise, law affirmatively gives employers permission to discriminate openly against gay, lesbian, or transgendered employees, by refusing to grant such employees a remedy for discrimination.[68]

Duncan Kennedy, who, as a critical legal scholar, can be seen as taking up where the realist project left off, contends that the pervasive distributional effects of law are felt not just in economic relations but in all relations of power.[69] The relative power of men and women or blacks and whites is primarily constituted not through culture but through law. For example, according to Kennedy, the historical legality of marital rape and battery as well as their current underenforcement are part of the legal background rules that define the possibilities of male behavior and hence structure the relations between men and women, even in the context of nonviolent relationships.[70] He goes on to say:

> Since we can imagine a legal program that would radically reduce the incidence of rape, the impact of rape on the relative bargaining power of nonviolent men and women is a function of the legal system.
>
> This is only the beginning of the story. The relative bargaining power of men and women when they confront one another from gendered positions is affected by hundreds of discrete legal rules. For example, the following legal choices structure women's bargaining power within marriage: the legalization of contraception and abortion, limited protection against domestic abuse, no-fault divorce, a presumption of custody in the mother, some enforcement of child support rules, and alimony without a finding of fault in the husband.[71]

One version of the critique offered by the realists and further developed by critical legal theorists is that virtually all human action, from going to bed to going to work, is either implicitly or explicitly defined and structured by law, which operates all the more effectively for appearing not to be law.[72]

The Power of Culture

Second, law as culture might mean emphasizing the pervasive power of culture, a power that might be conceived as either excluding the possibility of a legal realm that could be articulated without recourse to culture or establishing the possibility of cultural regulation that functioned independently of law.[73] Either way, law is a colony in culture's empire, and sometimes a rather powerless one.

For example, on most roads there is a legal speed limit; there are formal laws, usually enacted by state legislatures, that set the posted maximum speed.[74] Despite the existence of formal law, it is culture that actually determines the "legal" speed limit. The speed limit that is enforced, by the police and in traffic court, and hence operates as the de facto "legal" speed limit, is the limit set by the conventions of drivers—conventions which vary depending on the stretch of road, the time of day, the prevailing conditions, or the habits of a particular city or geographic region.[75]

Moreover, changes in the formal speed limit often have little or no lasting impact on the speed at which motorists drive.[76] Montana, which has seen the most fluctuation in its legal speed limit, provides the most vivid example. For almost twenty years prior to the federally imposed 55-miles-per-hour speed limit in 1975, Montana had no set speed limit and operated under what it called its "Basic Rule," which simply required a daytime speed that was reasonable and prudent under the prevailing conditions.[77] In 1995, after almost twenty years under the federal speed limit, Montana returned to using its Basic Rule.[78] Robert King and Cass Sunstein have concluded, in reviewing the history of the Montana speed limit, that the changes in the law had little impact on the behavior of drivers.[79] Montana motorists effectively ignored the federal speed limit when it was imposed and did not drive significantly faster once it was rescinded.[80] Indeed, current speed limits suggest that, if anything, the impact appears to have moved in the opposite direction, with states setting the formal legal speed limit to correspond roughly with the general practice of motorists in that region.

Culture can also be said to dictate a "legal" speed limit that differs from either the formal speed limit or the one determined by driving conventions. The color of one's car or, more important still, the color of one's skin will change the legally enforced speed limit and traffic laws generally. In this case, the shared yet contested meaning of race, combined with a subculture of policing, means that African American drivers are far more likely to be stopped by police than white drivers, even when they are a smaller percentage of the total drivers in a particular area. This practice is so common that it is now popularly known as "DWB," Driving while Black.[81] David Cole, in his widely lauded book on race and class in the criminal justice system, has collected evidence suggesting that there is a consistent and gross disparity between the rate at which blacks and whites are subject to pretextual stops.[82] For example, a review conducted in the early 1990s of more than one thousand traffic stops on one stretch of interstate highway in Florida "found that while about 5 percent of drivers on that highway were dark-skinned, nearly 70 percent of those stopped were black or Hispanic."[83] On Interstate 95 in Maryland, between 1995 and 1997, 29 percent of the drivers stopped and 70 percent of those searched were black, although African American drivers made up only 17.5 percent of the traffic on that road.[84] The statistical disparity is striking and consistent with studies done in other states.[85]

A cultural practice of targeting minority drivers persists in spite of the posted speed limit or other formal traffic laws and, more seriously, in spite of the Equal Protection Clause's guarantee that the Fourth Amendment's promise of freedom from unreasonable searches and seizures applies equally regardless of race. In an interesting and ironic twist, the law has made it nearly impossible to use a constitutional challenge to halt this cultural practice—another, more sinister version of law acquiescing to culture. In 1996, in *Wren v. United States*,[86] the Supreme Court held that as long as there is an observed traffic violation, no matter how minor, a stop is reasonable under the Fourth Amendment, even if the traffic violation is pretextual and not ultimately enforced.[87] Because driving is so minutely regulated and technical traffic violations so common, *Wren* essentially allows officers to make stops for any motive.[88] Moreover, the Court explicitly rejected the argument "that the constitutional reasonableness of traffic stops depends on the actual motivations of the individual officers involved."[89] As Cole points out, *Wren* "allows officers who have no more basis for suspicion than the color of a driver's skin to make a constitutional stop."[90] Harris takes the point further, contending that *Wren* not only approves such stops but implicitly approves the actual practice of using such stops disproportionately against African Americans and Hispanics.[91] Hence the law here aids in the triumph of culture by providing some protection for a cultural practice that is otherwise potentially illegal.[92]

Law as Culture as Law

Third, law as culture might mean emphasizing the mutuality and endless recycling between formal legal meaning-making and the signifying practices of culture, demonstrating that, despite their denials and antagonisms, these processes are always interdependent. The Supreme Court's famous decision in *Miranda v. Arizona*[93] and its recent reconsideration of that case in *Dickerson v. United States*[94] exemplify the constitutive nature of law and culture: the legal rule laid down in *Miranda* so effectively infiltrated cultural practice that forty years later the cultural embeddedness of Miranda warnings provided the justification for recognizing the constitutional status of the rule.

In *Miranda*, the Court was confronted with the problem of confessions resulting from custodial interrogation practices by police that effectively infringed the privilege against self-incrimination afforded by the Fifth Amendment.[95] The Court consciously sought a rule that would change culture in the narrow sense, by altering law-enforcement practices that ranged from the psychologically menacing to the physically brutal.[96] By requiring that custodial interrogations begin with a warning to the suspect that "he has the right to remain silent, that anything he says can be used against him in a court of law, that he has the right to the presence of an attorney, and that if he cannot afford an attorney one will be appointed for him,"[97] the Court not only changed police practices but also altered culture in the broadest sense—it created new meanings which circulated globally. The legal rule found its way not only into police stations but into television stations, movies, children's games, as well as the popular imagination of Americans and foreigners alike. The Miranda warnings became part of culture.

While one might say that *Miranda* had a more profound impact on popular culture than it did on the specific practices of law enforcement,[98] its impact in both contexts is complex and intertwined. In one sense, the effects of *Miranda* fit within the first paradigm of law as culture in which most cultural acts, symbols, and practices are traceable to the presence or absence of legal rules. Certainly, the broad cultural salience of the Miranda warnings depended on their widespread adoption within specific legal contexts. This reading, however, misses the interdependence of legal and cultural meanings. Although the legal rule had dramatic cultural influence, the influence was not unidirectional. It is plausible that, as the warnings gained cultural significance, their very familiarity made them both more mandatory and less meaningful in the context of actual interrogations.[99] One might also argue that it was culture in the narrow sense that created the need for the warnings in the first instance; they were a legal safeguard against police interrogation practices that were themselves a kind of cultural struggle over law's reach and authority.

The Supreme Court's reconsideration of its famous *Miranda* decision in 2000 evinces the third paradigm, the near-total entanglement of law and culture. At issue in *Dickerson* was whether the warnings spelled out in *Miranda* were required by the Fifth Amendment of the Constitution or were merely a prophylactic evidentiary rule meant to safeguard constitutional rights, but not required by the Constitution itself. Two years after *Miranda*, Congress had enacted a statute that sought to undermine the Miranda warnings by making the admissibility of a confession depend only on a finding of voluntariness.[100] If the *Dickerson* Court had concluded that the Miranda warnings were not constitutionally required, then Congress would have had the authority to legislate evidentiary rules governing confessions, and the statute might have overruled *Miranda* more than thirty years ago. Despite some tough cases to the contrary,[101] the Court in *Dickerson* confirmed that *Miranda* was a constitutional decision entitled to stare decisis protection and thus upheld it.[102]

What is most interesting about *Dickerson* is that the majority seemed to uphold the constitutional status of *Miranda* without a majority of the Court actually believing that Miranda warnings were ever constitutionally required.

As Justice Scalia pointed out in dissent, Justices Kennedy, O'Connor, and Rehnquist, who each joined the *Dickerson* majority, had previously participated in undercutting the constitutional rationale of *Miranda*.[103] Moreover, the *Miranda* court itself had anticipated and encouraged legislative experimentation with warnings, admitting that "we cannot say that the Constitution necessarily requires adherence to any particular solution for the inherent compulsions of the interrogation process as it is presently conducted."[104] Although the *Dickerson* majority appeared united by a commitment to stare decisis, it was an odd sort of stare decisis, in that the Court was faithful less to legal precedent and more to what that precedent had come to signify in popular culture. After *Miranda*, law had transformed culture; in *Dickerson*, culture transformed law. The *Dickerson* Court quickly and confidently declined to overrule *Miranda* because the decision "has become embedded in routine police practice to the point where the warnings have become part of our national culture."[105] Precisely because of its cultural ubiquity, a decision that the Court had been retreating from for some time was explicitly upheld—and upheld as a constitutional rule. The twist, however, is that the Court found that the warnings were constitutionally required not because the Constitution demanded them but because they had been popularized to the point that they were culturally understood as being constitutionally required.

In *Dickerson*, the synthesis of law and culture is complete: law became so thoroughly embedded in culture that culture became the rationale for law. While it is possible to read *Miranda* as a triumph of law over culture and *Dickerson* as a triumph of culture over law, I think such readings overlook the way in which both opinions participate in a broader narrative, one where law and culture are mutually constituted and legal and cultural meanings are produced precisely at the intersection of the two domains, which are themselves only fictionally distinct.

Notes Toward a Cultural Interpretation of Law

Cultural analysis is intrinsically incomplete. And, worse than that, the more deeply it goes the less complete it is.—Clifford Geertz, *The Interpretation of Cultures*

The main task of this essay is not to inaugurate a novel methodology but rather to elaborate theoretically on the uneasy entanglement of law and culture. Even the best work being done in this area has not adequately conceptualized and detailed the possible ways of thinking about law as culture and culture as law within a constitutive perspective. There is value in this theoretical endeavor, quite apart from its practical applications and normative implications.[106] But it is also worth thinking about what this theorizing might mean for legal and sociolegal scholars and what cultural studies might do for legal studies. To that end, I want to sketch briefly one possible way of thinking about a cultural interpretation of law. The work being done in a number of different fields—in sociology,[107] anthropology,[108] literature,[109] history,[110] and economics,[111] to name only a few—could be called varieties of a cultural studies of law. In this part of the essay, I borrow from semiotic and ethnographic approaches in order to approximate one methodology of cultural studies that might be fruitfully applied to law.

An Object of Inquiry: Slippage

If law is culture, then all interpretations of law are cultural interpretations. While this is widely accepted in theory, it is rarely admitted in practice; given the insularity of much legal analysis, it is therefore useful to make a cultural interpretation of law more explicit. I suggest a cultural interpretation of law that incorporates the third, synthetic view of law as culture elaborated above, one that is sympathetic to semiotic and ethnographic approaches. This interpretation employs "thick description" to give a complex account of the slippage between the production and the reception of law and legal meanings, of the ways in which specific cultural practices or identities coincide or collide with specific legal rules or conventions, thereby altering the meanings of both. In the slippage between a law's aims and effects, you often see this collision of cultural and legal meanings.

To understand law as culture synthetically and dynamically—to acknowledge that institutionally legal actors participate in creating culturally specific meanings and that legal symbols embedded in culture feed back into law—does not tell you anything substantive about how cultural meaning and practice change in response to, say, a legal rule. "Slippage" is the term I give to the inconsistencies between the production of legal meaning and its cultural reception. A legal prohibition might effectively eliminate a social practice. Or, more likely, it will alter the meaning of the practice, hence changing the purposes and effects of the practice in a way not entirely contemplated by—and in some cases directly contrary to—the aims of the legal rule.

For example, in a recent juvenile justice bill, the U.S. House of Representatives approved an amendment of questionable constitutionality allowing states to permit displays of the Ten Commandments on public property.[112] While it seems unlikely that posting the Ten Commandments in classrooms will significantly reduce youth violence, it seems quite possible that it will increase the cynicism of kids who perceive a divergence between what adults preach and what they practice. Indeed, there is some possibility that posting the Ten Commandments in classrooms could have an effect opposite to the one Congress intended: it could actually *increase* youth violence, by increasing youth cynicism. In the case of the Columbine shootings, for example, this outcome is more plausible than it might initially appear. The two killers apparently targeted religious classmates and asked them whether they believed in God. Given that religion partly motivated the violence in that instance, it seems relatively safe to say that posting the Ten Commandments at Columbine would not have prevented the killings, and might have even helped precipitate them. Similarly, in a related but less speculative vein, a legal prohibition against wearing trench coats in schools might only increase their symbolic power, adding an outlaw status to their prior significance.[113] The point is that understanding the inevitability of slippage makes the relationship between law and culture, if not clearer, clearly inescapable.

The Indian Gaming Regulatory Act (IGRA)[114] and its reception among different Native American cultures provides another example of slippage.[115] The act allows a limited gaming monopoly on Indian reservations. The stated purpose of IGRA was to create economic opportunities for tribes that would help them increase their sovereignty and decrease their poverty and dependence on the federal government. Like most statutes, IGRA invoked a vision of its proper subjects—in this case, the most traditional and poorest tribes. Thus the legislation produced not just legal rules (about what tribes must do in order to provide gaming) but engaged other sorts of cultural meanings (about what it means to be Native American). At the level of reception, however, the legal meaning of IGRA and its implementing regulations was utterly transformed by its tension with cultural practice. The most traditional tribes—arguably those that needed economic opportunities the most—refused to take advantage of the statute's benefits because its requirements were seen as an affront to their sovereignty, its opportunities as an affront to their identity. The tribes that were most able to benefit from the statute were either those least likely to need it or those that were the products of the law itself—tribes that sought recognition in order to set up gaming.[116] Thus, once a law is implemented—a process that always takes place in culturally specific contexts—its intended and unintended meanings circulate and are transformed. Those whom the law seeks to govern may redefine the law, the law may redefine them, or both. Getting at how this happens is the object of a cultural interpretation of law.

A Method of Inquiry: Thick Description

Although many disciplinary methods can and should be used in cultural interpretation, I want to suggest that Geertz's famous ethnographic method, with some modification, is particularly well suited to the task. Geertz's concept of "thick description,"[117] from which I borrow, was itself borrowed from Gilbert Ryle, who used it to show that descriptively there is no distinction between a twitch and a wink, as both are accurately described as the rapid contraction of an eyelid.[118] Making sense of the difference between a twitch and a wink requires capturing, through thick description, the cultural context of the eyelid contraction—the social codes that give it meaning as a twitch, a wink, a fake wink, a parody of a wink, a rehearsal of a wink, and so on.[119] Geertz uses thick description to mean ethnography, the rendering of "piled-up structures of inference and implication" that give contingent meaning to gestures, acts, rituals, things.[120] It is evident, then, that Geertz understands ethnography as not just descriptive but also as explanatory and interpretive. As he says, "It is explication I am after, construing social expressions on their surface enigmatical."[121]

I propose to modify this method in order to emphasize the interpretive aspects of thick description as against its representational possibilities. Cultural anthropology has come under attack for its antique, anthropological renderings of other societies, which were represented as "organic, unified, and whole,"[122] and which were used to distinguish, through description, those unlike us. Obviously, even description can be implicitly interpretive or normative (for example, when you describe someone as a "heathen").[123] However, despite some legitimate conceptual ambiguity, the primary task of much classical cultural anthropology has been representation rather than interpretation. This is one use of thick description that I caution against.

In addition, despite the fact that Geertz stresses that thick description is essentially interpretive,[124] others have pointed out that thick descriptions can still render thin interpretations.[125] The emphasis of a cultural interpretation of law should not be on documentation but rather on the interpretive battles in the ongoing struggle over meaning. A cultural interpretation of law does not seek to sort out the informal rules of a particular culture or to speculate about the "cultures" of law and legal practice. Instead, it involves the slightly more convoluted investigation of two intertwined social discourses and aims less at interpreting the rules of each and more at explaining the nature of their necessary intersection.

Ideally, there are three distinct interpretive aspects of what I am calling a cultural interpretation of law. The first is an interpretation of law at a site of production (the courtroom, the committee room, etc.),[126] which would make use of both traditional and nontraditional modes of legal interpretation.[127] The second is an interpretation of the cultural practices that might be said to inspire the law and those that the law confronts when applied. Ethnography or thick description is particularly well suited to this investigation. The third, and most crucial, is an interpretation of the encounter between law and culture—an interpretation of the interventions of culture in law and law in culture, of the dissolution of production and reception into a circulation of the interdependencies, contradictions, and conspiracies in meaning.

Some Implications of a Cultural Interpretation of Law

At this point, I want to return to an example in order to discuss in very broad terms how these strands of inquiry might come together. To attribute the Columbine shootings to "a culture of violence" is to invoke culture as a political device devoid of content.[128] A cultural interpretation of the legal responses to Columbine specifically, and youth violence generally, could be an opportunity to investigate the slippage between the production and reception of legal meanings. In this context, such an inquiry might begin at various sites of legal production and investigate their legal and cultural significance in relation to the shootings. The most obvious starting point might be the Second Amendment of the Constitution,[129] including the scholarly debates about its scope and interpretation, as well as its symbolic power (invoking, as it does, potent myths about pre-legal, individualistic norms of structured violence and freedom).[130] Judicial opinions interpreting the Second Amendment would be another important source of legal meaning.[131] In addition, Congress's role in supporting the presence and absence of gun control regulation is also significant in the legal debate over youth violence. Here, the lack of strong gun control laws and the political pressure on both sides of the issue contribute to the meaning of guns and the increased possibilities for legal violence.

Congress has been an especially potent producer of meaning in the recent debates over gun control and youth violence. Legislators have seemed to assume a direct causal link both between culture and youth violence and between legislative proposals and social behavior. The link between culture and the shootings at Columbine was repeatedly expressed in congressional debates over possible legislative responses.[132] The link between legislative regulation and behavior was assumed in the mammoth juvenile justice bill that grew out of the Columbine shootings.[133] The bill was heavy on cultural initiatives. It proposed redefining juvenile gangs;[134] directed the National Institutes of Health to study "the effects of violent video games and music on child development and youth violence";[135] established parenting training programs;[136] allowed for antitrust exemptions to entertainment-industry agreements aimed at alleviating the impact of violent and sexual subject matter in the media;[137] and sought to prevent juvenile delinquency through character education.[138] The congressional responses to Columbine attempted to change youth culture without acknowledging the participation of the law in the production of that culture. As a result, legislative proposals are less effective to the extent that they miss the salience of cultural practices that might contradict statutory goals and misjudge the ways in which statutes influence social life. For example, gun control advocates often overlook one cultural consequence and unintended effect of their proposals—namely, the likely increase in the symbolic power of guns.

Next, there is a whole category of sources that would be of secondary interest to an inquiry into the production of legal meaning surrounding the Columbine shootings: laws governing school funding, zoning, the distribution of mental health care, or law enforcement. A cultural interpretation of law would take up any or all of these laws and attempt to make sense of them as law and also as metaphor and symbol, understanding them as part of a larger set of social discourses of which they are an inextricable part. In other words, at the level of production, a cultural interpretation of law would try to account for the legal constructions that animate, and are animated by, the social practices at issue.

The legal discourse relevant to unpacking the significance of the Columbine shootings is bound up with the meanings of a number of cultural conventions and practices that would also be the object of a cultural interpretation of law. An ethnographic inquiry might focus on the relevant details of Goth subculture;[139] the rituals of Colorado suburban life; militias; and the hierarchies of social cliques at Columbine High School.[140] Alternatively, one might look at the extensive recent literature on youth culture more generally to help make sense of the event.[141] While I advocate the use of ethnography and semiotics to examine the social discourses that might give cultural meaning to these shootings, one could also use the methodologies of literature, history, psychology, or sociology to get a thicker, if different, description.

Finally, if there is a payoff to a cultural interpretation of law, it is in locating the entanglements of legal and cultural meanings. In the case of Columbine, the meanings of gun regulation and deregulation circulate in the world in which kids live and help inform their relationships to school, parents, and authority generally, their conflicts with peers, as well as their sense of agency and power-lessness.[142] As a result, the reception and reinterpretation of legal meaning are usually quite different from its production—different in ways that are made comprehensible by placing legal acts and omissions in their cultural contexts.

It might be the case that the story law tells about youth culture does not in fact bear any causal relationship to the story law tells about youth violence. As Andrew Sullivan observes, "The era that has seen the popular culture ratchet up its drug-addled, bigoted, violent messages to new levels of depravity has also seen one of the sharpest declines in teen violence, sex, and drug use ever."[143] On the other hand, the causation might exist but run in the opposite direction, with violent forms of popular culture functioning as a benign surrogate for the aggressive fantasies of teenagers.[144]

Another way to think about the interaction of legal and cultural meaning in the context of youth violence is to consider the ways in which the cultural power of gun advocates has influenced our notion of what is legally possible. Robin West has pointed out that when gun advocates are taken seriously, gun ownership is "invested with constitutional authority, and hence constitutional meaning. . . . The gun owner becomes an ideal, and an ideal which is constitutional. Her defiance *defines* us. Even if their legal claim ultimately fails, in other words, the NRA's depiction of our nature, and of what it means to be an American, remains, with respect to guns and gun ownership, the only constitutional story being told."[145] One implication of this argument is that the greatest obstacle to gun control legislation may not be politics or the Constitution, but the cultural power of guns.

From this perspective, there will be double slippage between law and culture: first, between the aims of the legislative initiatives directed at popular culture and their significance among consumers of movies and video games; second, between virtually any form of gun control that might pass Congress and the cultural saliency of guns and gun ownership. The inevitability of slippage is not a politically inspiring story, but it is truer to the webs of signification that bind law and culture.

If rage expressed through gun violence is part of culture (road rage, school rage, ethnic rage), then we need to make sense of how and why this is so, beyond the platitudes and easy indictments of popular culture. If law is culture, then the reception of legal meaning in social practices and the equation of guns with personal freedom and self-realization do not begin in either law or culture; rather, they tend to make clear that they are part of the same economy of signification. To dismiss and distance such rage as a product of a "culture of violence" misses the opportunity to make sense of it as a deeper part of our culture and a product of our laws. In this case, the interpretation is "thick" to the extent that it can explain how legal violence is constructed and understood in both legal and cultural practices, and how those specific practices help constitute each other.

Conclusion

I have tried to explore three different versions of what law as culture has meant and might mean. I have also briefly sketched a method for trying to apply the synthetic version of law as culture. Outlining the task of a cultural interpretation of law this broadly has the advantage of leaving room for variations on the theme, improvisations of approach, and engagement with the tools of other disciplines. Whereas a positivist scholar of law and culture might consider theoretical variety to be a vice,[146] I consider it a virtue. To my mind, one of the gifts of cultural studies is the hybrid vigor of theoretical mixing. I agree with Geertz that the object of analysis should determine the theory and not the other way around;[147] to script a theoretical method tightly would risk "locking cultural analysis away from its proper object, the informal logic of actual life."[148]

This raises the problem of formulating abstract theories at all, such as the one in this essay. I have provided a provisional framework for a cultural interpretation of law that I realize will (or will not) be persuasive only in the context of specific applications. While I cannot dispute that theoretical formulations "stated independently of their applications . . . seem either commonplace or vacant,"[149] I think that such a sketch, as well as the formulations of law as culture that animate it, is valuable to the extent that it enables scholars of law and culture to work toward some sort of agreement, however tentative, about what it is that we are doing. As scholars in a field that is still forming, more theoretical guidance, with plenty of room for dissent, would, I think, be helpful. A more coherent framework and a more consistent vocabulary would encourage this sort of work—work that at its best invites attention to issues of justice, power, recognition, and self-definition. To focus on culture is to locate the ways in which law influences who we are and who we aspire to be, and it moves us beyond the standard critique of what the law is and what we want it to be. Kahn is right to insist that the crucial "issue is not whether law makes us better off, but rather what it is that the law makes us."[150] As Sarat and Kearns so eloquently note, "we come, in uncertain and contingent ways, to see ourselves as the law sees us; we participate in the construction of law's 'meanings' and its representations of us even as we internalize them, so much so that our own purposes and understandings can no longer be extricated from those meanings."[151] Thus we all, in the most intimate sense, stand to gain from understanding law as culture.

There is, lastly, the issue of the complexity and uncertainty that attends scholarship of this kind. Some consider it a serious drawback that it is messy and makes appraisal so difficult.[152] With respect to appraisal, Guyora Binder and Robert Weisberg suggest that we judge legal representations of the social and law itself "aesthetically rather than epistemologically . . . according to the society it forms, the identities it defines, the preferences it encourages, and the subjective experience it enables."[153] My hope is that the appraisal of such work could be both aesthetic and epistemological. With respect to its messiness, I suspect that the cultural study of law will never attain the status of law and economics within law schools, precisely because, rather than simplifying law, it complicates it.[154] I count myself among those who consider the complexity of the endeavor a virtue. That is why our agreements as to method can and should be only rough. A cultural interpretation of law, like interpretive anthropology, is an enterprise "whose progress is marked less by a perfection of consensus than by a refinement of debate. What gets better is the precision with which we vex each other."[155]

Notes

My thanks to Heidi Li Feldman, Mark Kelman, David Luban, Leti Volpp, and Robin West for their comments on earlier drafts of this essay and to Rachel Taylor and Philip Ferrera for superb research assistance. The many comments I received from my colleagues at the Georgetown Faculty Workshops and from the participants of the Legal Studies as Cultural Studies Conference have improved this paper in ways large and small; I am particularly grateful for the insights of Lama Abu-Odeh, Sam Dash, Katherine Franke, Michael Gottesman, Angela Harris, Gillian Lester, Michael Musheno, Gary Peller, Milton Regan, Mike Seidman, Girardeau Spann, and Mark Tushnet. Thanks finally to Austin Sarat, Jonathan Simon, and the *Yale Journal of Law and the Humanities* for the opportunity to write and present this essay, and to Clifford Rosky and John Pellettieri for their very fine editing suggestions.

1   See, e.g., Flood v. Kuhn, 407 U.S. 258 (1972); Toolson v. N.Y. Yankees, 346 U.S. 356 (1953); Federal Baseball Club v. Nat'l League, 259 U.S. 200 (1922).

2   Austin Sarat and Thomas Kearns have been indefatigable champions of this cause with

their series of books in law, jurisprudence, and social thought. E.g., *Cultural Pluralism, Identity Politics, and the Law* (Austin Sarat and Thomas R. Kearns eds., 1999); *Law in the Domains of Culture* (Austin Sarat and Thomas R. Kearns eds., 1998); *Law in Everyday Life* (Austin Sarat and Thomas R. Kearns eds., 1993). See also Guyora Binder and Robert Weisberg, *Literary Criticisms of Law* (2000); Rosemary J. Coombe, *The Cultural Life of Intellectual Properties: Authorship, Appropriation and the Law* (1999); Robert M. Cover, *Narrative, Violence, and the Law: The Essays of Robert M. Cover* (Martha Minow et al. eds., 1993); Patricia Ewick and Susan S. Silbey, *The Common Place of Law: Stories from Everyday Life* (1998); Paul W. Kahn, *The Cultural Study of Law: Reconstructing Legal Scholarship* (1999); *Legal Studies as Cultural Studies: A Reader in (Post)Modern Critical Theory* (Jerry Leonard ed., 1995). However, many of the important predecessors in this area have worked primarily in anthropology and American studies. E.g., James Clifford, *The Predicament of Culture: Twentieth-Century Ethnography, Literature, and Art* (1988); Jane M. Gaines, *Contested Culture: The Image, the Voice, and the Law* (1991); Clifford Geertz, *Local Knowledge: Further Essays in Interpretive Anthropology* (1983).

3 See infra "Notes Ttoward a Cultural Interpretation of Law" (text accompanying notes 107–46).

4 Juvenile Justice Reform Act, H.R. 1501, 106th Cong. (1999).

5 I do not want to suggest that regulating guns is not an act with cultural implications, merely that legislators are increasingly overt in their attempts to use law to reform culture, however cynical those attempts might be. "The House did not entertain measures to make parents pay more attention to their children, or to expand mental health coverage, or to encourage jocks to treat Goths with more respect, but it discussed just about every other Columbine explanation. The widespread sense among members was that the era of big government may be over, but when tragedy strikes, Americans still expect at least the appearance of action from their politicians. In a typical swipe, Rep. Louise M. Slaughter (D-NY) described the debate as 'full of solutions in search of problems.'" Michael Grunwald, "Culture Wars Erupt in Debate on Hill," *Wash. Post*, June 18, 1999, at A1.

6 See infra "Law as Culture as Law" (text accompanying notes 93-105); see also Romer v. Evans, 517 U.S. 620 (1996). In Romer, the majority found that a Colorado referendum targeting homosexuals violated the Equal Protection Clause because it could not be explained by anything other than animus toward the class it affected. 517 U.S. at 632. Justice Scalia, writing in dissent, claimed that the majority had "mistaken a Kulturkampf for a fit of spite" by a group of tolerant Coloradans who were merely trying to express their cultural preference for heterosexuality. Id. at 636. Because Scalia found that nothing in the law prevented Coloradans from doing so, he argued that the Court should not resolve the issue based on its own preferences in an otherwise purely cultural debate. Id.

7 Austin Sarat and Thomas R. Kearns, "The Cultural Lives of Law," in *Law in the Domains of Culture*, supra note 2, at 1, 6.

8 A note on this part's title, "What We Talk about When We Talk about Culture." Among those who talk about culture, there seems to be a prevailing taboo against saying anything that might be understood as definitive on so delicate a topic, even while at the same time purporting to elucidate it. In the face of this trend, I thought I would try to say something definitive without aspiring to elucidation. A nod to Raymond Carver strikes me as a fitting way to acknowledge that culture, like love, is not something you can hold at arm's length

and analyze; because there is no escape from culture, to theorize about it is to theorize within it; to talk about it with others is to make it. See Raymond Carver, *What We Talk about When We Talk about Love: Stories* (1981).

9   Adam Kuper, *Culture: The Anthropologists' Account*, at xi (1999).

10   Adam Gopnik, "Culture Vultures," *New Yorker*, May 24, 1999, at 27, 28.

11   For example, Kuper, supra note 9, gives an account of the history of the concept within anthropology and, to a lesser extent, within sociology.

12   Clifford, supra note 2, at 10.

13   See, e.g., *Writing Culture: The Poetics and Politics of Ethnography* (James Clifford and George E. Marcus eds., 1986); Lila Abu-Lughod, "Writing against Culture," in *Recapturing Anthropology: Working in the Present* 137 (Richard G. Fox ed., 1991). These authors criticize the implicit hierarchy in ethnography, which articulates "the authority of the anthropologist by telling anthropology's essential(ist) story—that most modern triangle—of the grand encounter between the West and the rest, with the anthropologist as hypotenuse." Richard G. Fox, "For a Nearly New Cultural History," in *Recapturing Anthropology: Working in the Present*, supra, at 93. Renato Rosaldo puts it more pointedly: "The Lone Ethnographer's mask of innocence (or, as he put it, his 'detached impartiality') barely concealed his ideological role in perpetuating the colonial control of 'distant' peoples and places. His writings represented the human objects of the civilizing mission's global enterprise as if they were the ideal recipients of the white man's burden." Renato Rosaldo, *Culture and Truth: The Remaking of Social Analysis* 30 (1998).

14   See Rosemary J. Coombe, "Contingent Articulations: A Critical Cultural Studies of Law," in *Law in the Domains of Culture*, supra note 2, at 21.

15   Id.

16   Kuper, supra note 9, at 9–10.

17   Raymond Williams, *Keywords: A Vocabulary of Culture and Society* 87 (rev. ed. 1983). Others have more thoroughly summarized Williams's genealogy. See, e.g., Clifford, supra note 2, at 233–34; Dick Hebdige, *Subculture: The Meaning of Style* 6–7 (1979). Coombe provides a genealogy of the concept of culture that, drawing extensively from the work of Robert Young, links it more explicitly to law. Coombe, supra note 14, at 22–25; see also Kuper, supra note 9; Robert J. C. Young, *Colonial Desire: Hybridity in Theory, Culture, and Race* (1995).

18   Williams, supra note 17, at 87–89; see also 3 *Oxford English Dictionary* 257 (2d ed. 1971). Culture as civilization was meant to be the antithesis of nature or barbarism. Coombe, supra note 14, at 23.

19   Williams, supra note 17, at 89.

20   Williams attributes this innovation to Johann Gottfried von Herder, who, sounding exceedingly modern, attacked the idea of culture as universal; he decried the use of the term to naturalize the progress of human development at the expense of those cultures that Europe subjugated. Williams quotes Herder: "Men of all the quarters of the globe, who have perished over the ages, you have not lived solely to manure the earth with your ashes, so that at the end of time your posterity should be made happy by European culture. The very thought of a superior European culture is a blatant insult to the majesty of nature." Id. at 89 (quoting Herder without citation).

21 Id. at 90–91.

22 Matthew Arnold, *Culture and Anarchy and Other Writings* 79 (Stefan Collini ed., 1993). Although Arnold's is perhaps one of the most frequently quoted phrases on the meaning of culture, much less often quoted is the passage from which this phrase is taken. It demonstrates the moral and egalitarian impulses behind Arnold's formulation, which is most often referenced for its elitism. See, e.g., Clifford, supra note 2, at 337–38. According to Arnold, culture is about perfection—not the perfection of artistic production but the perfecting of human beings. Arnold, supra, at 59. Culture, he adds, "seeks to do away with classes; to make the best that has been thought and known in the world current everywhere; to make all men live in an atmosphere of sweetness and light, where they may use ideas, as it uses them itself, freely,—nourished, and not bound by them. . . . [T]he men of culture are the true apostles of equality." Id. at 79.

23 Williams, supra note 17, at 91.

24 In *The Long Revolution*, Williams identifies three categories in the definition of culture that correspond to some of the themes already mentioned: (1) the ideal, which understands culture as "a state or process of human perfection" according to universal values; (2) the documentary, where culture is "the body of intellectual and imaginative work"; and (3) the social, described above. Raymond Williams, *The Long Revolution* 41 (rev. ed. 1966).

25 Id. Stuart Hall identifies this "culturalism" (as opposed to structuralism) of Williams, Hoggart, and Thompson as the dominant paradigm within cultural studies. Stuart Hall, "Cultural Studies: Two Paradigms," in *Culture/Power/History: A Reader in Contemporary Social Theory* 520, 527 (Nicholas B. Dirks et al. eds., 1994).

26 Williams, supra note 24, at 43; see Hall, supra note 25 (contextualizing Williams's discussion of culture in *The Long Revolution*).

27 William H. Sewell Jr., The Concepts of Culture (1996) (unpublished manuscript, on file with author).

28 Raymond Williams, *Culture and Society: 1780–1950*, at 295 (1958).

29 Hall, supra note 25, at 527.

30 Rosaldo, supra note 13, at 28.

31 See id. at 20–21.

32 Clifford's essay about the Mashpee is an exceptional discussion of this proposition as well as of the repercussions of our assumptions otherwise. In the essay, Clifford points out that "the culture idea, tied as it is to assumptions about natural growth and life, does not tolerate radical breaks in historical continuity. . . . Metaphors of continuity and 'survival' do not account for complex historical processes of appropriation, compromise, subversion, masking, invention, and revival." Clifford, supra note 2, at 277, 338.

33 Coombe, supra note 14, at 37.

34 Rosaldo, supra note 13, at 20–21. Clifford notes, "The increased pace of historical change, the common recurrence of stress in the systems under study, forces a new self-consciousness about the way cultural wholes and boundaries are constructed and translated." Clifford, supra note 2, at 231. Edward Said links this reassessment of cultural boundaries more explicitly to imperialism: "Partly because of empire, all cultures are involved in one another; none is single and pure, all are hybrid, heterogenous, extraordinarily differentiated, and unmonolithic." Edward W. Said, *Culture and Imperialism*, at xxv (1993).

35 See Leti Volpp, "Blaming Culture for Bad Behavior," 12 *Yale J.L. and Human.* 89 (2000) (using examples of forced and voluntary adolescent marriages).

36 Id. at 94 (discussing Paul Gilroy's contention that "[w]hen culture is brought into contact with 'race' it is transformed into a pseudo-biological property of communal life" (quoting Paul Gilroy, *Small Acts: Thoughts on the Politics of Black Cultures* 24 (1993)); see also Dorothy E. Roberts, "Why Culture Matters to Law: The Difference Politics Makes," in *Cultural Pluralism, Identity Politics, and the Law,* supra note 2, at 85; Rosaldo, supra note 13, at 198–204. Rosaldo argues that one problem with conflating culture with difference is that it masks power: "[T]he more power one has, the less culture one enjoys, and the more culture one has, the less power one wields." Rosaldo, supra note 13, at 202.

37 See Hebdige, supra note 17, at 14.

38 Id. at 2.

39 Id. at 3.

40 Sewell, supra note 27, at 19.

41 Kahn, supra note 2, at 36.

42 Sewell does not address law specifically, but he makes the important point that "much cultural practice is concentrated in and around powerful institutional nodes—for example, religions, communications media, business corporations, and, most spectacularly, states." Sewell, supra note 27, at 31.

43 See infra note 113 and accompanying text.

44 Geertz, supra note 2, at 184.

45 Sarat and Kearns, supra note 7, at 10.

46 Pierre Bourdieu, "The Force of Law: Toward a Sociology of the Juridical Field," 38 *Hastings L.J.* 814, 839 (1987); see also Ewick and Silbey, supra note 2, at 39 (1998) (describing "a reciprocal process in which the meanings given by individuals to their world become patterned, stabilized, and objectified. These meanings, once institutionalized, become part of the material and discursive systems that limit and constrain future meaning-making.").

47 Ewick and Silbey, supra note 2, 34–35.

48 See, e.g., Alan Hunt, *Explorations in Law and Society: Toward a Constitutive Theory of Law* (1993); *Law in Everyday Life,* supra note 2, at 27–32; Susan S. Silbey and Austin Sarat, "Critical Traditions in Law and Society Research," 21 *Law and Soc'y Rev.* 165 (1987).

49 Naomi Mezey, "Out of the Ordinary: Law, Power, Culture and the Commonplace," 26 *Law and Soc. Inquiry* 145 (2001).

50 See Hunt, supra note 48, at 304–5.

51 Id. at 3.

52 Ewick and Silbey use the term "legal consciousness" "to name participation in the process of constructing legality. . . . [E]ach person's participation sustains legality as an organizing structure of social relations." Ewick and Silbey, supra note 2, at 45.

53 Id. at 19.

54 Austin Sarat and William L. F. Felstiner, *Divorce Lawyers and Their Clients: Power and Meaning in the Legal Process* 11 (1995).

55 Robert Gordon gives one of the classic statements of the hegemonic power of law: "[T]he power exerted by a legal regime consists less in the force that it can bring to bear against violators of its rules than in its capacity to persuade people that the world described in its

images and categories is the only attainable world in which a sane person would want to live." Robert Gordon, "Critical Legal Histories," 36 *Stan. L. Rev.* 57, 108 (1984). For the original source on "hegemony," see Antonio Gramsci, *Selections from the Prison Notebooks of Antonio Gramsci* 242, 245–46 (Quintin Hoare and Geoffrey Newell Smith eds. and trans., 1971).

56 Robert M. Cover, "Violence and the Word," reprinted in Cover, supra note 2, at 203.

57 Sarat and Felstiner offer a valuable corrective when they describe the power in the lawyer-client interactions they observed as "not possessed at all. It is mobile and volatile, and it circulates such that both lawyer and client can be considered more or less powerful, even at the same time." Sarat and Felstiner, supra note 54, at 19.

58 Dworkin continues: "It is sword, shield, and menace: we insist on our wage, or refuse to pay our rent, or are forced to forfeit penalties, or are closed up in jail, all in the name of what our abstract and ethereal sovereign, the law, has decreed. . . . We are subjects of law's empire." Ronald Dworkin, *Law's Empire*, at vii (1986).

59 While this story has been told many times by many different scholars, I rely here primarily on Gary Peller, "The Metaphysics of American Law," 73 *Cal. L. Rev.* 1151 (1985); Joseph William Singer, "Legal Realism Now," 76 *Cal. L. Rev.* 465 (1988).

60 Lochner v. New York, 198 U.S. 45 (1905), is the now infamous expression of the classical approach to contract. The *Lochner* Court understood the power of the state to legislate and the power of the individual to contract as two separate and competing powers, and concluded that the statute at issue was "an illegal interference with the rights of individuals, both employers and employes [*sic*], to make contracts regarding labor upon such terms as they may think best. . . . Statutes of the nature of that under review, limiting the hours in which grown and intelligent men may labor to earn their living, are mere meddlesome interferences with the rights of the individual." 198 U.S. at 61.

61 See, e.g., Morris Cohen, "The Basis of Contract," 46 *Harv. L. Rev.* 553, 562 (1933); cf. Jay M. Feinman and Peter Gabel, "Contract Law as Ideology," in *The Politics of Law: A Progressive Critique* 373 (David Kairys ed., 1990) (tracing the history of contract law through its ideological imagery).

62 Morris Cohen, "Property and Sovereignty," 13 *Cornell L.Q.* 8, 12 (1927).

63 See id. at 13 ("The extent of the power over the life of others which the legal order confers on those called owners is not fully appreciated by those who think of the law as merely protecting men in their possession."); Robert L. Hale, "Coercion and Distribution in a Supposedly Non-Coercive State," 38 *Pol. Sci. Q.* 470, 478 (1923) ("The distribution of income, to repeat, depends on the relative power of coercion which the different members of the community can exert against one another. . . . The resulting distribution is very far from being equal, and the inequalities are very far from corresponding to needs or to sacrifice.").

64 Singer, supra note 59, at 489. Put bluntly, "Property law, when combined with contract law, delegates to property owners the power to coerce nonowners to contract on terms imposed by the stronger party." Id. at 490. The only pressure operating to counteract the power of coercion is the relatively weak power of the nonowner to withhold her labor. Id.

65 Id. at 488.

66 Peller, supra note 59, at 1237 (explaining that the realist contention "was that the distinctions between the terms public and private, free will and coercion, were constructed in the very opinions which purported to proceed from them").

67 Hale, supra note 63, at 473; see generally Barbara H. Fried, *The Progressive Assault on Laissez Faire: Robert Hale and the First Law and Economics Movement* (1998). Hale's position can be distinguished from the standard Marxist critique of capital by the emphasis he puts on the ability of both workers and consumers to exert some countercoercion on labor. Hale, supra note 63, at 474.

68 Title VII of the Civil Rights Act of 1964 prohibited discrimination on the basis of race, color, religion, sex, or national origin. 42 U.S.C. § 2000e-2(a) (1964). With passage of the Age Discrimination in Employment Act, 29 U.S.C. § 621 (1967), and the Americans with Disabilities Act, 42 U.S.C. § 12,102(2) (1991), age and disability have been added as protected categories. Federal legislation to prohibit discrimination on the basis of sexual orientation has been introduced in Congress but has not passed. Employment Non-Discrimination Act, S. 2056, 104th Cong. (1996); S. 1276, 106th Cong. (1999). The Employment Non-Discrimination Act has been reintroduced in the 107th Congress as Title V to the Protecting Civil Rights for All Americans Act, S. 19, 107th Cong. (2001).

69 Duncan Kennedy, "The Stakes of Law, or Hale and Foucault!" in *Sexy Dressing, Etc.: Essays on the Power and Politics of Cultural Identity* 83 (1993).

70 Id. at 103–4; see also Duncan Kennedy, "Sexual Abuse, Sexy Dressing, and the Eroticization of Domination," in *Sexy Dressing, Etc.*, supra note 69, at 126. In other respects, Kennedy's book is a great example of a synthetic approach to law and culture.

71 Kennedy, supra note 69, at 104.

72 Mark Tushnet suggested to me a wonderful example of the invisibility of ground rules: there are implicit rules that most people recognize governing whether it is okay to let someone cut into a line, and whether it is better to let them in ahead of you or behind you, but the more powerful and less visible ground rule is evinced by the fact of the line itself.

73 I associate this second version of the power of culture with some social norms scholarship. See, e.g., Robert Ellickson, *Order without Law: How Neighbors Settle Disputes* (1991).

74 In 1974, in response to the Arab oil embargo, Congress passed a federally imposed 55-miles-per-hour speed limit in an effort to save fuel. Law of Jan. 4, 1975, Pub. L. No. 93–643, § 102(b), 88 Stat. 2281 (1975), repealed by National Highway System Act of 1995, 23 U.S.C. § 101 (1995). With full federal highway funds as an incentive, every state eventually complied. See Tyce Palmaffy, "Don't Brake for Big Government," *J. Am. Citizenship Pol. Rev.*, Sept.–Oct. 1996, at 11. In 1995 the newly Republican Congress, with the reluctant support of President Clinton, repealed the federal speed limit and returned authority to the states. National Highway System Act of 1995, 23 U.S.C. § 101 (1995). All states except Hawaii have since raised their highway speed limits to between sixty-five and seventy-five miles per hour for cars. "Maximum Speed Limits in Each State," at http://web.missouri.edu/7Ec669885/ncasl/limits.html (last updated Feb. 13, 2000).

75 See Ronald J. Krotoszynski, "Building Bridges and Overcoming Barricades: Exploring the Limits of Law as an Agent of Transformational Social Change," 47 *Case W. Res. L. Rev.* 423, 424 n.3 (1997) ("[N]on-compliance was greatest in the western United States, whose long expanses of sparsely populated land created a culture among Westerners that demanded higher speed limits.").

76 See id. (suggesting that lower speed limits imposed in response to the oil crisis in the 1970s did not change most people's driving habits); Quentin Hardy, "Transportation: Westerners Rev Up to Speed Legally Again," *Wall St. J.*, Nov. 13, 1995, at B1 (citing both federal and

local statistics to show that changes in the speed limit "don't seem to affect driving behavior much").

77 Mont. Code Ann. § 61-8-303 (1973).

78 Tom Kentworthy, "New Life in the Fast Lane: Wide Open Throttles in Wide Open Spaces," *Wash. Post*, Dec. 9, 1995, at A3. Montana subsequently imposed a numerical speed limit in 1999. Mont. Code Ann. § 61-8-303 (1999).

79 Robert E. King and Cass R. Sunstein, "Doing without Speed Limits," 79 *B.U. L. Rev.* 155, 162–68 (1999).

80 Id. at 160, 163. Their ability to flout the federal speed limit was undoubtedly aided by the law in Montana that required a mere five-dollar fine for speeding, payable in cash on the spot. Kentworthy, supra note 78, at A3. King and Sunstein report that during the first few months of Montana's return to the Basic Rule, total average speeds increased only negligibly, from seventy-two to seventy-four miles per hour. King and Sunstein, supra note 79, at 163. Tourists were the one exception to the constancy of driver behavior. According to King and Sunstein, the "repeal of the national speed limit turned Montana into a national speed magnet." Id. at 164 (recounting the exploits of "speed tourists" and test drivers).

81 See, e.g., David A. Harris, "'Driving while Black' and All Other Traffic Offenses: The Supreme Court and Pretextual Traffic Stops," 87 *J. Crim. L. and Criminology* 544 (1997) [hereafter Harris, "Driving while Black"]; David A. Harris, "The Stories, the Statistics, and the Law: Why 'Driving while Black' Matters," 84 *Minn. L. Rev.* 265 (1999) [hereafter Harris, "Stories"]; Katheryn K. Russell, "'Driving while Black': Corollary Phenomena and Collateral Consequences," 40 *B.C. L. Rev.* 717 (1999); David A. Harris, "Driving while Black: Racial Profiling on Our Nation's Highways," ACLU Special Report (June 1999); John Lamberth, "Driving while Black; A Statistician Proves That Prejudice Still Rules the Road," *Wash. Post*, Aug. 16, 1998, at C1.

82 David Cole, *No Equal Justice: Race and Class in the American Criminal Justice System* 25, 34–41 (1999) (discussing studies done in California, Maryland, Florida, Colorado, and New Jersey). While the studies vary in the size of the area under investigation and in design, Cole's conclusion that "traffic stops are routinely used as a 'pretext' to stop minority drivers" is compelling and widely regarded as sound. Id. at 38; see also Harris, "Stories," supra note 81, at 275–88 (detailing the studies done in New Jersey, Maryland, and Ohio).

83 Cole, supra note 82, at 37. This study also suggests that the practice is more accurately called "Driving while Brown."

84 Lamberth, supra note 81, at C1. The results of this study are even more astounding once we consider that it was conducted *after* the Maryland State Police had settled a lawsuit against them alleging racial profiling practices. As part of the settlement, the police agreed to issue a policy barring the practice, to train police in the new policy, and to submit to monitoring of all stops that resulted in a search. Cole, supra note 82, at 36.

85 The rolling study that Lamberth conducted in Maryland used the same technique as a study he had done of a stretch of the New Jersey Turnpike. In the New Jersey study, African Americans made up 13.5 percent of the total number of drivers, 15 percent of the speeders, and 35 percent of those pulled over. Lamberth, supra note 81, at C1. As Lamberth points out, "blacks were 4.85 times as likely to be stopped as were others." Id. While Lamberth did not study the rate of searches, he notes that police data showed that over 73 percent of those arrested along the turnpike were black. Id.

86 517 U.S. 806 (1996).

87 Id. at 819. The case arose out of a stop of two black men in a new car. The plainclothes vice-squad officers contended that the car was stopped for too long at a stop sign, made a turn without signaling, and proceeded at an unreasonable speed. Id. at 808.

88 Id. at 810.

89 Id. at 813. While intentionality does not matter for Fourth Amendment purposes, it may form the basis of an Equal Protection Clause challenge. Id.

90 Cole, supra note 82, at 39.

91 Harris, "Driving while Black," supra note 81, at 560.

92 It is also possible to characterize this practice as the power of law over culture in that it takes law to protect the cultural practice; however, given the conflicting and unresolved impulses in the law (between protecting police discretion and protecting people equally from police abuses of discretion), it makes more sense to think of this problem as the power of culture over law. One might also argue that it could be thought of as the third option of synthesis—law as always culturally informed and culture as always legally informed to the extent that it is nearly impossible to distinguish between them. Here a cultural practice conflicts with the law, but with law's approval. Likewise, the meaning of race and racial discrimination is both culturally and legally informed.

93 384 U.S. 436 (1966).

94 120 S. Ct. 2326 (2000).

95 384 U.S. at 439.

96 Id. at 445–55. The Court dedicated considerable time to documenting historical and contemporary interrogation practices that it gleaned from studies and police manuals. It concluded that "such an interrogation environment is created for no purpose other than to subjugate the individual to the will of his examiner" and such coercion is incompatible with the principle "that the individual may not be compelled to incriminate himself." Id. at 457–58.

97 Id. at 479.

98 Mike Seidman has argued that Miranda did not change the methods by which police obtained confessions, but instead provided a relatively easy way to sanitize confessions against claims of coercion. Louis Michael Seidman, "Brown and Miranda," 80 Cal. L. Rev. 673, 744–45 (1992).

99 For a discussion of the cultural feedback loop between Miranda and television, see Susan Bandes and Jack Beerman, "Lawyering Up," 2 Green Bag 5, 11, 13–14 (1998).

100 18 U.S.C. § 3501 (1994).

101 In his dissent in Dickerson, Justice Scalia made effective use of Michigan v. Tucker, 417 U.S. 433 (1974); Oregon v. Hass, 420 U.S. 714 (1975); New York v. Quarles, 467 U.S. 649 (1984); and Oregon v. Elstad, 470 U.S. 298 (1985) on this score. See 120 S. Ct. at 2340–42 (Scalia, J., dissenting).

102 Interestingly, the Dickerson Court did not quite conclude that the Miranda warnings were constitutionally required. Rather, it held more obliquely that "Miranda announced a constitutional rule that Congress may not supersede legislatively." 120 S. Ct. at 2336 (emphasis added). Needless to say, this rhetorical avoidance sent Scalia, writing in dissent, into mouth-foaming fits. See id. at 2337–38 (Scalia, J., dissenting).

103 Id. at 2337 (citing Davis v. United States, 515 U.S. 452 (1994); Duckworth v. Eagan, 492 U.S. 195 (1989); Elstad, 470 U.S. at 298; Quarles, 467 U.S. at 649).

104 384 U.S. at 467.

105 120 S. Ct. at 2336.

106 Kahn, supra note 2, at 91–92 (urging a cultural inquiry of law that resists the pervasive insistence on a normative conclusion about what the law should be).

107 E.g., Ewick and Silbey, supra note 2.

108 E.g., Carol J. Greenhouse et al., *Law and Community in Three American Towns* (1994).

109 E.g., Binder and Weisberg, supra note 2.

110 E.g., *Law as Culture and Culture as Law: Essays in Honor of John Phillip Reid* (Hendrik Hartog and William E. Nelson eds., 2000).

111 E.g., Eric A. Posner, *Law and Social Norms* (2000).

112 Juvenile Justice Reform Act, H.R. 1501, 106th Cong. (1999). The amendment was offered by Representative Aderholt and passed by the House on June 17, 1999. It declared in its findings: "The organic laws of the United States Code and the constitutions of every state, using various expressions, recognize God as the source of the blessings of liberty." H.R. 1501, 106th Cong. § 1201(2) (1999).

113 This is similar to the regulation of "gang-related apparel" in California, which has been found to be "hazardous to the health and safety of the school environment." Cal. Educ. Code § 35,183(a)(2) (West 2000). The state has given school districts the authority to adopt dress codes, including restrictions on "gang-related apparel" and mandatory uniforms. Cal. Educ. Code § 35183(b) (West 2000). The prohibitions that many schools have on wearing Los Angeles Kings or Oakland Raiders jackets, baggy pants, and bandanas contribute to the saliency of those symbols.

114 25 U.S.C. §§ 2701–21 (1988).

115 See generally Naomi Mezey, "The Distribution of Wealth, Sovereignty, and Culture through Indian Gaming," 48 *Stan. L. Rev.* 711 (1996).

116 The Pequots have gotten the most attention and criticism for their ability to profit handsomely from IGRA. Whether they are seen as having been invented by IGRA, or as using a fortuitous statute to reassemble a tribe that was almost entirely annihilated by the colonists, is a matter of one's cultural lens. Mezey, supra note 115, at 724–28.

117 Clifford Geertz, *The Interpretation of Cultures* 3 (rev. ed. 2000).

118 Id. at 6–7.

119 Id. at 7.

120 Id. "Doing ethnography is like trying to read (in the sense of 'construct a reading of') a manuscript—foreign, faded, full of ellipses, incoherencies, suspicious emendations, and tendentious commentaries, but written not in conventionalized graphs of sound but in transient examples of shaped behavior." Id. at 10.

121 Id. at 5.

122 Coombe, supra note 14, at 23.

123 Frederick Schauer, "Instrumental Commensurability," 146 *U. Pa. L. Rev.* 1215, 1222 (1998) (recognizing that "descriptive sentences containing seemingly descriptive words arrayed in a seemingly descriptive semantic structure often mask statements and conclusions that are in important ways normative, evaluative, and prescriptive," such as when you describe some behavior as "rude"); see also Heidi Li Feldman, "Objectivity in Legal Judgment," 92 *Mich. L. Rev.* 1187, 1188–90, 1191–1212 (1994).

124 Geertz, supra note 117, at 14–15, 20.

125 Renato Rosaldo, "While Making Other Plans," 58 *S. Cal. L. Rev.* 19, 24 (1985) (noting the "slender interpretation" in Geertz's own example of thick description, which "for all the insight it displays in the sheer telling, raises interpretive issues that outstrip Geertz's concluding efforts to contain it within a model of mutually uncomprehending cultural systems").

126 I want to be clear that by looking at the passage of law or at its "legal" interpretation as the site of the production of legal meaning, I am not suggesting that the meanings generated or rearticulated there are not cultural; indeed, they are, and they could not be otherwise. That is the point of constitutive theory. But we need an entrance into the analysis and an explanation of the inseparability of law and culture, so I am rather artificially suggesting this distinction between sites of production and reception.

127 By suggesting the use of "traditional" legal interpretation, I do not mean to imply a narrow range of formalist choices about the mode of inquiry. Rather, I mean to make clear that I think that there is some value in exploring those interpretations of law that lawyers recognize as legal.

128 This was the basic approach of Representative Tancredo of Colorado. 145 Cong. Rec. H2328 (daily ed. Apr. 27, 1999) (statement of Rep. Tancredo); see supra note 10 and accompanying text.

129 "A well-regulated militia, being necessary to the security of a free State, the right of the people to keep and bear arms shall not be infringed." U.S. Const. amend. II.

130 See, e.g., *Gun Control and the Constitution: Sources and Explorations on the Second Amendment* (Robert J. Cottrol ed., 1994).

131 Compare Presser v. Illinois, 116 U.S. 252 (1886), with United States v. Miller, 307 U.S. 174 (1939).

132 Representative Tancredo was especially prolific on this point: "Ours is a culture wrapped in cotton candy nihilism. Poses and attitudes of nihilism are struck and celebrated. The academy has its au courant ideologies. Feminism, postmodernism, structuralism, scientific materialism all presuppose a purposeless universe without any transcendent order where society is predicated on power and violence. Entertainment has its explicit nihilistic messages (the Goth rock of Marilyn Manson and KMFDM), its ironically hip ones (the accomplished, but immoral, films of Quentin Tarantino), and its implicit nihilism (Jerry Springer, or the titillation cum therapy of MTV's Loveline). Indeed, nihilism in a soft and weak form is everywhere." 145 Cong. Rec. H2328 (daily ed. Apr. 27, 1999) (statement of Rep. Tancredo).

133 H.R. 1501, 106th Cong. (1999); S. 254, 106th Cong. (1999).

134 H.R. 1501, at tit. II, § 204.

135 Id. at tit. III, § 302.

136 Id. at tit. III, subtit. D.

137 Id. at tit. IV, subtit. A.

138 Id. at tit. XIII.

139 There is not a clearly defined Goth subculture, and there have been disavowals by self-proclaimed Goths that the clique at Columbine known as the Trench Coat Mafia was not Goth. See Gersh Kuntzman and Ed Robinson, "Goths: Those Loonies Aren't with Us,"

N.Y. Post, Apr. 22, 1999, at 6. Although they favored a dark aesthetic and fantasy games, Harris and Klebold parted from Goths by admiring Hitler, white supremacy, and German techno music. Tina Griego et al., "Quiet Loners Worried Other Students: Trench Coat Mafia Spoke about Violence, Carried Reputation for Being Outsiders," *Rocky Mtn. News,* Apr. 21, 1999, at 6A; Robin McDowell, "Outcasts Linked to Killings: 'Trench Coat Mafia' Not Liked by Students," *Det. News,* Apr. 21, 1999, at A5.

140 See, e.g., Randy Holtz, "Shootings Fuel Debate over 'Jock Elitism' at Columbine," *Rocky Mtn. News,* Apr. 27, 1999, at 28A ("Joe Stair, one of the original members of the Trench Coat Mafia, said the group formed about four years ago to protect its members from harassment by jocks."); see also Renate Robey, "Cliques: A Fact of Life but Violence a Recent Reaction by Outcasts," *Denv. Post,* Apr. 25, 1999, at A8.

141 See generally *Cool Places: Geographies of Youth Cultures* (Tracey Skelton and Gill Valentine eds., 1998); Jonathan S. Epstein, *Youth Culture: Identity in a Postmodern World* (1998); Patricia Hersch, *A Tribe Apart: A Journey into the Heart of American Adolescence* (1999); Mike Males, *Framing Youth: 10 Myths about the Next Generation* (1999).

142 See Calvin Morrill et al., "Telling Tales in School: Youth Culture and Conflict Narratives," 34 *Law and Soc'y Rev.* 521 (2000).

143 Andrew Sullivan, "Real World," *New Republic,* Oct. 2, 2000, at 10.

144 Id.

145 Robin West, "Gun Rights," *Tikkun,* Sept./Oct. 1999, at 25.

146 See, e.g., Ellickson, supra note 73, at 149 (criticizing the failure of the law-and-society school to develop a unified, monolithic theory of human nature, culture, and social control).

147 Geertz, supra note 117, at 24–25 ("This is the first condition for cultural theory: it is not its own master. As it is unseverable from the immediacies thick description presents, its freedom to shape itself in terms of its internal logic is rather limited.").

148 Id. at 17.

149 Id. at 25.

150 Kahn, supra note 2, at 6.

151 Sarat and Kearns, supra note 7, at 7–8.

152 Ellickson, supra note 73, at 149.

153 Binder and Weisberg, supra note 2, at 463.

154 Jeffery Cole, "Economics of Law: An Interview with Judge Posner," 1 *Litig.* 23, 26 (1995) (quoting Judge Posner as saying, "There are simplifiers and complicators, and I'm a simplifier. I don't much like it when postmodern scholars talk about nuance and thick description and complexity and the need for constant qualification.").

155 Geertz, supra note 117, at 29.

What It Is and What It Isn't: Cultural Studies Meets Graduate Student Labor

Toby Miller

This essay performs two functions. First, it surveys cultural studies in the United States and elsewhere, providing a historically and geographically comparative genealogy and some points of differentiation from other forms of academic discourse. Second, the essay takes issue with criticisms of cultural studies for being socially irrelevant. This is done by pointing to its capacity for galvanizing opposition to exploitation in a practical way, even though many of its operating assumptions pose problems for governmental normativity. I challenge the reduction of cultural studies to interpretive reading, as per hermeneutics and other forms of textual analysis, psycho- or otherwise, just as I reject the shibboleth that cultural studies lacks actionable, political engagement.

Cultural studies is a tendency across disciplines, rather than a discipline itself. This is evident in practitioners' simultaneously expressed desires to refuse definition, insist on differentiation, and sustain conventional departmental credentials (as well as pyrotechnic, polymathematical capacities for reasoning and research). Cultural studies is animated by subjectivity and power—how human subjects are formed and how they experience cultural and social space. It takes its agenda and mode of analysis from economics, politics, media and communication studies, sociology, literature, education, the law, science and technology studies, anthropology, and history, with a particular focus on gender, race, class, and sexuality in everyday life, commingling textual and social theory under the sign of a commitment to progressive social change. Cultural studies' continuities come from shared concerns and methods: the concern is the reproduction of culture through structural determinations on subjects versus their own agency, and the method is historical materialism.[1] In this sense, it is vitally connected to issues of collective self-determination—how social movements gain control over the means of their existence. This link became manifest to me via the significance of cultural studies to struggles by graduate student employees at U.S. universities to attain the right to vote for or against unionization, then through the way in which legal proceedings to determine that struggle excluded certain approaches associated with cultural studies; hence my interest in bracketing these topics. I deal with them serially, such that the second section provides a demonstration-effect for some of the first section.

Rather than focusing on canonical works of art, governmental history, or quantitative social data, cultural studies devotes time to subcultures, popular media, music, clothing, and sport. By looking at how culture is used and transformed by "ordinary" and "marginal" social groups, cultural studies sees people not simply as consumers but as potential producers of new social values and cultural languages. The political significance of popular cultural practices is perhaps best exemplified in subcultures. Subcultures signify a space *under* culture, simultaneously opposed to, derivative of, and informing governmental and commercial forms of life. Examining subcultures entails a shift of intellectual focus away from culture as a tool of domination and toward culture as a tool of empowerment. This move wants to find out how the socially disadvantaged use culture to contest their subservient position. Historical and contemporary studies conducted through the 1960s and '70s on slaves, crowds, pirates, bandits, and the working class emphasized day-to-day noncompliance with authority. For example, U.K. research into Teddy Boys, Mods, bikers, skinheads, punks, school pupils, teen girls, and Rastas selected truants, drop-outs, and magazine readers as its magical agents of history—because they deviated from the norms of schooling and the transition to work by entering subcultures that generated moral panics within dominant culture. Such research examined the structural underpinnings to collective style, investigating how *bricolage* subverted the achievement-oriented, materialistic, educationally driven values and appearance of the middle class. The working assumption was that subordinate groups adopt and adapt signs and objects of the dominant culture, reorganizing them to manufacture new meanings. Consumption was thought to be the epicenter of such subcultures; paradoxically, it also reversed their members' status as consumers. They became producers of new fashions, inscribing alienation, difference, and powerlessness on their bodies. (The decline of the British economy and state across the 1970s was said to have been exemplified in punk's use of rubbish as an adornment: trash-bag liners, lavatory appliances, and ripped clothing.) But then capitalism appropriated the appropriator. For even as the media were denouncing punks as folk devils, and setting in train various moral panics, the fashion and music industries were sending out spies in search of new trends to market.[2]

An awareness of this double-edged investment in commodities—that they may be appropriated by subcultures as acts of resistance, then commodified again, with their rebellious connotations resignified as gimmicks—makes socioeconomic analysis via critical political economy a good ally of textual and audience analysis via cultural studies. A certain tendency on both sides has maintained that they are mutually exclusive—that one is concerned with structures of the economy and the other with structures of meaning. But this need not be the case. Historically, the best critical political economy and the best cultural studies have worked through the imbrication of power and subjectivity at all points on the cultural continuum: "Critical political economy is at its strongest in explaining who gets to speak to whom and what forms these symbolic encounters take in the major spaces of public culture. But cultural studies, at its best, has much of value to say about . . . how discourse and imagery are organized in complex and shifting patterns of meaning and how these meanings are reproduced, negotiated, and struggled over in the flow and flux of everyday life."[3] Ideally, blending the two approaches would heal the division between fact and interpretation and between the social sciences and the humanities and attend to the material and textual sides of citizenship, under the sign of cultural democracy. To that end, cultural studies aims to provide a dynamic way of "politicizing theory and theorizing politics" that combines abstraction and grounded analysis. This requires a focus on the contradictions of organizational structures and their articulations with everyday living, textuality, the polity, and the economy, refusing any bifurcation that opposes the study of production and consumption or fails to address overlapping axes of subjectification such as class, race, nation, and gender.[4] As noted above, following some historicization of cultural studies, I shall address in the second half of the essay a key site where political economy and cultural studies have forged an ongoing and practical connection—academic labor.

Fathers and Other Origins

Richard Maxwell has provided a useful representation of global cultural studies,[5] shown in figure 1. Four founding parents of British cultural studies are listed, all of them post–World War II, English-based intellectuals: Richard Hoggart, E. P. Thompson, Stuart Hall, and Raymond Williams. These men were adult educators and university professors on the left who wanted to understand the intersection of class and nation at the level of lived experience and social structure by foregrounding "the culture and sensibilities of industrial workers."[6]

Hoggart was a left Leavisite who favored the uplift of working-class people through literary study, at the same time that he took their popular pursuits seriously. His classic work *The Uses of Literacy* appeared in the 1950s while he was at the University of Leicester, after which he became a celebrated member of various public-review bodies examining questions of culture, a star defense witness at the trial of Penguin Books for publishing *Lady Chatterley,* and in the mid-1960s, the founder of the Centre for Contemporary Cultural Studies (cccs) at the University of Birmingham. He went on to be a senior culturecrat at unesco and latterly a memoirist.[7] Thompson's key contribution came through his work on the history of the English working class,[8] a focus on labor that concentrated on the past from "below," rather than from on high, and eschewed abstraction in favor of ordinary people's accounts of their lives. This rejection of theory was opposed to structuralist Marxism,[9] which had entered British cultural studies of the 1970s under the sign of Louis Althusser.[10] Thompson was also active in Britain's Campaign for Nuclear Disarmament, in both its 1960s and 1980s heydays. Hall started as a left Leavisite and worked as Hoggart's deputy at the cccs for some years, ultimately running the Centre for a decade from 1968 and marking out its classic period of collaborative, engaged Gramscian scholarship that investigated state stereotyping and ritualistic resistance. He concluded his career at the Open University with a shift toward Foucauldianism and the Fanonian postcolonial, brokering cultural studies' relationship to sociology and media studies, and becoming a key influence in the United States. Throughout, Hall sought a means of analyzing signs, representations, and ideology.[11] Williams drew heavily on his experiences growing up in Wales to make sense of cultural change and power dynamics. He has provided the largest body of theory for ongoing cultural studies work, via a wide array of noted volumes on literary history and theory, media and communications, culture, and society. That work models a hybrid between critical political economy and cultural studies, so I shall dedicate some space to its concerns and methods.

Williams is critical of idealist conceptions that assume culture is a march toward perfection as determined by universal values basic to the human condition, as if these were timeless rather than grounded in particular conditions of possibility. He also questions documentary conceptions of culture that seek to record artistic work so as to preserve specific insights and highlight them through criticism. Instead, Williams proposes that we concentrate on the ways

Figure 1 Cultural Studies Source: Richard Maxwell "Cultural Studies" in *Understanding Contemporary Society*: *Theories of the Present*, ed. Gary Browning, Abigail Halci, and Frank Webster (London: Sage, 2000), 292. Copyright R. Maxwell 2000. Reproduced with permission.

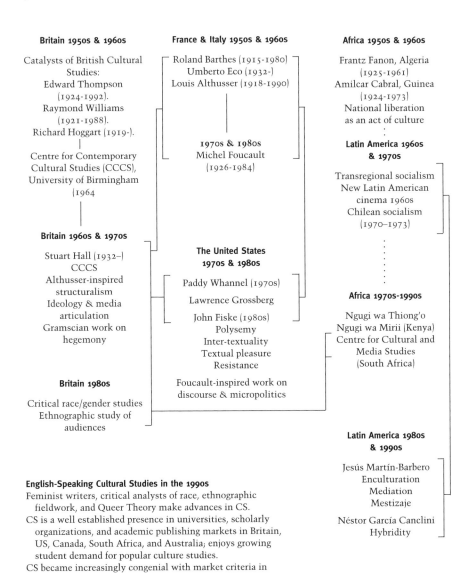

Britain 1950s & 1960s

Catalysts of British Cultural
Studies:
Edward Thompson
(1924-1992).
Raymond Williams
(1921-1988).
Richard Hoggart (1919-).

Centre for Contemporary
Cultural Studies (CCCS),
University of Birmingham
(1964

Britain 1960s & 1970s

Stuart Hall (1932–)
CCCS
Althusser-inspired
structuralism
Ideology & media
articulation
Gramscian work on
hegemony

Britain 1980s

Critical race/gender studies
Ethnographic study of
audiences

France & Italy 1950s & 1960s

Roland Barthes (1915-1980)
Umberto Eco (1932-)
Louis Althusser (1918-1990)

1970s & 1980s
Michel Foucault
(1926-1984)

**The United States
1970s & 1980s**

Paddy Whannel (1970s)

Lawrence Grossberg

John Fiske (1980s)
Polysemy
Inter-textuality
Textual pleasure
Resistance

Foucault-inspired work on
discourse & micropolitics

Africa 1950s & 1960s

Frantz Fanon, Algeria
(1925-1961)
Amilcar Cabral, Guinea
(1924-1973)
National liberation
as an act of culture

**Latin America 1960s
& 1970s**

Transregional socialism
New Latin American
cinema 1960s
Chilean socialism
(1970–1973)

Africa 1970s-1990s

Ngugi wa Thiong'o
Ngugi wa Mirii (Kenya)
Centre for Cultural and
Media Studies
(South Africa)

**Latin America 1980s
& 1990s**

Jesús Martín-Barbero
Enculturation
Mediation
Mestizaje

Néstor García Canclini
Hybridity

English-Speaking Cultural Studies in the 1990s

Feminist writers, critical analysts of race, ethnographic
   fieldwork, and Queer Theory make advances in CS.
CS is a well established presence in universities, scholarly
   organizations, and academic publishing markets in Britain,
   US, Canada, South Africa, and Australia; enjoys growing
   student demand for popular culture studies.
CS became increasingly congenial with market criteria in
   Neoconservative political context of 1980s and 1990s.
Cultural Policy Studies emerges.
CS undergoes fragmentation and depoliticization of its history.

of life and values of particular communities at particular times, noting benefits and costs in how they are represented.[12] As we shall see later, this has been suggestive for revisions to the U.S. academy's model of the liberal arts as a civilizing agent of moral uplift for cultural citizens and its teachers as the genteel poor.

Williams's method, cultural materialism, works with Karl Marx's insight that people manufacture their own conditions of existence, but often without a conscious or enabling agency. Social practices, not nature, genius, or individuality, make a way of life and change it over time. This insight directs us away from views of historical and contemporary culture that privilege aesthetic civilization, the experiences of rulers, or the impact of religion delivered from on high.[13] Instead, we should engage culture by reading its products and considering their circumstances of creation and circulation. Art and society—Williams calls them "project" and "formation" respectively—intertwine, with no conceptual or chronological primacy accorded to either term. The relations of culture, their twists and turns, the often violent and volatile way in which they change, are material parts of society. So language neither precedes nor follows the social world. That means allowing a certain autonomy to intellectual work from the prevailing mode of economic production, but not from its own micro-economies of person, place, and power.[14] There can be no notion here of an organic community that produces a culture of artworks or of a culture of artworks that reflects an organic community. Each has its own internal politics, as well as connections to the wider economy. The same is clearly true of private-sector graduate student employees and their moment of critique examined below—a case of realizing that "great books" and "great empires" have local politics not only to their content and form but also to the labor conditions that transmit them.

Cultural materialism articulates material culture (buildings, film, cars, fashion, sculpture, and so on) with sociohistorical change, explaining how the culture produced *by* ordinary people is repackaged and sold *to* them. Williams divides culture into *dominant* versus *residual* and *emergent* forms, as per Antonio Gramsci's model of hegemony, a process of securing consent to the social order that makes dominant culture appear normal and natural.[15] It exists alongside extant residual cultures, which comprise old meanings and practices that are no longer dominant but still influential, and emergent cultures, which are either propagated by a new class or incorporated by the dominant, as part of hegemony. These maneuvers find expression in what Williams terms a "structure of feeling": the intangibles of an era that explain or develop its quality of life. Such indicators often involve a contest—or at least dissonance—between official culture and practical consciousness. In short, Williams's view of culture insists on the importance of community life, the conflicts in any cultural formation, the social nature of culture, and the cultural nature of society. His dialectical interplay of seemingly profound opposites models the struggle between education and work that is played out in the second half of this essay, where such stark binary distinctions are shown to have been duly compromised.

Of course, there are many other sources of today's cultural studies apart from these four men. Manthia Diawara has provided a multicultural trace of U.K.-U.S. cultural studies that complicates the standard fatherly narrative, albeit foregrounding the later work of Hall. Diawara connects the Birmingham CCCS with London-based black cultural workers and people of color in black and feminist studies programs of U.S. colleges. This trajectory involves certain key transformations of perspective. The initial animating force to cultural studies came from a desire to understand British culture in terms of class dominance and resistance, and from the search for an agent of history that could propel radical politics. But that agency fell into doubt, with masculinity and Britishness/Englishness up for debate in ways that criticized sexism and white nationalism.[16]

It could be argued that Maxwell's diagram discloses both more and less than it should, claiming authors for cultural studies who would never have heard of it (such as Fanon and Cabral) and excluding influences such as critical theory and deconstruction. But however tendentious it may be to collect them, the focus of these writers on belonging and public identity clearly connects these tendencies. And as per Maxwell's schema, other semiautonomous forces have shaped cultural studies.[17] Latin American influences include the socialism manifested in New Latin American Cinema and Paolo Freire's pedagogy of the oppressed,[18] the Marxist media analysis done for Salvador Allende's Chile by Michèle and Armand Mattelart,[19] hegemony studies in Colombia by Jesús Martín-Barbero,[20] and anthropologist Néstor García Canclini's integration of social and cultural theory to analyze Mexico.[21] Ngugi wa Thiong'o, Ngugi wa Mirii, and others at the Kamiriithu Centre linked cultural critique to production.[22] In South Asia, the work of subaltern studies intellectuals such as Ranajit Guha[23] and Partha Chatterjee[24] and postcolonial critic Ania Loomba[25] has been pivotal for postcolonial and historical research, and the Sarai formation at the Centre for the Study of Developing Societies in Delhi[26] is a node between research and activism. Hong Kong has produced significant cultural studies work by Eric Kit-wai Ma[27] and Ackbar Abbas,[28] among many others. Across an array of sites, there has been significant feminist work by Judith Butler,[29] Donna Haraway,[30] Lesley Johnson,[31] and Angela McRobbie,[32] to name just a few.

What It Is (and What It Isn't)

What do these different legacies mean for cultural studies today? John Frow and Meaghan Morris contrast the view of hegemonic power brokers, who see culture as a route to economic efficiency, with cultural studies, which questions power and subjectivity rather than seeking to extract surplus value from ordinary people or educate them into obedience (as per the U.S. liberal arts model referred to earlier). Frow and Morris want to audit the denial, assimilation, and invention that occur each time such words as nation, community, or society are brought into discourse. They favor a move away from essentialist definitions of national identity and toward plural accounts of person and polity.[33] Morris glosses the concerns of cultural studies as "racial, ethnic, sexual, gender, class, generational and national differences (roughly in that order), as these are produced and contested in history," along with "a critique of cultural universals."[34]

At the same time as categorical devices from the social sciences are deployed here as grids of investigation, their status as machines obliterating difference is brought into question, the result being a productive intellectual polyphony that draws out contradictions and dissonances. If we link this to Frow and Morris's litany of interdisciplinarity,[35] we can specify a desirable cultural studies as a mixture of economics, politics, textual analysis, gender theory, ethnography, history, postcolonial theory, material objects, and policy, animated by a desire to reveal and transform control of the means of communication and culture, and undertaken with a constant vigilance over one's own raison d'être and modus operandi (for instance, graduate student employment). This could be connected to Grossberg's map of cultural studies along twin axes of cultural method and social theory, on a grid comparing five methods (literary humanism, dialectical sociology, culturalism, structuralist conjunctures, and postmodern conjunctures) with eight theories (epistemology, determination, agency, social formation, cultural formation, power, specificity of struggle, and the site of the modern) to produce historicized cultural analyses.[36]

So what is cultural studies *not*? Clearly, attempts to list what does and doesn't count as cultural studies are fraught with difficulty, especially when they engage in an absolute binarization (cultural studies frequently disavows binary oppositions for failing to acknowledge the logocentric interdependence of supposed opposites, such as that whiteness depends for its sense of self on blackness, for example).

But binaries are good to think with and good to tinker with, like any form of inclusion and exclusion. So table 1 presents my list of what's in and what's out.

Table 1 Cultural Studies

What It Is	What It Isn't
Ethnography	Physical anthropology
Textual analysis of the media	Literary formalism and canon formation
Social theory	Regression and time-series analysis
Science and technology studies	Mathematics, geology, and chemistry
Political economy	Neoclassical economics
Critical geography	Planning
Psychoanalysis	Rational-choice theory and cognitive psychology
Postmodern art	Art history
Critical architecture	Engineering and quantity surveying
Environmentalism	Industrial development
Feminism	Human biology
Queerness	Deviance
Globalization	Nationalism
Postcolonialism	World literature
Continental philosophy, structuralism, and poststructuralism	Analytic philosophy
Popular music	Musicology
Social semiotics	Formalist linguistics
Fashion	Technical design
Cultural and social history	Political history
Critical public health	Medical training
Critical legal studies and critical race theory	Legal training and legal formalism
Subcultures	Interest groups

The *left* side articulates knowledge with social change. It represents a will to link the professoriat to social movements as primary loci of power, authorization, and responsibility. The *right* side articulates knowledge with social reproduction. It represents a will to link the professoriat to universities and professions as primary loci of power, authorization, and responsibility. One is concerned with transforming the social order, the other with replicating it—the educational side to cultural citizenship as a transformative versus functionalist sphere.

Table 2 Cultural Journals

Journals of Tendency	Journals of Profession
Avowed political project seeking to make interventions, situated in time and space	Avowed truth project seeking a universalist, timeless pursuit of knowledge
In-house manuscript reviewers who argue for and against authors' mss. along grounds of politics and cohesiveness	External manuscript reviewers who engage in double-blind review of mss. in terms of disciplinary competence and falsifiability
Open calls for mss., theme issues, response to contemporary social questions	Access restricted to members of professional associations, lengthy period of review and revision
Seeks hegemony of a position across disciplines	Seeks hegemony over entry and success within disciplines
Editorial collectives that are self-selecting	Editors chosen by disciplinary associations
Prone to sudden bursts of energy and newness, inefficiency, and an eventual sense that the "moment" of particular journals has passed	Prone to efficiency, "normal science," and journals that are joined at the hip to their sponsoring disciplines
Social Text, Public Culture, Socialist Review, camera obscura, Radical History Review, Positions, Feminist Media Studies, Critique of Anthropology, Topia	pmla, *American Sociological Review, Cinema Journal, Journal of Communication, American Historical Review, Current Anthropology*

We can see the force of this divide in a raft of journal publications that stand for the impact of cultural studies on a host of disciplines.[37] There is a rough bifurcation in academic publishing between journals of tendency and journals of profession, each seeking to establish hegemony within particular spheres. They operate in binary opposition to one another, although there can be overlap of topic and authorship in certain cases. Table 2 provides a schema of this opposition.

Journals on the right-hand side of the grid are refereed. Double-blind refereeing (where the author's identity is hidden from reviewers and vice versa) arose in the social sciences as compensation for not being methodologically falsifiable (as per their fantasies about the sciences) or amenable to utilitarian auditing (in the case of some humanities sectors). The system gradually spread across universities, although some of the sciences have stayed with single-blind review (where the author's identity is revealed to reviewers). Most refereed journals are financially and intellectually supported by professional organizations. PMLA only publishes papers submitted by dues-paying members of the Modern Language Association, and all such offerings are read by fellow initiates. Your work is not even reviewed unless you're a member of the club. The results leave many of us ambivalent. An editor of *Nature*, for example, has bemoaned the fact that refereeing would have prevented publication of the letter announcing the double helix, which appeared in the journal in 1953, while research on peer review shows that it generates caution and reproduces an "invisible college" of elite scholars and disciplines.[38] Of course, this putatively highly professional, politically neutral college is prepared to be *very* political, as required—the high-Tory American Medical Association (AMA) dismissed George Lundberg, the editor of its house review, the *Journal of the American Medical Association (JAMA)*, for daring to print a paper during the controversy over Bill Clinton and Monica Lewinsky that showed 60 percent of undergraduates at "a large midwestern university" (how many times have we read that expression in survey research?) in 1991 did not think they had "had sex" if it involved oral contact rather than vaginal or anal intercourse.[39] Lundberg, who had held the job since 1982, was deemed by AMA executive vice president E. Ratcliffe Anderson Jr. to have "threatened the historic tradition and integrity of [the journal] by inappropriately and inexcusably interjecting JAMA into a major political debate that has nothing to do with science or medicine."[40] But, as an editorial in the equivalent Canadian journal noted, the AMA had given US$14 million over the previous decade to political parties—favoring the Republican side by a two-to-one ratio.[41] Despite the AMA's qualms, there is evidence of similar beliefs about what constitutes sex among New York City teens, British university students, and a cross-section of U.S. residents, while ethnic and racial distinctions are at play as well.[42]

Some journals cross the divide between tendency and profession. Over a five-year period, *Continuum: A Journal of Media and Cultural Studies* was transformed from four of us in Western Australia obtaining manuscripts, editing them, and putting in desktop codes, to a journal that had a senior editor, an editor, a photography editor, two reviews editors, four corresponding editors, seven members of an editorial collective, fifty-nine editorial advisers, and a British commercial publisher, with only one of those earlier artisans numbered among the above. So this schema is not a comprehensive divide. The editors of the journal *Cultural Studies* in fact "welcome" certain processes of academic formalization. They view publishing growth in the area as "signs of its vitality and signature components of its status as a field," but they continue to call for "knowledge formations" that are "historically and geographically contingent" rather than obedient to disciplines.[43] The inaugural issue of the *International Journal of Cultural Studies* promised to localize knowledge and be *"post-disciplinary,"* making "academic research itself" into an object of inquiry and engaging the fact that " 'cultural studies' is now a management and marketing skill."[44] These instrumental uses of cultural studies put at risk its flexibility, innovativeness, openness to critique, and relationship to radical democracy. At the same time, they ensure having a place at the table, as links to recent union action suggest.

The brigands to the left of the grid have gathered force in book publishing as well. Since 1990, we have seen the appearance of numerous cultural studies anthologies, such as feminist readers edited by Sarah Franklin et al.,[45] Terry Lovell,[46] and Morag Shiach;[47] an omnibus internationalist survey;[48] a volume on black British cultural studies;[49] and national mixtures of solid gold and future memories about Australia, Germany, France, Spain, Italy, Asia, Russia, Canada, the United States, and Britain.[50] Textbooks have been available for some time.[51] The gigantic *Cultural Studies* collection came out in 1992,[52] and family-resemblance volumes exist in lesbian/gay/queer, legal, multicultural/postcolonial, regional, sports, political theory, and alterity studies, while there is a call within biomedicine to adopt a cultural studies research agenda, and notable contributions have been made in areas such as AIDS.[53] Several "Cultural Studies at the Crossroads" conferences have been held, and Honolulu convened a major event in 1993, with one block dedicated to cultural studies journals from New Zealand/Aotearoa, Australia, India, the Philippines, and the United States. Major scholarly bodies have been transformed from within by cultural studies tendencies, notably the International Communication Association, the International Association for Media and Communication Research, and the National Communication Association. Finally, there is the inevitable raft of Web sites.[54]

Cultural studies has not avoided the eyes of academic and political invigilators, for the right-hand side of the publishing grid has analogues on the right of politics, as per the AMA. Cultural studies' concerns with identity, and its struggles against a canon of supposedly elevating aesthetic work, lead to accusations of a fall, respectively, from *e pluribus unum* and the grace of connoisseurship.

Kenneth Minogue polemicizes in the *Times Literary Supplement* about cultural studies as a "politico-intellectual junkyard of the Western world,"[55] while neo-conservative readers of *Partisan Review* and the *New Criterion* are alert to the danger as well.[56] Chris Patten, former Conservative member of the U.K. parliament and the last British governor of Hong Kong, calls cultural studies "Disneyland for the weaker minded,"[57] and Simon Hoggart, son of Richard and a notable journalistic maven, is an implacable foe. He could be seen on British television in February 2000 chiding local universities for wasting time on this nonsense when they should be trying to be in step with Harvard and MIT. But there have been several conferences at Harvard Law School about cultural studies, and MIT is forever promoting itself as a site for related work. Cultural studies has penetrated even these hallowed redoubts. On the other hand, some right-wing libertarians welcome it. Virginia Postrel, then the editor of *Reason* magazine, wrote a 1999 op-ed piece for the *Wall Street Journal* in which she described cultural studies as "deeply threatening to traditional leftist views of commerce" because its notions of active consumption were so close to the sovereign consumer beloved of the right: "The cultural-studies mavens are betraying the leftist cause, lending support to the corporate enemy and even training graduate students who wind up doing market research."[58]

In the United States, some sociologists, confronted by departmental closures, amalgamations, or transmogrifications into social policy, bury their heads in methodological anguish when confronted by cultural studies, or claim the turf and terminology as their own. What do you get when you cross Talcott Parsons with Émile Durkheim and Harold Garfinkel? "A New Proposal for Cultural Studies."[59] This position says Marxism has been overtaken by a revised functionalism that uses interpretative cultural anthropology and "subjective perceptions" to link meaning with social structure. Symbols and ideals, not power relations, are the appropriate focus. To underline the point, Cambridge University Press's "Cultural Social Studies" series is an avowedly Durkheimian project. It echoes the "Editor's Note" that inaugurated *Prospects: An Annual Journal of American Cultural Studies* twenty-five years ago as an attempt to "elucidate the essential nature of the American character,"[60] as well as claims that cultural studies is just symbolic interactionism.[61] So conventional critics either throw up their hands in horror or seek to incorporate the upstart hybrid as normal science or as part of the communitarian project of prayer and care.[62]

On the left, cultural studies' concerns with identity have led to accusations of a fall from the grace of "real" politics. (This recalls Don DeLillo's character in the postmodern novel *White Noise,* who complains of his university that "[t]here are full professors in this place who read nothing but cereal boxes" or Colson Whitehead's pop poststructuralist academic Godfrey Frank in *John Henry Days* who composes the lines *"Roland Barthes got hit by a truck / That's a signifier you can't duck / Life's an open text / From cradle to death"* for a song by Fire Drill and the Orderly Fashions.)[63] *New Yorker* journalist Adam Gopnik has accused radicals in the United States of being overcommitted to abstract intellection and the assumption that "consciousness produces reality," such that the "energy on the American left is in cultural studies, not health care."[64] To this one can only reply that work on consumption should include questions of pleasure and resistance as well as domination and that debates over health care are partially *conducted* through the popular. The long-standing cultural studies journal *Social Text* (1979–) became mired in public controversy over social constructionism and scientific truth claims in 1996–97, when it published a paper by a physicist who stated things he did not believe, then announced this in a populist academic magazine. He claimed his hoax was a sign of the area's sloppy thinking and its weakness as a site for radical politics. The story was picked up by major wire services and thereafter drew massive media attention. Given the deceitful nature of this conduct, we can see why it is necessary for the U.S. government to house a full-time bureau dedicated to scientific fraud by holders of federal research grants![65]

What is going on with these critiques? It seems as though cultural studies occupies the space of 1960s British sociology—an irritant to hegemonic forces because of its radical anti-elitist critique. This antagonizes both traditional academic disciplines and media mavens, who see it as the humanities' sacred duty to elevate the population (or at least segments of it) through indoctrination into a sacred array of knowledges carefully removed from the everyday. The DeLillo and Whitehead quips about full professors reading cereal boxes and so forth are funny and pointed—in a myriad of ways. Of course, it is odd to turn away from high-cultural pursuits and invest one's academic capital in the banal, to shift direction from the Bauhaus to the Mouse House. The Patten quip about "Disneyland for the feeble-minded" is also funny and pointed. But in each case, there is something behind the remark. Understanding the iconic significance and material history of U.S. food is important, while acknowledging the pleasures of ordinary people rather than privileging the quasi-sacerdotal pronouncements of an elect may not be so much "feeble-minded" as threatening to cultural elites and the corporate university.

For in addition to querying traditional humanities work, cultural studies has also questioned co-opted knowledge. In the research domain, today's college system clearly endorses partnerships between state, education, and industry. Such relationships merit scrutiny rather than an amiable blind faith. In the United States, university consultancies date to nineteenth-century museums, observatories, and agricultural-experimentation outposts, but the shop was really set up in the late 1950s. Considerable effort since then has gone into tailoring research priorities to contemporary political parties and corporations: "pork-barrel science," as it is known. Ralph Nader's Center for Universities in the Public Interest was set up because of such concerns, which are even evident to former supporters of government/college/industry relationships who have experienced the obstacles they can pose to disinterested research outcomes. The complications are obvious in a hot topic such as bioethics, but there are also issues for other fields. Anthropology, for example, has been stung by the unfolding controversies over the Yanomami in Venezuela and Brazil, sociobiology, measles vaccines, and money from the Atomic Energy Commission. Then there is the less spectacular case of psychology's common requirement that undergraduates present themselves as research subjects as a condition of enrollment, with the results—publication, presentation, or commodification—of no tangible benefit to them, and frequently undertaken without their knowledge.

And there is a problematic history to much academic participation in democratic government. Consider language-spread policy and the part played in it by linguists, let alone the work of economic advisers (Robert Triffin acting as plenipotentiary for the United States to the European Economic Community and then as a European delegate to the International Monetary Fund, just a few months apart, in the 1980s), political scientists (Project Camelot in the 1960s), biomedical researchers (relations with pharmaceutical companies), public relations consultants (a critical concern of the professional associations), and nuclear physicists (red-baiting of scientists). The very existence of communication research raises questions of ideological distortion, given the discipline's formation under the sign of war, clandestine government activity, and corporate and foundation support.[66] The policy sciences, originally conceived of as a connection between democracy and executive action, have degenerated into "unrepresentative expertise" that lacks articulation with the everyday. Communications researcher Thomas Streeter points out that in the United States "policy" frequently connotes a pro-corporate position that turns highly contestable positions into absolutes, with consultant professors simultaneously performing objectivity and applicability. (For example, the policy and program management of our national parks has consistently owed much more to bureaucratic *force majeure*, tourism money, and "development" than to ecological science.)[67] This sorry history long predates contemporary concerns about the corporatization of the U.S. university, which arose once we lost the frequently hands-off, sometimes hands-on Cold War stimuli to big science from government sources.

Of course, applied research does not have to be carried out on behalf of corporations or government offices that back corporate welfare. When we think about oppositional theory, the Italian semiotician and novelist Umberto Eco, linguistics professor and corporate media critic Noam Chomsky, French philosopher of the postmodern Jean-François Lyotard, García Canclini, and contemporary queer theory recur as signs. Some of their most famous work was born of cultural consultancy and applied research: Eco's TV semiotics was undertaken in the 1960s for Italian state broadcasting; Chomsky's transformational generative grammar arose from research funded by the Joint Services Electronics Programs of the U.S. military; Lyotard's report on the postmodern was written for the government of Québec; García Canclini's theory of hybridity derived from a report on indigenous crafts; and queer theory's *ur*-archaeological text, Harold Garfinkel's study of transsexuality, was funded by Cold War contract research.[68] Cultural studies intellectuals like García Canclini design policy recommendations to elude the production and reception parameters fostered by corporate interests. Research with the U.S.-Mexico Fund for Culture and other Latin American governmental and nongovernmental initiatives is predicated on respecting citizen and cultural rights over capital accumulation and traditional elites. Critiques of applied research can be too knee-jerk, putting into the same category radical democratic actors like Sonia Alvarez (formerly of the Ford Foundation) and Tomás Ybarra Frausto (of the Rockefeller Foundation) with those who promote the interests of capital from the offices of RAND, Olin, or Brookings.

In fact, cultural studies connections between universities and social movements can ground research in cultural citizenship. Consider how the place of indigenous cultures in the representational apparatuses of Mexican national identity was put into question from the late 1970s by pressure from indigenous groups and anthropologists and sociologists who worked with them, like Guillermo Bonfil Batalla, Rodolfo Stavenhagen, and García Canclini. They challenged the role of intellectuals in maintaining essentialized constructions of nativeness that restricted indigenous people to empirically erroneous and politically debilitating representations of their culture. Stavenhagen, for example, denounced the assimilation to Mexican identity promoted by anthropological, museological, and social-service institutions. Bonfil called for a redefinition of the researcher as a collaborator with subaltern communities—a necessary retooling for social scientists who were seeing their traditional functions disappear due to such political and economic transformations as neoliberalism and privatization. García Canclini sought to influence institutions of popular culture. Such struggles center key deliberations in the areas of citizenship and consumption: identity, authenticity, aesthetics, postcoloniality, capital, and the state. Clearly, this is appropriate terrain for applying the insights of the professoriat, with two questions always kept in mind: What controls exist on applied research that has no links to social movements? And what can social movements do without ties to research?

There is a strong lineage to applied cultural studies, and cultural studies in the United States has been in the forefront of activism and documentation of contemporary labor conditions, especially in education.[69] *Social Text* published "The Yale Strike Dossier," an "Out Front" dossier on sexual politics and the labor movement, which included an essay by AFL-CIO president John J. Sweeney, and "Academic Labor at NYU."[70] These issues have circulated as organizing material and archival records for these and other struggles. Perhaps most notably, it was cultural studies advocates from the left among graduate students and professors in the Modern Language Association who pressed for the landmark study on labor produced in late 2000 by the Coalition on the Academic Workforce. The coalition was formed from areas where cultural studies has been strongest: literature, cinema, anthropology, foreign languages, and history were prominent.[71] This does not mean, of course, that all these activists were either affiliated with cultural studies or even sympathetic with it—but the consanguinity is marked, especially given the claim that cultural studies lacks a "real" politics or a materialist link.

I offer an instance of cultural studies' relevance to this domain below, in two forms. First, I foreground my own experience in the U.S. labor relations system, as someone operating from a cultural studies framework. Second, I offer a rebuttal of an anti-unionization diatribe from a management *apparatchik*. There is a transformation in prose and reasoning between the essay up to this point and what is about to follow. Up to now, although I have been writing a polemical history in support of cultural studies, I have used a predominantly academic prose style, one that foregrounds citational support and allusion rather than an overtly tendentious and personal position. As a means of performing the slippage between these categories in the spirit of compromising the binaries I erected earlier between practices of tendency and profession, the remainder of these remarks is alternately autobiographically idiosyncratic and aligned with movement politics, but always with the link to subjectivity and power that characterizes cultural studies.

Before the National Labor Relations Board

For the first time in my adult life, I'm in a nonunionized industrial sector. As if in some communistic utopia, I work for a self-managed autonomous collective. It's called a privately owned U.S. university. These places are so extraordinarily collaborative and nonhierarchical that they transcend employer-employee relations. Why? We are all embarked on a collegial quest for truth. So it's essential that we don't know the truth about what other people earn, that our pay not be set through transparent categories of productive labor, that our rights and responsibilities rest uncodified, and that those studying under and working for us also join the party on these terms. Such truths, if known, would break down a sense of trust and common purpose. Ah huh.

I came to this country in 1993 from Australia, where faculty had recently (ten years earlier) won the right to collective bargaining once the courts held that education was an industry. Because I was paid a third of the money given to certain people I worked with who performed identical tasks (except that they didn't publish), I felt able to say: "You are paid a lot of money; kindly do some expletive-deleted work." Suddenly, at New York University (NYU), I did not know what anybody was being "compensated" (such a sweet euphemism—where I came from, it referred to payments to those injured at work). I had no idea what the norms of performance were, and no sense of the poles of collaboration and competition that I was seemingly meant to swing between. This became all the more puzzling once people around me sought to organize.

A 1999–2002 struggle by graduate students at NYU to be granted the right to have a democratic vote about affiliation with the International United Automobile, Aerospace and Agriculture Implement Workers of America (UAW) put me in conflicted subject positions. I am not a reliable student's "friend" or "co-worker." I am a professor who wants extremely dull, decidedly nondevelopmental tasks, such as endless photocopying and the filling out of forms, to be performed by others. As someone who has held many jobs where such duties were constitutive, I have no hesitation in describing them as routine and awful. Their execution is, of course, vital to a chain of labor that produces, one hopes, an active and empowered citizenry through the educational process. That's what we're here for. Right? Coming to this realization about the means of education derived from many of Williams's precepts explicated earlier. The "structure of feeling" of this genteel, civilizing mission didn't seem right, and neither did the labor relations that enabled it.

For most of this struggle, I was also the director of graduate studies (DGS) in my department, with responsibility for graduate degrees and students' progress through them. In that subject position, I spoke with incoming graduate assistants (GAS), who are assigned to professors to do banal administrative and research tasks. I told them that the performance of these tasks is crucial, both to the success of the department and to their selection as suitable Teaching Assistants (TAS) further down the track. Then I moved into another mode, driven by ideology and a commitment to unionism: I encouraged them to recognize my DGS subject position for what it is—managerial, nonconsultative, and directive. How might they deal with "people like me"? By organizing. Facing up to this constitutive contradiction of my position was facilitated by the cultural materialism of my intellectual formation.

This Janus face was clearly on display when I was called by attorneys for the UAW to give evidence and submit to cross-examination by NYU's union-busting attorneys in Case No. 2-RC-22082 of the National Labor Relations Board (NLRB) in late August 1999. My technical competence to testify derived from my professional position as DGS, and my comments were juridically restricted to that competence. Many things germane to the topic that an ordinary and reasonable cultural studies person might have thought crucial—such as the unsustainability of a binary opposition between learning and labor—were essentially unsayable. The attorneys for NYU argued vigorously that GAS' tasks are critical to obtaining the doctorate and moving on to professorial rank (aka the serried ranks of the gentried poor). Anything that is done for money is not done because NYU needs it done, but because it will assist students someday in telling their own GAS what to do. It is postulated that if some of these tasks involve learning on the part of the GA, they are "developmental." Photocopy thousands of pages of *Social Text* in a semester on behalf of a professor and you might learn something. Somehow.

It struck me during the proceedings that this position implies a dim view indeed of U.S. employers and hence NYU itself (I presume it does actually employ someone—they must be blue-collar, and the University must welcome their unionization, as that doesn't impair collegiality. Right?). The dim view is this: employers should not seek to develop their employees by training them, thereby precluding opportunities to learn and increase their labor power–income potential. If such development occurs, then the employer-employee relationship is undercut. This is the corollary of arguing that a smidgen of development puts an end to claims for student unionization. Development excludes employment—it is a pure category of learning.

I endeavored to explain to the NLRB that the primary task of GAS was to provide a cheap labor pool for crucial but dull tasks that we didn't want to undertake ourselves. I also explained that there was very little time available for such students to undertake research for the faculty, so onerous were these clerical duties. And that what research they did manage was of no necessary benefit to their studies. Most of these remarks were ruled inadmissible.

Some of the difficulties I experienced before the NLRB derived from my desire to speak colloquially. So when I said that GAS were expected to "keep their noses clean," this was incomprehensible, as was the idea that something was "as rare as hen's teeth." I promised to eschew metaphor from that point on, so that the assembled attorneys would be able to follow. Other communicative problems flowed from my attempt to talk about a contradiction at the heart of NYU and other such institutions: we rely on discounted labor performed by students, even as we claim that they need these "fellowships" to become more like us. The NLRB's presiding officer and the cross-examining lawyers for NYU may have been so troubled by my figures of speech that they appealed to a House Un-American Metaphors and Similes Committee (HUMsic), but they were much more deeply disturbed by my use of the word "contradiction." The identification and explication of contradiction were deemed "opinion," and hence unsayable, before I had detailed why I found the concept helpful and what the relevant contradictions were. "Contradiction" as a category was, in this sense, inadmissible. Why am I not surprised that this useful wee word should so exercise the minds of those assembled before it? Might it be that its lineage lies in a conflictual view of social thought rather than an integrative one—that it stresses power inequalities over behavioral norms? The claim that this went beyond my technical capacity to testify seems highly procedural, rejecting even the conceptualization of practices as laden with contradiction. In trying to make sense of this environment, I drew on both *Social Text*'s Yale strike dossier and my reading of Williams's negotiation of binaries.

The other unsayable aspects of my testimony detailed the respective career benefits of teaching as a TA and an adjunct. The learned gentleman cross-examining me for the university sought to establish that I saw the sale of this labor power as part of financial aid assisting study, rather than remuneration. Of course, it is both. To compete with other leading schools for graduate students, we have to offer money. At the same time, to sustain our undergraduate cash crop, the graduate students must provide cheap services. The GAS and TAS exist to perform both these functions, as well as to undertake such administrative tasks as fronting the offices of those departments that NYU elects not to staff with qualified full-timers. In a tuition-driven institution like NYU, TAS are crucial to the delivery of a credible and profitable undergraduate curriculum. Their noses clean and their interpersonal fumbles as rare as hen's teeth, GAs are unleashed onto recitation sections, where they in a sense replicate and develop what they have done as GAs in the new subject position of TA. They are still performing tasks that professors would rather not do (intersubjectivity with the Great Unwashed, aka undergraduate students) and that the university would rather not fund through people who are fully qualified in their discipline, regularly available to students, and in a position to vouch for the curriculum. Adjunct professors at NYU, who were organized by the UAW in 2002, are crucial educational workers. These are also key positions for graduate students, since many of our doctoral candidates who have finished their course work receive no financial assistance in order to write up their research. They must compete to teach as adjunct professors in the curriculum, occasionally with their own TAs selected from the student cohort behind them. So TA and adjunct labor is different from GA work, in that it presumes a mastery of academic material and pedagogy. How these abilities are attained is a mystery—they just burst forth from the collegiality that is allegedly native to nonunionized workplaces.

The inadmissible nature of what I had to say was, clearly, not only about HUMSIC's views on my turn of phrase. It had to do with revealing the unsaid, the abject, that which covertly enables the entire system—undervalued labor disguised as self-improvement. In a university that places science at the heart of knowledge, I find NYU's position on unions and collegiality not only politically dubious but analytically spurious. Let's leave to one side ideological issues and focus on methodology and truth claims. How does anybody know that there is collegiality at NYU? How would they know if it were absent? Where is it deemed strongest and weakest on the campus, and how is this divined? What is done to rectify the loss (or worse still, the absence) of collegiality? And what is the who/what/when/where/how of the negative correlation that is claimed to inhere to unions and collegiality, at NYU and elsewhere? Definitions and data please—and testing. Otherwise, NYU's blithe, arrogant assertion would mean that the unionized faculty at the University of Massachusetts and Rutgers University and unionized graduate student employees at the Universities of Wisconsin and Michigan lacked collegiality.[72] Would NYU like to endorse such a position?

In short, let's have some rigor in this discussion. First, NYU is claiming that something (collegiality) exists—good, let us know how to define and identify its presence and absence. Second, NYU claims that a relation (unions destroy collegiality) exists—good, let us know the same answers. Otherwise we are dealing with a set of assertions that lack any basis whatsoever. I think a TA would not give good grades to a term paper that demonstrated such tendencies. That is, a TA committed to the collegial quest for truth, of course.

The Dean

Early in 2000, many months after my testimony, the NLRB found in the union's favor and against NYU. An election was held, permitting the students to decide whether they wished to be represented by the UAW. But the results were then sealed pending the outcome of an (ultimately unsuccessful) appeal by the employer-that-says-it's-not-an-employer. The NYU administration certainly had some support among the faculty, but a significant group was opposed to managerial superstition. One hundred and seventy faculty members signed a petition requesting that the university not appeal the NLRB's decision to grant graduate student employees an open and free electoral process to determine whether a majority favored collective bargaining machinery as a means of improving their material conditions of existence. Of those 170, many supported the principle of unionization, and some did not. But all were horrified by the administration's automatic denunciation of the right to vote. That violated the principle that democratic self-expression about the desirability of union representation should be the right of a financially disadvantaged, but intellectually, administratively, and professionally important, fraction of the university population, whose contribution to everyday life is both crucial and systematically undervalued in material terms.

While all this was going on, Catharine Stimpson, the dean of the university's Graduate School of Arts and Sciences, wrote an opinion piece in the *Chronicle of Higher Education*.[73] Her remarks represent one—managerial—view of the issue from within NYU, but they dovetail with widely held academic superstitions that are implacably opposed to (a) student-employee unionization and (b) the opportunity for students to express their democratic views on this matter. Importantly, they also come from someone occasionally associated with progressive politics, but whose position places her well to the right of cultural studies work at her institution.

Stimpson's article is a farrago of *non sequiturs* and distortions. I shall deal with its manifold misrepresentations serially. First, she claims that unionization institutionalizes an adversarial versus a collegial means of governance. This is simply asserted without evidence. While there may well be profound differences of standpoint and interest generated by the division of labor, these do not always color the interactions of employers and employees. At NYU, which is fervently anti-union at each and every level of its operation, such difficulties do arise—from the administration's implacable opposition to industrial organization. As for the claim that the current modus operandi is collegial and not adversarial, I shall turn to that below.

Second, Stimpson asserts that graduate students "do valuable work, but they aren't employees." This fudges, for the umpteenth time, the dirty little secret of U.S. university life that was ruled unsayable in my testimony before the NLRB—student workers function as discounted labor, allowing these institutions to operate at a fraction of the cost that would be incurred if proper salaries were paid in return for the discharge of innumerable professional duties, such as teaching, photocopying, and waiting at functions. The only relevant national data suggest that in the humanities, graduate student labor sustains up to 42.5 percent of introductory classes and between 7 percent and 34 percent of all undergraduate instruction.[74] If these folks are not employees, perhaps the NYU administration might care to use the resources at its disposal to calculate and publish the cost of substituting their work for people paid at rates set by the market, or collective bargaining, rather than with "stipends." Of course, the dirty little secret was not Stimpson's alone—it was shared by the elitists who filed amicus briefs against the NYU student employees. The list includes the administrations of Princeton, Yale, Columbia, MIT, Hopkins, and Stanford. They knew, as did cultural politicians from the left, that the idylls of academia rested on discounted labor performed by those working from necessity, or bought off with the elusive promise of a future share in this "life of the mind." The critiques of elitism via the canon that have characterized cultural studies segue easily into rejection of graduate student life as a pastoral idyll and recognition of the wage apparatus that underpins this system of work.

Third, Stimpson claims that the industrial model generated by union membership cheapens the historic mission of the university. But this begs the question of where that process of industrialism began and how it is currently managed. The short answer lies in the corporatization of university life. This is not a function of graduate student organizing. It is the outcome of universities' adherence to forms of funding and social influence that have to do with providing research and development services to government and business. Equally involved is the borrowing of fashionable forms of managerialism from corporations, such as practicing divide-and-rule forms of administration to centralize power deconally and keep faculty at private schools from participating in the actual versus the apparent allocation of resources on campus, despite legal obligations to do so under the Supreme Court's *Yeshiva* decision from twenty years earlier. This is a clear undermining of traditional academic values of collegiality and self-management, and it comes not from the brigands of cultural studies but from the avowed custodians of a historic mission of elevation.

Fourth, Stimpson quotes approvingly an anonymous alumnus hurrumphing that the graduate students are "damn well paid." This is amateur-hour economic analysis. It can hardly be indicative of her fellow managers' methods of financial planning and prudentialism—at least I hope it's not. But more than that, it shows a shocking disregard for questions of a living wage in New York City in terms of the costs of health care, housing, and basic subsistence.

Fifth, Stimpson maintains that the UAW's representing student concerns over these basic questions of life and limb would stifle debate and influence basic academic decisions at NYU. My understanding is that this is not intended by the union, the NLRB, or anyone else. Mandatory collective bargaining does not typically include such issues—they fall into the voluntary category and require the agreement of both sides in order to be included in negotiations. The idea that there would be a loss of "shared and collegial academic governance" presumes, in any case, that such governance exists at NYU. The huge centralization of power in the hands of deans (for example, routinely denying departments the right to select their own chairs and centralizing admissions decisions) makes a mockery of such claims and has led to the revival of an American Association of University Professors chapter by the faculty.

Sixth, Stimpson says that graduate students are a transient population, and as such they should not be permitted to vote on matters that will bear on others. At another point in the piece, she describes herself as a feminist. Perhaps she might ruminate on the arguments made against women workers gaining similar representation on the grounds that they are transient populations, engage in piece work, and so on.

Last, Stimpson objects to the NLRB's exclusion of certain students from the vote. It seems incredibly bad faith, even from an NYU dean, to make this point, since it arose because NYU's own claims on this issue were backed up by both the UAW and the NLRB—that students funded by professorial grants to undertake collaborative work that directly addressed their dissertation topics were not undertaking labor on behalf of the university, such as photocopying course outlines or grading papers.

This entire affair has laid bare NYU's desire to prevent graduate student employees from expressing their views on a key topic that differentiates open from repressive societies—namely, the right to organize. Whatever your views on unionism, this is a shocking breach. New York University's antidemocratic conduct has seen the self-styled "global university" attract global and national condemnation for its authoritarianism from the *Economist*, the *New York Times*, *Doonesbury* cartoons, and New York legislators.[75] The list goes on and on. As its notoriety spread, the administration and its antidemocratic *confrères* looked uglier and uglier and lonelier and lonelier, until finally they lost legally and gave in.

To repeat, opposition to NYU's administration has seen cultural studies students and faculty at the forefront, as was the case during an earlier Yale strike (which drew similarly barren ideas and brutal reactions from that administration, including many faculty nominally on the left, and resulted in the university being obliged by the federal government to post notices disavowing its appalling threats during the action). It is no accident that numerous activists at both NYU and Yale have been associated with cultural studies and anti-sweatshop activism, much to the chagrin of leading U.S. reactionaries.[76] And it is no accident that their opponents have hewed more closely to disciplinarity.

New York University's humiliating backdown led to additional graduate student employee activism at elite schools. The Ivy League campuses have seen a remarkable, if not absolute, split between pro-union humanities leftists and anti-union social scientists and scientists over the issue.[77] The very styles of analysis associated with cultural studies, such as the constitutive nature of conflict and contradiction, the myth of collegiality in corporate universities (aka student-maintenance organizations), and the iniquities of discounted labor and casualization, have facilitated a pragmatic understanding of the conditions of existence that have led to and sustained the situation of these workers.

This returns us to some of the issues raised earlier, in my summary of cultural studies. First, the NYU action confirms the power of seeing culture as ordinary. Being a graduate student employee is not tantamount to an avocational calling such as the priesthood or a search for a few scattered additions to the cv en route to becoming a gentleman scholar on a modest stipend—it is a job. Second, culture is a tool of action, as the NYU case demonstrated, via forms of cultural protest such as teach-ins, rallies to obtain support from undergraduate students and their parents, and media coverage. This extended to a non-hierarchical form of representation within the student-employee movement. Third, the story models a rapprochement between political economy and cultural studies, where issues of everyday life are equally about subsistence and self-definition and where claims for recognition are equally and indivisibly about both material well-being and a redefined sense of public identity. Fourth, it also illustrates the heuristically helpful, but ultimately problematic, dichotomy of my "tendency versus profession" ideal-type grids. Committed young workers are *both* professionals *and* politicos, and the moves blurring that distinction also query the mysticism promulgated by Stimpson and her ilk.

This is not to forward a blanket anti-institutional politics at all, either for cultural studies or its graduate student militants. It *is*, however, to argue with the pieties that criticize reformist "deals" with traditional power blocs. I was happy to appear before the NLRB, as were these activists. We may not have been able to put on the record our deeper analyses of what produced this tale of oppression, but we *were there*, and that illustrated to the administration, the NLRB, and the media that there were real differences of opinion—that cultural politics was at work.

Conclusion

Any undertaking that aims to map cultural studies is partial, and potentially controversial, because the terrain is up for grabs in definitional and power terms and is avowedly political. Let it be so. My own view? For what it's worth, I maintain that cultural studies should look at social movements and actionable policy as lodestones and direction-finders. In recognition of this, we must turn our gaze onto shifts in public discourse between self-governance and external governance and track the careers of the commodity sign and the state sign as they travel through time and space—Stuart Hall's "circuit of culture" that focuses on practices of representation, identity, production, consumption, and regulation.[78] This means recalling Foucault's provocation that the modern has as much to do with the governmentalization of the state as of the social. Then we shall have something to say about the institutional control of culture and the democratic promise of everyday life, pointing out erasures in the former and the potential of the latter. As Justin Lewis puts it, a concern with political power exercised over majorities need not be at the expense of specificity and marginality; rather, it should be regarded as a precondition to empowering the marginal.[79] Richard Maxwell stresses articulations between the two:

> People work to make culture. Not only the writers, technicians, artists, carpenters and all those who put together movies, books and such; culture is also made by labour not directly involved in the culture industries. Consider your own daily works of judgement and interpretation about a film plot, your grammar or a classmate's joke. Think of all those whose efforts built the bridges you have crossed, the roads travelled, the means of trans-

port and human relationship . . . your love story, a brief encounter . . . and all the hardship, strikes, solidarity, death, wage negotiations, debt and satisfaction embodied in those structures.[80]

So graduate students are definitely at work, no? And not just in a Marxist sense —they are paid money by an employer in return for making things happen.

I argued at the beginning of this chapter that cultural studies' continuities come from a concern with the reproduction of culture through structural determinations on subjects versus their own agency and from a method of analyzing that via historical materialism—no surprise, then, that key activists in the new wave of private-sector graduate student activism should find some inspiration in cultural studies. The links between study and labor should not be so difficult for higher education to conceptualize—they are the stuff of our world. And cultural studies also puts together seeming opposites that are actually natural syntagms. I recall my excitement when I first saw the front cover of the Birmingham Centre's *Working Papers in Cultural Studies 4* of 1973. Alongside a *bricolage* graphic of a thoughtful cherub, some compass points with dollar and pound signs, and a few printers' codes, the bottom center-left read like this:

LITERATURE ~~ SOCIETY

MOTOR RACING

It seemed natural to me for these topics to be together (as is the case in a newspaper). But of course that is not academically "normal." To make them syntagmatic was *utterly sensible* in terms of people's lives and mediated reality and *utterly improbable* in terms of intellectual divisions of labor and hierarchies of discrimination. By the same token, the efforts of cultural studies graduate students (and others) to strike a blow for their own democratic rights, and secure livable remuneration, have sent shock waves through Catharine Stimpson and her fellow travelers. The *New York Times* says, "American graduate programs, the envy of the world, are not so fragile they cannot coexist with unions, or provide workers the rights they enjoy elsewhere in the economy."[81] Bravo.

Notes

Thanks to Marie Leger, Jonathan Simon, Austin Sarat, Raphael Allen, and the editorial group of the *Yale Journal of Law and the Humanities* for their comments and to Rick Maxwell for permitting me to reproduce his diagram.

1   Raymond A. Morrow, "The Challenge of Cultural Studies," 22 *Canadian Review of Comparative Literature/Revue Canadienne de Littérature Comparée* no. 1: 3, 6 (1995).

2   Laurence Wei-Teng Leong, "Cultural Resistance: The Cultural Terrorism of British Male Working-Class Youth," 12 *Current Perspectives in Social Theory* 29–58 (1992).

3   Graham Murdock, "Across the Great Divide: Cultural Analysis and the Condition of Democracy," 12 *Critical Studies in Mass Communication* no. 1: 94 (1995).

4   Lawrence Grossberg, *Bringing It All Back Home: Essays on Cultural Studies* 4–5, 9–10 (1997).

5   Richard Maxwell, "Cultural Studies," in *Understanding Contemporary Society: Theories of the Present* 281–95 (Gary Browning et al. eds., 2000).

6   Id. at 282.

7   Richard Hoggart, *The Uses of Literacy: Aspects of Working-Class Life with Special Reference to Publications and Entertainments* (1957). The inaugural issue of the *International Journal of Cultural Studies* features an interview with Hoggart and a bibliography of his work: Mark Gibson and John Hartley, "Forty Years of Cultural Studies: An Interview with Richard Hoggart, October 1997," 1 *International Journal of Cultural Studies* no. 1: 11–23 (1998).

8   E. P. Thompson, *The Making of the English Working Class* (1968).

9   E. P. Thompson, *The Poverty of Theory* (1978).

10 Louis Althusser, *Lenin and Philosophy and Other Essays* (Ben Brewster trans., 1977).

11 A festschrift, *Stuart Hall: Critical Dialogues in Cultural Studies* (Kuan-Hsing Chen and David Morley eds., 1996), collects some of his work, reacts to it, and provides a useful bibliography.

12 Raymond Williams, *The Long Revolution* 57 (1975).

13 Raymond Williams, *Marxism and Literature* 19 (1977).

14 Raymond Williams, *The Politics of Modernism: Against the New Conformists* 151–52, 164–66 (Tony Pinkney ed., 1989).

15 Antonio Gramsci, *Selections from the Prison Notebooks* (Quentin Hoare and Geoffrey Nowell-Smith trans., 1971).

16 Martha Diawara, "Black Studies, Cultural Studies, Performative Acts," in *Race, Identity and Representation in Education* 262–63 (Cameron McCarthy and Warren Crichlow eds., 1994); see also Women's Studies Group of the Centre for Contemporary Cultural Studies, *Women Take Issue: Aspects of Women's Subordination* (1978).

17 Maxwell, supra note 5, at 286–87.

18 Paolo Freire, *Pedagogy of the Oppressed* (M. B. Ramos trans., 1970).

19 Armand Mattelart and Michèle Mattelart, *Rethinking Media Theory: Signposts and New Directions* (James A. Cohen and Marina Urquidi trans., 1992), and Michèle Mattelart, *Women, Media and Crisis: Femininity and Disorder* (1986).

20 Jesús Martín-Barbero, *Communication, Culture, and Hegemony: From the Media to Mediations* (Elizabeth Fox and Robert A. White trans., 1993).

21 Néstor García Canclini, *Hybrid Cultures: Strategies for Entering and Leaving Modernity* (Christopher L. Chiappari and Silvia L. López trans., 1995).

22 Handel Kashope Wright, "Take Birmingham to the Curb, Here Comes African Cultural Studies: An Exercise in Revisionist Historiography," 65 *University of Toronto Quarterly* no. 2: 355–65 (1996).

23   *Subaltern Studies* (Ranajit Guha ed., 1982–).

24   Partha Chatterjee, *The Nation and Its Fragments: Colonial and Postcolonial Histories* (1993).

25   Ania Loomba, *Colonialism/Postcolonialism* (1998).

26   *The Sarai Reader 02: The Cities of Everyday Life* (Ravi S. Vasudevan et al. eds., 2002).

27   Eric Kit-wai Ma, *Culture, Politics and Television in Hong Kong* (1999).

28   Ackbar Abbas, *Hong Kong: Culture and the Politics of Disappearance* (1997).

29   Judith Butler, *Gender Trouble: Feminism and the Subversion of Identity* (1990).

30   Donna Haraway, *Simians, Cyborgs, and Women* (1991).

31   Lesley Johnson, *The Modern Girl: Girlhood and Growing Up* (1992).

32   Angela McRobbie, *Feminism and Youth Culture* (1991).

33   John Frow and Meaghan Morris, "Introduction," in *Australian Cultural Studies: A Reader*, at viii–xv (John Frow and Meaghan Morris eds., 1993).

34   Meaghan Morris, *Ecstasy and Economics: American Essays for John Forbes* (1992).

35   Id.

36   Lawrence Grossberg, "The Formations of Cultural Studies: An American in Birmingham," in *Relocating Cultural Studies: Developments in Theory and Research* 21–66 (Valda Blundell et al. eds., 1993).

37   On the journals front, there have been special issues on "Asia/Pacific as Space of Cultural Production," 21 *boundary 2* no. 1 (1994); "Cultural Studies in the Asia Pacific," 22 *Southeast Asian Journal of Social Science* (1994); "Cultural Studies," 6 *Critical Studies in Mass Communication* no. 4 (1989); "Cultural Studies/Cultural Politics: Articulating the Global and the Local," 6 *Politics and Culture* (1994); "Cultural Studies/Les études culturelles," 22 *Canadian Review of Comparative Literature/Revue Canadienne de Littérature Comparée* no. 1 (1995); "Cultural Studies: Crossing Boundaries," 3 *Critical Studies* no. 1 (1991); "The Future of the Field—Between Fragmentation and Cohesion," 43 *Journal of Communication* no. 3 (1993); and "Rethinking Black (Cultural) Studies," 19 *Callaloo* no. 1 (1996).

The *Quarterly Journal of Speech* asks whether "neo-Marxism as a metadiscourse" is "alien to rhetorical sensibilities," in evaluating the impact of the *arriviste*, while *Victorian Studies* is anachronistically moved to run a review symposium on work about the 1980s and 1990s. Thomas Rosteck, "Cultural Studies and Rhetorical Studies," 81 *Quarterly Journal of Speech* no. 3: 397 (1995); and "Review Forum on Cultural Studies," 36 *Victorian Studies* no. 4: 455–72 (1993).

The journal *Cultural Studies* has been relaunched in the United States, its origins in Australia wiped from the slate of history; the *Review of Education* has been redesignated as the *Review of Education/Pedagogy/Cultural Studies*; and *African Literatures and Cultures* has been transformed into the *Journal of African Cultural Studies*. Other significant related journals include *French Cultural Studies*; *Social Semiotics*; *UTS Review*; *Strategies: Journal of Theory, Culture and Politics*; *Positions*; and *Travezia: The Journal of Latin American Cultural Studies*. The turn of the twenty-first century saw the launch of the *International Journal of Cultural Studies*, the *European Journal of Cultural Studies*, the *Journal of Spanish Cultural Studies*, *Inter-Asia Cultural Studies*, *Nepantla: Views from South*, and *Feminist Media Studies*.

38   Elisabeth S. Clemens et al., "Careers in Print: Books, Journals, and Scholarly Reputations," 101 *American Journal of Sociology* 433–94 (1996); John Maddox, "Where Next with Peer-

Review?" 339 *Nature* 11 (1989); and Cecil L. Willis and Stephen J. McNamee, "Social Networks of Science and Patterns of Publication in Leading Sociology Journals," 11 *Knowledge: Creation, Diffusion, Utilization* 363–81 (1990).

39   Vincent Kiernan, "Journal Editor Loses His Job over a Paper on How Students Define 'Having Sex,'" *Chronicle of Higher Education*, Jan. 29, 1999, at A20.

40   Quoted in John Hoey et al., "Science, Sex, and Semantics: The Firing of George Lundberg," 160 *Canadian Medical Association Journal/Journal de l'association médical canadienne* no. 4: 507 (1999).

41   Id.

42   Maggie Paley, *The Book of the Penis* (1999); Marian Pitts and Qazi Rahman, "Which Behaviors Constitute 'Having Sex' among University Students in the UK?" 30 *Archives of Sexual Behavior* no. 2: 169–76 (2001); Laura M. Carpenter, "The Ambiguity of 'Having Sex': The Subjective Experience of Virginity Loss in the United States," 38 *Journal of Sex Research* no. 2: 127–39 (2001); and Laura M. Bogart et al., "Is It 'Sex'?: College Students' Interpretations of Sexual Behavior Terminology," 37 *Journal of Sex Research* no. 2: 108–16 (2000).

43   Lawrence Grossberg and Della Pollock, "Editorial Statement," 12 *Cultural Studies* no. 3: 2 (1998).

44   John Hartley, "Editorial (with Goanna)," 1 *International Journal of Cultural Studies* no. 1: 5–7 (1998).

45   *Off-Centre: Feminism and Cultural Studies* (Sarah Franklin et al. eds., 1991).

46   *Feminist Cultural Studies*, vols. 1 and 2 (Terry Lovell ed., 1995).

47   *Feminism and Cultural Studies* (Morag Shiach ed., 1999).

48   *The Cultural Studies Reader* (Simon During ed., 1993).

49   *Black British Cultural Studies: A Reader* (Houston A. Baker Jr. et al. eds., 1996).

50   *Australian Cultural Studies: A Reader* (John Frow and Meaghan Morris eds., 1993); *Nation, Culture, Text: Australian Cultural and Media Studies* (Graeme Turner ed., 1993); *French Cultural Studies: An Introduction* (Jill Forbes and Michael Kelly eds., 1996); *Spanish Cultural Studies: An Introduction: The Struggle for Modernity* (Helen Graham and Jo Labanyi eds., 1996); *Contemporary Spanish Cultural Studies* (Barry Jordan and Rikki Morgan-Tamosunas eds., 2000); *Italian Cultural Studies: An Introduction* (David Forgacs and Robert Lumley eds., 1996); *Trajectories: Inter-Asia Cultural Studies* (Kuan-Hsing Chen ed., 1998); *Russian Cultural Studies: An Introduction* (C. Kelly and D. Shepherd eds., 1998); *Relocating Cultural Studies: Developments in Theory and Research* (Valda Blundell et al. eds., 1993); *American Cultural Studies* (John Hartley and Roberta Pearson eds., 2000); and *British Cultural Studies: Geography, Nationality, and Identity* (David Morley and Kevin Robbins eds., 2001).

51   Patrick Brantlinger, *Crusoe's Footsteps: Cultural Studies in Britain and America* (1990); David Chaney, *The Cultural Turn: Scene-Setting Essays on Contemporary Cultural Theory* (1994); *Culture/Power/History: A Reader in Contemporary Social Theory* (Nicholas B. Dirks et al. eds., 1994); *Studying Culture: An Introductory Reader* (Ann Gray and Jim McGuigan eds., 1993); Fred Inglis, *Cultural Studies* (1993); *Cultural Reproduction* (Chris Jenks ed., 1993); Jim McGuigan, *Cultural Populism* (1992); *Introduction to Contemporary Cultural Studies* (David Punter ed., 1986); John Storey, *An Introductory Guide to Cultural*

Theory and Popular Culture (1993); Andrew Tudor, *Decoding Culture: Theory and Method in Cultural Studies* (1999); and Graeme Turner, *British Cultural Studies: An Introduction* (1990).

52 *Cultural Studies* (Lawrence Grossberg et al. eds., 1992).

53 *The Lesbian and Gay Studies Reader* (Henry Abelove et al. eds., 1993); *Legal Studies as Cultural Studies: A Reader in (Post) Modern Critical Theory* (Jerry D. Leonard ed., 1995); *Colonial Discourse/Post-Colonial Theory* (Patrick Williams and Laura Chrisman eds., 1993); *Out of Bounds: Sports, Media, and the Politics of Identity* (Aaron Baker and Todd Boyd eds., 1997); *SportCult* (Randy Martin and Toby Miller eds., 1999); *Cultural Studies and Political Theory* (Jodi Dean ed., 2000); Mary-Jo Delvecchio Good, "Cultural Studies of Biomedicine: An Agenda for Research," 41 *Social Science and Medicine* no. 4: 461–73 (1995); and Paula Treichler, *How to Have Theory in an Epidemic: Cultural Chronicles of AIDS* (1999).

54 Sarah Berry and Toby Miller, *Blackwell Cultural Theory Resource Centre* (2002), at http://www.blackwellpublishers.co.uk/cultural.

55 Kenneth Minogue, "Philosophy," *Times Literary Supplement*, Nov. 25, 1994, at 27–28.

56 Alan Wolfe, "The Culture of Cultural Studies," 53 *Partisan Review* no. 3: 485–92 (1996); Roger Kimball, " 'Diversity,' 'Cultural Studies,' and Other Mistakes," 14 *New Criterion* no. 9: 4–9 (1996).

57 Quoted in David Morley, "So-Called Cultural Studies: Dead Ends and Reinvented Wheels," 12 *Cultural Studies* no. 4: 476–97 (1998).

58 Virginia Postrel, "The Pleasures of Persuasion," *Wall Street Journal*, Aug. 2, 1999.

59 Jeffrey C. Alexander and Philip Smith, "The Discourse of American Civil Society: A New Proposal for Cultural Studies," 22 *Theory and Society* no. 2: 151–207 (1993).

60 Jack Salzman, "Editor's Note," 1 *Prospects: An Annual Journal of American Cultural Studies*, at iii (1975).

61 *Symbolic Interaction and Cultural Studies* (Howard S. Becker and Michael M. McCall eds., 1990).

62 Robert N. Bellah et al., *The Good Society* (1992).

63 Don DeLillo, *White Noise* (1985); Colson Whitehead, *John Henry Days* (2001).

64 Adam Gopnik, "Read All about It," *New Yorker*, Dec. 12, 1994, at 84–102.

65 I have been involved with *Social Text* since 1994 and was its coeditor from summer 1997 to 2001. I did not bear the brunt of this crisis, but I was present throughout. It became clear that the desire to attack cultural studies was very intense indeed, regardless of the alibi of the moment.

66 Christopher Simpson, *Science of Coercion: Communication Research and Psychological Warfare, 1945–1960* (1996); and Herbert I. Schiller, *Living in the Number One Country: Reflections from a Critic of American Empire* (2000).

67 John S. Dryzek, *Discursive Democracy: Politics, Policy, and Political Science* (1994); Richard West Sellars, *Preserving Nature in the National Parks: A History* (1997); and Thomas Streeter, *Selling the Air: A Critique of the Policy of Commercial Broadcasting in the United States* (1996).

68 Noam Chomsky, *Aspects of the Theory of Syntax* (1965); Umberto Eco, "Towards a Semiotic Inquiry into the Television Message" (Paola Splendore trans.), *Working Papers in Cul-*

tural Studies no. 3: 103–21 (1972); Harold Garfinkel, *Studies in Ethnomethodology* (1992); Jean-François Lyotard, *La Condition Postmoderne: Rapport sur le Savoir* (1988); and Nestór García Canclini, *Hybrid Cultures: Strategies for Entering and Leaving Modernity* (Christopher L. Chiappari and Silvia L. López trans., 1995).

69 *Chalk Lines: The Politics of Work in the Managed University* (Randy Martin ed., 1998); *Will Teach for Food: Academic Labor in Crisis* (Cary Nelson ed., 1997).

70 "The Yale Strike Dossier," *Social Text* no. 49 (1996); "Academic Labor at NYU," *Social Text* no. 70 (2002); "Out Front," *Social Text* no. 61 (1999); and American Historical Association, *Summary of Data from Surveys by the Coalition on the Academic Workforce* (2000), at http://www.theaha.org/caw/cawreport.htm.

71 Ana Marie Cox, "Study Shows Colleges' Dependence on Their Part-Time Instructors," *Chronicle of Higher Education*, Dec. 1, 2000, at A12–A14.

72 Gordon Lafer, "Graduate Student Unions Fight the Corporate University," 48 *Dissent* no. 4: 63–71 (2001).

73 Catharine R. Stimpson, "A Dean's Skepticism about a Graduate-Student Union," *Chronicle of Higher Education*, May 5, 2000, at B7.

74 Cox, supra note 71.

75 "Pupil Power," *The Economist*, Nov. 18, 2000, at 40, and "Unions and Universities," *New York Times*, Nov. 25, 2000, at A18.

76 David Glenn, "A Free Trader Today," *Chronicle of Higher Education*, Mar. 29, 2002, at A14.

77 Scott Smallwood, "Union? No Thanks," *Chronicle of Higher Education*, May 17, 2002, at A12–A14.

78 Stuart Hall, "Introduction," in *Representation: Cultural Representations and Signifying Practices* 1 (Stuart Hall ed., 1997).

79 Justin Lewis, "The Opinion Poll as Cultural Form," 2 *International Journal of Cultural Studies* no. 2: 199–221 (1999).

80 Maxwell, supra note 5, at 281.

81 *New York Times*, supra note 75.

Telling a Less Suspicious Story: Notes toward a Nonskeptical Approach to Legal/Cultural Analysis

Paul Schiff Berman

Those of us who labor in academia—either in law or in the humanities—are, at a very basic level, storytellers. Both in my scholarly writing and in the classroom, I find that most of my effort is focused on constructing narratives of meaning from the complicated and multifaceted material that makes up our lived reality. Philosopher Wilhelm Dilthey wrote that "reality only exists for us in the facts of consciousness given by inner experience."[1] But for every experience there is a wide range of possible meanings that can be assigned. And for every possible meaning there is a range of stories we can tell. As anthropologist Edward Bruner has pointed out, "If we write or tell about the French Revolution, for example, we must decide where to begin and where to end, which is not so easy, so that by our arbitrary construction of beginnings and endings we establish limits, frame the experience, and thereby construct it."[2] On this view, "Every telling is an arbitrary imposition of meaning on the flow of memory . . . every telling is interpretive."[3] Thus, although we may not always be conscious of it, scholars are constantly engaged in the process of articulating a vision both of our culture and of the nature and shape of reality itself.

Moreover, I'm not sure that I at least am able to say definitively that any particular vision is necessarily the most "accurate." Certainly, if a scholar argued that the U.S. government consisted of Martians who were inhabiting the bodies of our national leaders, we might think that such a narrative was so removed from the everyday experience of most people that it was unhelpful. But, in the main, I find that there are a wide variety of critical stances available about any given subject and that it cannot necessarily be said that one approach is more "true" than another.[4]

If there are a range of plausible critical stances available about any given subject, then it is not inevitable that we choose one perspective over another. So how do I, as someone embarking on a project aimed at discussing law's role in American culture, choose the type of story I wish to tell? What sort of critical stance should I adopt, and what are the ramifications—political, psychological, spiritual—of that choice? These are the questions I wish to explore in this essay. In the end, I will pursue the possibility of viewing law in an extremely sympathetic light, as a useful forum for discourse among multiple worldviews. Other scholars, of course, have provided more skeptical accounts of law's pervasive cultural influence. I will examine some of these accounts as well and offer reasons why, though much of this scholarship has been extremely useful, I wish to move in a different direction. But regardless of the critical stance one ultimately adopts, I hope that, simply by musing about these questions in a fairly personal way, I will encourage others to consider the ethical choices inherent in their own scholarship as well.

Nevertheless, before beginning I must first acknowledge that, merely by conceiving of one's critical perspective as a choice, I may have already committed myself to a particular point of view. For example, some might question just how free the choice of stories actually is. Our critical perspectives are, of course, influenced by many factors, including psychological predispositions, cultural and class backgrounds, concerns about career advancement, and so on. Or one might go even further and contend that the very idea of a free choice is illusory because embedded cultural and political forces may determine our choices without our conscious knowledge.[5]

Part of the point of this essay, however, is to suggest that we might want to resist precisely this type of argument on the ground that such a perspective is ultimately disempowering, debilitating, and insufficiently useful from a pragmatic point of view. In addition, it seems reasonable to think that, at least as compared to most of the population, tenured academics are among the most free to choose their own critical stance. Nevertheless, I readily admit that the "choice" on which I focus may be constrained in significant ways. Even with this caveat, though, I believe that it may still be useful to think self-reflectively about the critical perspectives we generally take and consider to what extent other possibilities exist. This exploration will necessarily be a personal one for each of us, but I think it is essential that we remember periodically to ask such questions about the kinds of stories we tend to tell.

In the generation of law and society research that emerged with the formation of the Law and Society Association, sociolegal scholars, building on the legal realist attack on formalism, told a story primarily about the possibility of social progress through law. Law was seen in instrumental terms as a means to a more just society, and scholars focused on the "gaps" between legal doctrine and legal practice in order to foster reform.

Over the past two decades, however, sociolegal scholars have become increasingly disenchanted with the reformist project. These writers, influenced by Michel Foucault and other postmodern theorists, have begun to see law not as an instrument for dispensing justice but as a constitutive societal force shaping social relations, constructing meaning, and defining categories of behavior. Such a constitutive theory of law takes seriously Clifford Geertz's observation that law is not simply an instrument for enforcing a system of morality or justice but is also "part of a distinctive manner of imagining the real."[6] Accordingly, scholars have emphasized that law cannot be distinguished from the rest of social life; rather, "law permeates social life, and its influence is not adequately grasped by treating law as a type of external, normative influence on independent, ongoing activities."[7] As Paul Kahn has written recently, echoing a generation of critical legal scholars,[8] "We experience the rule of law not just when the policeman stops us on the street or when we consult a lawyer on how to create a corporation. The rule of law shapes our experience of meaning everywhere and at all times. It is not alone in shaping meaning, but it is rarely absent."[9]

As part of the move to view law as a constitutive force in social *relations*, many sociolegal scholars have chosen to go even further and emphasize law's role as a pervasive form of social *control.* On this view, "Law constrains not by force but by creating the very categories of action that define social life."[10] Law is seen as inherently "implicated in the maintenance of inequality rather than its amelioration."[11] Accordingly, the focus of more recent sociolegal scholarship often involves uncovering how law's coercive power is inscribed in all legal discourse and practice.

This is certainly one possible story to be told about the constitutive power of law, but I wonder if there are others. For example, might we tell a story that emphasizes law's generative possibilities, one that envisions law not merely as an instantiation of embedded power but as an activity that might have true intellectual, imaginative, ethical, and political value? Moreover, could we tell this story while still embracing a constitutive theory of law, and while refusing to return either to legal formalism or to the instrumental reformist vision of the first generation of law and society scholarship? And, if we can imagine such an alternative story, why might we choose to tell that story, rather than adopt the more familiar sociolegal focus on law as hegemonic discourse?

These questions form the basis of a larger project that I am just beginning, and so my aim in this essay is to take a frankly impressionistic, unsystematic "first cut" at them. Such issues are of particular interest to me as an emerging scholar seeking a way both to embrace the antifoundational insights characteristic of postmodern thought and to acknowledge law's role as a discourse of cultural meaning, while at the same time trying to articulate a more optimistic and pragmatic story about law's power and potential.

But before attempting to articulate such a vision, it is necessary to examine the more skeptical story and to try to speculate about how that story came to be so dominant in cultural and sociolegal discourse. In this regard, it may be useful to reconsider Paul Ricoeur's famous analysis of the "hermeneutics of suspicion."[12] Ricoeur discussed the work of three influential thinkers: Nietzsche, Marx, and Freud. According to Ricoeur, Nietzsche believed that human beings are in a constant state of deluding themselves that they actually possess foundational knowledge; Marx attempted to show that all societal institutions and ideological constructs were the product of economic relations; and Freud explained human behavior in terms of underlying unconscious impulses and desires. Thus, all three employed what Ricoeur called the hermeneutics of suspicion. According to Ricoeur, this approach is characterized by the desire to unmask, demystify, and expose the real from the apparent. Although Ricoeur's ideas on this topic have been widely disseminated, I will review them briefly in the first part of this essay.

It seems to me that the move in law and society scholarship away from a legal-realist-inspired reform agenda toward a focus on law as a pervasive and inescapable force in defining social relations can be viewed as an ongoing elaboration of this same hermeneutics of suspicion. In the second part of the essay, I will sketch the evolution in sociolegal scholarship toward an ever more suspicious critical stance. Because it is beyond the scope of this essay to attempt a systematic review of such scholarship, I will use as an illustrative case study a recent volume of essays, *Justice and Power in Sociolegal Studies*, edited by Bryant G. Garth and Austin Sarat.[13] This collection exemplifies the constitutive view of law, and by examining several of the essays, we can perhaps begin to see how the skeptical approach operates more generally in contemporary sociolegal scholarship.

The hermeneutics of suspicion obviously has much to recommend it, and we have all learned a tremendous amount from the efforts of scholars to expose the pervasive discourse of power that may underlie lofty rhetoric, "neutral" philosophical systems, or even well-intentioned efforts at reform. In law, for example, sociolegal scholars have worked successfully not only to question the ability of the legal system to live up to its ideals but also to challenge "the very ideals and principles that law claims for itself."[14] There can be little doubt that this suspicious stance has yielded substantial fruit. I emphasize this point because I do not want this essay to be misread as yet another polemic against postmodern critical theory.

Nevertheless, the question remains: do we *always* want to tell a story that seeks to challenge "the very ideals and principles that law claims for itself"?[15] And, if we choose to tell a different story, must we jettison the constitutive view of law altogether? In the third part of the essay, I explore two potential drawbacks of the hermeneutics of suspicion. First, such an approach may situate the writer (and perhaps the reader as well) in a superior position to those who are the objects of study. By unmasking ideologies and power dynamics unacknowledged by those participating in the systems being analyzed, the writer may imply that he or she is able to get beyond the mystification and see the situation more accurately than those caught "within" the system.[16] Thus, for example, a critical scholar might attempt to show that, even when litigants report their satisfaction with the procedural justice system, such reports are unreliable because the litigants are unwittingly in the thrall of the legal system's dominance. Likewise, a critic who views law as a constitutive language may focus on the inherent power relations within that language, regardless of the subjective intentions of the participants who are actually engaged in the discourse. This type of analysis may, by its very nature, suggest that the writer has discerned a truth unavailable to those who are participating in the social practice. Such a perspective may not give sufficient value to the lived reality of those participants and may therefore provide a distorted picture of the social practice itself.[17]

Second, and perhaps even more importantly, relentless practice of the hermeneutics of suspicion may, over time, have a corrosive effect both on our psyches and on society as a whole. What does it mean for us to be consistently skeptical of all human efforts to make the world more just, more beautiful, or more joyful? In what ways might skepticism discourage such noble striving? To tell stories of beauty, of optimism, and of hope might be a profoundly important task in and of itself. And, even from the more earthbound perspective of political mobilization, a less suspicious story might actually be more effective at achieving social reform. As Richard Rorty has recently argued, "Those who hope to persuade a nation to exert itself need to remind their country of what it can take pride in as well as what it should be ashamed of. They must tell inspiring stories about episodes and figures in the nation's past—episodes and figures to which the country should remain true."[18]

Thus, from both a spiritual and a pragmatic standpoint, we may wish to adopt a sympathetic reading rather than a suspicious one and to emphasize what is worthwhile in the efforts of people to construct ideas, systems, or principles, flawed though they might be. We must remember that if the ideas of law and justice are inherently compromised by the practice of power and ideology, it may become more difficult even to envision a satisfactory response short of revolution.

Having discussed some limitations to the hermeneutics of suspicion, this essay then offers notes toward a less skeptical approach to legal/cultural analysis. This approach builds on Ronald Dworkin's theory of how judges reach legal conclusions.[19] According to Dworkin, the legal decision-making process is akin to a group of authors constructing a chain novel. In adding each new chapter, the author must interpret the work of the other authors in the preceding chapters so as to make of the overall shared enterprise the best work of art possible. Whether or not Dworkin is correct in his interpretation of judicial decision-making, I believe his analysis holds much promise as an *attitude* with which to undertake scholarly criticism. Rather than attempting to debunk, unmask, and demystify a particular legal or cultural practice and tell a story that makes the practice seem more oppressive than before, we might instead seek an interpretation that makes the best case on behalf of the practice and that makes it into the best practice it can be, at least according to the values and philosophies of the critic.[20]

In conclusion, I offer one possible alternative story as an example of the type of less skeptical scholarship I have in mind. Significantly, this story also derives from the constitutive theory of law. And it resists the move, championed by some communitarian critics, to return to a prerelativist world where one version of truth was to be considered authoritative. Rather, I suggest what might be called a doctrine of multiple perspectives, which views law[21] as a potentially generative site for the play of discourses and the encounter with the Other.

Such a doctrine need not replace the more suspicious story altogether. Indeed, it should go without saying that there are multiple stories to be told, and any and all of them are likely to be useful at one time or another.[22] In addition, my discussion here only begins to raise the complicated question of how one decides, in any given circumstance, whether to adopt a suspicious or sympathetic approach. Nevertheless, I think that, simply by recognizing the possibility of alternatives, we will open a creative space for such a self-reflective question, which may be a positive development in and of itself.

For myself, I ultimately choose to tell a story that may help remind us of what is best about our nation's legal environment and that may help instill a sense of optimism about our ongoing shared enterprise. I neither expect nor desire that all scholars embrace the same perspective. Rather, I suggest only that our critical stance is, in part, an ethical choice and that we should each consider the subtle but significant ramifications of the types of stories that we tell.

Paul Ricoeur and the Hermeneutics of Suspicion

Paul Ricoeur speaks not of stories but of hermeneutics. Yet his inquiry is similar: what are the methodological principles we use to interpret and describe reality? Although it is beyond the scope of this essay to attempt a comprehensive analysis of Ricoeur's discussion of hermeneutic styles, I believe it may be useful to invoke Ricoeur's categories briefly, because they can provide a framework for considering trends in sociolegal scholarship.

Ricoeur contrasts two different "poles" among hermeneutic styles. At one pole, hermeneutics is "understood as the manifestation and restoration of . . . meaning."[23] At the other pole, hermeneutics is "understood as a demystification, as a reduction of illusion."[24] It is not entirely clear to me precisely what Ricoeur means by these two categories. Nevertheless, I understand a hermeneutics of faith to be one that treats the object of study as possessing inherent meaning on its own terms. In contrast, the hermeneutics of suspicion seeks to expose societal practices as illusory edifices that mask underlying contradictions or failures of meaning. I will return to the first pole in the fourth part of this essay, but for now I wish to focus on the hermeneutics of demystification and suspicion.

Ricoeur locates in the work of Nietzsche, Marx, and Freud the central hallmarks of this suspicious approach. He argues that each of these thinkers makes "the decision to look upon the whole of consciousness primarily as 'false' consciousness."[25] Ricoeur sees this perspective as an extension of Descartes's fundamental position of doubt at the dawn of the Enlightenment. According to Ricoeur, "The philosopher trained in the school of Descartes knows that things are doubtful, that they are not such as they appear; but he does not doubt that consciousness is such as it appears to itself; in consciousness, meaning and consciousness of meaning coincide."[26] The hermeneutics of suspicion takes doubt one step further, by distrusting even our perceptions.

This suspicious position questions the so-called correspondence theory of truth. As we go through our lives, most of us generally assume that our mental perceptions accord with reality because we believe we have direct access to reality through our senses or through reason. This is the legacy of the Enlightenment, the "answer" to the fundamental Cartesian doubt. But the hermeneutics of suspicion maintains that human beings create false truths for themselves. Such false truths cannot be "objective" because they always serve some interest or purpose.

By discovering and revealing those interests or purposes, suspicious analysis seeks to expose "false consciousness" generated through social ideology or self-deception. False consciousness may arise in many different ways. Nietzsche looked to people's self-deceit in the service of the "will to power." Marx focused on the social being and the false consciousness that arises from ideology and economic alienation. Freud approached the problem of false consciousness by examining dreams and neurotic symptoms in order to reveal hidden motivations and desires. Thus "the *Genealogy of Morals* in Nietzsche's sense, the theory of ideologies in the Marxist sense, and the theory of ideas and illusions in Freud's sense represent three convergent procedures of demystification."[27]

Although these three "masters of suspicion" aim to destroy false consciousness, they do so in the service of greater consciousness. For all three, there is some better, healthier perspective to which we should aspire. As Ricoeur points out, they are attempting to "clear the horizon for a more authentic word, for a new reign of Truth."[28]

This move is significant, and it is perhaps what allows us to characterize these three thinkers as modern, rather than postmodern, critics. Although they attack false consciousness, they cling to the possibility of a "truer" consciousness. Nietzsche wants to recapture the meaning of the will to power by meditating on the deceptions of "superman," "eternal return," and "Dionysus."[29] Marx argues for a "conscious insight" that will counteract the mystification of false consciousness.[30] And, as Ricoeur explains, "[w]hat Freud desires is that the one who is analyzed, by making his own the meaning that was foreign to him, enlarge his field of consciousness, live better, and finally be a little freer and, if possible, a little happier."[31]

Thus the hermeneutics of suspicion as practiced by these three modernist thinkers involves demystifying illusion and fable but then replacing that false consciousness with something "better" and "truer." Postmodern thinkers take this hermeneutics of suspicion one step further by questioning whether the "true" consciousness that emerges through demystification is any truer than the "false" consciousness that existed previously. On this view, Nietzsche, Marx, and Freud, no matter how suspicious they were, can still be characterized as part of the Enlightenment project. This project, as David Harvey has written, "took it as axiomatic that there was only one possible answer to any question. From this it followed that the world could be controlled and rationally ordered if we could only picture and represent it rightly."[32] Likewise, Nietzsche, Marx, and Freud offered particular forms of order that they advocated as the more accurate picture of the world.

By contrast, in his seminal work, *The Postmodern Condition*, Jean-François Lyotard defines postmodern existence as the inability to believe in any such "metanarratives."[33] And, in his explication of metanarratives, Lyotard includes as an example Marx's political story of class conflict and revolution.[34] He could easily have included the metanarratives asserted by Nietzsche and Freud as well. Indeed, Jean Baudrillard makes the point starkly when he writes that, whereas modernity is concerned with "the immense process of the destruction of appearances . . . in the service of meaning," postmodernism addresses the "immense process of the destruction of meaning, equal to the earlier destruction of appearances."[35]

This is a kind of "hyper-suspicion." From this perspective, *all* explanatory stories are contingent, even those offered by the skeptical critic. It is this constant questioning that leads some people to view such postmodern suspiciousness as nihilistic or paranoid.[36] For these critics of postmodernism, it is one thing to undertake a process of dismantling that also provides for rebuilding. It is quite another to take a stance "where the point is precisely to dismantle with no ground left, but only a multiplicity of standpoints which amounts to no standpoint—an everywhere which is nowhere."[37] On this view, "The enabling suspicion of the older tradition is extended and intensified into paranoia—and thus becomes disabling."[38]

I do not share this view, although I am sympathetic to its concerns. It is undoubtedly the case that some postmodern scholars, in both law and the humanities, have focused so much on dismantling that they are left with no constructive story to tell. However, I do not think that nihilism is a necessary feature of postmodern thought.[39] Indeed, I will argue in the culmination of this essay that, by recognizing the existence of multiple stories, all with potentially legitimate claims to truth, we can focus on the play of opposing discourses and the creative possibilities that arise from conversation among competing narratives. The view from postmodernism need not be so bleak.[40] Nevertheless, it is clear that the basic approach of both modern and postmodern critics in the twentieth century has been characterized by a general suspicion about truth claims.

The Hermeneutics of Suspicion and Sociolegal Scholarship

In legal scholarship, we might view some of the key theoretical movements in the twentieth century as a similar progression of the hermeneutics of suspicion. First, scholars attacked the purportedly neutral principles underlying legal doctrine in order to spark progressive reform. Next, they turned to the question of whether law reform could achieve the aims of justice. And finally, they began to envision law as a pervasive and inescapable form of social control. As a way of summarizing these moves, I will consider a collection of essays published in 1998, *Justice and Power in Sociolegal Studies*. Because the editors and many of the contributors to the collection are leading figures in contemporary law and society scholarship, the volume provides a useful snapshot of current perspectives in the field as well as a "native" account of scholarly trends over the past several decades written by two active participants, Bryant G. Garth and Austin Sarat. Then I will discuss several specific scholarly projects in order to see how the hermeneutics of suspicion operates in practice.

An Overview of Trends

In the first decades of the twentieth century, legal realists asserted that legal doctrine was inherently indeterminate and that therefore decisions about contested doctrinal issues were always decided based on nondoctrinal factors. Law and society research in the 1960s extended this critique, pushing a progressive agenda that sought to use law instrumentally to achieve distributional justice. As described by Garth and Sarat in the introduction to *Justice and Power in Sociolegal Studies*, "At this stage in the development of law and society research, there was a taken-for-granted understanding of the nature of justice and an unembarrassed commitment to the project of using social research to promote justice through law."[41] Thus scholars focused on the gap between "law on the books" and "law in action" in order to suggest better ways of implementing a just legal order. For example, Garth and Sarat cite an American Bar Foundation Survey of Criminal Justice in the 1950s and 1960s finding that the exercise of discretion among regulators and the police was one factor preventing the criminal justice system from operating consistently with the progressive ideals being articulated by the U.S. Supreme Court in that era.[42] The focus, in this and other "gap studies," was to identify and explain deviations from the regulatory ideal. "Implicit in most of this research," however, "was the assumption that the state regulatory policies, like the goals of the criminal justice system, represented an appropriate starting point for a researcher strongly committed to social justice."[43]

The legal realist critique and sociolegal gap studies can be viewed as equivalent to the modernist version of the hermeneutics of suspicion described by Ricoeur. Just as Nietzsche, Marx, and Freud (in Ricoeur's view) attacked false consciousness but remained committed to the existence of a "truer" consciousness, so too did legal realists challenge the truth claims of legal formalism, while remaining committed to using law instrumentally to achieve justice.[44] Similarly, early law and society scholarship employed the hermeneutics of suspicion to expose the failure of specific legal efforts to enact meaningful reform, but it did not question the fundamental assumption that the legal order was an appropriate site for seeking justice.

The next move in the progression toward greater suspicion came from those (to use Garth and Sarat's taxonomy) who criticized gap studies and "raised questions about the ability of the liberal state, even in the best of times and with the best intentions, to realize social justice."[45] Here, law was still seen in instrumental terms, but as a force that actually thwarts meaningful reform. Thus Garth and Sarat cite the work of scholars who, they say, viewed "the entire regulatory effort [as] some kind of hoax, unlikely ever to contribute to the progressive goals implicit in early enthusiasm for regulation."[46] These scholars expressed "skepticism about the power of litigation to promote social change, about claims of right generally, about the helpfulness of due process hearings for welfare recipients, the usefulness of consumer rights, the proliferation of alternative dispute mechanisms, and the autonomy of the legal profession."[47]

Here we see the hermeneutics of suspicion deployed in order to expose not only the *failure* of law reform but also the *very impossibility* of law reform. This perspective questions the power of even well-intentioned people to bring us closer to justice through law. As Garth and Sarat comment, "Loss of confidence in research-inspired progressive legal reform led law and society scholars away from the strategy of 'delivering legality' as a way of delivering justice."[48] It is in this period that we also see the emergence of critical legal studies scholarship challenging the classic doctrines of American law and legal education, including contracts, torts, and corporations, as well as antidiscrimination and labor law. Some analyses argued that appeals to reason or principle are inevitably incoherent and that the resolution of legal questions is therefore inherently political.[49] Others focused on the suppression of alternative values by dominant ideologies.[50] Still others argued that legal education was an indoctrination of individuals into a dominant elite.[51] Finally, some critical scholars challenged assumptions underlying communication itself by claiming that all meaning is ultimately determined by the listener/reader.[52]

These moves exemplify a further elaboration of the suspicious approach.

There is again a distrust of stated rationales and a desire to expose false consciousness. But now, under the influence of postmodern critical theory, we begin to find a new level of unmasking—not merely that one particular justice claim is ineffective, but that *any* justice claim is inevitably compromised by the legal language and institutional context in which it is framed. In the ongoing discourse between law and power, power was beginning to triumph as the fundamental "truth" to be revealed through critical (that is, suspicious) scholarship.

Finally, Garth and Sarat identify the move toward a constitutive, rather than an instrumental, vision of law. Such an approach focuses not on how law might serve progressive goals but instead on how law works within a society to help shape social relations. "The study of ideology and legal consciousness, in particular, became part of the quest for an understanding of this side of law's power."[53]

A constitutive view of law sees legal discourse, categories, and procedures as a framework through which individuals in society come to apprehend reality. Thus, law is not merely a coercive force operating externally to affect behavior and social relations; it is also a lens through which we view the world and actually conduct social relations. On this view, "[L]aw shapes society from the inside out by providing the principal categories in terms of which social life is made to seem largely natural, normal, cohesive, and coherent."[54] Clifford Geertz perhaps provided a manifesto for the constitutive view in 1983:

> [L]aw, rather than a mere technical add-on to a morally (or immorally) finished society, is, along of course with a whole range of other cultural realities . . . an active part of it. . . . Law . . . is, in a word, constructive; in another constitutive; in a third, formational. . . .[55]
>
> Law, with its power to place particular things that happen . . . in a general frame in such a way that rules for the principled management of them seem to arise naturally from the essentials of their character, is rather more than a reflection of received wisdom or a technology of dispute settlement.[56]

For at least the past fifteen years, sociolegal scholars have largely pursued a constitutive vision of law and therefore have treated law as (1) a belief system that helps define the roles of individuals within society; (2) a system of organization that determines societal roles; and (3) a language for conceptualizing reality, mediating social relations, and defining behavior. Following Geertz, they have deployed various interpretive methods to study the "webs of signification"[57] found within law.

Significantly, taking a constitutive view of law need not commit one to the hermeneutics of suspicion. Indeed, in the final part of this essay, I will attempt to point toward a less skeptical constitutive approach. Nevertheless, as Garth and Sarat point out, many of those who have adopted a constitutive view of law's power have focused on law as a particularly pervasive form of social control. "Studying the power of law as social control has led scholars to consider the mechanisms through which liberal legality works to limit our conceptions of justice as well as our efforts to promote social change."[58] Indeed, the deployment of the hermeneutics of suspicion has become so complete that it is difficult for its adherents to remain committed to any instrumental social reform task. As Garth and Sarat observe, "[R]esearch on law's constitutive power generally shows how law disciplines potential challengers to the social order rather than serving to promote change and reform."[59] From such a perspective, even the idea of justice is unmasked and demystified. "Justice becomes at best an external, political critique—and otherwise an inevitable disciplinary ally of law's hegemony."[60] As Susan Silbey has written, "[T]he ideals and principles that legal institutions announce, even though they fail to support them, are part of how legal institutions create their own power and authority."[61]

Thus the progression of sociolegal scholarship charted by Garth and Sarat can be seen as stages in the further elaboration of a hermeneutics of suspicion. As they acknowledge, "Recognition of law's hegemony and its constitutive power [has] undermined the optimism of the vision of 'social justice through law' that animated so much early scholarship."[62] And, now that many sociolegal scholars take as a given the idea that law is constitutive, it is not surprising to see a substantial body of scholarship predicated on the idea that law is fundamentally a language and structure of social control and a means by which entrenched power relations are constructed and legitimized. Even the more recent turn in sociolegal scholarship to a focus on "agency"—the ways in which individuals contest and resist legal categories—tends to build from the assumption that law inevitably operates as a force of power, thereby engendering the resistance.[63] Moreover, although I have focused on the development of law and society scholarship in particular, the basic scholarly approach will no doubt be familiar to those who identify with movements in feminist legal theory, critical race theory, and other similar areas. Employing the hermeneutics of suspicion, these scholars too have attempted to uncover the ideological biases in legal categories, the stories excluded or distorted through law, and the inequities inherent in legal discourse, procedure, and adjudication.[64] As Garth and Sarat observe, "[M]any scholars would say that they now study power, not justice."[65]

Specific Scholarly Projects

So far, the discussion has been fairly abstract. In this section, therefore, I will explore how the hermeneutics of suspicion plays out in several articles. My aim is neither to criticize these projects nor to show the ways in which they are wanting. Indeed, I have deliberately attempted to select strong examples of suspicious scholarship in order to avoid the accusation that I am setting up a straw man. Thus I attempt to identify some of the consequences of a suspicious approach even in works that make useful contributions.

Turning again to *Justice and Power in Sociolegal Studies*, I begin by looking at Carol J. Greenhouse's essay in that volume, "Figuring the Future: Issues of Time, Power, and Agency in Ethnographic Problems of Scale."[66] Greenhouse focuses on two concepts, diversity and community, and seeks to describe law's role with regard to both. She offers two case studies. First, she discusses press coverage of the 1992 violence in Los Angeles after the verdict in the trial of four police officers accused of beating Rodney King. Then, she analyzes the U.S. Supreme Court's decision in *Brown v. Board of Education*,[67] as well as the text of three major federal civil rights statutes enacted from 1964 to 1991.[68]

Starting from these two case studies, there are a number of different stories Greenhouse might have told about the role of law with regard to diversity and community. For example, she might have discussed the way in which the civil rights laws attempted to construct a more inclusive conception of community by providing more space for diversity in society. Or she could have discussed the circumstances under which civil rights lawsuits might provide a community forum for discussion among diverse voices. Or she might have talked about the ways in which law could speak usefully about diversity or help construct community.

But Greenhouse instead chooses to tell a story that *equates* the various civil rights statutes with the police crackdowns in Los Angeles. She acknowledges that the two case studies seem to be opposites: one "involves massive disruption and violence," and the other "involves the legal poetics of equality."[69] But she argues that the differences between the two case studies "are superficial. In fact, they *both* associate diversity axiomatically with violence, and both associate diversity with a corollary need for active legal intervention. The interventions differ in form—police action in Los Angeles and judicial and legislative action in the civil rights context—but not in their operative premise that diversity is intrinsically uncivil without the intervention of the law."[70]

It is important to recognize how the hermeneutics of suspicion works here.

We might at first think that civil rights statutes are an attempt to acknowledge diversity and protect it by preventing discrimination. But Greenhouse attempts to demystify the statutes. She reads them to be as hostile to the idea of diversity as was the newspaper coverage of the Los Angeles riots that focused on the supposedly inherent volatility of multiethnic neighborhoods. And she argues that law is not so much about *mediating* the *effects* of diversity in order to foster community as about *claiming* the *power* to transform diversity into civility.

Greenhouse views the civil rights statutes as an assertion of state power, an attempt to "construct 'community' around the central axis of the state's role in the management of diversity in physical space."[71] Thus a disorderly community "call[s] forth the law's coercive powers of physical social control."[72] But an orderly community that resorts to courts rather than violence is also squelching diversity by invoking the state as mediator among diverse groups that are "implied as being ordinarily inimical to each other."[73]

Greenhouse also focuses on the constitutional basis for the federal civil rights statutes. Historically, the ability of Congress to enact such statutes has been justified as an exercise of its power to regulate interstate commerce. Although most observers would agree that justifying civil rights legislation as a regulation of commerce is counterintuitive, there are historical and jurisprudential reasons that such an approach proved to be a pragmatic strategy to persuade the U.S. Supreme Court of the constitutionality of the statutes.[74] Greenhouse chooses to tell a different story, however. From this jurisprudential choice, she makes the observation that, in the civil rights law, "commerce emerges as an ongoing materialization of the state's agency that . . . takes up its vigil over the public space through law enforcement."[75] In Greenhouse's account, the interstate commerce rationale is itself somewhat suspicious. She argues that the civil rights statutes "imply . . . that the colonization of the future will be financed with capital borrowed from the meanings of difference."[76]

Thus Greenhouse's story subverts the idea that the civil rights statutes represent any kind of advance toward justice or societal tolerance for diversity. Instead, she argues that, in both the fears about urban violence and the enactment of civil rights legislation, "the state's centrality in the public management of 'diversity,' the materialization of that agency in investment and commerce, and the commoditization of identity emerge as inextricably linked ideas and social processes."[77] Moreover, she rejects the idea that the concept of "community" might even provide a meaningful aspirational goal. Rather, she views "community" as merely a rhetorical conceit that is "deliberately reworked as legal and political strategies by architects and adversaries of change."[78]

These are provocative ideas, and I do not here wish to take issue with any of Greenhouse's contentions. Instead, I note only the choice of stories. What are the narratives that we take from the essay? Federal civil rights statutes are ultimately hostile to diversity because they implicitly associate diversity with violence. These statutes inevitably inscribe the state's role in managing and enforcing the transformation of diversity into civility. Such state control is linked to commerce, commoditization, and colonization. And "community" is a strategic construct used to enforce these norms of civility and control. Thus Greenhouse effectively challenges our faith in the aspirational goals of civil rights as diversity-protecting, community-building, or civility-enhancing.

My second example of the way in which sociolegal scholarship chooses among multiple available stories comes from the study of procedural justice. Tom R. Tyler's essay "Justice and Power in Civil Dispute Processing"[79] provides an overview of the substantial literature in this area. The literature consists largely of empirical studies about litigant satisfaction with various dispute resolution mechanisms. "Instead of evaluating litigation experiences against objective criteria specifying desirable features of procedures or outcomes, experiences are evaluated in terms of the subjective experiences of the litigants."[80]

Such studies use interviews with disputants to examine the degree to which people care simply about "winning" and the extent to which they care about other elements of the dispute resolution process, including notions of fair procedure. For example, one study of civil litigation[81] reached two basic conclusions. First, just looking at outcome turns out to be a poor predictor of litigant satisfaction. "Whether assessed in terms of length of time to case resolution (delay), costs to the litigant, and/or amount won or lost, objective indicators do not explain much about people's postlitigation feelings."[82] Second, litigant satisfaction is closely correlated with subjective perceptions of whether the process was just. Moreover, the factors that influenced such a determination, rather than being related to outcome, focused more on process issues such as whether the participant had the opportunity to address the decision-maker, whether the decision-maker appeared to be honest, and whether the participant was treated with dignity and respect.[83]

From this research, two alternative stories (at least) can be told, both of which are consistent with a constitutive theory of law's power. The first story starts from the evidence that, even for its participants, law is not solely (or perhaps even primarily) an instrumental means for achieving a desired outcome. Rather, the legal process can be a substantive end in itself. Law provides a forum for storytelling, a set of rules for constructive discourse, and a site for subjective observations about fairness. As a result, so this story goes, it is essential for achieving substantive justice that the legal system *seem* just and provide an effective locus for discourse. Indeed, on this view, such factors would need to be a basic part of any analysis of what justice is.

The second, more skeptical story challenges the first one in two significant ways. As an initial challenge, this story questions why we should think that the subjective experiences of litigants provide any truly useful information about conceptions of justice. This is because people's beliefs may reflect false consciousness. As Susan Silbey has argued, unequal power in society allows certain groups to establish hegemony in a society's ideology. By hegemony, she means "those circumstances where representations and social constructions are so embedded as to be almost invisible, so taken for granted that they 'go without saying, because, being axiomatic, they come without saying.'"[84] If, as Silbey contends, liberal law is hegemonic, then people's evaluations of their experiences may simply be a reproduction of a society's ideology rather than an "objective" statement of their actual interests.

A further challenge transforms the idea of procedural fairness into a view about the legitimation of power. On this view, procedural justice is not so much a worthwhile aspiration as it is a means for law to *appear* fair while in reality perpetuating power dynamics in the society. Indeed, Garth and Sarat question the procedural justice literature for precisely this reason: "The justice that is described in research on procedural justice is fully compatible with, and may be an essential part of, the processes through which law legitimates itself and *unjust* social arrangements. Thus, . . . studies of procedural justice may tell us less about justice as an ideal and more about the power of law to get its way."[85]

Again, I do not argue that there is anything more "correct" about the first story than the second, with its dual skeptical challenges. But notice the difference in tone and emphasis. The first story discusses the potential ways in which the justice system might actually provide a helpful forum and might generate a sense of fairness, justice, and satisfaction through procedural or ritual mechanisms. The second story argues that, even if people gain a sense of satisfaction, their perceptions are irrelevant because the participants are in the thrall of false consciousness and are therefore reproducing hegemonic ideologies about which they are unaware. Moreover, this story argues that the quest for procedural justice is inevitably compromised because creating the appearance of justice is merely a way of legitimating law's power.

In recent years, sociolegal scholars such as Patricia Ewick, Susan Silbey, Austin Sarat, Barbara Yngvesson, Sally Engle Merry, and David Engel have offered somewhat more optimistic variations on the idea of law as hegemony discussed above. Although they still present legal narratives as hegemonic, they insist that law is always locally contested. Accordingly, they refuse to accept a depiction of law's subjects as mere passive victims of law's power. Rather, these authors see active "agents" who may sometimes manipulate the legal system to win partial but consequential victories, both material and symbolic.[86]

Yet even in these accounts, law tends to be viewed not as an enabling language that actually *provides* the opportunity for engagement among conflicting narratives, but as a form of power "emanating outward from the sources of sociocultural production to shape the practices of everyday life,"[87] and therefore allowing a space for alternative worldviews only through an act of resistance. Moreover, although disempowered people may contest the categories imposed on them by law, such contests are seen as temporary, their effects short-lived. In these analyses, law is no longer a rigid hegemony—dictating categories and determining meaning in an absolute way—but it is still viewed as a "moving hegemony." This moving hegemony "allows for the coexistence of discipline and struggle, of subjection and subversion, and directs attention toward a dynamic analysis of what it means to be caught up in power."[88] Yet the tactical resistance of disempowered groups ultimately does not "dislodge the power of law or the dominance of legal rules and practices."[89] Indeed, "Even when relatively powerless persons adopt a counterhegemonic view of the world . . . they construct it around the cultural shapes and forms that law helps to create."[90] Thus, although these scholars offer a picture of law that allows for the possibility of multiple narratives, those narratives are seen as oppositional, not as inherent and empowering features of legal discourse itself. Accordingly, these accounts still tend to be framed in a suspicious language focused on exposing the inevitable and largely unnoticed dominance of legal categories.

Two final examples of the hermeneutics of suspicion should suffice. First, I point to the work of Pierre Schlag, even though he is not represented in the *Justice and Power in Sociolegal Studies* collection, because he has continued to offer a forceful critique of legal discourse from the perspective of critical legal studies. Schlag, in numerous articles and in his book *The Enchantment of Reason*,[91] argues that judges and legal academics are trapped in a jointly constructed maze of incoherent justifications for the legal system. He contends that judges refuse to acknowledge "all that law is and all that law does" and instead insist on "a romanticized and inflated shadow image" of the law that legitimizes the inherently violent nature of legal practice.[92] Moreover, he argues that legal academics tend to perpetuate this mythology because most academics were formerly judicial clerks and so are invested in the judicial enterprise. As a consequence "of the legal academic's primal identification with the persona of the judge,"[93] Schlag concludes, legal scholarship devolves into "the legitimization and rationalization of judicial opinions."[94] Thus Schlag argues that legal scholarship is devoted to obscuring the "real" workings of the legal system.

This perspective exemplifies the extreme skepticism of much critical sociolegal scholarship. Other scholars, working in a more realist mode, have similarly sought to demonstrate that legal doctrine is inevitably a product of political partisanship by using empirical data to show that judges decide cases based on nondoctrinal factors. One recent example is Richard Revesz's work regarding the United States Court of Appeals for the D.C. Circuit.[95] Revesz argues that ideology "significantly influences" judicial decision-making on the D.C. Circuit; that ideological voting is more prevalent in cases where purely procedural challenges are raised; and that a judge's vote is greatly affected by the party affiliation of the other judges sitting on the panel.[96]

Both Schlag and Revesz tell stories that aim to strip away the veneer covering legal doctrine, though Schlag obviously takes this critique much further than Revesz. They view judicial decisions (and legal doctrine more generally) as a form of subterfuge, disguising law's power and the play of ideology. The story that remains untold in these accounts, of course, is the story of principled decision-making, the idea that judges strive, however imperfectly, to articulate principles in their adjudication of cases and aim to be faithful to the decisions and articulated principles of the past. This may again be a story that allows law to *seem* principled and therefore disguise its hegemonic power, but it is also a story that might inspire us to think of law as more than just an exercise in power politics, and thereby to look past our own parochial interest, acknowledge an opposing view, and try to develop a language for mutual accommodation and understanding. A language of principle might therefore be useful, regardless of whether or not such principles are truly determinative.

To the extent that practice of the hermeneutics of suspicion in twentieth-century scholarship has successfully eroded notions of legal method as a science and legal rules as formalist truths, there can be little doubt that such scholarship has opened up a more varied and subtle set of inquiries and understandings about law. Moreover, much of this scholarship has been vitally important both in exposing many legal principles and procedures to be the product of hierarchy, ideology, and language and in bringing previously unheard voices to debates about legal doctrine. Finally, the constitutive theory of law, which views law as a lens for constructing reality, holds much promise as an interpretive framework because it allows us to see the ways in which law influences both our comprehension of and discourse about social and political conflicts.

Yet, as some of the previous discussion indicates, there are also potential drawbacks to these kinds of skeptical stories, and we should be self-conscious about the ramifications of our choice to tell them. The next part revisits the articles just discussed in an attempt to identify some of these potential drawbacks.

The Hermeneutics of Suspicion and Its Limitations

I see at least two reasons to be concerned about the use of the hermeneutics of suspicion as the primary method for legal/cultural scholarship. First, the focus on unmasking a cultural practice may tend to situate the observer outside the practice being studied, thereby robbing the observer of empathy and perhaps distorting the ultimate account. Second, oversuspiciousness may actually discourage efforts toward political change and may have a disempowering or dispiriting effect on society as a whole.

The Importance of Empathy

The hermeneutics of suspicion tends to place the scholarly observer in a position superior to those who are the objects of study. The skeptical critic tends to point out what is "really going on" in a particular social practice, and what is "really going on" is almost never acknowledged or understood by those who work within that practice. Indeed, because the participants are understood to be deluded by false consciousness, their perceptions and understandings of the world are easily discredited, or at least discounted.[97]

The Revesz piece provides an example. Harry T. Edwards, chief judge of the D.C. Circuit, wrote an article responding to Revesz's charge that the D.C. Circuit judges resolve disputes based on political partisanship.[98] Aside from criticizing Revesz's statistical analysis (a debate that is not relevant here), Edwards argues that Revesz's work, and those by others in a similar vein, is fundamentally flawed because it treats as irrelevant the subjective experience of the judges themselves. According to Edwards, "[S]erious scholars seeking to analyze the work of the courts cannot simply ignore the internal experiences of judges as irrelevant or disingenuously expressed. The qualitative impressions of those engaged in judging must be thoughtfully considered as part of the equation."[99]

Revesz's response to this charge might well be that he *must* discount the stated motivations of the judges. Indeed, if his attempt is to uncover the judges'

"real" motivations rather than their "conscious" motivations, then the pro-
testations of the judges are worse than irrelevant—they may actually be evidence of the judges' false consciousness!

We have already discussed this same approach with regard to the empirical
studies of dispute processing. A skeptical critic might well discount a litigant's
reported satisfaction with the legal system on the ground that the individual has
succumbed to the illusion spun by law's embedded power. Greenhouse's reaction would likely be similar. For example, we could imagine that all those who
drafted the civil rights statutes considered in her article reported that, in drafting the statutes, they were attempting to encourage diversity. We could imagine
further that all the litigants who have successfully pursued claims under these
statutes over the years reported that filing the suits had encouraged tolerance of
diversity in their communities. Even with this testimony, it is unlikely that
Greenhouse's analysis would change. And, of course, anyone attempting to
refute Schlag with discussions about the importance of legal rules or principles
would, in Schlag's terms, be exhibiting the very pathology that Schlag is attempting to expose.

Thus, not only is the critic situated in a position of superior perception, any
objection by the participants can easily be dismissed as a product of the delusion
itself. One can see how this logic operates among Ricoeur's "masters of suspicion" as well. The rhetoric of suspicion creates a dichotomy: those ensnared by
false consciousness versus those who can get out from under it and see the snare.
Whether this snare is deluded Christian mythologies (Nietzsche), capitalist false
consciousness (Marx), or repression (Freud), the basic strategy is the same.[100]

At first blush, it appears that postmodern critics should be able to answer
this objection. Unlike the modernists, they purport not to be saying what is
"really" going on beneath the surface because they believe that the interpretations are no more real than the surface behavior.[101] However, the basic move is
the same because the critic is able to recognize that truth is a contingent notion,
while the people being discussed do not. Thus such critics tend to adopt a
"super-perspectival" version of reality, a view from Olympus, if you will.[102]
Moreover, the view that truth is contingent tends to mean that contests about
truth claims are inherently questions of politics, ideology, and power. Thus,
like the skeptical critiques discussed above, most postmodern critical approaches tend to view human behavior through this lens, even while denying
that any one lens is authoritative.

One might well ask, of course: why should we be concerned that a scholarly
approach tends to place the critic and reader in a position of greater perception

than those working within a societal practice? After all, most of us probably have had the experience of seeing a situation more clearly with the benefit of hindsight or from a more emotionally detached perspective. Why shouldn't critics have the same privilege? My answer is that of course they should. Indeed, as I will stress later in this essay, a less suspicious hermeneutics does not mean that critics lose their ability to be critical. Thus there certainly may be times when a critic is able to recognize the significance of an issue that was unnoticed by the participants.

But a less suspicious, more empathetic reading has the virtue of acknowledging that the lived experience of the participants is at least relevant to the discussion. To take the Revesz/Edwards debate as an example, an empathetic hermeneutics would most certainly find it significant that judges believe themselves to be acting based on precedent and principle rather than political partisanship. Indeed, only by taking the judges' belief seriously will we become aware of the possibility that the belief itself might function as a constraint on judicial discretion. Thus judges who believe in legal principle and repeatedly tell themselves and the world a story about both the nonideological nature of their work and the substantial constraints on their discretion may, in fact, be more constrained in their decision-making, regardless of whether or not a critic can "prove" that such constraints are illusory.[103]

As a result, less suspicious scholarship may have two benefits in this regard. First, it encourages critics both to be empathetic toward their subjects and to resist the urge to take a God's-eye view.[104] Second, it forces the critic to include in the analysis the lived reality of the people being studied, leading to a richer, more textured perspective.

Paranoia and the Corrosive Effects of Suspicion

The second drawback of the hermeneutics of suspicion is perhaps even more important. As some scholars have noted, the hermeneutics of suspicion can easily slip from healthy skepticism into a kind of rhetorical paranoia. Paranoia, of course, is a loaded term, and probably a bit unfair. Nevertheless, because it is used frequently in the academic literature about the hermeneutics of suspicion, I will use it as well—though I want to make clear that I believe paranoia to be the hypothetical extreme in the movement toward skeptical scholarship. I do not mean to imply that any actual scholars necessarily display such paranoid logic.

Critics of the hermeneutics of suspicion describe the "paranoid style of functioning"[105] as "an intense, sharply perceptive but narrowly focused mode of attention" that results in an attitude of "elaborate suspiciousness."[106] Paranoid individuals constantly strive to demystify appearances; they take nothing at face value because "they regard reality as an obscure dimension hidden from casual observation or participation."[107] On this vision, "The obvious is regarded as misleading and as something to be seen through. So, the paranoid style sees the world as constructed of a web of hints to hidden meaning. . . . The way in which the paranoid protects fragile autonomy is by insuring, or at least insisting, that the paranoid's interpretation of events is *the* interpretation."[108]

Such a paranoid style may, over time, have a potentially corrosive effect on society.[109] Consider the long-term consequences of repeated exposure to suspicious stories. An appeal to religious ideals is portrayed as an exercise of political power or the result of deluded magical thinking. A canonical work of art is revealed to be the product of a patriarchal "gaze." The programs of politicians are exposed as crass maneuverings for higher office or greater power;[110] the idealistic rhetoric of judicial opinions is depicted as an after-the-fact justification for the exercise of state-sanctioned violence; the life choices of individuals are shown to be responses to psychological neurosis or to social pathology.

All of these are exaggerations, but they increasingly represent the rhetoric that is used to describe human interaction both in contemporary society and in the past. As Richard Rorty puts it,

> In this vision, the two-hundred-year history of the United States—indeed, the history of the European and American peoples since the Enlightenment —has been pervaded by hypocrisy and self-deception. Readers of Foucault often come away believing that no shackles have been broken in the past two hundred years: the harsh old chains have merely been replaced with slightly more comfortable ones. Heidegger describes America's success in blanketing the world with modern technology as the spread of a wasteland. Those who find Foucault and Heidegger convincing often view the United States of America as . . . something we must hope will be replaced, as soon as possible, by something utterly different.[111]

If that is one's viewpoint, it will inevitably be difficult to muster one's energy to believe in the possibility of positive action in the world, short of revolution (and even revolution is probably inevitably compromised). As Rorty points out, though the writers of supposedly "subversive" works "honestly believe that they are serving human liberty," it may ultimately be "almost impossible to clamber back down from [these works] to a level of abstraction on which one might discuss the merits of a law, a treaty, a candidate, or a political strategy."[112]

Of course, one might view this as a positive development. One might think people should stop being lulled into a false sense of believing that the rhetoric of public life really matters. If people began to view such rhetoric as a construction of entrenched power, so the argument might go, they would form the nucleus of a truly revolutionary political movement.

I doubt that such an eventuality is likely to occur. Moreover, I am not sure that a culture of suspiciousness is the most effective way to seek political (or personal) change anyway. Suspicious analysis seeks to expose the dangers of our enchantment with reason or truth or collectivity, but there are dangers that arise from relentless disenchantment as well. As Richard K. Sherwin has observed, "[W]ithout the means of experiencing more profound enchantments, without communal rituals and social dramas through which the culture's deepest beliefs and values may be brought to life and collectively reenacted, those beliefs ultimately lose their meaning and die. . . . Forms of enchantment in the service of deceit, illicit desire, and self-gratification alone must be separated out from forms of enchantment in the service of feelings, beliefs, and values that we aspire to affirm in light of the self [and the] social and legal realities they help to construct and maintain."[113]

If all we have is relentless suspicion, we are unlikely to be inspired to create a better world. Instead, we are likely to feel a kind of collective guilt and self-loathing (or, worse, a fatalistic apathy) because of the hopelessly compromised system we have created or to which we have acquiesced. Such guilt, self-loathing, and apathy is, as Rorty argues, a luxury that agents who need to act in the world cannot afford to maintain.[114]

Paul Kahn, in his recent book, *The Cultural Study of Law*, indirectly suggests a possible response to this critique. Kahn encourages sociolegal scholars not to worry so much about being political or social agents of the sort Rorty describes. Instead, he argues that scholars studying law as a cultural system should move "away from normative inquiries into particular reforms and toward thick description of the world of meaning that is the rule of law."[115] If we resist being seduced into focusing on the policy ramifications of our work, Kahn believes, we could better study law the way a religious studies scholar studies religion: not from the perspective of one who is a part of the practice under consideration, but as an independent observer seeking to understand the cultural meaning of the practice from a greater distance. Thus Kahn argues that it is a mistake for scholars to be too invested in legal practice, regardless of whether they see themselves as law's custodians or law's reformers. Rather, Kahn contends that we would be better off suspending our belief in law's rule altogether,[116] thereby allowing us to analyze legal practice without a normative agenda.

Although I agree with Kahn that sociolegal scholarship need not include explicitly normative policy ramifications to be effective, his approach still requires the scholar to choose a hermeneutic stance. Even if we adopt the more distanced "observer" perspective Kahn advocates, we still must choose to analyze legal and cultural practices through a suspicious lens or through one that is more sympathetic. And this choice inevitably has social and political consequences of the sort described above. Moreover, I am concerned about Kahn's particular articulation of the legal scholar's task: to *suspend belief* in law's rule. Such a formulation seems to invite a more skeptical stance than I find appropriate. Nonetheless, there is nothing about his call to study law as a cultural system rather than as a set of policy prescriptions that requires us to study law from the perspective of disbelief. Indeed, as I argue below, studying any cultural practice (whether literature or religion or law) from a perspective of belief—as long as it is not completely uncritical belief—may ultimately be more fruitful. Regardless of one's position on that issue, however, it seems to me that, at the very least, the move toward less normative scholarship cannot extricate scholars from the fundamental questions that I am discussing.

A Hermeneutics of Meaning, Faith, and Sympathetic Interpretation

Ricoeur contrasts the hermeneutics of suspicion with a hermeneutics of meaning. This hermeneutics is based on a conception of faith. In Ricoeur's words, "The contrary of suspicion, I will say bluntly, is faith. What faith? No longer, to be sure, the first faith of the simple soul, but rather the second faith of one who has engaged in hermeneutics, faith that has undergone criticism, postcritical faith."[117] Such faith is difficult if one employs the hermeneutics of suspicion because such a skeptical approach tends to promote "knowingness" rather than belief. Once one has exposed or demystified a cultural practice, it will inevitably be more difficult to believe in that practice whole-heartedly. One might accept it as the best of a bunch of poor alternatives, but it will lose its power to inspire.

As Rorty argues, "Knowingness is a state of soul which prevents shudders of awe. It makes one immune to romantic enthusiasm."[118] For example, he points out that it is difficult to be inspired by a cultural practice while at the same time viewing that practice "as the product of a mechanism of cultural production."[119] To view a work in this way, he contends, may yield understanding, but not self-transformation.

The hermeneutics of suspicion tends to require that the cultural practices under observation be placed within the framework of the critic. But if a practice, such as the work of the U.S. Supreme Court, is to have inspirational value, it must be allowed to recontextualize much of what the observer previously thought she knew; it cannot, at least at first, be itself recontextualized by what the observer already believes.[120] Thus if we begin with the suspicious premise that justices of the U.S. Supreme Court are articulating hopelessly indeterminate legal principles that merely mask the inevitable assertion of power inscribed within legal discourse, then we will have precluded the possibility that we could be surprised or inspired by the beauty, poetry, or idealism of the Court's project.[121]

But how might we fashion an alternative approach? In order to pursue one possibility, I wish to draw on Ronald Dworkin's work on interpretation. Dworkin was writing primarily about how judges decide cases, but his approach is generalizable into a theory of interpretation that may be a useful model. Thus, for my purposes, it is less important whether Dworkin accurately describes the process of judging than whether he offers a helpful metaphor through which we might consider the idea of sympathetic interpretation more generally.

Dworkin's metaphor is the chain novel. He asks us to assume a group of novelists get together and decide collectively to write a novel. One writer will contribute the first chapter, pass it on to the second writer, who will contribute the next chapter, and so on. In this scenario, "every writer but the first has the dual responsibilities of interpreting and creating because each must read all that has gone before in order to establish, in the interpretivist sense, what the novel so far created is."[122]

How then might, say, the writer of the sixth chapter go about interpreting the preceding five chapters? Notice that the hermeneutics of suspicion may not work very well here. Even though the author of the chapter must decide what the book is "really" about, what the motivations of the characters "really" are, and so on, it is unlikely that unmasking the descriptions provided in earlier chapters as the product of false consciousness will make a very successful novel. Similarly, if the novel through five chapters is an Agatha Christie–like mystery, the writer will be likely to refrain from turning the sixth chapter into a philosophical exegesis on the nature of human relationships. Such an approach might well make the book seem disjointed and poorly written. Notice that this is true even if the writer of the sixth chapter honestly prefers philosophical works to Agatha Christie novels. In the act of interpretation, the writer of the sixth chapter must attempt to make the overall work into the best possible work of art it can be, not transform it into a different one. As Dworkin points out, "Interpretation of a text attempts to show *it* as the best work of art *it* can be, and the pronoun insists on the difference between explaining a work of art and changing it into a different one."[123]

Of course, my sixth chapter may differ from yours, because we have different ideas of what makes a work of art good. But the point is that both of us must attempt to make the work as it exists into the best work it can be. As with the Agatha Christie example above, we are not free simply to ignore the first five chapters merely because we have a very different idea of how those chapters should have been written. "An interpretation cannot make a work of art more distinguished if it makes a large part of the text irrelevant, or much of the incident accidental, or a great part of the trope or style unintegrated and answering only to independent standards of fine writing."[124]

In likening this process to the act of common-law judging, Dworkin articulates an attractive theory of sympathetic interpretation:

> Each judge must regard himself, in deciding the new case before him, as a partner in a complex chain enterprise of which these innumerable decisions, structures, conventions, and practices are the history; it is his job to continue that history into the future through what he does on the day. He *must* interpret what has gone before because he has a responsibility to advance the enterprise in hand rather than strike out in some new direction of his own. So he must determine, according to his own judgment, what the earlier decisions come to, what the point or theme of the practice so far, taken as a whole, really is.[125]

Again, I am not interested here in whether this is an accurate description of how judges decide cases, nor am I interested in taking sides in the long-running scholarly debates about Dworkin's approach to interpretation.[126] Instead, I want to consider Dworkin's conception solely as a thought experiment that might suggest a useful *attitude* for scholars to adopt. Notice how this attitude differs in tone and emphasis from the hermeneutics of suspicion. For example, I argued above that one drawback of the suspicious approach is that it may appear to place the commentator apart from the pathologies or delusions of the people operating within a given social practice. Thus, in the act of pointing out others' "false consciousness," one implicitly exempts oneself from that consciousness. In contrast, Dworkin's model requires the interpreter to treat herself as a "partner" in the endeavor being analyzed.

Moreover, because the interpreter is in partnership with the activity or text being analyzed, she will be more likely to think of it as a *joint* enterprise and therefore construct the best explanatory framework she can. Accordingly, she

will try to understand what this enterprise amounts to and develop an interpretation that both fits the contours of the enterprise and offers the best justification for it.[127] This again is very different from the hermeneutics of suspicion.
A suspicious reading generally seeks to undermine the practice being studied. If
one is attempting to expose, unmask, or demystify in order to show the "real"
unvarnished truth, one is, by definition, not attempting to create the best justification for it or make it into the best practice it can be. To the contrary, the
hermeneutics of suspicion usually seeks to show the essentially compromised
nature of the practice.

Again, I want to step back from the argument for a moment because I do not
want it to be misread. I am not condemning skepticism as a critical stance
altogether. Nor do I advocate merely accepting all human practices at face value
without employing any critical judgment at all. It is important to recognize
that, in describing the hermeneutics of meaning, Ricoeur defined it as *post*critical faith, not *un*critical faith.

More importantly, my aim is not to advocate that either critical stance be
eradicated. Indeed, I must leave to another day a key question: how does one
decide in any given situation which scholarly stance to take? The answer to this
question is not at all clear to me, and I hope to pursue the issue in a future essay.
For now, I must be content merely to open up space so that such a question can
be asked. Thus I suggest only that we examine the stories that we as scholars
tend to tell and then think about whether there are others that we might tell but
do not, simply because we reflexively fall into using one critical stance instead
of another.

Let me use an example that is closer to home. My experience has been that,
at academic conferences, reading groups or colloquia, or in humanities or law
classes, much of the conversation centers on all the issues the book or article
under discussion failed to address. Thus we hear that the author left out a
consideration of x, which would have complicated her analysis, or that she
failed to recognize the ways in which issues of power were embedded in y, so she
missed a key part of what was "really" going on, etc. Almost inevitably, the
piece that was "left out" happens to be the focus of the critic's own scholarly
agenda. These are not sympathetic readings. Because human experience is
widely varied and multifaceted, there will always be aspects of an issue that are
omitted in any given scholarly account. But instead of focusing on what the
author *failed* to do, we might look at what *her particular project* was and see if
we can form the best possible understanding of that project. I remember when I
was in an undergraduate anthropology course, we would read book after book

from the history of anthropological theory, and, with regard to each book, all we would discuss was what that account had missed. By the end of the semester, I was left feeling that there were no examples of worthwhile anthropology scholarship. This is precisely what can happen if the stories we tell are unrelentingly suspicious. We deprive our listeners of a sense of inspiration, of models to follow, of belief in possibilities.

A Less Skeptical Approach to Thinking about Legal Discourse

Having proceeded this far, I feel compelled to provide an example of a less skeptical approach to understanding legal practice in the United States. My aim here is not to lay out a complete theory—or even to convince you that it is correct. Rather, I offer a sketch in order to suggest one possible way in which a more sympathetic story about law in American culture might be told.

One possible sympathetic story, of course, is simply to accept the status quo and argue that it should be preserved. This approach, however, might fail Ricoeur's requirement that a hermeneutics of meaning be "postcritical." In any event, I want to try something different from that. Moreover, I want to accept and adopt many of the antifoundational insights of postmodern theory and *then* construct a story about legal discourse and practice in America that is aspirational.

Recently, Richard K. Sherwin's *When Law Goes Pop: The Vanishing Line between Law and Popular Culture*[128] has attempted a similar project. Sherwin argues (as I have earlier in this essay) against what he calls "skeptical postmodernism." Referring to Baudrillard, Sherwin observes that skeptical postmodernism "manifests a marked inclination toward pessimism and disenchantment."[129] If truth, meaning, and reality are no longer discernible, and if any sense of the unified self or of human agency is illusory, he argues, we risk living in a world where "individuals can no longer be held accountable for having 'authored' their acts or caused an event to happen."[130] According to Sherwin, "In the end the skeptical postmodern is left with nothing more than endless play and detached irony."[131]

Nevertheless, like me, Sherwin refuses to jettison postmodern theory altogether. He contends, instead, that "[p]ostmodernism need not be skeptical. . . . A story might concede the demise of the autonomous modern subject, but still find meaning through the distributed self: an identity made up of multiple cultural and social constructs shared by others in particular communities."[132] Similarly, taking Sherwin's "affirmative postmodern" view, we might recognize that concepts such as truth and justice are contingent, but still see those ideas as coherent. "Abstraction may give way to particularity, contextuality, multiplicity; judgment may turn toward characteristic voices and localized accounts. But localization and contextualization are not fatal to meaning. It remains possible to seek rather than abandon meaning for concepts like truth and justice— even in the face of contingency, unpredictability, and spontaneity."[133]

Following Sherwin's suggestion, I wish to pursue a story about law that makes no attempt to return to a formalist world where legal rules are "truths" to be "discovered" by judges. Rather, I accept the idea that there are an infinite number of possible narratives for describing reality and that each narrative is inevitably a product of many cultural forces. Further, I will accept that, at least within a certain range, none of these narratives necessarily has a stronger claim to truth than any other. In such a world, how might one understand and justify law practice in America?[134]

My suggestion is that we might develop a doctrine of multiple perspectives that conceives of law as a site for encounter, contestation, and play among various narratives. I draw on Hannah Arendt's conception of the "public" as a space of appearance where actors stand before others and are subject to scrutiny and judgment from a plurality of perspectives.[135] The public, on this view, "consists of multiple histories and perspectives relatively unfamiliar to one another, connected yet distant and irreducible to one another."[136] By communicating about their differing perspectives on the social world in which they dwell together, people and communities can collectively constitute an enlarged understanding of the world.[137] In this part of the essay, therefore, I will first outline a prominent conception of "communicative democracy" that builds on Arendt, one offered by political theorist Iris M. Young. Then, I will begin to elaborate this doctrine of multiple perspectives by considering law's potential as a site for the type of idealized public discourse Young envisions.[138]

In recent decades, political philosophers and legal theorists,[139] drawing on the ideas of such thinkers as Arendt[140] and Jürgen Habermas,[141] have developed a conception of deliberative democracy as an alternative to what might be called an "interest-based" model of democracy. Using an interest-based model, democracy is seen primarily as a way of expressing one's interests and registering them in a vote. The goal of democratic decision-making, on this view, "is to decide what leaders, rules, and policies will best serve the greatest number of people, where each person defines his or her own interests."[142] As a result, democratic decisions will be the outcome of competition for self-interested votes.

Deliberative theorists, in contrast, conceive of democracy as a process that actually helps to create a public sphere. They argue that "[d]emocratic processes [must be] oriented around discussing [a] common good rather than competing for the promotion of the private good of each. Instead of reasoning from the point of view of the private utility maximizer, through public deliberation citizens transform their preferences according to public-minded ends, and reason together about the nature of those ends and the best means to realize them."[143] Building on this view, deliberative theorists attempt to define those societal settings most conducive to such public deliberation.

The vision of deliberative democracy does not necessarily mean that all debates must reach consensus or that differences of economic power, education, and cultural background must be bracketed in the search for some mythical common good.[144] Indeed, as Young has argued, to the extent that deliberative theorists may have overemphasized such requirements, we might adjust this model so that it is less about deliberation toward consensus and more about communication across differences. Indeed, Young points out, one of the problems of focusing on consensus is that "such a conception cannot account well for the transformation the communicative process should often produce in the opinions of the participants. If we are all looking for what we have in common—whether as a prior condition or as a result—then we are not transforming our point of view."[145] Accordingly, she calls her alternative conception a model of communicative, rather than deliberative, democracy.

Young's conception of communicative democracy may be particularly useful in helping to articulate a generative vision of law. She views the goal of democratic discourse to be the process of encountering differences of meaning, social position, language, background, and perspective. Inclusion of multiple points of view is obviously important because it is a means of demonstrating equal respect for those views. But, Young argues, the inclusion of multiple voices serves two other important functions as well: "First, it motivates participants in political debate to transform their claims from mere expressions of self-regarding interest to appeals to justice. Second, it maximizes the social knowledge available to a democratic public, such that citizens are more likely to make just and wise decisions."[146] Both functions are deserving of further consideration.

As to the first, Young argues that when a debate includes multiple voices, we must each pursue discourse that is not framed in the rhetoric of pure self-interest. "Because others are not likely to accept 'I want this' or 'This policy is in my interest' as reasons to accept a proposal, the requirement that discussion participants try to make their claims understandable and persuasive to others means they must frame the proposals in terms of justice."[147] This does not mean, of course, that others will necessarily agree with the justice claim, but, at least on a rhetorical level, the claim must be framed from a broader point of view. Because such a view must take into account a range of socially differentiated perspectives, we are forced to recognize that our own perspective is merely one among many. "Listening to those differently situated than myself and my close associates teaches me how my situation looks to them, in what relation they think I stand to them."[148] This acknowledgment of multiple stories is particularly important for those with more power in society: "Those in structurally superior positions not only take their experience, preferences, and opinions to be general, uncontroversial, ordinary, and even an expression of suffering or disadvantage . . . but also have the power to represent these as general norms. Having to answer to others who speak from different, less privileged, perspectives on their social relations exposes their partiality and relative blindness."[149] Thus the requirement that people speak in a language that acknowledges multiplicity may help moderate some of the normalizing tendencies of dominant discourse.

As to the second function, Young argues that including multiple points of view not only has the potential to alter the rhetoric of public discourse but also provides an opportunity to gain knowledge about a broader cross-section of society. People in differentiated social positions may have (1) different understandings of their social position in relation to others; (2) a particular point of view about the perspectives of others; (3) a unique understanding of their society's history; (4) a distinctive conception of "how the relations and processes of the whole society operate"; and (5) a position-specific narrative about the natural and physical environment.[150] As a result, if people are going to address collective problems, they must acknowledge and embrace each other's perspective and thereby recognize their own perspective as only partial. "Such an enlarged view better enables them to arrive at wise and just solutions to collective problems to the extent that they are committed to doing so."[151]

Having briefly sketched a scenario for ideal communicative democracy, we now face the question of whether we can tell a story about legal practice that envisions legal discourse and procedure as a potential site for such communication. I believe such a generative story—a doctrine of multiple perspectives—is available.

To begin, there can be little doubt that law, at least as practiced in this country, holds a privileged place as a forum for addressing social and political issues. Indeed, de Tocqueville's famous observation that "scarcely any political question arises in the United States that is not resolved, sooner or later, into a judicial question"[152] has been repeated so often that it has itself become a part of our national lore. Moreover, the pervasive presence of law in American society grew still greater in the twentieth century, penetrating more spheres of social and domestic life.[153] Thus, even though lawyers are often objects of derision, when the chips are down, we Americans are apt to frame our struggles in the language of competing rights and fight our battles in a legal forum.[154]

This forum could be envisioned to be a model for multivocal discourse of the sort Young advocates. Indeed, law is a social practice that both recognizes the existence of many different narratives and provides the opportunity to create new narratives that may help forge group identities.[155] Legal proceedings, therefore, function in part as a site for adjudicating among various explanatory narratives for describing reality.[156]

Both trials and judicial opinions, for example, ultimately construct a narrative about a disputed event by rendering a decision or verdict. They do so, however, only after first enacting a performance in which the society "creates, tests, changes, and judges" the various competing discourses that could make up our social knowledge.[157] As James Boyd White has observed, "The judicial process not only recognizes the individual but compels him to recognize others. For the litigant, the lawyer, and the observer alike, the central ethical and social meaning of the practice of the adversary hearing is its perpetual lesson that there is always another side to the story, that yours is not the only point of view."[158] In this vision, law's strength is precisely in its ability to provide a forum for testing the persuasive power of competing narratives: "The multiplicity of readings that the law permits is not its weakness, but its strength, for it is this that makes room for different voices, and gives a purchase by which culture may be modified in response to the demands of circumstance. It is a method at once for the recognition of others, for the acknowledgment of ignorance, and for cultural change."[159] In its ideal state, therefore, law provides a set of institutions that emphasize the fact that "we are a discoursing community, committed to talking with each other about our differences of perception, feeling, and value, our differences of language and experience."[160]

Consider, for example, the paradigmatic exchange between teacher and student in a first-year law school classroom. The student has an initial reaction to a case or an issue. Immediately, that student is forced to confront multiple alternative narratives for understanding the question. For example, the student might be asked to consider a less sympathetic set of facts or to argue the issue from the opposing party's point of view. Or the student might be forced to address the question from the perspective of law and economics or of critical legal studies. The teacher might point out some of the historical reasons that the law might have evolved in a contrary fashion. Ultimately, the debate might include questions of public policy, judicial competence, the appropriate division of responsibility among branches of government, and the practical impediments to reaching a solution. In the end, the student is encouraged to develop a more nuanced viewpoint, one that takes greater account of all the various available narratives on the issue. At its best, this process should be a lesson in tolerance for opposing viewpoints, an exercise in humility. The student can develop a greater understanding and appreciation for other ways of conceptualizing issues. From this idealized exchange, we can envision law as a "method of individual and collective self-education, a way in which we teach ourselves, over and over again, how little we can foresee, how much we depend on others, and how important to us are the practices we have inherited from the past."[161]

Thus we can perhaps tell a story of law as a useful site for discourse among multiple worldviews. And when we think of law in this way, we need not be limited to the idea that law is only the official discourse that takes place in courtrooms and legal memoranda. Rather, as the constitutive view makes clear, law talk is dispersed throughout the culture—in the newspaper accounts of legal decisions, in the everyday conversations that invoke conceptions of legal rights, and in the way law is portrayed in movies, on television, and in books.[162] Accordingly, law is not simply a form of pervasive hegemonic control dictated and managed by elites. We are all continuously producers and consumers of our legal culture, and the story is always in flux. Moreover, all of these multiple understandings and perspectives can be seen as an inevitable *part* of the language of justice, not simply as a set of stories generated *in opposition to* law's power.[163] As one commentator has pointed out, justice "involves reconciling diversities into a restored and new multiple unity. Justice requires a unity of differences; mutuality and incorporation rather than annihilation of opposites and distinctions."[164]

Such a unity is always provisional, always contingent, always contested. As Sherwin observes, "It is precisely the proximity of disorder—deriving from constant contestation among conflicting discourse communities as well as from the various irrational forces that surround and suffuse them—that compels new forms of legal self-organization. . . . This is how law adapts to the contingencies and vicissitudes of shifting social, cultural, and technological (among other) developments."[165] In the end, law's generative potential in American culture rests on its availability as a site for continuous self-criticism and re-creation. And the effort to articulate principles of justice, the creation of forums for debating those principles, the commitment to a culture of conversation about them, and the recognition that clashes among various forms of knowledge are inevitable and desirable—these are the aspects of law we might want to celebrate, tell stories about, and strive to achieve.

These stories about law strike me as particularly important ones for those of us within the legal academy to communicate to our students. Law professors and students have long wrestled with the issue of why so many students enter law school with a strong sense of idealism about law and a clear set of intuitive personal values, only to lose their grip on both during the first year of law school. This process is often derisively referred to as "learning to think like a lawyer" and is treated as synonymous with being forced to abandon one's own sense of moral truth. It strikes me that the disillusionment many feel during the first year of law school arises because students are forced to acknowledge that, on any given issue, there are multiple competing views, many of which are valid even if one does not agree with them. Thus students are having their preconceptions or prejudices challenged. Such challenges are useful, but professors are often content merely to challenge; we do not take the next step, which is to show students that there is *an independent ethical value* in trying always to see and respect multiple points of view. The oft-criticized willingness of lawyers to espouse any point of view regardless of personal belief does not necessarily signal a cynical lack of conviction. Rather, it is an acknowledgment that all points of view deserve to be aired. It is a recognition that human truths are contingent, that it is always possible to use many different narratives to describe any single event. Indeed, one might even say that the very language and structure of our legal processes are premised on the idea of a discourse among multiple worldviews. Learning to think like a lawyer is, ideally, a lesson in tolerant, creative, civic discourse.

This is, of course, merely a sketch of a more systematic analysis of law in American culture that must await future elaboration. However, even this brief account may offer a sense of what a less skeptical approach to legal/cultural analysis might look like. I also realize that my vision of law as a potentially generative cultural practice is an idealistic one and that there are many objections that could be raised. For example, it could be argued that official legal discourse, far from embracing multiple points of view, is severely limited by formal rules[166] and that it actually distorts alternative stories or shuts them out altogether by privileging only certain types of rhetoric, which must be spoken by an elite, trained, professional class.[167] Moreover, even the legal norms that tend to conflate discussion with argument may tend to mute certain types of voices.[168] These objections are significant, and any generative story about law requires that we not accept legal discourse uncritically.

Nevertheless, the idealized story still plays an important role. In a less skeptical approach to conceptualizing legal discourse and practice it is essential for us to look at law, not as it exists in any particular place and time, but "as a collective activity of mind and spirit, which has the possibility of goodness, of value, even of greatness."[169] The aim is similar to that expressed by James Boyd White:

> [I]t is with the possibility, not the often lamentable current conditions, that I am concerned. Perhaps I am answering a voice, in myself or in the culture, that says that there is no such possibility; that law is only the exercise of power by one person or group over another, or only a branch of bureaucracy, or only money-making, or only instrumental; that it has no real and independent value for the person or the community. Thus I ask whether we can imagine law as an activity that in its ideal form, at least on occasions, has true intellectual, imaginative, ethical, and political worth. If we can, this would give us both something to aim for and a more workable and trustworthy ground for the criticism of what we see around us.[170]

Moreover, the vision must be idealistic because we need stories to tell that offer hope for the future and a goal to achieve.[171] As academics, we need not gloss over injustice, nor should we accept the status quo blindly or uncritically. But we are responsible for the stories we choose to tell. We can choose to understand the efforts of our fellow human beings sympathetically or cynically. We can see our country as a fallen nation that is irredeemably corrupt, or we can describe it in terms we passionately hope it will embody. We can view our society as inevitably divided by class, race, ethnicity, gender, and ideology, or we can search for stories that help us see a shared enterprise. As postmodern theory has made us understand, the narrative we tell is not truth; it is a choice. I believe it is a choice we should make solemnly and with full understanding of both the power and the potential of our tales.

Postscript

Although this essay was written prior to the events surrounding the presidential election of 2000, the ideas I explore seem particularly pressing in light of the legal controversy over ballots in Florida and the disillusionment that many feel about the U.S. Supreme Court's role in the outcome. The news coverage of the ongoing court battles demonstrated just how far the hermeneutics of suspicion have pervaded popular culture, at least with respect to the legal system. Indeed, for a full month, nearly every mention of a court or a judge was accompanied with a phrase identifying the purported political makeup of the court or the presumed party affiliation of the judge. Thus the media sent a clear message: regardless of what judges say or what the ideals of the justice system demand, the courtroom is simply another partisan political forum where people vote their partisan preferences. Unfortunately, the U.S. Supreme Court's ultimate decision did little to temper this suspicious attitude. Fundamentally flawed as a matter of both logic and jurisprudence, the opinion of the narrow five-member majority is difficult to explain on any grounds other than partisanship.

The result of all this is that any faith we may have had in our legal institutions as a place where we struggle, however imperfectly, to articulate useful principles for living together or attempt to engage in constructive dialogue has been sorely tested. As one commentator has noted, it is possible that, especially in the wake of the election, "we are all 'crits' now."[172]

So how do I, as one who has argued for the generative potential of law in American culture, respond to *Bush v. Gore*?[173] First of all, I reject the assumption that the partisan nature of this decision simply made manifest that which is present in every judicial decision. The actions of five justices in a truly anomalous case cannot be allowed to speak for the work of the entire judiciary around the nation. Second, I reiterate that the optimistic vision I have begun to articulate here is an aspiration and therefore, by definition, is not always fulfilled. Nevertheless—and perhaps this is the most important point of my essay—an ideal does not lose its value simply because human beings inevitably fall short of it. Indeed, even if we know in advance that it *cannot* be reached, we might be better off with the ideal than without it. Both our willingness to believe in the ideal and our dedication in striving toward it may, by themselves, encourage us to create better social institutions. And if even one person who was unheard by the political process can gain a forum for change through the legal system, that is a miracle that cannot be sloughed off as inconsequential. We can certainly decry injustice or disingenuousness in our legal system, but I think we should resist the temptation to insist cynically that justice is not possible or is an incoherent category altogether. Rather, we might wish to remember the little miracles and continue to insist on the possibility of possibility.

Notes

This essay was presented at a Symposium on Cultural Studies and Law held at Yale Law School and organized by Austin Sarat and Jonathan Simon. I am grateful to both for their comments and for providing me the opportunity to explore these ideas in such interesting company. In addition, this essay was presented at the annual meeting of the Law and Society Association in Miami, Florida, and at the annual conference of the Association for the Study of Law, Culture, and the Humanities at Georgetown University Law Center, and I wish to acknowledge the numerous insights offered in response to the paper by audience members at both of these occasions. Finally, I thank Jerome Bruner, Anne Dailey, Laura Dickinson, Martha Ertman, Jeremy Paul, Thomas Morawetz, Richard K. Sherwin, and Susan Silbey for helpful suggestions on earlier drafts. A slightly different version of this essay first appeared in 13 *Yale J.L. and Human.* 95 (2001).

1   *Wilhelm Dilthey: Selected Writings* 161 (H. P. Rickman ed. and trans., Cambridge Univ. Press 1976).

2   Edward M. Bruner, "Experience and Its Expressions," in *The Anthropology of Experience* 3, 7 (Victor W. Turner and Edward M. Bruner eds., 1986).

3   Id; see also Louis O. Mink, "Narrative Form as a Cognitive Instrument," in *The Writing of History: Literary Form and Historical Understanding* (Robert H. Canary and Henry Kozicki eds., 1978) (describing the way in which narratives shape historical writing); Dan Slobin, "Verbalized Events: A Dynamic Approach to Linguistic Relativity and Determinism," 198 *Current Issues in Linguistic Theory* 107 (2000) ("One cannot verbalize experience without taking a *perspective,* and . . . the language being used often favors particular perspectives. The world does not present 'events' to be encoded in language. Rather, in the process of speaking or writing, experiences are filtered through language into *verbalized events."*).

4   See, e.g., Renato Rosaldo, *Culture and Truth: The Remaking of Social Analysis,* at xviii (1989) (proclaiming that "classic modes of analysis, which in their pure type rely exclusively on a detached observer using a neutral language to study a unified world of brute facts, no longer hold a monopoly on truth. Instead, they now share disciplinary authority with other analytical perspectives.").

5   See, e.g., Pierre Schlag, "The Problem of the Subject," 69 *Tex. L. Rev.* 1627 (1991).

6   Clifford Geertz, "Local Knowledge: Fact and Law in Comparative Perspective," in *Local Knowledge: Further Essays in Interpretive Anthropology* 167, 184 (1983).

7   Bryant G. Garth and Austin Sarat, "Justice and Power in Law and Society Research: On the Contested Careers of Core Concepts," in *Justice and Power in Sociolegal Studies* 1, 3 (Bryant G. Garth and Austin Sarat eds., 1997) [hereafter *Justice and Power*].

8   See, e.g., Mark Kelman, *A Guide to Critical Legal Studies* 242–68 (1987); Robert W. Gordon, "Critical Legal Histories," 36 *Stan. L. Rev.* 57 (1984); Roberto Unger, "The Critical Legal Studies Movement," 96 *Harv. L. Rev.* 561 (1983).

9   Paul Kahn, *The Cultural Study of Law: Reconstructing Legal Scholarship* 124 (1999).

10 Nancy Reichman, "Power and Justice in Sociolegal Studies of Regulation," in *Justice and Power,* supra note 7, at 233, 250.

11 Garth and Sarat, supra note 7, at 8.

12 Paul Ricoeur, *Freud and Philosophy: An Essay on Interpretation* 32–36 (Dennis Savage trans., Yale Univ. Press 1970).

13 *Justice and Power,* supra note 7.

14 Susan S. Silbey, "Ideology, Power, and Justice," in *Justice and Power,* supra note 7, at 272, 274.

15 This question raises, in a different context, the issue of "double consciousness" first identified by W. E. B. Du Bois to describe the African-American experience. See W. E. B. Du Bois,
The Souls of Black Folk 3 (1903) ("The Negro is . . . born with a veil, and gifted with second-
sight. . . . [In] this double-consciousness . . . [o]ne ever feels his two-ness,—American, a
Negro; two souls, two thoughts, two unreconciled strivings; two warring ideals."). Although we need not deny the coercive power of law, we may simultaneously recognize that
law also provides a language and structure from which to construct alternative worlds.
Ultimately, we might insist on such a double consciousness: recognizing *both* the persistence of oppression *and* the potentially generative nature of law.

   In his seminal essay, "Nomos and Narrative," Robert Cover argued that law functions
in part "as a system of tension or a bridge linking a concept of a reality to an imagined
alternative." Robert M. Cover, "The Supreme Court, 1982 Term—Foreword: Nomos and
Narrative," 97 *Harv. L. Rev.* 4, 9 (1983). On this view, law is a language that allows us to
discuss, imagine, and ultimately even perhaps generate alternative worlds spun from present reality. Thus Cover envisioned law as that which connects "reality" to "alternity."
Robert M. Cover, "The Folktales of Justice: Tales of Jurisdiction," in *Narrative, Violence,
and the Law: The Essays of Robert Cover* 173, 176 (Martha Minow et al. eds., 1992) (citing
G. Steiner, *After Babel* 222 (1975)). If Cover's vision is correct, then law has enormous
potential as a creative and transformative language. Building on this vision, my ultimate
goal is to see whether one can use the idea of law as generative discourse to develop a more
optimistic story about law's role. It seems to me that this story should, at the very least, sit
alongside the suspicious one in our consciousness about law.

16 Thomas Morawetz, among others, has explored in detail the question of an "inside" versus
an "outside" perspective in critical theory. See, e.g., Thomas Morawetz, "Law as Experience: Theory and the Internal Aspect of Law," 52 *S.M.U. L. Rev.* 27 (1999); Thomas Morawetz, "Understanding Disagreement, the Root Issue of Jurisprudence: Applying Wittgenstein to Positivism, Critical Theory, and Judging," 141 *U. Pa. L. Rev.* 371 (1992) [hereafter
Morawetz, "Understanding Disagreement"].

17 Of course, the problems that may result from taking a "God's-eye view" are inherent in
almost all scholarship, regardless of whether or not one takes a particularly suspicious
critical stance. Nevertheless, a scholar who views the lived experience of participants
empathetically may be less likely to discount that experience. In contrast, if one specifically sets out to unmask aspects of culture that are hidden to the participants, these problems may be more acute.

18 Richard Rorty, *Achieving Our Country: Leftist Thought in Twentieth-Century America* 3–
4 (1998).

19 See Ronald Dworkin, *Law's Empire* 225–75 (1986).

20 It is important to make clear at the outset that the distinction I am attempting to draw
between hermeneutic approaches is not the same as the distinction between scholarship
that criticizes a legal practice and scholarship that supports it. For example, one could
imagine a law and economics scholar making an argument along the following lines: "The
judge may have thought she was deciding the case based on *X*, but *really* she was promoting
efficient economic relations, and we are all better off because she did so." Such an analysis
would be suspicious as I am using the term because it seeks to unmask the practice being

studied, even though it ultimately takes a position in favor of the decision. On the other hand, one could take a less skeptical approach by attempting to make the best possible case on behalf of a judicial decision, yet still conclude that the decision is incorrect. Thus suspicious scholarship is not necessarily negative scholarship, nor is less suspicious scholarship necessarily positive.

21 When I refer to "law" in this essay, I mean something very broad indeed. I refer not only to formal legal rules and procedures but also to "quasi-legal" discourses and practices that sometimes straddle the law/entertainment boundary. See, e.g., Austin Sarat, "Imagining the Law of the Father: Loss, Dread, and Mourning in *The Sweet Hereafter*," 34 *Law and Soc'y Rev.* 3, 5–10 (2000) (arguing that sociolegal scholars must "take on" cultural studies by considering how law exists in a world of film and television images); Alison Young, "Murder in the Eyes of the Law," 17 *Stud. L. Pol. and Soc'y* 31, 31 (1997) (exploring how law "appears and reappears in the cinematic text"); see generally Richard K. Sherwin, "Symposium, Picturing Justice: Images of Law and Lawyers in the Visual Media: Introduction," 30 *U.S.F. L. Rev.* 891 (1996). These include television court channels, legal talk shows, legal "thriller" novels and films, public memorials and ceremonies (such as the monument to victims of the Oklahoma City bombing or candlelight vigils to build community after hate crimes), and marches on Washington (such as the "Million Mom March" to lobby for stricter handgun regulations).

Even more broadly, my invocation of law is meant to refer to the often unnoticed practice of "law talk" in the society at large. By law talk, I mean the use of legal concepts in everyday language. Such talk includes abstract (and often inchoate) ideas of street justice, due process, civil disobedience, retribution, deterrence, and rights, all of which are frequently invoked both in public discussions and dinner-table conversations alike. Indeed, I deliberately use a conception of law aimed at expanding the law's generic constraints to encompass a broader spectrum of discourses talking in the "shadow" of official legal categories, but talking law nonetheless. See Patricia Ewick and Susan S. Silbey, *The Common Place of Law: Stories from Everyday Life* 20 (1998) ("Legality . . . operates through social life as persons and groups deliberately interpret and invoke law's language, authority, and procedures to organize their lives and manage their relationships. In short, the commonplace operation of law in daily life makes us all legal agents insofar as we actively make law, even when no formal legal agent is involved.").

The great variety of discourses that might be brought under the rubric of "law talk" not only attests to the conceptual power of law in the collective American consciousness but also simultaneously underscores the elusiveness of the very concept of "law." For example, even relatively well-established forms of "alternative" dispute resolution, such as mediation and arbitration, are accepted by many legal practitioners as legitimate quasi-legal mechanisms; to others, however, they are viewed as antithetical and even subversive to canonical law practice. This is merely one example of the way in which a narrow definition of "law" can serve as a hegemonic arbiter of what counts as sanctioned legal practice. Thus a methodical definition of "law" is not only unlikely to be satisfying, but it also may tend to privilege certain understandings of law over others. In any event, attempting such a definition is a project far beyond the scope of this essay. Accordingly, although I refer to "law" and "legal" discourse liberally, I do so with invisible quotation marks around them in order to acknowledge their broad interpretation and application. Cf. id. at 22 (choosing to use the term "legality" rather than "law" to describe a broader set of "meanings, sources of authority, and cultural practices that are commonly recognized as legal, regardless of who employs them or for what ends").

22 My focus on "usefulness" as the criterion for choosing among critical approaches echoes some of the core insights of pragmatist philosophy. See Richard Rorty, "Truth without Correspondence to Reality," in *Philosophy and Social Hope* 23, 27 (1999) ("Pragmatists—both classical and 'neo-'—do not believe that there is a way things really are. So they want to replace the appearance-reality distinction by that between descriptions of the world and of ourselves which are less useful and those which are more useful."). For further discussion of pragmatism, critical theory, and law, see Morawetz, "Understanding Disagreement," supra note 16, at 443–49. See generally *The Revival of Pragmatism* (Morris Dickstein ed., 1998); Steven D. Smith, "The Pursuit of Pragmatism," 100 *Yale L.J.* 409 (1990); Peter D. Swan, "Critical Legal Theory and the Politics of Pragmatism," 12 *Dalhousie L.J.* 349 (1989); "Symposium, the Renaissance of Pragmatism in American Legal Thought," 63 *S. Cal. L. Rev.* 1569 (1990).

23 Ricoeur, supra note 12, at 27.

24 Id.

25 Id. at 33.

26 Id.

27 Id. at 34.

28 Id. at 33.

29 See id. at 35.

30 See id. at 34–35.

31 Id. at 35.

32 David Harvey, *The Condition of Postmodernity: An Enquiry into the Origins of Cultural Change* 27 (1990).

33 See Jean-François Lyotard, *The Postmodern Condition: A Report on Knowledge*, at xxiv (Geoff Bennington and Brian Massumi trans., Univ. of Minnesota Press 1984) (1979).

34 See id.

35 Jean Baudrillard, *Simulacra and Simulation* 160–61 (Sheila F. Glaser trans., Univ. of Michigan Press 1994).

36 See, e.g., Paul D. Carrington, "Of Law and the River," 34 *J. Legal Educ.* 222, 227 (1984); Martha C. Nussbaum, "The Professor of Parody," *New Republic*, Feb. 22, 1999, at 37.

37 Linda Fisher, "Hermeneutics of Suspicion and Postmodern Paranoia: Psychologies of Interpretation," 16 *Philosophy and Literature* 106, 112 (1992).

38 Id.; accord Richard K. Sherwin, *When Law Goes Pop: The Vanishing Line between Law and Popular Culture* 129 (2000) ("in the end the skeptical postmodern is left with nothing more than endless play and detached irony"); James B. Twitchell, *Carnival Culture* 51 (1992) ("What characterizes the condition of culture since World War II is . . . that now we have more signs than referents, more images than meanings that can be attached to them. The machinery of communication often communicates little except itself—signs just refer to each other, creating a 'simulacra' of reality.").

39 My hopefulness about the possibilities that exist within postmodern legal discourse per-

haps distinguishes this essay from earlier attacks on critical legal theory. For example, in his well-known essay "The Death of the Law?" Owen Fiss criticized the "negativism" of critical legal studies and argued for the building of social and political movements reminiscent of the 1960s that would help foster "a belief in public values." Owen Fiss, "The Death of the Law?" 72 *Cornell L. Rev.* 1, 14–15 (1986). In many respects, my aims are similar to Fiss's. He too sought "[a]n appreciation of law as a generative force of our public life," id. at 15, and identified the skeptical stories of critical legal theory as potentially destructive of that aim. Unlike Fiss, however, I do not pin my hopes on a revival of the political activism of the 1960s (though I would certainly be pleased to see the return of such an activist spirit). Nor do I decry critical theory as inherently destructive. Rather, I suggest that the very antifoundational insights of postmodern theory that Fiss criticizes might be used to open an imaginative space for understanding law in ways that might generate the public values Fiss seeks.

40 See Sherwin, supra note 38, at 128–33 (distinguishing between "skeptical" and "affirmative" postmodernism).

41 Garth and Sarat, supra note 7, at 4.

42 See id. at 4–5.

43 Id. at 5.

44 See Richard Michael Fischl, "Some Realism about Critical Legal Studies," 41 *U. Miami L. Rev.* 505, 521 (1987): ("Realism undertook its rule-debunking program in the service of exposing the law for what it really was: social policymaking. But the Realists did not intend to leave the Emperor naked. The law's 'ought' could be . . . discovered by a fact-sensitive adjudication overtly and consciously informed by the methods of social science.").

45 Garth and Sarat, supra note 7, at 6.

46 Id.

47 Id. (citing Gerald Rosenberg, *The Hollow Hope: Can Courts Bring about Social Change?* (1991)); see also Joel Handler, *Social Movements and the Legal System* (1978); John Heinz and Edward Laumann, *Chicago Lawyers: The Social Structure of the Bar* (1982); Robert Nelson, *Partners with Power: Bureaucracy, Professionalism, and Social Change in the Large Law Firm* (1987); Stuart Scheingold, *The Politics of Rights: Lawyers, Public Policy, and Political Change* (1974); Richard L. Abel, "The Contradictions of Informal Justice," in 1 *The Politics of Informal Justice* 267 (Richard L. Abel ed., 1982); Marc Galanter, "Why the 'Haves' Come Out Ahead: Speculations on the Limits of Legal Change," 9 *Law and Soc'y Rev.* 95 (1974); Stewart Macaulay, "Lawyers and Consumer Protection Laws," 14 *Law and Soc'y Rev.* 115 (1979).

48 Garth and Sarat, supra note 7, at 6–7 (citation omitted).

49 See, e.g., *The Politics of Law: A Progressive Critique* (David Kairys ed., 1982).

50 See, e.g., Gerald E. Frug, "The Ideology of Bureaucracy in American Law," 97 *Harv. L. Rev.* 1277 (1984); Mary Jo Frug, "Rereading Contracts: A Feminist Analysis of a Contracts Casebook," 34 *Am. U.L. Rev.* 1065 (1985); Duncan Kennedy, "Form and Substance in Private Law Adjudication," 89 *Harv. L. Rev.* 1685 (1976).

51 See, e.g., Kelman, supra note 8; Duncan Kennedy, "Legal Education as Training for Hierarchy," in *The Politics of Law*, supra note 49.

52 In 1988, Sanford Levinson and Steven Mailloux observed that, in light of "ambiguities of

interpretation, many legal theorists have substituted for the hermeneutics of objective interpretation what Gerald Graff has termed a "hermeneutics of power," where one emphasizes the political and social determinants of reading texts one way as opposed to another." *Interpreting Law and Literature*, at xiii (Sanford Levinson and Steven Mailloux eds., 1988) (quoting Gerald Graff, "Textual Leftism," 49 *Partisan Rev.* 566 (1982)).

53 Garth and Sarat, supra note 7, at 8 (citation omitted).

54 Austin D. Sarat, "Redirecting Legal Scholarship in Law Schools," 12 *Yale J.L. and Human.* 129, 134 (2000) (reviewing Kahn, supra note 9).

55 Geertz, supra note 6, at 218.

56 Id. at 230.

57 Id. at 182 (quoting A. M. Hocart, *Kings and Councillors: An Essay in the Comparative Anatomy of Human Society* 128 (1970)).

58 Garth and Sarat, supra note 7, at 8.

59 Id. at 9.

60 Id. at 9–10.

61 Silbey, supra note 14, at 274.

62 Garth and Sarat, supra note 7, at 10.

63 See, e.g., Sarat, supra note 54, at 140 ("Contests over meaning in courts or communities . . . become occasions for [sociolegal scholars to observe] the play of power. Meanings that seem natural, or taken-for-granted, are described as hegemonic, but because the construction of meaning through law is, in fact, typically contested, scholars show the many ways in which resistance occurs.") (citation omitted). For examples of such work, see Sally Engle Merry, *Getting Justice and Getting Even: Legal Consciousness among Working-Class Americans* (1990); Barbara Yngvesson, *Virtuous Citizens, Disruptive Subjects: Order and Complaint in a New England Court* (1993). For a further discussion of the agency critique, see infra notes 86–90 and accompanying text.

64 Surprisingly, even interdisciplinary scholars in public choice theory and law and economics, who are not generally associated with a progressive agenda, employ a "watered-down" hermeneutics of suspicion by positing that self-interest (rather than stated values) is the "true" explanation of political and social processes. See also supra note 20.

65 Garth and Sarat, supra note 7, at 10.

66 Carol J. Greenhouse, "Figuring the Future: Issues of Time, Power, and Agency in Ethnographic Problems of Scale," in *Justice and Power*, supra note 7, at 108.

67 347 U.S. 483 (1954).

68 See Civil Rights Act of 1964, 78 Stat. 241 (1964); Voting Rights Act of 1965, 79 Stat. 437 (1965); Civil Rights Act of 1991, 105 Stat. 1071 (1991).

69 Greenhouse, supra note 66, at 114.

70 Id.

71 Id. at 125.

72 Id.

73 Id.

74 Indeed, as many critics have observed, the clause of the Fourteenth Amendment guaranteeing the "privileges or immunities of citizens of the United States" would seem to be a more likely source for Congress's power to enact civil rights legislation. The Supreme Court

construed this language so narrowly in the Slaughterhouse Cases, 83 U.S. 36 (16 Wall.) (1872), however, that proponents of such legislation were forced to look elsewhere to justify congressional power. For further discussion of more recent calls to overrule the Slaughterhouse Cases, see, e.g., Charles L. Black Jr., *A New Birth of Freedom: Human Rights, Named and Unnamed* 146–48 (1997); John Hart Ely, *Democracy and Distrust: A Theory of Judicial Review* 28–30 (1980); David A. J. Richards, *Conscience and the Constitution: History, Theory, and Law of the Reconstruction Amendments* 199–232 (1993); Laurence H. Tribe, *American Constitutional Law* §§ 7–2 to 7–4 (1978); Akhil Reed Amar, "The Bill of Rights as a Constitution," 100 *Yale L.J.* 1131, 1149 (1991); Richard L. Aynes, "On Misreading John Bingham and the Fourteenth Amendment," 103 *Yale L.J.* 57, 103–4 (1993); Philip J. Kurland, "The Privileges or Immunities Clause: Its Hour Come Round at Last?" 1972 *Wash. U.L.Q.* 405 (1972); William Winslow Crosskey, "Charles Fairman, 'Legislative History,' and the Constitutional Limitations on State Authority," 22 *U. Chi. L. Rev.* 3, 3–10 (1954). See generally Michael Kent Curtis, *No State Shall Abridge: The Fourteenth Amendment and the Bill of Rights* 216–20 (1986).

75   Greenhouse, supra note 66, at 124.

76   Id.

77   Id. at 127.

78   Id.

79   Tom R. Tyler, "Justice and Power in Civil Dispute Processing," in *Justice and Power*, supra note 7, at 309.

80   Id. at 313.

81   See E. Allan Lind et al., *The Perception of Justice: Tort Litigants' Views of Trial, Court-Annexed Arbitration, and Judicial Settlement Conferences* (1989); E. Allan Lind et al., "In the Eye of the Beholder: Tort Litigants' Evaluations of Their Experiences in the Civil Justice System," 24 *Law and Soc'y Rev.* 953 (1990).

82   Tyler, supra note 79, at 315.

83   See id.

84   Silbey, supra note 14, at 287 (quoting 1 Jean Comaroff and John Comaroff, *Of Revelation and Revolution: Christianity, Colonialism, and Consciousness in South Africa* 23 (1991)).

85   Garth and Sarat, supra note 7, at 11.

86   See, e.g., Ewick and Silbey, supra note 21; Merry, supra note 63; Yngvesson, supra note 63; Austin Sarat, "'. . . The Law Is All Over': Power, Resistance, and the Legal Consciousness of the Welfare Poor," 2 *Yale J.L. and Human.* 343 (1990). For a discussion of this turn in sociolegal scholarship, see David M. Engel, "How Does Law Matter in the Constitution of Legal Consciousness?" in *How Does Law Matter?* 109 (Bryant G. Garth and Austin Sarat eds., 1998).

87   Engel, supra note 86, at 131.

88   Yngvesson, supra note 63, at 121.

89   Sarat, supra note 86, at 376.

90   Engel, supra note 86, at 134.

91   Pierre Schlag, *The Enchantment of Reason* (1998).

92   Pierre Schlag, "Clerks in the Maze," 91 *Mich. L. Rev.* 2053, 2054 (1993).

93   Id. at 2067.

94 Id. at 2063.

95 Richard L. Revesz, "Environmental Regulation, Ideology, and the D.C. Circuit," 83 *Va. L. Rev.* 1717 (1997).

96 In the study, judges were assigned the party affiliation of the president who appointed them (which is, of course, in and of itself a debatable rubric for determining the ideology of any particular judge).

97 Note that this concern may exist regardless of whether the critic ultimately takes a position for or against the practice being studied. See supra note 20.

98 Harry T. Edwards, "Collegiality and Decision Making on the D.C. Circuit," 84 *Va. L. Rev.* 1335 (1998).

99 Id. at 1338.

100 See Frederick Crews, *Skeptical Engagements,* at xiii (1986) ("Just as Marxism divides humankind into those people illumined by proletarian consciousness and those entrapped in capitalist false consciousness, so Freudianism can acknowledge only deep knowers—roughly, the analyzed—and the repressed."). See generally John Farrell, *Freud's Paranoid Quest: Psychoanalysis and Modern Suspicion* (1996).

101 See, e.g., Stanley Fish, "Critical Self-Consciousness, or Can We Know What We're Doing?" in *Doing What Comes Naturally: Change, Rhetoric, and the Practice of Theory in Literary and Legal Studies* 436, 436–67 (1989) (arguing that the theorist, because he or she inhabits a particular way of thinking and speaking, cannot ever get "outside" a social practice in order to achieve an "objective" view).

102 See Jerome Bruner, *Making Stories: Law, Literature, Life* 23 (2002).

103 See, e.g., Brian C. Murchison, "Law, Belief, and Bildung: The Education of Harry Edwards," 29 *Hofstra L. Rev.* 127 (2000) (discussing the role that belief in neutral principles and the rule of law plays in the actual practice of judging).

104 See supra note 17.

105 Francis J. Mootz, "The Paranoid Style in Contemporary Legal Scholarship," 31 *Hous. L. Rev.* 873, 879 (1994).

106 William Bywater, "The Paranoia of Postmodernism," 14 *Phil. and Literature* 79, 80 (1990).

107 Mootz, supra note 105, at 879.

108 Bywater, supra note 106, at 80–81.

109 See Jean Bethke Elshtain, "Will the Real Civil Society Advocates Please Stand Up?" 75 *Chi.-Kent L. Rev.* 583, 585 (2000) (criticizing an "all-knowing skepticism [that] is skeptical about everything but skepticism").

110 See, e.g., James Fallows, *Breaking the News: How the Media Undermine American Democracy* 161–65 (1996) (criticizing the news media for repeatedly covering stories as if the content of political dialogue were irrelevant and only the immediate political advantage or disadvantage were worth discussing).

111 Rorty, supra note 18, at 7.

112 Id. at 93.

113 Sherwin, supra note 38, at 228–31.

114 See Rorty, supra note 18, at 33.

115 Kahn, supra note 9, at 91.

116 See id. at 3.

117 Ricoeur, supra note 12, at 28.

118 Richard Rorty, "The Inspirational Value of Great Works," in *Achieving Our Country*, supra note 18, at 125, 126.

119 Id. at 133.

120 See id.

121 As Rorty argues, the Foucauldian refusal to indulge in utopian thinking may not be the product of sagacity but rather a result of Foucault's "unfortunate inability to believe in the possibility of human happiness, and his consequent inability to think of beauty as the promise of happiness." Id. at 139.

  I recognize, of course, that for many the U.S. Supreme Court's decision in the recent presidential election, see Bush v. Gore, 121 S. Ct. 525 (2000), severely undermines any possibility of being inspired by the Court's work. I address this issue in a postscript to this essay, infra.

122 Ronald Dworkin, "How Law Is Like Literature," in *A Matter of Principle* 146, 158 (1985). Dworkin uses this metaphor again in his later work, *Law's Empire*, supra note 19.

123 Dworkin, supra note 122, at 150.

124 Id.

125 Id. at 159.

126 See, e.g., Stanley Fish, "Working on the Chain Gang: Interpretation in Law and Literature," in *Doing What Comes Naturally*, supra note 101, at 87; Ronald Dworkin, "My Reply to Stanley Fish (and Walter Benn Michaels): Please Don't Talk about Objectivity Any More," in *The Politics of Interpretation* 287 (W. J. T. Mitchell ed., 1983).

127 See Dworkin, supra note 19, at 228–38.

128 Sherwin, supra note 38.

129 Id. at 128.

130 Id. at 129.

131 Id.

132 Id. at 131.

133 Id.

134 Sherwin sees the challenge similarly. He asks: "[I]s it possible reflectively to reframe the myth of modernity . . . to avoid the excesses of skeptical postmodern irrationalism and disenchantment on the one hand, and of modernist rationality and repression on the other? Put differently: how are we to affirm a world of meaning in which law and democracy may flourish?" Sherwin, supra note 38, at 233.

135 See Hannah Arendt, *The Human Condition* 50–58 (1958).

136 Iris M. Young, *Inclusion and Democracy* 111 (2000) (discussing Arendt).

137 See Arendt, supra note 135, at 50–58; see also Lisa J. Disch, *Hannah Arendt and the Limits of Philosophy* 80 (1994); Anna Yeatman, "Justice and the Sovereign Self," in *Justice and Identity: Antipodean Practices* 195 (Margaret Wilson and Anna Yeatman eds., 1995). For an interpretation of the Arendtian public in terms of plurality, see Susan Bickford, *The Dissonance of Democracy: Listening, Conflict, and Citizenship* (1996).

138 My ultimate project, which seeks to apply theories of deliberation and discourse to legal practice, will also build on Thomas Morawetz's application of Wittgenstein to the process of legal discourse. See Morawetz, "Understanding Disagreement," supra note 16.

139 See, e.g., Benjamin R. Barber, *Strong Democracy: Participatory Politics for a New Age* (1984); John S. Dryzek, *Discursive Democracy: Politics, Policy, and Political Science* (1990); James S. Fishkin, *Democracy and Deliberation: New Directions for Democratic Reform* (1991); Thomas A. Spragens, *Reason and Democracy* (1990); James Bohman, "Public Reason and Cultural Pluralism," 23 *Political Theory* 253 (1995); Joshua Cohen, "Deliberation and Democratic Legitimacy," in *The Good Polity: Normative Analysis of the State* 17 (Alan Hamlin and Philip Pettit eds., 1989); Jane J. Mansbridge, "A Deliberative Theory of Interest Representation," in *The Politics of Interests: Interest Groups Transformed* (Mark P. Patracca ed., 1992); Frank Michelman, "Traces of Self-Government," 100 *Harv. L. Rev.* 4 (1986); Cass R. Sunstein, "Beyond the Republican Revival," 97 *Yale L.J.* 1539 (1988).

140 See generally Arendt, supra note 135.

141 See generally Jürgen Habermas, *The Structural Transformation of the Public Sphere: An Inquiry into a Category of Bourgeois Society* (Thomas Burger and Frederick Lawrence trans., MIT Press 1989) (1962); 1 Jürgen Habermas, *The Theory of Communicative Action: Reason and the Rationalization of Society* (Thomas McCarthy trans., Beacon Press 1984) (1984); Jürgen Habermas, "Three Normative Models of Democracy," in *Democracy and Difference: Contesting the Boundaries of the Political* 21 (Seyla Benhabib ed., 1996).

142 Iris Marion Young, "Communication and the Other: Beyond Deliberative Democracy," in *Democracy and Difference,* supra note 141, at 120, 120.

143 Id. at 121.

144 See generally James Bohman, *Public Deliberation: Pluralism, Complexity, and Democracy* (1996) (criticizing communitarian and neorepublican interpretations of deliberation as requiring too much consensus).

145 Young, supra note 142, at 127.

146 Young, supra note 136, at 115.

147 Id.

148 Id. at 116.

149 Id.; see also Martha Minow, *Making All the Difference: Inclusion, Exclusion, and American Law* (1990) (discussing the importance of multiple perspectives as a means of dislodging stated assumptions about social relations).

150 See Young, supra note 136, at 117.

151 Id. at 118.

152 Alexis de Tocqueville, *Democracy in America* 280 (Phillips Bradley ed., Henry Reeve trans., Vintage Classics 1990) (1835).

153 For example, the century saw the enfranchisement of women and the enforcement of civil rights protections for African Americans. In addition, we witnessed the establishment of public defender offices to represent criminal defendants, the expansion of the Bill of Rights to cover a range of police procedures and prison conditions, and the creation of an income tax law, bank deposit insurance laws, social security laws, and regulatory laws aimed at everything from environmental protection to the filing of corporate financial statements. Government agencies dispatched agents around the country to enforce legal rights and duties. Litigation among business corporations grew rapidly; see, e.g., William Nelson, "Contract Litigation and the Elite Bar in New York City, 1960–1980," 39 *Emory L.J.* 413 (1990). The size of law firms serving corporate clients increased as well; see, e.g., Marc

Galanter and Thomas Palay, *Tournament of Lawyers: The Transformations of the Big Law Firms* (1991). By the end of the twentieth century, the threat of legal liability permeated the operation of universities, public school systems, hospitals, and municipal governments, as well as tobacco companies, land developers, and product manufacturers. Perhaps most significantly, ordinary individuals increasingly came to think of themselves as possessing legal rights and therefore defined "the law" not only as a range of official demands and constraints but also as a universally available set of entitlements. See generally Ewick and Silbey, supra note 21. These examples are drawn from a useful discussion of law in twentieth-century America found in Robert A. Kagan et al., "Facilitating and Domesticating Change: Democracy, Capitalism, and Law's Double Role in the Twentieth Century," in *Looking Back at Law's Century* 5 (Austin Sarat et al. eds., 2002).

154 Whatever one might think about the role of the courts in the presidential election of 2000, there can be little doubt that the postelection contest is a testament to the extraordinary willingness of Americans to wage political battles in a legal forum. For a discussion of how the ideas in this essay relate to the election and its aftermath, see postscript, infra.

155 See Reva B. Siegel, "Collective Memory and the Nineteenth Amendment: Reasoning about 'the Woman Question' in the Discourse of Sex Discrimination," in *History, Memory, and the Law*, 131, 133–34 (Austin Sarat and Thomas R. Kearns eds., 1999).

156 See Cover, *Nomos and Narrative*, supra note 15; see also Paul Schiff Berman, "An Observation and a Strange but True 'Tale': What Might the Historical Trials of Animals Tell Us about the Transformative Potential of Law in American Culture?" 52 *Hastings L.J.* 123 (2000).

157 Robert Hariman, "Performing the Laws: Popular Trials and Social Knowledge," in *Popular Trials: Rhetoric, Mass Media, and the Law* 17, 29 (Robert Hariman ed., 1990).

158 James Boyd White, *Justice as Translation: An Essay in Cultural and Legal Criticism* 266 (1990).

159 James Boyd White, "Law as Language: Reading Law and Reading Literature," 60 *Tex. L. Rev.* 415, 444 (1982).

160 White, supra note 158, at 80.

161 Id. at 266.

162 See supra note 21.

163 This distinction may be why the view of law I suggest is different from the focus of some sociolegal studies of "agency"—the ways in which individuals resist law. See supra notes 86–90 and accompanying text.

164 Jane Flax, "The Play of Justice," in *Disputed Subjects: Essays on Psychoanalysis, Politics and Philosophy* 111, 123–24 (1993).

165 Sherwin, supra note 38, at 238–39.

166 For example, critical race theorists, feminists, and others have advocated relaxing the rules of evidence to encourage narrative testimony. See, e.g., Jacqueline St. Joan, "Law and Literature: Sex, Sense, and Sensibility: Trespassing into the Culture of Domestic Abuse," 20 *Harv. Women's L.J.* 263, 266 (1997) (arguing that "rules of evidence and the interrogatory format of the trial process suppress the female voice," and suggesting that a remedy to the problem lies in "broadening the scope of judicial inquiry at trial and loosening the restrictions on narrative-style testimony"); Kathryn Abrams, "Hearing the Call of Sto-

ries," 79 *Cal. L. Rev.* 971 (1991); Richard Delgado, "Storytelling for Oppositionists and Others: A Plea for Narrative," 87 *Mich. L. Rev.* 2411 (1988); Lynne N. Henderson, "Legality and Empathy," 85 *Mich. L. Rev.* 1574 (1987); Martha Minow, "When Difference Has Its Home: Group Homes for the Mentally Retarded, Equal Protection, and Legal Treatment of Difference," 22 *Harv. C.R.-C.L. L. Rev.* 111 (1987). Many other sources are collected in Barbara J. Flagg, "The Algebra of Pluralism: Subjective Experience as a Constitutional Variable," 47 *Vand. L. Rev.* 273 (1994).

167   See, e.g., Lucy E. White, "Subordination, Rhetorical Survival Skills, and Sunday Shoes: Notes on Hearing of Mrs. G.," 38 *Buff. L. Rev.* 1 (1990).

168   See, e.g., Marianne Constable, "Reflections on Law as a Profession of Words," in *Justice and Power*, supra note 7, at 19.

169   Milner S. Ball and James B. White, "A Conversation between Milner Ball and James Boyd White," 8 *Yale J.L. and Human.* 465, 468 (1996).

170   Id.

171   See Rorty, supra note 118, at 140 (describing the divide "between people taking refuge in self-protective knowingness about the present and romantic utopians trying to imagine a better future").

172   Linda Greenhouse, "Learning to Live with Bush v. Gore," 4 *Green Bag* 2d. 381, 383 (2001); see also Mark Tushnet, "Renormalizing Bush v. Gore: An Anticipatory Intellectual History," 90 *Geo. L.J.* 113, 113 (2001) ("Bush v. Gore seems to have let critical legal studies arise like Lazarus from the grave."). But see Jack M. Balkin, "Bush v. Gore and the Boundary between Law and Politics," 110 *Yale L.J.* 1407, 1443 (2001) (arguing that "in Bush v. Gore the Court did not even preserve the relative autonomy of law from politics that Critical Legal Studies assumed").

173   121 S. Ct. 525 (2000).

Freedom, Autonomy, and the Cultural
Study of Law
Paul W. Kahn

In the spring of 1999, I published a little book with a big title: *The Cultural Study of Law, Reconstructing Legal Scholarship.* The ambition of the book was to clear a space within law schools for a study of law that was not directed at the issue of legal reform. I urged a theoretical approach free of the insistent question: "What should the law be?" The reasons for my plea were not new. The rule of law, I argued, is not just a set of rules to be applied to an otherwise independent social order. Rather, law is, in part, constitutive of the self-understanding of individuals and communities. In particular, Americans often identify themselves as citizens within a polity characterized by the rule of law. This is not the only way in which Americans imagine themselves, but it is a powerful way for many people.

To achieve such a disciplinary stance with respect to law's rule is particularly difficult, I argued, because the study of law is itself a part of the practice of law. An openness to reform is characteristic of the legal order, and a significant source of reform is the study of legal rules and institutions that occurs within the law school. Thus, an effort to shift the disciplinary attitude confronts not merely resistance arising from the personal ambition of those in a professional school to "have an impact" on legal practice, but a deeper problem of the co-optation of reason by the very object of study: the rule of law. Law professors, for the most part, are not studying law, they are doing law. Even to see this, however, requires a kind of Cartesian division of the self, such that the law professor's ordinary beliefs and professional practices become the object of his or her inquiry.

Anyone reading my book would quickly see that the title is grander than the actual project. For the most part, I have explored the links between constitutional law and the constitutive character of law. The culture of law's rule on which I have focused is that which we acknowledge when we look to the Supreme Court as the literal embodiment of the belief that ours is "a government of laws, and not of men."[1] Because constitutional law rests its claim to legitimacy on the realization of self-government, it provides a particularly compelling point of entry for an inquiry into the ways in which law both reflects and constructs the self.[2]

Much of the cultural studies of law movement has been an effort to shift the location at which we study law from the opinions of the appellate courts to the expressions of ordinary people carrying out the tasks of everyday life. Because of my focus on the constitutional rule of law, my work moves in the opposite direction. There is an unfortunate, but understandable, tendency to think that I am resurrecting a conception of culture as "high culture"—that which ordinary people lack—and that my focus on legal elites rests on a normative assumption about the superior value of the judicial opinion as compared to the representations of law that appear in popular culture. For these reasons, my work has been received with some unease by those who I thought might be my natural allies.[3]

This skepticism has forced me to think further about the normative implications of my inquiry. In this essay, I first locate my work in the field of cultural studies. My work is in some respects narrower and in others broader than that of colleagues working in the field: narrower in its focus on the rule of law as an expression of self-government; broader in its use of a distinctly philosophical methodology. In the final part of the essay, I take up the issue of the normative implications of the differences in approach. At issue is not so much a difference over the character of law, but rather different conceptions of the relationship of the scholar to his or her project. Two different conceptions of freedom, and of the relationship of scholarship to freedom, lie behind this difference.

Where We Agree, or How We Got to Where We Are

Traditionally, the autonomy of the discipline of legal study was located within the doctrinal rules, which were thought to be capable of generating solutions to every actual controversy. The expert—a position claimed by both the judge and the law professor—could remain wholly within the domain of law in order to resolve social conflicts. To reach outside was to commit either the sin of "result-oriented" jurisprudence or that of "usurping the legislative role." Legal practice and legal study formed a seamless whole. The judge and the professor knew the same things: one wrote opinions, the other treatises—or, more likely, law review articles. The law review article could become a favored style of presentation because of background assumptions that were just those embodied in the treatise —for example, that every area of law has a systematic completeness already known to the experts. Accordingly, the law review article could make a discrete intervention aimed at reforming a small part of the law, while assuming the relevant domain would otherwise remain stable. Law reviews were like pocket parts—indeed, the new information technology has made law review articles accessible just as if they were pocket parts.

Legal scholarship had no other ambition than to systemize the knowledge claims implicit in the opinions it analyzed.[4] The world of the judge, of the professor, and of the elite legal practitioner was one world, staffed by the same individuals who would transit among all of these positions over the course of a career. This ambition is seen today in someone like Lawrence Tribe, who undertakes to write a treatise on constitutional law in order to systemize—to make into a single coherent whole—judicial doctrine. Having made a claim to this knowledge, he can now assume either of the other roles of practitioner or judge. This same vision is represented by Ronald Dworkin's mythic figure of Hercules, who personifies the perfect academic become the perfect judge. There is no longer any space between the different roles. Both aim to state what the law is by stating what they believe the law should be. The reform of law does not arise from knowledge claims external to law; it is the internal expression of the law itself.[5]

This world of traditional, doctrinal legal scholarship was thought to have been largely broken apart by the rise of legal realism in the first half of the twentieth century. From the perspective of intellectual history, legal realism represented the transformation of legal scholarship by the rise of the new empirical social sciences. For the first time, the judge and his product—the judicial opinion—became an object of study by those who were not themselves a part of the extended practice of law. Attacking the knowledge claims of the doctrinalists—both judges and academics—the legal realists defeated the claims for the autonomy of law by showing that doctrine alone could neither determine nor explain outcomes. An understanding of law had to work with a different vocabulary and a different set of explanatory rules from those deployed by the practitioners themselves. Here, the modern paradigm—and direct descendent of legal realism—is the law and economics movement. Law and economics, however, is only a particularly successful example of a set of epistemic assumptions embodied equally in a variety of disciplinary approaches, each of which sees law as epiphenomenal and seeks to reveal the "underlying" truth by deploying the tools and concepts of some other discipline.

Yet the capacity of the practice of law's rule to co-opt the scholars' claims to knowledge proved to be much stronger than the legal realists had imagined possible. Within a very short time, professors who alleged a loyalty to legal realism were themselves occupying the bench. Legal realism was no longer outside legal practice looking in but rather a dominant form of reason operating within the rule of law itself. The Brandeis brief anticipated this intersection in which the arguments made to the court drew from the insights and methodologies of the new social sciences.[6] Thus, the rise of the social sciences not only transformed the structure of government institutions—for example, with the rise of the administrative agency—but also transformed the nature of legal reasoning. The postrealist language of constitutional law is the language of measurable interests, of balancing, and of deference to the claims of agency expertise.[7] Instead of describing the competition of interests as what is "really" going on "behind" the legal rhetoric—the Holmesian critique of the pre–New Deal Court—interest balancing becomes the language of the Court itself and, accordingly, the material for doctrinal systematization. Not only was constitutional law transformed by the rise of new forms of knowledge, but a whole new domain of public law, characterized by its incorporation of bureaucratic rationality, arose to compete with constitutional discourse: administrative law.

This regular movement from critic to participant is a product of an epistemic self-reflection characteristic of law's rule. The rule of law is not just a set of rules like those one finds in a game that one can choose not to play. Rather, law appears as a legitimate source of authority; it could not do so if it appeared irrational or ignorant. Judges cannot speak of a flat earth for too long after everyone else in the society understands the earth to be round. The appearance of reason is not a sufficient condition of legitimacy, but it is a necessary condition—at least for a modern society.

The rule of law may be our tradition, but it is a tradition rooted in substantial part in Enlightenment beliefs about the place of reason in structuring a political association. If the legal order is committed to reason, and reason is understood to produce an ever-increasing growth of knowledge, then the order of law must hold itself open to knowledge-based reform. Sometimes that reform is dramatic and widespread. This was true of the rapid reform of law in the wake of the rise of legal realism.[8]

The character of knowledge claims within the legal order is a function of this need for legitimacy. Without attempting to set forth a necessary, formal logic of the legal order, we can still describe the general character of the epistemic conditions that a modern legal order must purport to satisfy. First, the law has to be objective: there must be a truth of the matter. If there were not an object external to the legal decision-maker, then there could be no assurance in advance that the experts would agree on a single answer to legal questions. Without this kind of objectivity, the claim to expert knowledge of the law would not be capable of solving any controversy.[9] Second, the law has to be neutral. If the product of legal inquiry depends on the character of the inquirer— or even worse, on the character of the parties making legal claims—then claims of expert knowledge would not merit deference from the parties to a controversy. Without neutrality, the autonomy of law would only be a statement about the interests of those who exercise power to decide under the law. Law would be no more stable than the flow of political power. Finally, law must be a system in the sense of a reasonably ordered whole. One has to be able to move from one proposition to another within the legal order by means of established procedures and justified inferences. There must be a reasonably supported chain of argument from common starting points to a common resolution. This requirement is analogous to that of "repeatability" with respect to scientific experiments. Without this transparency to reasons, law's legitimacy in a democratic order would again be in doubt.[10]

For the classic doctrinalist, the autonomy of law rested on the claim that the expert knowledge of law satisfied all three of these demands for objectivity, neutrality, and coherence. The claims of the doctrinal science of law, however, were thoroughly discredited by the legal realists, who left the law professor looking like a snake-oil salesman who had illegitimately worked his way into the university. Legal decisions and legal rules, the legal realists taught us, have to be understood in a social/political context that is not captured by the categories and descriptions of law. Law satisfies none of the normative criteria of autonomy: it is not objective, neutral, or coherent.

Despite the victory of legal realism, the power of these epistemic norms remained. If they serve a legitimating function, they cannot easily be discarded. Nevertheless, they had to find a new footing apart from the traditional science of law. Precisely as a result of the success of the legal realists at simultaneously colonizing the academy and the bench, this battle today is waged on two fronts at once—within the judiciary and within the university. Most famously, it is the framework within which many of our most pressing constitutional disputes are fought out. Here, the battle pits those who claim to be strict constructionists against those who are inappropriately labeled "noninterpretivists." But it is also fought on a daily basis in the law schools, which have experienced a constant methodological crisis for a generation as scholars have searched for and critiqued the epistemic grounds for legal reform. Behind the explosion of studies of "law and . . ." lies this legitimation crisis.

The strict constructionists claim that judges must restrict themselves to a narrow reading of the Constitution, although even here there is disagreement on whether a narrow reading sticks only to the text or also appeals to original intent (and whose intent matters). The point of this narrowness is to satisfy just those demands for objectivity, neutrality, and coherence described above. The fear is that a noninterpretivist approach provides the judge a space for free play of his or her own values, allowing legal decision-making to become another forum for political and moral disagreement. Thus the dispute over law's autonomy becomes a battle over the legitimacy of judicial decision-making. The reach of judicial decisions should not exceed the domain within which these norms of objectivity, neutrality, and coherence can extend. Beyond that domain, not knowledge but consent is the sole source of legitimate authority in a democracy. With consent, we move from legal to political institutions.

The noninterpretivists react defensively, claiming first that the resources of text and history cannot satisfy the epistemic demands that could ground the autonomy of law. Just as the legal realists delegitimized the claims of the doctrinalists early in this century, modern theorists use the same strategies to delegitimize the knowledge claims of the strict constructionists. Texts, they argue, are multivalent, and history is a wide-open field for interpretive disagreement.[11] Even to begin a legal inquiry requires decisions resolving complex questions of interpretation with respect to the level of generality at which questions are posed and answers articulated. Does one ask what the Framers said in 1789, or what they would have said 200 years later, or something in-between, such as what is the current meaning of what they said then? There is no end to these questions, and no agreement on the answers. Modern disputes over statutory interpretation reflect the transference of these same interpretive controversies from the problem of reading the Constitution to that of reading statutes.[12]

These are extremely bitter battles on the bench because the underlying issue is the legitimacy of the judicial claim to say what the law is. The dispute is framed as a question of whether one is engaging in law at all. Thus, on the abortion issue, Justice Antonin Scalia accuses the majority of abandoning "reasoned judgment [for] personal predilection" and declares that such an "unprincipled" approach is "more than one should have to bear."[13] Justice John Paul Stevens has returned the accusation in the recent federalism cases, accusing the states' rights majority of a "judicial activism [that] represents such a radical departure from the proper role of this Court that it should be opposed whenever the opportunity arises."[14]

Despite the dissenters' resistance to stare decisis, the strong role of precedent within legal reasoning inevitably creates a movement toward judicial self-regulation. However illegitimate a decision may appear to those who disagree with it at first, it nevertheless operates as a precedent. *Roe v. Wade*[15] is normalized by *Casey*, just as *Seminole Tribe v. Florida*[16] has been normalized by the numerous Eleventh Amendment cases in recent years. Within the law schools, however, there is no corresponding regulatory mechanism. One consequence of this has been a growing division within the academy among the diverse approaches to law and legal argument. Not bound to each other by a need to decide anything—apart from the occasional faculty appointment—disciplines continue to proliferate, with each discourse having less and less contact with its competitors.[17]

The modern law school lives with this burden of establishing the form of knowledge appropriate to law. Here, the noninterpretivists must confront the fact that they cannot simply dismiss the implicit norms behind claims for the autonomy of legal knowledge, since those norms ground the legitimacy of legal decision-making. The noninterpretivist must meet those standards of reason or provide an alternative legitimating ground. Modern constitutional theory, starting with Alexander Bickel's identification of the countermajoritarian difficulty,[18] is just such an attempt. In substantial part, this amounts to an effort to ground the incorporation of the legal realists' interest-balancing approach into constitutional law.[19]

The law school operates as a kind of funnel through which other disciplines are fed into the law itself. This is one half of the legal realists' legacy of turning to the resources of social science—resources outside the discipline of law—and insisting that the law be informed by an intellectual expertise that meets contemporary epistemic standards. Thus the critique of law as epiphenomenal continues as a theme common to scholars on both the left and the right. It runs from the variety of forms of Marxism and feminism, on one side of the political spectrum, to conservative charges that liberal judges have implemented a political program unsupported by legitimate legal sources, on the other. All want to get at the "truth" of the matter; all believe that having reached that truth, legal reforms should follow.

The other half of the legal realists' legacy is the movement of the boundaries of legal discourse such that what had been outside comes to have a place within the law itself. To speak of the autonomy of law in the law school today is to describe a domain capable of expanding to include virtually any kind of knowledge claim. Economics, for example, is not just an external perspective that can be applied to law. It also claims a place within the legal academy as yet another source of what the law is. The same is true of moral theory, as illustrated by the work of someone like Ronald Dworkin.[20] Institutionally, there is a characteristic movement of knowledge claims from the periphery to the center of the law school and from there into the patterns of judicial reasoning. The outsider regularly becomes the insider through the powerful need of law to claim the support of reason.

From this vantage point, we can see the similarities and differences of critical legal studies (CLS) and the law and economics movements, the two major claimants to the legal realist tradition. Both share the negative, critical theme of piercing the language of law and deploying in its place an expert language better able to grasp the truth on which law rests. They bring different resources to a shared perception that interests and the material capacities to realize these interests are foundational considerations. They differ, of course, in their understandings of the origins of interests and the way in which interests are realized. Nevertheless, they share a positive belief that the reform of law must follow from the realization of the truth each purports to recognize. Both believe that the practice of law should be informed by the truth revealed through legal study. One pursues reform under the norm of efficiency and the other under that of justice, but for each this is simply the affirmative side of the critical exposure of the epiphenomenal character of law.[21]

That law and economics has been far more successful in its critical and reformist ambitions than CLS reflects the same constellation of forces seen in the dominant place of economics in social science departments and in the formulation of policy. Again, we should not expect the truth operating in law to look very different—at least in the medium term—from that operating in the broader society. It is not surprising, therefore, to find some of the leaders of the CLS movement today pursuing a reformist enterprise that, in its focus on economic institutions, looks like some aspects of the law and economics movement.[22]

Those who pursue the cultural study of law often want to escape this entire matrix of thought in which the study of law becomes a contest over the legitimacy of knowledge claims and over the direction of legal reform. Like the CLS scholars, they too tend to think that legal claims are less a form of knowledge than a form of power—more precisely, that the truth of legal propositions rests not in some objective fact or principle accessible to rational inquiry but in the relationships of power that such claims sustain. These scholars are no less interested in recovering that which law's knowledge removes from sight. Recovery, however, no longer means discarding the language or practices of law as simply epiphenomenal. The power at issue substantially creates and sustains itself through the claims of law. Accordingly, there is a need to investigate the ways in which law is constitutive of group and individual identities and values.

If truth and power are bound together, there is no way to abandon one for the other or to view either from the perspective of the other. Neither provides a solid ground on which to stand without the other. The old opposition between claims for the autonomy of law, on the one hand, and for the epiphenomenal character of law, on the other, dissolves. Without a clear division between inside and outside, the critique of the autonomy of law no longer leads to the same process of co-optation by which the external becomes internal.

Cultural studies tend to see law as nothing in the abstract; rather, law is a set of sites of social conflict and a set of resources—institutional and rhetorical—for those involved in such conflict. Sites and resources, however, do not exist independently of the claims and conflicts. Individuals do not first have interests that they then take to the law. Individuals literally find themselves in these sites deploying these resources; we are always already there.

Scholars of law and culture focus on the materiality of law, the way in which law simultaneously embodies the interests of particular groups and shapes those interests—and even shapes the identities of those who understand themselves as members of such groups. Law must, on this view, be studied in ways that are historically specific and deeply contextualized. The turn to historical context reveals a dynamic process in which power is contested for the sake of ideas, values, and interests. The contest is often fought within, and over, the terms of legal claims for recognition of identity as well as of particular interests.

To understand law, accordingly, we have to investigate how it works in its multiple uses. Use is not simply in the Supreme Court, but just as much in the divorce court—not simply by the judges, but also by the parties. To know what the law means to people, we should ask them. Do not ask the chief justice. Instead, ask the ordinary person who comes into contact with the law at multiple sites in his or her daily life; ask those who must negotiate a divorce or pay a traffic ticket. Knowledge of the law begins with good survey data. The study of legal culture has its roots not only in the CLS concern for power but equally in the law and society concern for the empirical investigation of the social.[23] This turn to the social, away from the opinions of the legal elite, means that the study of the culture of law tends to slide toward law's representation in "popular culture." The concept of legal culture seems to require both forms of approach to the ordinary: statistical representation and analysis of the symbolic productions of everyday life.

Some who study the culture of law suspect that I may be on the wrong side of all of these divides. My inquiries tend to focus on the top of the legal hierarchy—on the judges and professors, rather than on ordinary citizens in their confrontations with, and deployments of, law. There is indeed implicit in my work a claim about the autonomy of law's rule. Moreover, many who study the culture of law approach the subject from the perspective of group interests—for example, minorities or women—that might provide a ground for resistance to, and thus for evaluation of, legal understandings. Since I do not take such a perspective, I face the threat that the subject will be swallowed up by law. Thus I need to save the subject from law's imperial claims.[24] These are the points I want to address. While doing so, I do not mean to discredit the work of others. The issue here is not who has the correct approach or who can properly claim the label "cultural study." There can be multiple forms of inquiry into the nature of law, even multiple forms of a cultural study of law's rule.

Moreover, we are in broad agreement on many of the underlying premises of the significance of the turn to culture. We share a similar frustration with the terms of legal inquiry as they have continued to cycle through the debate first realized in the opposition between the doctrinalists and the realists. We agree that law plays a constitutive role for individuals and communities and that interpretation and power go hand in hand. None of us believe that law is an objective or neutral set of propositions, yet we share an interest in the way in which claims of objectivity and neutrality operate within the law. We also agree that the culture of law needs to be understood in its relationship to other cultural products and that there is no law in the abstract. There is only a field of social relationships organized, in part, through assertions of law. We accept the hermeneutic turn, and for that reason are interested in exploring the contributions that the study of rhetoric and interpretation can make to understanding the culture of law. Our interdisciplinary interests are strong and reach as much toward the humanities as they do toward the social sciences. We agree on the need for historical inquiry into the forms and patterns of legal understandings. Like other cultural products, law has a history that sets the limits of possibility at any given time. To understand why we order the legal world as we do, we need to understand where these patterns came from and how they changed over time.

An interest in history does not commit one to any particular form of historical explanation or any propositions about historical causation. Nevertheless, a concern with the genealogy of legal understandings is common to many of those who study the culture of law, including myself.

Where We Disagree

More than anything else, we disagree on the sites at which a cultural analysis can be usefully applied. I have been particularly interested in using a cultural studies approach to understand the character of the legal imagination of those who consider themselves, and are considered by others, to be the spokespersons for the rule of law: law professors, judges, and justices. What is the structure of the legal imagination of those who are most deeply committed in their professional and personal lives to the rule of law? They engage in a constant process of reification and objectification of the categories of legal analysis: for example, the sovereign people, the judicial role, legislative intent, the permanent Constitution, and precedent. How do they imagine the world when they invoke such concepts? How does that world give meaning to their sense of their own identity and their understanding of the political community? How did this way of thinking come to seem so "natural"?

Of course, this inquiry would be of less interest if it failed to make contact with the beliefs maintained by a more substantial portion of the population. Studying the justices is not the legal equivalent of studying the string theorists in the physics department. There are deep resonances between what the judges and professors say, on the one hand, and some very basic beliefs central to a broadly available American culture of the rule of law, on the other. We find the elements of this set of beliefs in much of our public rhetoric, regularly deployed for over 200 years.

This set of beliefs is often referred to as our "national faith" or our "civic religion." Its standard terms are endlessly repeated in civics classes and on every occasion when someone—even if only a private citizen—must explain the legitimacy of a claim put forth for public acknowledgment and response. These terms are so basic that anyone who rejects them is seen as radical, dangerous, or, more likely, unstable. Just as they are repeated in the endless invocations of the rule of law in public discourse, they are repeated in the dominant forms of modern political theorizing, beginning with Hobbes's linkage of the concepts of sovereignty, the social contract, and political science. The rule of law in this tradition is a product of a sovereign people constituting itself through an act of constitutional construction founded on the insights of political science.[25]

Much about the set of beliefs that constitute law's rule is obvious. It is only obvious, however, because it is so deeply enmeshed in our political culture. That this is *our* culture, and not some universal order of law, becomes clear as soon as one compares it to the discourse and beliefs of other states and peoples—even other liberal democracies. Our immediate and easy recourse to the language of law is hardly universal. The export of our legal rules often fails to produce anything that looks to us like a polity under the rule of law. We often speak loosely about the need for certain habits of law-abidingness when we try to explain the failure of a government of law to work elsewhere. Habits are forms of practice that seem to come "naturally" because the world is imagined to have a character within which these forms of behavior make sense. This perception of the world is hardly natural. I have sought to explain the how and why of our perception of legitimacy under law.

Thomas Paine announced that in America "law is king." There has since been an unbroken, public commitment to the idea that we live under the rule of law, not men. Paine's proposition works as both a descriptive and a normative claim. Thus the deepest criticism that one can make of political behavior is that it is in violation of a legal norm. Who in this country does not believe that "not even the President is above the law"?[26] And who does not understand the deep resonance of the assertion, in the face of injustice, that the injured party is going to take the case "all the way to the Supreme Court"? Of course, we all know that the president can get away with much and that the Supreme Court is not in the business of doing justice. But even as we acknowledge the failures of these propositions as descriptive claims, we nevertheless feel those failures as points of illegitimacy in our political arrangements. Law should be king. Of this, we are quite certain.

One saw, for example, fascinating permutations on this theme in the recent impeachment process, in which both sides tried to claim for themselves the virtue of law and to cast the other as "mere politicians"—those who in bad faith would use the form of law to advance factional ends. The supporters of impeachment appealed to this norm of universal and equal application of the rule of law; opponents claimed that President Clinton was being singled out for prosecution on the basis of an alleged violation of law that would not be pursued against any other individual. The battle for public legitimacy was not fought over what happened—or over who could claim popular support—but over which side could claim the virtues of law's rule.[27] Each sought to label the opposing arguments a "perversion" of law for merely political purposes. Of course, an even deeper indication of our public commitment to law's rule is the fact that removal of the president takes the form of a legal proceeding: Our Constitution provides no room for a no-confidence vote based on a loss of political support. Here, as elsewhere, we find a deep inclination toward juridifying what might otherwise be seen as political disputes.[28]

The Supreme Court regularly appeals to an understanding of its own role as the guardian of law's rule in American political life, and the Court remains our most respected governmental institution. The Court started its career of judicial review by making three fundamental claims: ours is a government of law, not men; it is the Court's role to say what the law is; and the law is the expression of the opinion of the people.[29] When the Court speaks the law, it speaks in the name of the sovereign people. This was the vision of *Marbury,* and it remains the central normative claim of the Court, appealed to, for example, in *Casey* when the Court felt compelled to reassert the grounds of its own legitimacy in the face of the abortion controversy: "Like the character of an individual, the legitimacy of the Court must be earned over time. So, indeed, must be the character of a Nation of people who aspire to live according to the rule of law. Their belief in themselves as such a people is not readily separable from their understanding of the Court invested with the authority to decide their constitutional cases and speak before all others for their constitutional ideals. If the Court's legitimacy should be undermined, then, so would the country be in its very ability to see itself through its constitutional ideals."[30]

That this understanding is shared by other politicians—as well as the electorate—is suggested by the fact that it has become virtually inconceivable for a politician, including the president, to oppose a court order. For example, the widespread resistance to desegregation, following *Brown v. Board of Education,*[31] is not viewed as a story of democratic resistance to an unelected judiciary. Rather, that history is read as a story of the progressive triumph of law over a demagogic politics of special interests. Defiance of the Supreme Court by public officials appears to us as the equivalent of military defiance of civilian command. Indeed, these are linked aspects of belief in the rule of law: to defend the nation is to defend the Constitution. The object of the oath of office required of representatives and governmental officers is to "support this Constitution."

The ambition of the cultural study is not just to delineate the substantive character of these beliefs of the Court and its audience but also to understand how it all works. How has the Court created an appearance of itself as the voice of the people? What is it that we see, and fail to see, when we look to the Court?

This language of law's rule is our dominant, although not exclusive, language of legitimacy. We are, of course, quite capable of speaking the language of majority rule and electoral politics. But even that language rarely works against the rule of law. When it does—for example, Jefferson's resistance to Marshall, Lincoln's to Taney, and Franklin Roosevelt's confrontation with the *Lochner* Court—it is a strong indication of a national crisis. Moreover, the resolution of such crises usually includes a claim to recovery of the larger narrative of law's rule. The crisis is contained, localized, and resolved by the identification of a specific error that is then excised from the legal corpus: consider *Dred Scott v. Sanford*,[32] *Plessy v. Ferguson*,[33] and *Lochner v. New York*.[34]

The narrative offered in support of the legitimacy of every political act or actor moves to the plane of constitutional order surprisingly quickly. When challenged, a governmental action will be justified by reference to some particular regulation or decision, which will be supported by some statutory authority, which will find its source in the Constitution. Because we assume these levels of support, judicial review is easily sought and widely expected as the test of legitimacy. There is no point at which politics is visibly unleashed from law.[35] Political opposition to judicial rulings will, for this reason, inevitably be framed as an opposing legal claim. In this instance, it will be said, the Court misinterpreted the truth of the Constitution.

The recent dispute over the appropriate course of action with respect to the six-year-old Cuban boy, Elián Gonzales, is a good example of the role of the legitimating discourse of law's rule. The Clinton administration immediately took the position that his disposition was a matter to be determined by law, not by the politics of our relationship with Cuba or by politics in the streets of Miami. When "application" of the legal rule led to a decision to send him back to his father, there were massive demonstrations by the Cuban American community. But when asked about the grounds for this demonstration, the leadership's response was not framed in terms of the political power of the community or in terms of their political opposition to Castro. Rather, a counterclaim of law's rule was put forth: the protestors accused the administration of sacrificing a claim of legal right to the political goal of rapprochement with Castro. They wanted to make sure that the child had "his day in court." Law, it seems, can only be opposed by law, even in the middle of spontaneous forms of political action.[36]

Of course, law does not eliminate politics in any dispute. But what is striking is the need for all sides to frame their actions in terms of law's rule. We do not capture what is going on by approaching the legal contest as if it were merely a rhetorical cover for the political disputes. Not only does the invocation of law have institutional consequences, but it is offered as a normative justification that can settle disputes on terms common to all sides. To win the contest at law really is to win the controversy.[37]

These are the sorts of disputes in which I have been interested: contests that go to the issue of the legitimacy of the entire structure of governmental authority. This is the point at which issues of legitimacy become issues of citizen identity. The language of law's rule appeals to our understanding of who we are as citizens. Much of my work has tried to offer a kind of phenomenology of this distinctive American political culture of the rule of law.[38]

This is a key point of difference between my work and that of many others in the field of cultural studies of law. I have not been writing about the culture of law per se, here or anywhere else, but about the American culture of political legitimacy through law's rule. My concern has not been with the operation of the multiple bodies of law—such as tort, contract, family—but with the nature of the understanding of a constitutional order of law that appears to citizens to make legitimate claims on them. Other domains of law are not entirely beyond my vision, but I approach them from the perspective of the constitutional construction of self and nation.

Our discourse of law's rule is not primarily a discourse of rights—a point about which both liberal theorists and their communitarian critics are often mistaken. Rather, the American discourse of legitimation through law's rule is a discourse of popular sovereignty. We only get to the discourse of rights when we ask what it is that the popular sovereign "says." Combining the who and the what of this speech gives us the deeply felt, but weakly conceptualized, relationship of will and reason at the foundation of our concept of political legitimacy.[39] This relative priority of popular sovereignty over rights is not a universal characteristic of legal discourse. It points to a uniquely American culture of law's rule.

My point has never been to praise or to condemn this set of beliefs in law's rule. I have not urged it on people or expressed regret that it may be a cultural form of ultimate meanings that is dying for many. I have no doubt that many people do not experience popular sovereignty and law's rule as something affecting their own lives, let alone defining their own identity. Some, because they have a less political understanding of what is important in their lives; some, because they understand themselves to be oriented toward an emerging global order that has displaced their identification with the nation-state; and some, because they understand themselves through an identification with a group that sees itself as victimized by the majority's actions and beliefs, which they perceive to be embodied in the law. Yet I suspect that many of these people can still understand the pull of the culture of law's rule; they still feel something of the effects of this set of beliefs. They are likely still to think that what needs to be done is to fulfill the promise of the rule of law, that is, the promise of the Constitution. They may fight for group recognition and an expansion of rights, but they are hard pressed to find a language outside our rhetoric of law's rule, and a set of institutions outside our legal practices, within which to frame their political struggles.

I have sought to understand where this cultural form of law's rule comes from, how it holds together, and what meaning of self and community is maintained by those who operate with this set of beliefs. Avoiding advocacy of law's rule, I have, nevertheless, tried to maintain a respectful attitude toward the culture of law; not because it is better than other cultural forms or somehow represents a higher truth, but because it has provided a matrix of meanings for generations of Americans. Kant argues that what deserves our respect is the individual's capacity to formulate a moral rule. Accordingly, respect is due to that in which every individual is the same. But respect is also due to the capacity for difference: for who we *are*, as well as for an ideal we all might be. Respect is due not only to the universal, but formal, capacity of every individual to appeal to reason; it is due also to the substantive capacity to create and maintain a culture. We cannot respect that capacity without respecting its products, any more than we can respect the artist but not her art.

Respect hardly means that one should ignore the injustices, repressions, and inequalities sustained in the name of the rule of law or of any other cultural form, whether religious, political, or familial. None of the forms of our cultural inheritance is free of guilt in this respect. The barbarism done in the name of beliefs—of what we call high as well as low culture—does not lurk very far below the surface of most of our ideals.[40]

Central to my inquiry has been an investigation of the way in which popular sovereignty appears to those who participate in the culture of law's rule. This inquiry into the appearance of popular sovereignty, in turn, has raised a host of questions about the imaginative shape of time, space, representation, and authority within the rule of law, as well as about the nature of legal texts, the authorial voice, and interpretation. These are only the general topics under which I have organized the inquiry, not an exhaustive list of categories. In one form or another, all of these inquiries are directed at the subject's imagination of the self as a citizen under law's rule. To borrow a phrase from Charles Taylor, I have explored the "sources of the self" at work in the American conception of the citizen under law's rule.

I have tended to focus on the strongest claim that we imagine possible within the political order: that is, the claim for self-sacrifice made on the citizen. For many Americans, the rule of law has been a deadly serious affair, providing an ultimate meaning and meriting an ultimate sacrifice. The rule of law is a kind of shorthand way of referring to a matrix of beliefs and practices within which the citizen acknowledges the possibility that the state will make a demand on his or her life and that, regardless of personal interests, the legitimacy of that claim will have to be acknowledged.[41]

If we try to imagine a state that could never make such a claim on the individual, we are either imagining an "illegitimate" state or we are imagining a political order very different from that which we have experienced within the modern nation-state.[42] Indeed, imagining the compelling quality of this claim is a way to begin to distinguish the symbolic form of political life from the symbolic form of our moral life. Politics and morality do not always intersect, as becomes obvious when we examine the political justice of warfare in which morally innocent combatants are thought to be appropriate targets of deadly force.[43] Conversely, the demand for an international law of human rights rests on an intuition that the moral and political orders must have some minimum contact.

I have sought to describe the substance of those beliefs that amount to a kind of faith in the popular sovereign, which is simultaneously the source and meaning of the rule of law. This inquiry takes no position on the validity of the truth claims put forward under the rule of law. Nor does it imply anything about the normative justifications that could be offered for such beliefs. Understanding the shape and the origins of the constellation of beliefs in the rule of law is a very different enterprise from the philosophical inquiry into the conditions under which a government can make legitimate claims on individuals. The latter is a project in political justification, an aspect of normative political theory.[44]

I have often used an analogy to the study of religion in order to explain my own work. As with the study of religion, I have argued that we must suspend belief in the truth of law's rule if we are to investigate the imaginative shape of the culture of law's rule. Just as a cultural study of religion focuses on religious experience rather than on the truth of religious doctrine, a cultural study of law should focus on the character of experience under belief in the rule of law.

We should not ask, for example, whether law's rule is really founded in the popular sovereign, but rather how it is that the popular sovereign appears in and through the categories of the legal imagination. Like the Judeo-Christian God, the popular sovereign is the reified subject of a process of interpretation. Both the divine and secular sovereigns are imagined as the point of origin of a text. Apart from moments of miraculous appearance through revelation or revolution, access to both sovereigns is achieved only through reading and interpreting texts. Similarly, we should not ask whether the rule of law maintains the neutrality and objectivity it claims, but rather how the belief in law's neutrality and objectivity operates in the citizen's understanding of his or her relationship to legal claims. Again, the analogy is to the equal position of all souls before God, regardless of worldly distinctions of wealth, power, or honor. We want to know how the denial of distinction works in religious belief, not whether that radical equality states an "objective truth."

The analogy to religion helps to sharpen the point of difference between myself and others pursuing the cultural study of law. Many of the latter assume that the way to pursue a cultural study of religion is to begin by investigating the beliefs of parishioners. I, on the other hand, would begin with an investigation of the theologians. These inquiries are not mutually exclusive. If we want to understand Christianity, it would be wrong to think that we can ignore Augustine, Aquinas, or Luther. But it would be equally wrong to think that the beliefs of the parishioner are irrelevant or that they fail to make contact with those of the theologians.

The theological analogy goes to one of the basic points of misunderstanding. Essentially, my critics have the genealogy of my work wrong. The point of intersection between my work and their own may be Clifford Geertz.[45] They often come out of a social science tradition for which empirical research—the gathering of data through the field study—is necessary to the scholarly enterprise. Geertz, for them, may represent a change in the understanding of the object of those field studies, but not in the essential character of the work. But the genealogy of my work is philosophical, not anthropological.

The cultural study of law's rule that I pursue figures in an enterprise that begins with Kant and the subjective turn to transcendental philosophy, moves through the historical objectification of reason in Hegel, and then expands into the study of diverse cultural forms with Ernst Cassirer[46] and Suzanne Langer.[47] This neo-Kantian approach takes a number of forms in the twentieth century, including Wittgenstein's *Philosophical Investigations*,[48] Foucault's inquiries into truth and power,[49] and Charles Taylor's work on the sources of the self.[50] Foucault refers to "the historical a priori,"[51] which is an accurate description of the kind of philosophical inquiry that I have pursued. Geertz is a critical figure linking these two genealogies, as he himself recognizes when he acknowledges the importance of Wittgenstein to his own investigations.

The most important influence on my work is neither Geertz nor Foucault but rather Cassirer's inquiries into the variety of symbolic forms.[52] This is just the spirit with which I approach the study of the culture of law's rule, as a distinct symbolic form that constructs one possible world of meaning. That world exists alongside others constructed by deploying other symbolic forms. Thus, while I have tried to sketch a picture of law's rule as a complete world, that is, one that can make sense of all the phenomena that can appear within it, I have been careful to describe this as a world that is deeply contested by other symbolic forms. These other forms also participate in constructing the meaning of our political life; they too make claims to completeness that compete with those of the rule of law. This leads me to emphasize points of contestation different from those my critics emphasize. While they are interested in the contests within law, I am interested in the confrontations between legal and nonlegal understandings of our experience. Again, these are not mutually exclusive inquiries.

In *The Reign of Law*,[53] I described a kind of symbolic competition between the rule of law and what I termed "political action." The latter describes an order of politics characterized by contrast to law's rule. It is a world in which meaning is located in individuals performing unique acts; it is not a world of preexisting rules to which individuals appeal in order to make sense of their experience. The ambition of political action is to create the new, rather than to preserve existing meanings. The political actor claims to represent the current people, while the legal subject understands the self to represent a transgenerational community. Political action takes revolution, not constitutional preservation, as its paradigmatic political act. The distinction can be thought of as one between the potential and the actual. Under the symbolic form of law's rule, all possible meaning is present before the act occurs: the event only has meaning as the realization of a potential that was already there. This is what it means to recognize the act or event as an instance of a legal rule. Under the symbolic form of political action, the meaning of the event is established in its actual appearance as a unique product of contingent forces. Rules alone will produce no act; something must happen. Only then does the contest of meaning begin.

Our political life often appears as a competition between these different forms of perception and understanding. We honor both Revolution and Constitution. We experience the promise of the "New Frontier," the "New Deal," or a new "Contract with America": we yearn for a kind of individual political heroism. But we also experience the claim of faith in the constitutional order of law that we inherit from our predecessors. This is a competition not between events and actions but between the forms of understanding within which we perceive their meanings. Consider, for example, an act of Congress. It can be understood as the realization of a constitutional rule establishing the possibility of a range of legislation—the issue before the Court when the constitutionality of the act is challenged. But it can equally be understood as a unique event, bringing policy innovations to a contemporary problem.

Although I describe these as two competing symbolic forms, that does not mean that they are somehow hermetically sealed off from each other, both in our actual experience and in the explanations and public justifications of events. We can appreciate the politically effective character of Chief Justice Earl Warren's leadership of the Supreme Court—and of the Court itself at times—just as we can admire the political actor who defends a rule of law even when it is against his or her self-interest.

In *Law and Love*,[54] I described a more elusive competitor with the symbolic form of law's rule: the world of love, in which law itself is identified with the fallen condition of mankind. Within this cultural form, the highest values realized in our mutual engagements are those of grace, forgiveness, and mercy. This Christian claim of a love beyond law is also an inescapable part of our imaginative construction of the domain of the political. We imagine the alternative to law's rule to be not just a state of nature in which life is short, nasty, and brutish—the natural world of the social contact theorists. Alongside of that image, we imagine a state of grace that is beyond, not below, law. Political meanings are perceived against this horizon of self-transcendence.

The rule of law appears as both a triumph over nature and a tragedy of our fallen condition. In the midst of the constitutional project, James Madison writes that "if men were angels no government would be necessary."[55] This idea of law as tragedy remains a powerful belief at the heart of the symbolic form of love.[56] This belief is continuous with the early colonial experience of religious exiles seeking to create utopian, Christian communities. American experience, I suspect, remains far more oriented toward religion than that of other Western nations.

Again, the point is not to offer a defense of law's rule but to understand it as a structure of experience. That experience maintains itself against competing possibilities. We always speak of the "rule of law, not men." But the "rule of men, not law" has its own possibilities that we can value over the virtues of law. The competition with law's rule comes from both the experience of revolution as a form of political action and that of love as a form of religious experience.

Each of these symbolic forms is complete within itself; each offers an understanding of the entire world of possible experience. "Complete" here does not mean bounded or conceptually determined. It means only that there is no point at which the symbolic form—for example, the rule of law—confronts an act, event, or actor that is beyond its capacities of cognition. In the same way that there is nothing beyond the reach of an aesthetic, religious, or scientific understanding, there is nothing outside the possible domain of legal and political sensibilities. There is nothing to which law does not extend, nothing to which love does not extend, and nothing that cannot be understood as the beginning of the new rather than the continuation of the old. Most of us are quite good at organizing discrete areas of experience under different cultural forms: we do our religion in church and our aesthetics at the museum.[57] But we also understand the unlimited potential of each form and the ever-present possibility of conflict among them. Aesthetic sensibilities can surface in the laboratory, and love can appear within the courtroom. Most obviously, law's rule can appear as a form of political contest, and political contest can appear as a form of the rule of law. We can find the meaning of a presidential contest, for example, in political action or in its realization of the constitutionally established rule for presidential succession.

In pursuing this claim for completeness of a symbolic form, some may suspect me of returning to the traditional claims for the autonomy of law. But this is a misunderstanding. Indeed, it is a senseless proposition within the structures of experience that I describe. The autonomy of law suggests a kind of objectivity, a form of reasoning in which law alone can—and should—determine outcomes of particular controversies. On my understanding of a symbolic form, however, no outcomes are determined by the form itself. Belief in the rule of law, played out in the deployment of legal categories and the legal imagination, is what unites all sides in a legal controversy. Whatever the outcome of a controversy, it will be formulated as the consequence of law's order. But so, then, would the opposite outcome. If, for example, *Roe*[58] had been reversed in *Casey*,[59] that reversal would have been justified in an opinion celebrating the "recovery" of the rule of law. That recovery would have been no less true than the celebration of stare decisis we find there instead.

David Hume describes a kind of completeness of a symbolic form in his *Essay on Miracles*.[60] His point there is that our commitment to a scientific understanding is such that nothing that happens—however miraculous it may appear—is beyond our commitment to this order of meaning. That which we do not understand, we describe as still an open question—an area for further scientific inquiry, not an appearance of the miraculous. There is no point at which the scientific form of explanation simply ends, no point beyond which we say all else is God's mystery. The same is true from the other side—that is, for those who hold deeply religious beliefs. For example, the problem of the evidence of evolution is, for them, not one that shakes the foundations of faith, but rather a puzzle to be solved within the terms of faith. The rule of law is equally a way of making sense of an entire world of experience. About every controversy, we are sure that there is a legal resolution. There is always an answer. We have this faith before we know what that outcome is; we maintain our faith even after we know the outcome is not what we might have hoped.

Neither the positions of the parties nor the outcomes of the cases can be determined by appeal to these shared understandings alone. To think that it could be otherwise would be like saying that disputes among different Protestant sects can be determined within the autonomy of the religious form. There would be a kind of confusion of levels of explanation here. Of course, each side to the dispute believes that law—or religion—supports their position; each will make their own truth claims. But bracketing belief in all such claims is exactly the first step of self-distancing that I described above as a necessary condition of the form of cultural study that I pursue.

Here, one model for my work has been that of Thomas Kuhn on the history of science.[61] Kuhn engaged in the same sort of neo-Kantian project as the others I mentioned earlier.[62] In *Legitimacy and History*,[63] I took a specifically historical approach to the American belief in self-government under law, tracing the way in which this idea has undergone successive Kuhnian crises, each of which has caused a reimagining of the basic form of the idea of constitutionalism. I do not deny that particular groups will use legal categories to advance their own interests. Just as Kuhn would not deny that the parties engaged in scientific disputes at any particular moment will lay claim to all the truth that is available within the existing categories, so legal disputants will reach for all the truth available within the general understanding of law's rule.[64] In neither science nor law are the results of these particular controversies irrelevant to the changing character of the symbolic form itself.

Although belief in the rule of law is quite independent of the outcome of particular controversies at any given moment, this does not mean that nothing could ever force us to forsake the belief. After all, for many people God did die sometime in the last 200 years. The same thing may be going on with respect to the nation-state—and the rule of law is a way of understanding the meaning of the nation-state. The globalization of legal rules through the development of international law may be a good thing, but it is a profound mistake to believe that the emerging culture of a global order of law is simply an enlargement of our traditional culture of law's rule. Most importantly, the new global order of law puts rights, not sovereignty, at its foundation. A cultural study of law's rule warns us not to take any comparisons for granted; it suggests that we will make little progress understanding what is at stake if we look only to the content of legal rules.[65]

In truth, religion has operated as more than an analogy in my work. Running throughout my work have been two claims not shared by many of those doing cultural studies of law. First, I have been struck by the way in which the American belief in law's rule is continuous with many large religious themes in the West.[66] There has been a substantial migration of religious conceptions into legal thought.[67] For example, in both the religious and the secular traditions, law is founded on the expression of sovereign will; in both, the rule of law maintains through ordinary time the meaning of the sovereign's revelatory act. The history of the nation for both is understood as the narrative of maintenance of a legal order suspended between these extraordinary moments in which the sovereign reveals itself. The rule of law constitutes one historical community—religious or secular—even as generations, concerns, and material interests shift.[68] I have traced this intertwining of our most basic religious narratives with our "secular" conception of ourselves as a people living under a rule of law that we have given to ourselves.

Second, I have also suggested that it is not just the forms of the imagination that migrate from the religious to the political; the locus of ultimate concern does as well. An ultimate concern provides a life-defining good—one that can make a compelling claim on the self. The issue is not whether such claims are justified, but rather whether they are acknowledged by the subject. The rule of law is a system of beliefs capable of calling forth individual sacrifice on a massive scale. This is the language within which generations of Americans have understood the legitimacy of the claim that the state may make on their own lives. Much in my work has, accordingly, focused on the violence of law.

This concern for law's violence is shared by others in the field of cultural studies, but I have approached it a bit differently. Where others are often interested in the violence done in the name of law to individuals and groups, I am interested in violence as a form of sacrifice.[69] I explore the forms within which individuals understand the possibility of sacrifice as an expression of ultimate commitment. For example, I have written of the relationship between the rule of law and nuclear weapons, trying to understand the imagination of self that makes it possible to see mutual assured destruction as an affirmation of a community of equal citizens under law.[70]

The rule of law is a deadly serious business, calling forth our capacities for sacrifice. Its seriousness differentiates this symbolic form from others—for example, art or science—and places it within a genealogy of ultimate concerns. In modern political cultures, nationalism has absorbed much of our faith in ultimate meanings. American nationalism has been linked to a particular understanding of the rule of law—one in which law is thought to be the imposition of a constitutional order on the people, by the people themselves. Belief in the rule of law draws as much on myth as on reason, on faith as on evidence. I have studied these elements of our faith.

What Is at Stake?

One characteristic of a cultural approach to law is that it positions itself on the line separating internal and external accounts of law.[71] This capacity to participate within a cultural form for the purposes of description and interpretation, yet to suspend belief in its norms, has been critical to my endeavors in two ways: first, in defining the normative attitude of respect characteristic of a cultural study; second, in offering a kind of transcendental proof of individual moral freedom. These two points are related, and in that relationship lies the only kind of normative implications that this cultural study can claim.

If it were not possible to bracket one's normative commitments in the course of the scholarly inquiry, we would have no way of ever escaping the very conceptual forms that we are endeavoring to understand. Without an Archimedean point on which to stand either intellectually or morally, we would be able to say only that the forms of positive analysis are yet another deployment of the available symbolic tools within which we comprehend experience. There would be no point from which we could say that the reflective, analytic stance gives us a better understanding than the nonreflective stance. Recategorization of ordinary experience in the name of truth is not necessarily a more accurate representation. Alchemy, astrology, or reading the signs of divine revelation in the ordinary experience of nature may all be examples of "false sciences." Some people make the same claims against Marxist, neoliberal or feminist forms of analysis—and, indeed, against the prevailing forms of legal analysis.

The only way out of the limitless claims of the hermeneutic circle is self-reflexive. That is, we must be able to take the categories of experience as a subject of reflection even as we deploy them. This does not guarantee their truth, as if we can establish a correspondence with an external reality. We can never get to the thing itself in this sense. It does mean, however, that there is no point of our experience against which we cannot construct a critical space from within which we can examine the structure of that experience. We try to reveal the sense of the subject's world from within, but we take up that task by simultaneously standing without.[72]

The concern with method, as I have pursued it, is a concern with setting forth the analytic conditions of such a critical approach, that is, with establishing the conditions under which this bracketing of normative belief and distancing from conceptual structure can occur. This is a kind of modern counterpart to the Cartesian effort to deploy radical doubt in order to reach a firm foundation from which to rebuild a system of knowledge. Instead, however, of establishing a well-founded order, the end now is simultaneously to grasp contingency and system—again the idea of the historical a priori. The methods of inquiry I have urged have been genealogical and architectural, which together represent this double aspect.

Legal concepts, particularly the large, framing concepts—sovereignty, constitutionalism, the judicial role, or even the rule of law itself—have their own histories. The point of the genealogical inquiry is not simply to show the historically contingent character of our beliefs, but to grasp the way in which these concepts continue to bear remnants of their past. This form of inquiry forces us to see the ways in which we remain bound to the long history of Western structures of belief about claims of ultimate authority, even as we may think of ourselves as citizens of a modern age of reason.

Today, freedom has become embedded in the realization of our own contingency. It is no longer found in the certainty of a moral rule or the fulfillment of desire; neither Kantianism nor utilitarianism offers a model of freedom adequate to modern understandings of the deep contingencies of belief and desire. The self has been irretrievably historicized. This means that the free subject must comprehend both the self and the whole course of history at the same moment. In our knowledge of the physical universe, we have reached just such an awareness. We grasp our own position in time, but we simultaneously see the whole, from the big bang to the final collapse of the sun. We have a god's-eye view of the whole, as a matter not of theological speculation but of scientific knowledge. This awareness is too much for most of us, most of the time. Yet we insist that the only possibility of free thought is to stand apart and force ourselves to contemplate the whole. The same is true of that reduced scale of being that amounts to our position in political life.

Pressing the genealogical inquiry is a way of stepping out of one's own historical moment, that is, of suspending belief long enough to understand the contingency of contemporary beliefs. The order of law is not the product of abstract reason, nor is it the product of an objective reason working itself pure through some sort of evolutionary, historical process. At various moments, claims of both sorts have been put forward as the ground of the reasonableness of law's rule. These claims, however, are made from within the legal order; that is, they are expressions of self-legitimation within legal practice. I have called such internal, legitimating efforts the "auto-theory" of law; they too are objects for cultural study. Without the security of a myth of progress or a belief in the formal logic of law, we comprehend beginning and end while remaining just where we are. In that comprehension, we realize the characteristic freedom of the contemporary period.

While the genealogical approach creates distance by emphasizing historical contingency, the architectural inquiry creates distance by holding up a standard of coherence. This form of inquiry assumes that the rule of law is an entire system of order and that each of its elements rests on a network of meanings constitutive of the whole. Thus we can start at any point—for example, any judicial opinion—and work through it to the whole.

The philosophical rigor of the idea of system again forces on us a kind of Cartesian abstraction from the self. We can always ask whether we can better express the system of related ideas on which each part draws and to which it contributes. The point is not that there is a provable logic to the whole; nor is the point that there is a single position outside the cultural form that gives us a kind of comprehensive view of the whole. The external position is an attitude or an ambition.

A symbolic form is not a formal, logical order; it does not even follow the principle of noncontradiction. The resources of legal reasoning are predominantly analogical. They are quite capable of reaching mutually exclusive answers to a single question. Legal controversy is resolved, in the end, by an assertion of authority, not by agreement on a single interpretation.[73]

An appropriate analogy is to the interpretation of a novel, in which we can ask how each aspect makes sense in light of all the others and how the whole appears from the perspective of each aspect. Even to begin such an interpretive inquiry, we have to be able to imagine a position outside the whole. If we were wholly outside, however, the novel would be a closed book. Conversely, if we were wholly within, we would be limited to the terms and sequence of positions within the plot. We cannot pursue this relationship of part to whole without positioning ourselves simultaneously inside and outside the world created by the novel. The same is true with a cultural form: we are of it and beyond it.

Together, the two approaches make us observers of our historical moment and critics of our own beliefs. Yet it remains our moment and they are our beliefs. We do not find an absolute point of justice or the good; nor do we find the pure voice of the popular sovereign speaking the law. Nevertheless, this critical distance is enough to establish the transcendental conditions that support a claim for moral freedom. Precisely because we can construct this distance from our ordinary ways of knowing and responding, we always stand apart from context. This critical space represents the possibility of surprise. We imagine that we can act differently, that we can come to a new insight about the world or ourselves. We imagine and are entitled to imagine that the future is open and that it is open to us. We do not know where the inquiry will lead us theoretically or practically.

The freedom that is the condition of this inquiry is both negative and positive. Negative, because one must withdraw from one's commitments, at least temporarily. But positive as well, because the very act of interrogating one's beliefs implies the existence of some measure beyond those beliefs. No cultural form is immune from the inquiry that begins with the Socratic elenchus: are the practices and beliefs supported by that form justified on examination? Thus, we have some idea of a substantive norm that founds the free inquiry. The negative space of critical inquiry does not overwhelm us, leaving us with nothing to say and nowhere to go. We do not fall into an abyss of silence. Rather, the negative freedom of inquiry establishes a discourse in which we inevitably feel that we are approaching an ultimate good. We know there is an end—a telos—to our discourse, even as we acknowledge that we may never reach that end.

The capacity to ask the Socratic question is an affirmation of a freedom necessary to the human condition: We are never so bound by culture, historical circumstance, or social practices and beliefs that we cannot establish a critical distance from our ordinary selves. We cannot help but believe that we are free agents precisely because of this capacity for normative and intellectual bracketing. Nor can we help but believe that this capacity exists in others. This belief is the foundation of a recognition of the possibility of a free discourse with every other subject. The openness of both participants in such a discourse to surprise at the outcome of this mutual engagement expresses this experience of freedom.[74] Knowing what we do of ourselves, and of how we have come to be ourselves, we cannot help but believe that we might be moved by others. Historicized and historicizing, we become aware of our own contingency. Recognizing that contingency, we are free to recognize others as equal participants in a common discursive endeavor.

Just at this point, the cultural study of law's rule—or any other symbolic form—crosses from positive to normative. It is another version of the oldest form of proof of the good that we have, for it states the conditions of belief in the Platonic forms. It is what Kant called a transcendental proof and what Charles Taylor has referred to as the "best account" of our moral experience.[75] It is that form of an account without which we cannot make sense of the experience of ourselves as simultaneously a part of and apart from the world within which we find ourselves. We cannot help but acknowledge the possibility of free inquiry and freedom of the will, even if we do not always put a positive value on that possibility.

Liberal political philosophers believe that we can construct a political order out of this experience of a kind of transcendental freedom. The "original position" is a metaphor for this capacity to bracket all of one's commitments, to divide the self and become the critical observer. I, on the other hand, take the Socratic view that the experience of this freedom is an end toward which we always have to work from within a cultural practice. This critical capacity is a transcendental condition of inquiry; it serves as a kind of regulative idea. It is not a substantive position that we can obtain or from which we can build a political order.

The freedom at issue here is moral, not political. It exists only as a possibility within a critical inquiry. That inquiry will take a discursive form whether or not the interlocutor is the self or an other. The discursive experience of freedom can never be institutionalized in a political form because it can give no ground to any authoritative voice or hierarchical position. It always unsettles our commitments. In this respect, a neo-Kantian study of symbolic forms produces a kind of super-liberalism beyond even that imagined by Roberto Unger.[76] Where I see an ultimate incommensurability between the political and the moral, his super-liberalism remains a political project.[77]

Not just liberal philosophers, but all who take the reform of law as the limit of their ambition remain bound to a political conception of freedom. Even the best of legal orders is an inadequate field for this experience of a radical freedom. We cannot escape the burden of trying to reform the law, but we should not mistake that end for a complete account of freedom. Critical inquiry is a philosophical practice commensurate with the idea of a free self that is never exhausted within the conditions of experience.

In sum, the normative implications of the cultural study of law, as I have described it, have nothing to do with the affirmation of "high culture" against popular culture, or an affirmation of the legal achievements of the dominant interests of the society against the legal experiences of ordinary citizens. The normative implications arise out of the necessary understanding of freedom that lies at the foundation of the possibility of such an inquiry. The different forms of cultural inquiry reflect, therefore, not only different intellectual genealogies—philosophy and social science—but different conceptions of the free character of the subject.

In the end, my critics would bring their inquiry into line with the great reformist ambition of the law: to build a political order commensurate with their vision of truth. It is not an accident, for example, that Sarat and Kearns's book *Law in the Domains of Culture* ends with an essay called "Components of Cultural Justice."[78] There is an inevitable movement from the cultural study of law's power to marginalize, suppress, and exclude to an embrace of the reformist ambitions of liberation politics and the politics of identity. I do not disapprove of that end, but it is not the end at which I aim. In the capacity for critical distance, I find a free self that is always beyond the reach of any symbolic form to exhaust. Beyond politics and law, even beyond language, is a self and an ultimate good that we necessarily affirm each time we take up the Socratic inquiry.

In these competing conceptions of freedom lies the deepest ground for my effort to focus the cultural study of law on the discourse of the bench and the academy. A commitment to anti-elitism threatens to relieve the inquirer of too much responsibility. Some argue that no one but a small elite reads Supreme Court opinions or law review articles; no one hears the self-justifying rhetoric of our high public officials. We must, they claim, look to the popular representations of law's order. Yet when we look there, we may not find ourselves. For law professors are participants in the debate among the politically powerful.

We are seriously in and of the law, while television, movies, and popular literature are forms of entertainment that may not engage our deepest beliefs. While we may occasionally find ourselves in local courts, the Supreme Court occupies our own image of the legitimate rule of law. One can too easily end up studying the beliefs of others, which means there is nothing at risk for the self. There is nothing wrong with such an inquiry as a discipline of study. But if the cultural study of law is to be a project of transcendental freedom, rather than another angle on the project of legal reform, then the beliefs exposed must be our own, and the distance created must be within ourselves.

Bringing cultural study into the heartland of the legal academy is a way of putting the self at risk. Here, I agree with the critical legal studies movement. In the end, I fear they were too often captured by the law professor's ambition for reform, but they did see that the study of law can be a practice of freedom. For me, this is central to the genealogy of my approach, which extends back through Kant to Plato and the origins of Western philosophy. The subject of that inquiry is always the self. Without putting the self at risk, there can be no experience of freedom. Philosophy, even in the form of a cultural study of law, need not justify itself at the bar of politics.

At stake, then, in this competition between social scientists and philosophers over the meaning of the cultural study of law, is a larger vision of the nature of freedom and the possibility that even an inquiry into the rule of law can be more than an intellectual inquiry and more than a plan for reform; it can be a practice of freedom. Philosophy must be a high-risk enterprise, or else it becomes only a continuation of politics under another name.

Notes

1   Marbury v. Madison, 5 U.S. (1 Cranch) 137, 163 (1803).
2   There is no reason to think that the self of constitutional self-government is a unified, single self that appears everywhere the same both here and abroad. Of course, from within constitutional law a hierarchical claim is made—all domestic law is regulated by, and ultimately a product of, the Constitution. That internal claim, however, does not tell us whether the diverse forms of law as they work in the many domains of experience are in fact experienced as subordinate parts of a single order. The more compelling issue today is not the unity of the domestic legal order but the relationship of the constitutional to the international rule of law. See Paul Kahn, "Speaking Law to Power: Popular Sovereignty, Human Rights and the New International Order," 1 *Chi. J. Int'l. L.* 1 (2000). Cf. Richard Posner, "Cultural Studies and the Law," 19 *Raritan*, Fall 1999, at 42.
3   See Austin Sarat, "Redirecting Legal Scholarship in Law Schools," 12 *Yale J.L. and Human.* 129 (2000).
4   See, e.g., Thomas Cooley, *A Treatise on the Constitutional Limitations Which Rest upon the Legislative Power of the States of the American Union* (1868); William Prosser, *Handbook of the Law of Torts* (1941); John Wigmore, *A Treatise on the Anglo-American System of Evidence in Trials of Law* (1923); Samuel Williston, *A Treatise on the Law of Contract* (1920–22). See generally A. W. Brian Simpson, "The Rise and Fall of the Legal Treatise: Legal Principles and the Forms of Legal Literature," 48 *U. Chi. L. Rev.* 632 (1981).
5   See Roberto Mangabeira Unger, *What Should Legal Analysis Become?* 36–40 (1996) (discussing rationalizing legal analysis).
6   See Brief for the Defendant in error, Mueller v. Oregon, 208 U.S. 412 (1908). See generally Ellie Margolis, "Beyond Brandeis: Exploring the Uses of Non-legal Materials in Appellate Briefs," 34 *U.S.F. L. Rev.* 197 (2000).
7   See T. Alexander Aleinikoff, "Constitutional Law in the Age of Balancing," 96 *Yale L.J.* 913 (1987).
8   The continuity of the legal order across time is at stake in the conception of reform. Because he emphasizes revolution over reform, Ackerman must locate the continuity of the legal

order in the unity of the acting subject: the people. See Bruce Ackerman, 1 *We the People: Foundations* (1991).

9 See Owen Fiss, "On Objectivity and Interpretation," 34 *Stan. L. Rev.* 739 (1982) (questioning how much epistemic certainty is required to satisfy a demand for objectivity).

10 See Robert Post, "Theories of Constitutional Interpretation," in *Law and the Order of Culture* 27 (1991) (arguing that authority of law "embodies the values of stability, predictability, and reliance which are necessary to the legitimacy of any modern legal system").

11 See, e.g., Jack Rakove, *Original Meanings: Politics and Ideas in the Making of the Constitution* 3–22 (1996); Paul Brest, "The Misconceived Quest for the Original Understanding," 60 *B.U. L. Rev.* 234 (1980); Lawrence Lessig, "Fidelity in Translation," 71 *Tex. L. Rev.* 1165 (1963).

12 See, e.g., Ronald Dworkin, *Law's Empire* 313–54 (1985); William Eskridge, *Dynamic Statutory Interpretation* (1994).

13 Planned Parenthood v. Casey, 505 U.S. 833, 984–85 (1992) (Scalia, J., dissenting).

14 Kimel v. Florida Bd. of Regents, 528 U.S. 62, 65–66 (2000) (Stevens, J., dissenting).

15 Roe v. Wade, 410 U.S. 113 (1973).

16 Seminole Tribe v. Florida, 517 U.S. 44 (1996).

17 This same phenomenon appears in the increasing proliferation of specialized law journals.

18 Alexander Bickel, *The Least Dangerous Branch: The Supreme Court at the Bar of Politics* (1962).

19 Compare Learned Hand, *The Bill of Rights* (1958) (objecting that the Court was becoming a legislative body), with Bickel, supra note 18, (embracing an educational and representational role for the Court); see also Paul Kahn, "The Court, the Community and the Judicial Balance: The Jurisprudence of Justice Powell," 97 *Yale L.J.* 1 (1987).

20 See generally Ronald Dworkin, *Freedom's Law: The Moral Reading of the American Constitution* 1–38 (1996).

21 Early participants in CLS focused on destabilizing—"trashing"—claims of legal knowledge and resisted the reformist ambition. See, e.g., Mark Kelman, "Trashing," 36 *Stan. L. Rev.* 293 (1984). Over time, critical legal scholars too had to answer the question "what should the law be?" Answering the question is a condition of participation in the practice of law.

22 See, e.g., Roberto Mangabeira Unger, *Democracy Realized: The Progressive Alternative* (1998). Duncan Kennedy lists among his current research interests "left wing law and economics," see www.law.harvard.edu/faculty/directory.

23 See Jonathan Simon, "Law after Society," 24 *Law and Soc. Inquiry* 143 (1999).

24 See Jack Balkin, "Ideology as Constraint," 43 *Stan. L. Rev.* 1133, 1137 (1991).

25 See James Tully, *Strange Multiplicity: Constitutionalism in an Age of Diversity* 62–70 (1995) (discussing the seven features of modern constitutionalism).

26 See generally Nixon v. Fitzgerald, 457 U.S. 731, 766–67 (1982) (White, J., dissenting); Clinton v. Jones, 520 US. 681, 697 n.24 (1997) (discussing American rejection of the absolute immunity that is an attribute of the British monarchy).

27 See Charles Collier and Christopher Slobogin, "Terms of Endearment and Articles of Impeachment," 51 *Fla. L. Rev.* 614 (1999).

28 On rereading these lines at the end of November 2000, I noted the repetition of this cycle of

claims and counterclaims in the postelection Florida controversy. See Paul Kahn, "The Call to Law Is a Call to a Faith in Higher Politics," *L.A. Times*, Nov. 24, 2000, at B7.

29 See Paul Kahn, *The Reign of Law: Marbury v. Madison and the Construction of America* (1997).

30 Planned Parenthood v. Casey, 505 U.S. 833, 868 (1992).

31 347 U.S. 463 (1954).

32 60 U.S. 393 (1856).

33 163 U.S. 537 (1896).

34 198 U.S. 45 (1905).

35 Even the political question doctrine represents only a judicial pronouncement that the Constitution has vested a substantial discretion in the political branches. See Louis Henkin, "Is There a Political Question Doctrine?" 85 *Yale L.J.* 597 (1976).

36 See Rick Bragg, "Judge Upholds Plan for Return of Boy to Cuba," *N.Y. Times*, Mar. 22, 2000, at A1 (quoting Luis Felipe Rojas, press secretary for Movimiento Democracia, saying that the "demonstrations had been organized to demand that Elián's case be heard by the courts."). As the Elián crisis continued, a claim on Elián surfaced from an entirely different dimension—a claim that he had deep religious significance, having been saved by God. This is a reminder that law and political action do not exhaust the dimensions of experience. The assertion of the miraculous may be more powerful than law for those who have faith, but it is not a claim toward which those who believe in our civic religion are likely to be sympathetic.

37 This is why overruling precedents is such a difficult subject both in the deliberative processes of the justices, see, e.g., Planned Parenthood v. Casey, 505 U.S. 833, 869 (1992) (O'Connor, Kennedy, and Souter, JJ.), and, as a matter of theory, see, e.g., Kevin Stack, "The Practice of Dissent in the Supreme Court," 105 *Yale L.J.* 2235 (1996).

38 See Paul Kahn, *Legitimacy and History: Self-Government in American Constitutional Theory* (1992); Kahn, supra note 29.

39 See Paul Kahn, "Reason and Will in the Origins of American Constitutionalism," 98 *Yale L.J.* 449 (1989).

40 See Walter Benjamin, "Theses on the Philosophy of History," in *Illuminations* 253, 256 (Hannah Arendt ed. and Harry Zohn trans., 1969) ("There is no document of civilization which is not at the same time a document of barbarism.").

41 Jefferson, in his first inaugural address, spoke of this: "I believe this . . . the strongest Government on Earth. I believe it the only one where every man, at the call of law, would fly to the standard of the law, and would meet invasions of the public order as his own personal concern." Thomas Jefferson, "First Inaugural Address," reprinted in 1 *Documents of American History* 187 (Henry Steele Commager ed., 1973).

42 Consider, in this regard, the struggle of the European Union states to unify foreign and defense policies and whether the European Union itself would properly be regarded as a state were it to achieve this unity.

43 See Paul Kahn, "Nuclear Weapons and the Rule of Law," 31 *N.Y.U. J. Int'l. L. and Pol.* 349 (1999).

44 In *Legitimacy and History*, Kahn, supra note 38, I take up the issue of legitimacy of constitutional authority. I conclude that the search for legitimacy is necessary, but ultimately

impossible to resolve, because the question of legitimacy takes constitutional thought beyond the capacities of constitutional institutions.

45 See Clifford Geertz, *The Interpretation of Cultures* (1973).

46 See 1–3 Ernst Cassirer, *The Philosophy of Symbolic Forms* (Ralph Manheim trans., 1953–57).

47 See Suzanne Langer, *Philosophy in a New Key* (1951).

48 See Ludwig Wittgenstein, *Philosophical Investigations* (G. E. M. Anscombe trans., 3d ed. 1999).

49 See Michel Foucault, *The Order of Things*, at xxii (1990).

50 See Charles Taylor, *Sources of the Self: The Making of the Modern Identity* (1992).

51 Foucault, supra note 49, at xi.

52 See Cassirer, supra note 46.

53 Kahn, supra note 29.

54 Paul Kahn, *Law and Love: The Trials of King Lear* (2000).

55 *The Federalist* No. 51, at 322 (James Madison) (Clinton Rossiter ed., 1961).

56 It would be interesting to explore President Clinton's invocation of this symbolic form following his confession of sin in the Lewinsky affair.

57 See generally, e.g., Michael Walzer, *Spheres of Justice: A Defense of Pluralism and Equality* (1983) (discussing the normative separation of distinct domains of experience).

58 Roe v. Wade, 410 U.S. 113 (1973).

59 Planned Parenthood v. Casey, 505 U.S. 833 (1992).

60 David Hume, *An Essay on Miracles* (Holyoake 1856).

61 Thomas Kuhn, *The Structure of Scientific Revolutions* (1962).

62 See supra notes 45–49.

63 Kahn, supra note 38.

64 See Richard Fallon, "A Constructivist Coherence Theory of Constitutional Interpretation," 100 *Harv. L. Rev.* 1189 (1987).

65 See Kahn, supra note 2.

66 *The Reign of Law*, supra note 29, explicitly links the internal structure of the symbolic form of law's rule to an Hebraic cultural inheritance; *Law and Love*, supra note 54, turns to the Christian inheritance.

67 See, e.g., Carl Schmitt, *Political Theology* 32 (1916) ("All the pregnant ideas and institutions of modern political thought are in essence secularized forms of theological doctrines and institutions.").

68 The problem of the continuity of the authority of law across generational change is an important point of contact between analytic jurisprudence, see, e.g., H. L. A. Hart, *The Concept of Law* (1961), and cultural studies of law.

69 Robert Cover shared this interest. See Robert Cover, "The Supreme Court, 1982 Term—Foreword: Nomos and Narrative," 97 *Harv. L. Rev.* 4 (1983); Robert Cover, "Violence and the Word," 95 *Yale L.J.* 160 (1986).

70 See Kahn, supra note 43.

71 See supra notes 1–23 and accompanying text.

72 See S. Lukes, "Moral Diversity and Relativism," 29 *J. Phil. Educ.* 173 (1995).

73 See Paul Kahn, "Interpretation and Authority in State Constitutionalism," 106 *Harv. L. Rev.* 1147 (1993).

74 See Hans Gadamer, *Truth and Method* 379 (J. Weinsheimer and D. Marshall trans., Crossroad 2d ed. 1989) (discussing the "fusion of horizons").

75 Taylor, supra note 50, at 58.

76 Roberto Mangabeira Unger, *The Critical Legal Studies Movement* 41 (1986).

77 See Paul Kahn, "Democracy and Philosophy," in *Deliberative Democracy and Human Rights* 247 (Hongju Koh and Ronald C. Slye eds., 1999).

78 Andrew Ross, "Components of Cultural Justice," in *Law in the Domains of Culture* 203 (Austin Sarat and Thomas R. Kearns eds., 1998).

II Deploying Law and Legal Ideas in Culture and Society

Ethnography and Democracy: Texts and Contexts in the United States in the 1990s

Carol J. Greenhouse

In some respects, the decade of the 1990s was an anachronism even in its own times. The crossed preoccupations with "posts" (postmodern, postcolonial, postindustrial, post-Marxist, among others) and "precedents" (the impending millennium) made it paradoxically easy to miss the moment. The debates over constructionist and interpretivist approaches to ethnography and the cultural analysis of texts make a case in point. Such theories gained widespread acceptance in the humanities and social sciences in the 1980s and 1990s (if always as counter-canons), but they never worked free of the persistent criticism that they lack attention to power. What and where is this "lack"? In this essay, I will suggest that it is not in the method but in the context of inquiry—the public sphere—as the civil rights era yields to neoliberalism and as the lines of confrontation take shape as both partisan divisions and competition among the branches within the federal government. Advocates and critics of constructionism and interpretivism alike take for granted these pragmatic circumstances; however, a reflexive analysis of interpretivism reveals assumptions about realism and readership (among other things) specific to the politics of this time and place. Interpretivism's power for projects of cultural critique is a power of association with the textual genres, tropes, and institutional practices of legal activism and citizens' movements of the previous generation—the civil rights era of the 1950s and 1960s. This remains part of their power, but in the places in the United States where ethnographers work, the law has moved on, and its power is recognizable in interpretative ethnography primarily in traces of that association, which are evident as nostalgia, irony, and allegory, among other things.

The 1990s are an ideal context in which to explore such issues, because the new proximity of cultural studies and legal studies brings these very questions to the fore, highlighting recent transformations of the state from standpoints afforded by the emergence of new forms of difference. In this essay, I concentrate on the horizons where the "crisis of representation"[1] implies a commitment to both social portraiture and democratic aspiration—indeed, it is political struggle that defines key stakes in social portraiture. My artifacts are texts of the 1990s from the three genres that give primary attention to "representation" in this double sense (the semiotics and politics of representation): ethnography, literature, and law. I explore these for their respective constructionist strategies and their mutual points of contact and strain. I focus especially on their literariness in relation to each other; indeed, my main interpretive claim is that these genres' literariness defines them as democratic practices in specific ways. Along this critical horizon in the United States, cultural studies and legal studies are adjacent practices specific to the context of their creation. This means that part of the ethnographic value of textual interpretation lies in the way it affords access to political and social contests in which the state is implicated as agent, addressee, or arena. Correspondingly, part of the value of contemporary ethnography is in its implicit demarcation of a relationship between social description (and its textual forms) and the limits of social inclusion.

The exchanges between cultural studies and legal studies over the last ten years or so are not merely an example of promising dialogues that have emerged between disciplines on some neutral ground, but evidence from the heart of the matter. The matter is social justice. In key respects, the cultural analysis of texts is predicated on a tacit critique of liberalism's limits, especially in the neoliberal context emerging in the 1990s. This can be seen most vividly, I will argue, in contexts where neoliberalism defeats the legislative expansion of rights by rendering its poetics moot. In the United States of the 1990s, as key elements of liberalism and its critique faded away (or were pushed away) from the legislative arena, they became objects of interdisciplinary dialogue and debate. Academics called for attention to text and narrative precisely at the junctures where mainstream political discourse foreclosed an older justice discourse anchored in the common sense notions of relief.[2]

State nationalism entails a classic story line: a "nationalist historicism that assumes that there is a moment when the differential temporalities of cultural histories coalesce in an immediately readable present."[3] That story line is partially endorsed by the classic conventions of human sciences and is partially an object of their critique. The conventions presuppose that collective identities are large-scale projections of individual affinity and character; that law is an expression of identity and a resource of socialization; that identities might become a fixed, coherent set of choices and standards over time. Such assumptions—"the dream of a unified field," to borrow poet Jorie Graham's phrase[4]—are deeply inscribed in liberal thought and its social science extensions, offering a certain (sometimes inspiring, sometimes chilling) poetics of democratic aspiration. Scholars who are critical of this vision elaborate the incommensurability of collective identities, the difference between self-identity and identification by others, and the place of law in fragmenting horizons of identification and consolidating collective interests as identifications. Such critics explore the mythical status of the nation itself, as well as the ways in which that myth supports patterns of exclusion, marginality, and invisibility. They propose the possibility that "culture" might be both a categorical displacement of politics and an affirmation of the possibility of solidarity and innovation.

These two formulations of the constitution of individual and collective identities in the nation are not mutually exclusive; they are different registers in the analysis of the United States as a diasporic site in which the (so-called) national culture monopolizes the terms of identification but not their significance.[5] Lisa Lowe writes: "Culture is the terrain through which the individual speaks itself as a member of the contemporary national collectivity, but culture is also a mediation of history, the site through which the past returns and is remembered, however fragmented, imperfect, or disavowed. Through that remembering—that recomposition—new forms of subjectivity and community are thought and signified."[6]

Constructivism and interpretivism are emergent from the fault lines between liberal and conservative approaches to equality and social justice, but it is important to note from the outset that these approaches need not inevitably belong to either side of the debate. For classic liberals, constructivism lends itself to pluralism, individual choice, and a methodology of color blindness, as solidarity is deconstructed to expose individual interests and choices. For conservatives, though, constructivism exposes key social categories and mainstream claims (race, for example) as empirically falsifiable. Both groups (and these binary categories are purely heuristic, as is perhaps already clear) regard identity as originating in antagonisms and displacements within the nation. This in itself is problematic, as Nikhil Pal Singh makes clear: "If we are ever to consider going beyond multiculturalism, we must first assess in a more thoroughgoing manner just what it has actually meant in recent history (and what it might mean in the future) to rely upon the U.S. nation-state *as a stable container of social antagonisms, and as the necessary horizon of our hopes for justice.*"[7] Or, to borrow Joan Scott's cautionary phrase on a related point: "It is not a happy pluralism that we ought to invoke."[8] Indeed, it is not: constructivism instead commits one to an ethnographic project of considering the fields of encounter where the term "identity" answers a question of political subjectivity. Such encounters are likely to be along lines that are uneven, fragmentary, and sometimes obscure. We should not invoke a "happy pluralism" because, as we shall see, the state, the nation, citizenship, and culture constitute different discursive topographies of possibility and contestation, not a unified field internally differentiated by sector or scale.

In the 1990s, ethnography, literature, and law were most alike in their attention to inequality and their common commitment to antiracism, but they differed in other key respects: their analysis of difference and the potential agencies of justice, the limits of law, and the place of the United States in a transnational order, among others. These differences give me my main themes. In the realm of fiction, I focus on works by authors of the 1990s who write explicitly about racism.[9] Such works have been a flourishing segment of the U.S. fiction market, in terms of the range of books (many by new authors), their critical acclaim, and their sales. There has also been a surge in publication of ethnographic accounts of American experience, particularly in inner city areas characterized by ethnic and racial diversity and, in general, sustained poverty. My legal text is the Americans with Disabilities Act of 1989 (ADA),[10] a harbinger of the contents of and contests over both the failed Civil Rights Act of 1990[11] and the Civil Rights Act of 1991.[12]

The rest of my discussion is in four main parts. The first part poses the central question of the essay (regarding the historical and political specificity of constructionist approaches to texts) in relation to the ethnography of the United States. I begin there partly because I am an ethnographer, but also because the problems and politics of realism (which constructionism and interpretivism tacitly address) are most clear in this hyper-realistic genre. In the second and third parts of the essay, I focus on narrative and narrative structure, concentrating on a comparison of ethnography and fiction. In the fourth part, I extend that comparison to a detailed discussion of the congressional hearings that led to the ADA. These texts are connected by their respective constructions of federal power. They are divided primarily by their very different expectations of law in practice.

U.S. Ethnography: Background and Prospects for New Beginnings

The ethnography of the United States is a vast literature, but it is strikingly resistant to self-reference as a literature. Knowing how to read such texts cumulatively is never obvious, since how things "add up" across texts implies some correspondence to knowledge of real-life processes "on the ground." In this sense, cumulative reading is itself an ethnographic practice of sorts, and its absence is noteworthy in relation to this genre. In the case of U.S. ethnography, as Hervé Varenne has convincingly argued, cumulative reading founders under the hectoring of constant disruption by anthropologists' ideological attachments to the notion of the United States as a culture of individualists.[13] In practice, the ethnography of the United States is a large collection of isolated works about local communities and institutions, which pays relatively little attention to the translocal dimensions of social life and contains few works of a comparative nature.

The localism in the U.S. ethnographic field is no doubt a hallmark of anthropology's tradition of studying village life, with the American "case" being a somewhat mimetic exercise. But in the context of ethnography's practice within the United States, this localism can also be read as a sign of the times in which it took shape as a genre. Arising in the civil rights era of the 1960s and its immediate aftermath, the localist emphasis of ethnography reflected the Civil Rights Movement's attention to "the local" as the site of customary (discriminatory) practices. But the localism is deceptive—or, rather, it is a localism constructed by federal architects for a national audience.

The community study, not too fashionable in the ethnography of elsewhere nowadays, is still very much in vogue among American anthropological authors who write about the United States.[14] These are studies of place: diaspora and arrival, ethnic neighborhoods, multiracial settings of various kinds. The localism of community tends to emphasize the marginality of communities—obviating critical aspects of context and historical process. By contrast, the ethnography of postmodernity (of institutions and media, for example)—the other major ethnographic register for the United States—tends to personify hegemony, ideology, and discourse in ways that displace questions of agency and, indeed, location in favor of the "new" and the now.

The possibility of bridging this divide tends to be concealed by conventions of scale. Those conventions are based in part on illusions imported into ethnography from the social distances that divide actual people in their everyday encounters: distances that divide institutions from the individuals they serve, governments from citizens, corporations from consumers, and so forth, yielding illusions capable of dividing even two people who are face-to-face. This appearance of incommensurability hints at other ethnographic domains that are not hidden but simply out of the usual range of ethnographers' attention: for example, the employees of large-scale institutions and government. Questions of agency—by which I mean the relevance of individuals' actions—should not be

suspended in the face of such conventions of scale, or in the silences that sometimes give rise to them.

How Does Ethnography Work?

U.S. community studies from the 1990s are books about American cities, neighborhoods in trouble or in ruins. They are stories of social distress, sometimes
extreme distress, as well as of resilience and survival. They are immigrant stories of successes and failures; they are stories of lives hemmed in by racism and
poverty, problematic access to needed resources, intergenerational tensions,
and pervasive uncertainty. They relate gripping human dilemmas, written in
ways that register direct appeals to readers' capacities for empathy and civic
resolve. They emphasize the details of individual situations. The works tend to
be strongly contained by their attention to local detail and the authorizing
details of ethnographic rapport. Their citations to other ethnographic works
(even in the same city) are rare, with the exception of ethnic communities,
whose origins are often reflected in a bibliography through references to studies
of their homelands.

Even while they tend to dissolve the time and space around the study site,
however, community studies in the United States are cast as direct appeals to a
general audience. I will focus on this feature of their narrative structure. In a prologue or an epilogue, or both, the authors invite readers to envision *this* community in some affirmative relation to the society at large. Tolerance, economics,
and democracy are the touchstones of such visions. Bracketed by prefaces and
endings in these terms, the moves from opening to main text and from main text
to closing provide a pair of performances—one from a personal discourse to a
discourse of discipline; the other from discipline to personal hope. These are
performances of conversion, accomplished through the works' narrative structures. The conversion is to *citizenship*: the ethnographer's identification with
readers (prologue or preface), the ethnographer's performance of learning and
liberal tolerance (the main text), the ironically hopeful endings envisioning
democracy's increase (the conclusion, final paragraph, or epilogue).

Since the market for ethnographic writing is not (or not yet) a general market, such narrative stagings would seem to be for the benefit of the anthropological profession or our students. What does it mean, then, that as anthropologists
we address each other as citizens, as if to create for other anthropologists a
mirror of our own craft in the convictions of an imaginary general public?

The answer depends on what kind of act reading is. The community studies

—written to citizens as if they were not anthropologists—invite readers to experience a break between the "real" world (in which anthropological knowledge is true but arcane) and an imagined world in which anthropological knowledge would be valued for its relevance to urgent social problems. Here is an example from the closing paragraphs of Philippe Bourgois's *In Search of Respect*:

> I hope to contribute to our understanding of the fundamental processes and dynamics of oppression in the United States. . . . Highly motivated, ambitious inner-city youths have been attracted to the rapidly expanding, multi-billion-dollar drug economy during the 1980s and 1990s precisely because they believe in Horatio Alger's version of the American Dream. . . .
>
> "Mainstream America" should be able to see itself in the characters presented on these pages and recognize the linkages. The inner city represents the United States' greatest domestic failing, hanging like a Damocles sword over the larger society. . . . From a comparative perspective, and in a historical context, the painful and prolonged self-destruction of people like Primo, Caesar, Candy, and their children is cruel and unnecessary. There is no technocratic solution. Any long-term paths out of the quagmire will have to address the structural and political economic roots, as well as the ideological and cultural roots of social marginalization. The first step out of the impasse, however, requires a fundamental ethical and political reevaluation of basic socioeconomic models and human values.[15]

Bourgois's epilogue, written after a visit back to the neighborhood as the book went to press, takes a cinematic form, listing each character and place, with accompanying notes to bring the action up to date. They are the notes of a nightmare. In the book's closing lines, he goes farther, presenting a moving testimony of his own distress:

> Witnessing [people's situations] during the few weeks that I spent back in El Barrio in the spring and early summer of 1994 made me realize I had lost the defense mechanisms that allow people on the street to "normalize" personal suffering and violence. For example, I still cannot forget the expression of the terrified, helpless eyes of the five-year-old boy who was watching his mother argue with a cocaine dealer at 2:00 a.m. in the stairway of a tenement where Primo and I had taken shelter from a thunder shower on my second night back in the neighborhood. Primo shrugged when I tried to discuss the plight of the child with him. "Yeah, Felipe, I know, I hate seeing that shit too. It's wack."[16]

I draw on Bourgois's text because he makes explicit what is implicit in many similar contemporary ethnographic works about the United States. In the book's double closure, Bourgois specifies two moments of loss. The first is the public one in the conclusion to the monograph: "There is no technocratic solution."[17] The second is the private one in the personal epilogue: "I had lost the defense mechanisms that allow people on the street to 'normalize' violence."[18] And then at the last instant, in a powerful moment of identification with the child, he aligns these as a problem of knowledge that remains his (not Primo's)— and now, ours. His text figuratively positions the reader—or, rather, he makes use of what is inevitably the reader's literal position, holding the book. The lines yield a strong impression of this terrified child, staring back from the page into the reader's eyes. The book's conclusion also has a performative aspect, in that the conclusion is not just in words but also in the arrayed distinctions among silences from which the reader cannot avoid choosing: indifference, numbness, terror, or excessive knowledge. The book ends, then, by encompassing the *reader's* very presence—through this ambiguous silence and the inescapability of choosing—within the scene itself. Asking, "What does this book mean?" becomes the same as asking, "What kind of person am I?"

Bourgois's text is a fine example of the genre, which relies on the structural form of allegory, as defined by Walter Benjamin:

> The immersion of allegory has to clear away the final phantasmagoria of the objective and, left entirely to its own devices, re-discovers itself, not playfully in the earthly world of things, but seriously under the eyes of heaven. And this is the essence of melancholy immersion: that its ultimate objects . . . turn into allegories, and that these allegories fill out and deny the void in which they are represented, just as, ultimately, the intention does not faithfully rest in the contemplation of bones, but faithlessly leaps forward to the idea of resurrection.[19]

I draw on Benjamin to make the point that while Bourgois's study—like other community studies—is intensely local, the allegorical form does the work of evoking "the economy of the whole."[20] The author's formal address to other anthropologists and their students commits these pages to a tacit transnationalism more than its contents and argumentation do.

The narrative structure of Bourgois's book, in other words, announces the social and political aspirations of the work; it situates the political in relation to the social at the point where readers are induced to reinterpret their own silence —inevitably, the silence of reading in solitude—as a field of knowledge and responsibility. These structural dynamics are legible, though, only to the extent that one brings to the book some broader knowledge of its times. The construction of knowledge as *both* moral and political is crucial to the book's ethical charge:[21] The challenge to defend ethnography's relevance in terms of ethical engagement is a tacit reference to a specific political and economic order. Only a knowing reader is capable of accepting this challenge and offering such a defense. Importantly, however, the empirical realm of that reader's reflection is itself placed outside the book, an exterior world constructed in the book's final pages as the domain of failed solutions within the liberal order. Other community studies share this book's allegorical structure, lending them the form of a morality play in which the reader is confronted at the last minute with the possibility that tragedy might be averted if ethnographic knowledge can be redeemed as democracy.[22] I call this structural feature "the democratic envoi"—the happy ending that is the sign that the book should be read *in time*; this, indeed, is the time of the nation.[23] The following examples of democratic envois are drawn from recent ethnographies of New York City:

[1] Thus, immigrants—legal or not—breathe new life into an American dream that has proven elusive to many native-born. The transformation of successful immigrant groups into "model minorities" goads Americans in general, and less successful minority groups in particular, into believing, much as immigrants do, that success is more the product of individuals' hard work and sacrifice than of differences in their levels of education and economic resources. Imported rugged individualists and American dreamers, immigrants buttress the foundational ideology, the primal myths of Americana. In sum, though they are often accused of alien beliefs and practices, they fundamentally contribute to the nation's cultural reproduction.[24]

[2] Since they are saving less money for the future and the return home, their original monetary goal remains illusive, and they stay on in the host country for another year and yet another. As more and more immigrants go through this process, a community of sojourners is transformed into a community of settlers.

This scenario will likely hold for Brazilians as they become a permanent ingredient in New York's vibrant ethnic medley. Having been sojourners, many will turn settlers. They will become true transnationals. They will continue to live in the United States, but they will not abandon Brazil; they will not stop thinking of themselves as Brazilians or stop going home on visits to see family and friends; they may even retire in their native land. But like so many immigrants to these shores before them, Brazilians will see their lives and future as intimately tied to the fortunes and future of their adopted home.[25]

[3] Small business activities today are a symbol, perhaps the *key* symbol, of Korean American identity and success. But today, some Korean immigrants are considering the warning from the overconfident rabbit in the race with the turtle. They find it necessary to reassess the Korean American dream. As they experience life in America, Korean Americans create new identities, new cultural forms, and new ideologies. Ultimately, through these acts of creation, they reshape American dreams.[26]

[4] With the tense racial and ethnic climate in the United States today, the slogan "a second Chinatown" might well cause non-Chinese to fear that the Chinese are "taking over" and produce resentment. Anti-Chinese feeling has indeed been expressed in recent years as more and more Chinese and Asians have migrated to Queens. But no part of Queens is a second or third Chinatown. Queens is a *world town* for those people who come from many parts of the world to contribute, like the Chinese, their talents and strengths to make this diverse community more prosperous, more beautiful, and more peaceful.[27]

[5] Nothing is impossible if we believe that people can change.[28]

Such patterned flourishes establish a break just inside the books' back covers between the present (the manifest subject of the monograph) and the future. Ethnographic narrative structure projects concern for the future both in the organization of the ethnographic substance and (more especially) in the sharply drawn juxtaposition between the book's contents and the fantasy version of its reception. (By "fantasy," I do not intend a dismissal; I mean an indication of how ambiguous power gaps among authors and readers are incorporated into the text via substitution, as a time gap.) Prologues are less patterned (and less concise), but they stage similar demonstrations of ethnographic discipline as personal narratives of the circumstances of field research give way to the scientific discourse of the main texts.

By methods such as these, the narrative structure of the monographs is organized around intention and disappointment in the democratic public sphere, though their substance is oriented elsewhere, generally toward assimilation.[29] Read cumulatively, the refrain is striking: the snares of the American dream and the widening income gap within racial and ethnic communities. But the word "refrain" is not quite right here. In twelve recent books about New York City, for example, the refrain is merely a passing reference in each book; it becomes a refrain only in the context of a cumulative reading.[30] It is only in the repetition of passing references, across New York City and elsewhere, that a window opens onto key developments of the 1980s and 1990s, that a glance can become the time-space of a gaze. The ethnographic problem ultimately emerges from the increasing gap between the rich and the poor; the significant decline in real wages; the resegregation of U.S. cities and suburbs; the feminization of poverty; the criminalization of identity; the expansion of poverty among the full-time employed; the lessened impact of education on personal income prospects; the political imperatives linking welfare to work and immigration to costs; the shift of employment in the major cities from manufacturing into the service sector and into the suburbs; the high rates of uninsured and underinsured in the cities; and the crisis of self-care. These are some of the developments that surface in the spaces within the monographs and (even more obviously) between them, as well as between the ethnographies, fiction, and civil rights law.

How Do Novels Work?

If ethnography makes for powerful reading, its power is contingent on the knowing reader's ability to break through the monograph's strategies of containment.[31] The narrative structure of the monographs stages the act of reading itself as the precondition of power, in Hannah Arendt's sense of this word: "Power is actualized only where word and deed have not parted company, where words are not empty and deeds not brutal, where words are not used to veil intentions but to disclose realities, and deeds are not used to violate and destroy but to establish relations and create new realities."[32]

Fiction's "essential gesture"[33] involves a different critique and a different formulation of critical agency. In comparison with the ethnographic literature, the novels of the 1990s are striking, first, for their abandonment of the optimism of the civil rights era and, more generally, "the ethnic success story."[34] The novels contemplate tragedy—or realize tragedy fully. Furthermore, the novels complicate difference by entwining color, ethnicity, class, and gender in ways that defy any singular set of identity categories; the community studies—which include narratives of rapport—highlight the bonds and barriers of gender, age, race, and ethnicity, and, to some extent, class. Novelists do not segregate their neighborhoods; they portray them as numerous "others," all unequally unequal.

Against the intentions of their authors, I believe, conventional modes of anthropological presentation tend to reinforce an essentialist view of difference —for example, by equating discrimination with identity, concentrating on the distinctive character of "ethnic" neighborhoods, and treating assimilation as culture loss. Further, in the ethnographic texts, color and/or national origin are treated as primary markers that define individuals within "their" groups, locally and temporally. The novels, on the other hand, often connect current American experience to other geographies and histories.

Ethnographies are organized by social field, their narrative breaks reserved for the transit to and from the monograph proper, just inside the preface or epilogue. Fiction offers abundant heteroglossia and narrative breaks. Shifting points of view, the interior presence of the narrator, frequent disjunctions of time and space—these devices clarify the authors' analyses of the unsteady environments of living, as well as their own claims to a place in the transnational circulation of postcolonial novel forms.[35] Individuals are present in the novels, offering figurations of the varied modes of consciousness and the challenges of consciousness: of knowing who one is in others' eyes, of knowing oneself as "simultaneously the subject and object of the socio-historical process."[36] The resolute individualism of the ethnographies provides some access to these kinds of crises, but ethnographers are only beginning to contemplate the possibility that an individual's life might be so fractured as to preclude a first-person rendering of his or her life course, or (for that matter) a steady narrative standpoint for the ethnographer him- or herself.[37]

In one respect, the novels are more optimistic than the monographs, namely, in their consideration of the agentive aspects of knowledge itself. Knowing is not forgetting in the novels, as it sometimes is in the assimilation stories. Still, knowing is not necessarily saving, even in fiction. Where public discourse inserts a hyphen between identities, one refrain in the novels is the image of rending or explosion—"the world cracked open"[38] and "cracks . . . were . . . dark fissures in the globe light of the day,"[39] where the self and the public script break apart from the contending forces of self-knowledge and the image others hold. Another refrain is the figuration of the narrator as an author: the imaginary author presents narrative as confirmation of survival or (in more technical terms) confirmation of the limits of representation.

This is the context in which first-person narration is especially interesting —since it *performs* this critique. The critical burden of narrative performance in antiracist fiction evokes the prose experiments of Fanon[40] and Du Bois,[41] who explicitly associate the necessity of first-person narrative with the limits of liberalism and the condition of double consciousness. In their work, the techniques of realism and the critique of the limits of public discourse converge in an evocation of law's absence and (consequently) the imperative of *self*-representation.[42] In modern fiction, too, the absence of law is sometimes specifically figured: as a presence (for example, as the policeman who will not be called or the teacher who accuses unjustly); or in the form of the slave-hunter, marauders, or borders; or as an injury or a broken desire—physical and spiritual woundings, poverty, the beloved (a child, lover, or parent) who is missing, or cries for justice that go unanswered. In these figurations of law's absence, first-person narration is constructed as the law's textual Other.

As in the monographs, it is beside the point to ask what specific law has gone awry or what injury hurts the most. At the same time, the rejection of law is not a rejection of the social or of hope. The narrative structure and substance hold certain aspects of the social to one side, offering these back to the reader at critical moments. For example, in novels with first-person narration the narrator's voice tends to monopolize the place of dialogue, displacing other representations of direct speech. Such dialogue between the fictional narrator and the (real) reader underscores the instability of "the real." The reader, listening in silence, receives this testimony and in so doing enters into a compact of trust that is inherently also a (fictional? real?) position of power, freedom, and responsibility.

The ambiguity of this position is, I think, crucial to the agency that fiction offers readers. Writing, presented as a representation of narrative in a context of transference that is private and (in effect) uninterrupted, situates reading within a question of countertransference—that is, stipulating reading as a function of readers' ability to respond from their personal capacity for identification and responsibility. Inescapably, this means setting aside any question of identity cast in racial, gendered, or other singular terms, at least as *the first* question. In this way, fiction makes the categories of identity within the contemporary state disappear—however momentarily—to yield place to the problem of knowledge and the capacity for love.[43]

The conclusion of Toni Morrison's *Jazz* invites countertransference; the first person narrator is the book itself—a speaking book that (who?) fuses writing and reading.[44] The narrator (the book "itself") wistfully evokes a couple's "public love" and then says:

> I envy them their public love. I myself have only known it in secret, shared it in secret and longed, aw longed to show it—to be able to say out loud what they have no need to say at all: *That I have loved only you, surrendered my*

*whole self reckless to you and nobody else. That I want you to love me
back and show it to me. That I love the way you hold me, how close you let
me be to you. I like your fingers on and on, lifting, turning. I have watched
your face for a long time now, and missed your eyes when you went away
from me. Talking to you and hearing you answer—that's the kick.*

But I can't say that aloud; I can't tell anyone that I have been waiting for
this all my life and that being chosen to wait is the reason I can. If I were
able I'd say it. Say make me, remake me. You are free to do it and I am free to
let you because look, look. Look where your hands are. Now."[45]

Indeed, this very gesture (the demand for the reader's agency from within
the narrative itself) *is*, in a sense, the novel's work. By this gesture, the fictional
work displaces the very notion of singular identity—such as constitutes the
federal menu of categories of race, ethnicity, gender, and sexual orientation—
from the agentive realm. The identification fiction invites a reader to make
with a speaking or writing subject does not await a sequel; it is its own transformative work. It does not directly empower the reader; in this, it is like ethnography. In contrast to ethnography, though, it gives the reader an experience of
according agency to another by the fact of the reader's attentiveness. It does not
matter that the other is fictional, so long as the end of the book is not the end of
the matter. The act of reading is real, just as the analyses that inform the stories
are real, and the knowledge that makes the stories matter is real, too. The
agency of identification goes beyond comforting and understanding another
person; it is an end in itself. But here, as in the ethnography, consciousness
implies awareness of an actual sociolegal order. Fiction is not before or after the
law, but perhaps in its fissures, or in its unsteady margins.

Law's Silence

U.S. ethnography, fiction, and civil rights law are easily distinguished by their
different sites of production and modes of circulation. While all three offer
important critiques of racism, they do so with distinctly different substantive
visions of antiracism. At the risk of oversimplifying, one could say that fiction
offers a progressive vision anchored in expressive community; that civil rights
law—in the 1990s—offers a conservative vision anchored in the market; and
that ethnography, for the most part, offers a centrist vision, firmly rooted in a
liberal pluralist endorsement of diversity and its democratic potential. There is
more to say about their substance, of course; I have emphasized the issue of

narrative structure because it is at the level of structure that their differences can be put into dialogue most efficiently. That would be a dialogue about federal power, inequality, racism, and poverty, among other things. To reach this conversation from the ethnographies, we considered where and how the works' narrative structure is predicated on the wider context of the contemporary urban milieu. To reach it from the fiction, we considered the way authors—again, through narrative structure—choreograph specific displacements of federal policy discourse and key terms of public debate with a vindication of mutual recognition and self-expression in the public sphere.

Let us turn now to the public sphere of law, in the specific circumstances of the times. In 1989, a liberal Congress was pitched for a partisan contest with the conservative administration. Partisan divisions within the Congress ran deep. The last years of the Reagan administration had seen the Iran-Contra hearings and the defeat of the Bork nomination. The controversy over the Bork nomination illuminated the centrality of the judiciary in the field of partisan division during the Reagan years. But the confirmation process was not the only lightning rod for partisan politics within the federal government. Those partisan divisions were also, importantly, divisions among the branches of government, specifically over the expansion or containment of civil rights legislation. The contests took the form of debates over costs and profitability for American business in an increasingly transnational (global) economic order. My last example involves such a debate.

In 1990, Edward Kennedy, as chair of the Senate Committee on Labor and Human Resources, opened hearings by announcing a project of reclaiming for the Congress a civil rights agenda that had been led off course (he claimed) by a conservative Supreme Court: "When the Court misinterprets the legislative intent of Congress, Congress can correct the mistake by enacting a new law. And that is what we intend to do."[46] But that is precisely what they failed to do.

Although the would-be Civil Rights Act of 1990 was vetoed by President Bush,[47] it suggests what was at stake in the hearings over a slightly earlier bill— the Americans with Disabilities Act of 1989 (ADA)[48]—which passed with bipartisan and administration support. The proposed safeguards for people with physical and mental disabilities were already guaranteed in forty-five out of the fifty states; it had numerous cosponsors from both sides of the aisle. Perhaps this made the ADA a useful context for rehearsing the arguments for a broader renewal of the civil rights agenda in the affirmative action context.

Like the proponents of the later Civil Rights Act of 1990, the proponents of the ADA invoked the Civil Rights Act of 1964 as their refrain.[49] Indeed, the hearings on the ADA began on the twenty-fifth anniversary of the passage of Civil Rights Act of 1964, to the day. The invocations of the earlier law were broadly celebratory—notwithstanding the awkwardness of the constructed parallels between "race" and "disability." Congressman John Moakley's statement is an example: "As you know, Mr. Chairman, the Civil Rights Act of 1964 prohibits employment discrimination on the basis of race, color, religion, sex, or national origin, but provides no protection for disabled workers. Handicapped individuals share a host of deprivations very similar to deprivations directed toward minority groups which are now protected under the CRA. *Realizing the parallels between disabled individuals and minority groups, I strongly believe that the best way to combat flagrant discrimination is through a remedy which has proven successful in the past, the Civil Rights Act of 1964.*"[50]

Advocates of the ADA presented their support in terms of a range of identifications with specific experiences of disease and disability, with other groups who had historically experienced discrimination, such as Jews, and with universal problems such as old age. These opening statements in support of the bill were rhetorically keyed to other minority groups or to women. For example, Senator Tom Harkin said, "Today under our Nation's civil rights laws, an employer can no longer say to a prospective employee, 'I will not hire you because of the color of your skin, or because you are a woman, or because you are Jewish.'"[51] In some cases, these associations involved intertextual allusions to the slogans of other social movements, for example, Senator James Jeffords's invocation of "one simple right, the right to control their own lives, to make choices and to choose."[52] Senator Kennedy drew the widest circle:

> I think, as you listen to those who have spoken today, you realize that there probably has not been a family in the country that has not been touched by some form of physical or mental challenge. . . . I bet if you go across this country, there really is not a member of a family or an extended family that has not been touched.
>
> This legislation will become law. . . . There is a movement and it is alive and it is growing. And it should grow.
>
> This legislation will become law. It will become law not because of the people up here, although all of us want it to become law, but because of you all across this Nation, in the small towns and communities, in the plants and factories all across this Nation, that are really challenging this country to ensure that we are basically going to have an even playing field and we are going to eliminate the barriers that keep people out, so that people can become a real part of the American dream.[53]

The allusions to the legislative agenda of 1964–65 were highly literal. For example, Sandra Parrino, chairperson of the National Council on the Handicapped, said in her testimony: "Martin Luther King had a dream. We have a vision. Dr. King dreamed of an America 'where a person is judged not by the color of his skin, but by the content of his character.' ADA's vision is of an America where persons are judged by their abilities and not on the basis of their disabilities; 36 million Americans, our Nation's largest and no longer silent minority."[54] Congressman Tony Coelho later set the figure at 43 million, noting, "That is a tremendous political force."[55]

The Reverend Jesse Jackson, president of the National Rainbow Coalition, spoke in favor of the bill, comparing the rights struggle of people with disabilities to that of the students in Tiananmen Square, and closer to home, the protest against the appointment of a hearing person to the presidency at Gallaudet College earlier that year.[56] Congressman Donald Payne spoke for the bill on behalf of the Congressional Black Caucus—in an eloquent statement also in support of the Civil Rights Act of 1990, which was emerging by then.[57] The many other statements in this vein from congressmen, senators, and witnesses drew explicitly on the making of the Civil Rights Act of 1964, invoking the reality of justice, the urgency of inclusion, the practical benefits—political and economic—of extending full employment rights and other rights to people with disabilities. Those had been the arguments in 1964: here, those principles were marshaled for service in both the ADA and the future Civil Rights Act of 1990.

Principle and pragmatics were compatible lines of argument only so long as these cost issues were beyond question. Advocates minimized costs, balancing them against overall gains to the economy—as civil rights advocates had in 1964. For example, a sympathetic Congressman Matthew Martinez raised the cost issue on the first day of the hearings in the opening question to Congressman Moakley, referring to "hav[ing] heard on several occasions . . . that the cost would be prohibitive to providing access for these handicapped workers."[58] Moakley replied: "Well, actually we wouldn't expect an employer to build a certain type of entranceway to hire one employee in his plant. There might be a little cost of moving a desk from here to there or a machine, to give a certain entrance, but, Mr. Chairman, if you look at the overall picture, there would be one billion dollars more in the economy . . ." And he continued, elaborating the consequent reductions in welfare costs.[59] As in the earlier era's contests over the Civil Rights Act of 1964, the defenders of the ADA argued that (in the words of Congressman Moakley) "[t]he contributions of disabled workers would clearly benefit our economy."[60]

But precedent and principle were repeatedly confronted with cost questions. The rhetorical appeal to 1964 as the promise of universal rights now threatened to make any implementation of this new law seem uncontrollably expensive. Awkwardly, congressmen and witnesses sought to insert some distinctions within their earlier all-inclusive circles of potential beneficiaries. Congressman John LaFalce, chair of the House Committee on Small Business, put it this way: "But there is a difference, is there not, in the type of discrimination? . . . If you are discriminating against a woman or if you are discriminating against a minority, it is usually not going to involve the issue of expense on your part, is it? For some reason or another, you just do not want to deal with women or do not want to deal with minorities. . . . You are talking about the will, and you are talking about the mind really discriminating."[61]

Kenneth Lewis, representing the National Federation of Independent Business, sought to introduce some distinctions: "When I was attempting to study this bill, I was informed there are over 900 different disabilities the bill addresses. We need to have a definite understanding of what type of disabilities that we need expect [sic] provisions made for readily available accommodations."[62] Another witness, Les Frieden, professor of rehabilitation at Baylor College, responded immediately: "Please forgive me as I do not intend to offend anyone, but there are over 900 shades of black and brown, and the law says you cannot discriminate on the basis of color."[63] To this, Congressman Jim Olin interjected:

> I do not know. There are innumerable numbers of different types of disabilities. It would be endless, obviously. They are the same variety as we have people. But nevertheless there are some big categories that you are certainly going to want to be sure are covered such as putting a seat behind a post for a disabled person. Certainly you would not want that done. If that can be defined a little bit better or some kind of limits put on this, I think that you would find the business community much more amenable to trying it out for awhile and see how it works.[64]

Indeed, the expansion of the democratic appeal to identify people with disabilities as "everyone" raised, for some, the specter of endless litigation against businesses. Olin continued: "You do not want to end up in court all of the time. You do not want a great controversy. You want people to work out reasonable solutions."[65] Joseph Dragonette, representing the U.S. Chamber of Commerce, encouraged this line of conversation, drawing a line between productive discussion of pragmatics and lofty talk of rights: "When you start using words like practical, that makes sense. It makes sense to me a lot more than words like undue burden or readily achievable. . . . Now let's specify those things that we can in the bill to make it understandable and workable for business. I mean this is not an opposing kind of thing."[66]

But the problem of fusing promise to practice—that is, of fusing democratic inclusiveness to costs—produced some awkward syntax. While improvised speech, especially under stress, is likely to produce infelicities, my interest in these crumbling sentence structures is in the way the fractures isolated significant key terms and/or stopped phrases short of lending full expression to the idea that equality should be limited by cost considerations—as in this passage from David Pinkus, testifying for a small business interest group:

> You brought up the term *full and equal* and Mr. Frieden talked about the Astrodome. I agree that putting seats behind the posts is not within the spirit of what we are trying to achieve here. But when you say full and equal, this is one of the terms that we feel should be deleted from the bill. Because full and equal to me in relation to the Astrodome would mean that you have to provide all of the seats on the 50-yard line to accommodate wheelchairs. *I mean you can carry some of these terms.*
>
> *Full and equal.* The term full is a pretty broad definition, and it is not really defined. If you leave that up to the courts, some day somebody is going to say that means that every seat in the movie theater needs to accommodate disabled people. I am not sure that is what we are doing, or I am not sure that is what you are looking for either, and we just need to clarify that.[67]

As the democracy rhetoric confronted costs considerations, the fulsome invocations of citizenship and equal rights became more condensed. They crumbled to mere key phrases—especially the phrase "full and equal" drawn from the 1964 act and in play again in this context. For Congressman LaFalce, the cross-pressures arising from the universalistic appeal to democratic inclusion entailed in the 1964 law and the various current special interests yielded this lament (tellingly built on the rhetorical opposition of an able body and disabling legislation):

> I want to assure you that every fiber in my body wants to see passage of a bill. But also, I have had such bad experiences with so many other laws. I do not trust anybody these days. I do not trust other Members of Congress or other committees because they come in and they say, oh, yes, we have thought of all these things, and then all of a sudden it is a law and you say,

my God, I was relying upon you and you did not think about the most simple, basic elementary things. . . .

Sure enough, once the law is being implemented there are a million and one horror stories. Unfortunately, this has more often been the rule than the exception with legislation. . . . People do not want to be opposed to legislation that will deal with discrimination.[68]

Caught between a precedent that was beyond question and a set of challenges on the cost question, LaFalce could only lament the law itself and the lawmaking process (of which he was a part). This scissoring was precisely what scored the Civil Rights Act of 1990 with risk, contributing to its eventual defeat. The ADA, on the other hand, passed. The costs questions were handled with a series of phase-ins, limits on retroactive lawsuits, and adjustments of the requirements to the scale of the business in question.

The broader partisan debate over separation of powers at that time created a context in which democratic universalism could not be answered by the cost question. Instead, it was consumed by the question, leaving the speakers' syntax in a shambles, and the efficacy of legislation itself explicitly in doubt. One can literally (and literarily) hear the rights discourse yield to a market discourse in the following exchange between James Turner, acting assistant attorney general in the U.S. Department of Justice Civil Rights Division, and Congressman Olin:

> Turner: Certainly, Mr. Chairman, there will be costs associated with this law. There are costs associated with not having this law that are at least as expensive. . . . To see wasted human resources is a very significant cost for our country.
>
> Olin: I'm not arguing that point. Excuse me for interrupting you. I am talking about the potential of huge economic consequences and the need for putting some kind of a ceiling on that so we understand to what extent we are going to expect enterprises, public enterprises to respond to situations that they will be faced with.
>
> Turner: I think that is true. The language that you quoted, the full and equal enjoyment of the accommodation or the facility, was drawn out of Title II of the Civil Rights Act of 1964. That has never—
>
> Olin: I think that is a non sequitur all by itself. It is probably impossible to achieve that.
>
> Turner: It may be.
>
> Olin: Even as much as you might try.[69]

In this passage one can hear the production of silence—here, literally cutting off the speech of the witness at critical junctures where he presumably would have defended "full and equal" as necessitating costs. In unfinished statements such as these—and not in the content of the legislation alone—the contradictions between universal equality and the market took form. In the 1960s, equality had been free, in market terms—even efficient—as dual accommodations were merged for an integrated citizenry. In this context, though, the content of the legislation and its costs pulled in different directions, producing (or perhaps extending) the same fault line that makes the shifts of register among the genres so telling—and aligns them with the debate over the limits of federal power.

Authors and speakers in the different genres address the dynamics at the edges of this gap and attempt to cross it in characteristic ways, but the point to emphasize is that the genres themselves can be differentiated in terms of their emergence from and responses to the specific curtailments of liberalism in the 1990s. To address these, congressmen look to the market, novelists look to their readers' capacity for love, and ethnographers appeal to their readers through the allegorical potential of citizenship. Moreover, the gap between the ethnographic genres—divided by their placement of American communities and translocal or "large-scale" institutions under separate rubrics—is also the gap within the other texts to which I have been referring. Indeed, the gap is to be found in the social field itself, as an ambiguous silence in the public sphere—even, as my last example demonstrates, at the sentence level.

Conclusion

The silences within ethnography and between fiction, ethnography, and lawmaking mark the places where—literally and figuratively—sentences begun as affirmations of civil rights cannot be completed in the language of costs. In saying this, I would not wish to be misunderstood as minimizing the pragmatic challenges of delivering equality or other objectives of reform. I acknowledge these, and for that very reason I place neoliberalism at the center of the contemporary need to join cultural studies and sociolegal studies through ethnography. Neoliberalism, in experiential terms, entails both the necessity and impossibility of maintaining a rights discourse that is not at some point vulnerable to questions of costs. This contradictory situation occasions realignments of power and the formation of new coalitions, as well as new social identities.[70] It is also therefore at the center of ethnography's importance—the mode of inquiry par excellence for exploring the performative dimensions of culture that exceed the settled scripts of markets and legislation, among others. Interpretative ethnography is not everywhere shaped by the discourse of the state as I am claiming it (primarily) is in the community studies of the United States; however, its starting point is inevitably a hegemonic order against which ethnography lodges its critical specificity. In the contexts I have discussed in this essay, interpretive ethnography reveals performative and discursive aspects of state power by its own textual practices, even when the state is not its object. Correspondingly, its textual limits trace the horizons where liberalism and citizenship are most sharply contradicted in the conditions of life.

The broad connections I have in mind between ethnography and the state are illustrated by Claude Lévi-Strauss in his essay on "New York in 1941," a reminiscence of the war years.[71] He recalls ethnic performances in the city—storytellers from Central and Eastern Europe, Chinese opera, an Indian in feathered headdress taking notes with a Parker pen in the New York Public Library—as fragile ephemera from a world on the wane:

> Naturally, we sensed that all these relics were being assaulted by a mass culture that was about to crush and bury them—a mass culture that, already far advanced in America, would reach Europe a few decades later. This may be the reason so many aspects of life in New York enthralled us: it set before our eyes a list of recipes thanks to which, in a society each day ever more oppressive and inhuman, the people who find it decidedly intolerable can learn the thousand and one tricks offered, for a few brief moments, by the illusion that one has the power to escape.[72]

Dressing up, dining out, these performances—as presented by Lévi-Strauss—provided ordinary men and women with a chance to enact their own presence (if only as arrival or imminent exit) on a stage of flavors, fabrics, or folklore in the midst of the city, poised on the shore opposite the war. Today, too, under different circumstances, the ethnic palette—in politics, the media, and retailing—veils the distinction between arriving and staying, belonging and alienage, hegemony and resistance.[73] The act of claiming identity is therefore always double-edged, and redactions of identity (whether in speech or literature) are themselves potent technologies of inclusion and exclusion.[74]

Difference conceived in these terms is not automatically a charter for pluralism; nor is the illusion of escape always so neatly contained within the bounds of the retail trade, where it can be fused with and confused for multicultural celebration. For some theorists, the move toward difference is an affirmative political movement, across a space of solidarity and contestation.[75] It politicizes creativity and artistic innovation.[76] Such signs are in wide circulation, linking the circuitries of juncture and disjuncture. Sometimes, difference signifies erotic space[77] or violence and outrage.[78] It can be an object of highly fetishized power (I am thinking of the militias, the Klan, segregationists, and separatists)[79] or the nourishment of vernacular ritual.[80] In some contexts, it is a space of madness[81] or addiction[82]; in others, it is a space for prayer.[83] For all of these, as for Lévi-Strauss, the allusion to escape positions a response to the discursive framework of the nation-state by rendering illusory a reclaiming of significance as a matter of personal physical presence.[84]

Without such associations with personal presence, "difference" would not have theoretical meaning or political resonance. But the empirical significance of difference is not inherent in the presence of *particular* groups "within" the nation. Rather, the discursive framework of citizenship creates the *universal* possibility of difference as a subject position vis-à-vis the state.[85] These two meanings of difference (demography versus subjectivity) may be historically related (as they are in the United States), and they may even unfold simultaneously in their respective or overlapping spheres. But they are very different, both as visions of pluralism and social justice and as theoretical rationales for the human sciences. Lisa Lowe evokes these positions as an ambivalence in relation to the empirical life of the nation:

> Cultural forms are not inherently "political," indeed in the modern nation-state, culture has been traditionally burdened to resolve what the political forms of the state cannot, but the contradictions that produce cultural differences are taken up by oppositional practices that are brought to bear on the political institutions that currently exist. Alternative cultural forms and practices do not offer havens of resolution but are rather often eloquent descriptions of the ways in which the law, labor exploitation, racialization, and gendering work to prohibit alternatives. Some cultural forms succeed in making it possible to live and inhabit alternatives in the encounter with those prohibitions; some permit us to imagine what we have still yet to live.[86]

This brings us back to the texts that are the main subject of this essay. The constitution of "culture" within such ambiguous frameworks of possibility and prohibition is *in itself* a contextualization of the question of representation in the political spaces of the city, nation, and transnation.[87] The breaks between genres (or, more accurately, the breaks that mark them as genres), as well as some of the tensions within the genres, may come to the page as silences (narrative breaks, evasions, or elisions). Such silences do not suspend questions of agency or the possibility of ethnography—any more than the fracture and isolation of urban neighborhoods in the United States or elsewhere in the midst of globalization suspend questions of responsibility or democratic aspiration. To the contrary, the silences reveal something of the impressive discursive compressions at the junctures of personal, local, national, and transnational power. These junctures are very immediate and concrete. As academics, we face them daily, even as readers and writers. Anthropologist Nicholas Dirks articulates the excitement and risk in the present moment: "The epistemological battles we fight are not mere abstract debates but struggles that take on their particular meanings in discrete and different terrains. Culture can be used to critique the West at the same time that it can be deployed to deflect any interrogation of local politics. . . . We are still uncertain about our place as intellectuals, and wherever we position ourselves, we are not completely sure what these places signify in relation to concerns of constituency and representation, let alone the politics of criticism."[88]

My purpose has been to suggest that the histories that produced the contemporary genres and their narrative forms—histories of movements and crosscurrents in struggles for justice—have also produced the present complications to which Dirks refers. My main suggestion in this regard is that authors mobilize identification and agency differently through their texts; this aspect of their work articulates a "crisis of representation" that is more telling than issues of ethnographic authority or verisimilitude of social description. By attending to the relative literariness of our texts, we can pursue such issues and stakes, pushing ethnography farther toward the unsteady core of its necessity. I have considered fiction and law alongside ethnography, not just because we can borrow from our colleagues' creativity and craft to do more with words, but more specifically because key aspects of our craft and theirs are today molded to the shape of silence. That silence implicates federal power in its present state of pressure and torque under conditions of globalization, and makes it a parameter of constructionist ethnography and interpretive approaches to texts.

The experiential horizons of state power—in this case, federal power, past and present—in the subjective and material conditions of ordinary men's and women's lives lend cultural studies its critical force. Interpretivism commits the human sciences to exploring the silent imprint of law's presence and absence for particular groups at particular times in the layeredness of texts and the association of textual practices with various publics. My purpose here has been to name that silence, trace some of its channels along the edges of liberalism, and explicitly connect the interpretivist commitment to commitments of other kinds.

Notes

My thanks to Austin Sarat and Jonathan Simon for their invitation to contemplate the relationship of cultural studies and sociolegal studies in such a hospitable setting, and to colleagues at the Yale Symposium—participants and editors alike. Thanks, too, to student and faculty colleagues whose comments on earlier versions or portions of the essay in seminars at the Ecole des Hautes Etudes en Sciences Sociales (Paris), Indiana, Princeton, and Purdue, as well as at the annual meeting of the American Anthropological Association in Chicago (1999), helped shape the present essay. In those contexts, special thanks to Joëlle Bahloul, Richard Bauman, James Boon, John Bowen, Don Brenneis, Andrew Buckser, Nahum Chandler, Jean Heffer, Robert Ivie, Emily Martin, Phil Parnell, and Lawrence Rosen.

1 George E. Marcus and Michael M. J. Fischer, "A Crisis of Representation in the Human Sciences," in *Anthropology as Cultural Critique: An Experimental Moment in the Human Sciences* 7, 7 (1986).

2 For a discussion of nineteenth- and early-twentieth-century legal liberalism, see Michael Grossberg, "The Politics of Professionalism: The Creation of Legal Aid and the Strains of Political Liberalism in America, 1900–1930," in *Lawyers and the Rise of Western Political Liberalism* 309 (Terrence Halliday and Lucien Karpik eds., 1997).

3 Homi K. Bhabha, "DissemiNation: Time, Narrative and the Margins of the Modern Nation," in *The Location of Culture* 139, 152 (1994).

4 Jorie Graham, "The Dream of the Unified Field," in *The Dream of the Unified Field: Selected Poems, 1974–1994*, at 176 (1995).

5 *See* Avtar Brah, *Cartographies of Diaspora: Contesting Identities* (1996).

6 Lisa Lowe, "The Power of Culture," 1 *J. Asian-Am. Stud.* 5, 19 (1998).

7 Nikhil Pal Singh, "Culture/Wars: Recoding Empire in an Age of Democracy," 50 *Am. Q.* 471, 472 (1988).

8 Jean Wallach Scott, "The Sears Case," in *Gender and the Politics of History* 167, 176 (1988).

9 My selection was from the best-seller and new fiction shelves (including some reissues) in major chain bookstores; my effort was to be comprehensive and current but I make no claims for a systematic sampling. In this essay, I draw especially on the following books: Sandra Cisneros, *The House on Mango Street* (1994); Sandra Cisneros, *Woman Hollering Creek* (1991); Christina Garcia, *Dreaming in Cuban* (1992); Oscar Hijuelos, *Mambo Kings Sing Songs of Love* (1989); Gish Jen, *Typical American* (1991); David Wong Louie, *Pangs of Love* (1991); Jaime Manrique, *Latin Moon in Manhattan* (1992); Paule Marshall, *Praisesong for the Widow* (1983); Paule Marshall, *The Timeless Place, the Chosen People* (1969); Toni Morrison, *Beloved* (1987); Toni Morrison, *The Bluest Eye* (1970); Toni Morrison, *Jazz* (1992) [hereinafter Morrison, *Jazz*]; Darryl Pinckney, *High Cotton* (1992); Leslie Marmon Silko, *Ceremony* (1977); Amy Tan, *The Joy Luck Club* (1989); Amy Tan, *The Kitchen God's Wife* (1991); Alfredo Vea Jr., *La Maravilla* (1993); Alice Walker, *Possessing the Secret of Joy* (1992)

[hereinafter Walker, *Secret of Joy*]; Alice Walker, *Temple of My Familiar* (1989); Sylvia Watanabe, *Talking to the Dead* (1992).

10 42 U.S.C. §§ 12,101–12,213 (Supp. V 1993).

11 Two bills comprised the 1990 anti-discrimination legislation: H.R. 4000, 101st Cong. (1990), and S. 2104, 101st Cong. (1990).

12 Pub. L. No. 102–166, 105 Stat. 1071 (1991) (codified as amended at scattered sections of 2 U.S.C., 29 U.S.C., and 42 U.S.C.).

13 See Hervé Varenne, "Collective Representation in American Anthropological Conversations About Culture: Culture and the Individual," 25 *Current Anthropology* 281 (1984).

14 See, e.g., Micaela di Leonardo, *Exotics at Home: Anthropologists, Others, American Modernity* (1998); Michael Moffatt, "Ethnographic Writing about American Culture," 21 *Ann. Rev. Anthropology* 205 (1992).

15 Philippe Bourgois, *In Search of Respect: Selling Crack in the Barrio* 326–27 (1996).

16 Id. at 337.

17 Id. at 326.

18 Id. at 337

19 Walter Benjamin, *The Origin of German Tragic Drama* 232–33 (John Osborne trans., Verso 1998) (1963).

20 Id. at 234; accord id. at 186.

21 See id. at 230–31 (discussion of the ethical implications of knowledge in the tragic context).

22 Ralph Ellison distinguishes tragedy from the absence of solutions, referring to the latter as the "blues." Ralph Ellison, *Shadow and Act* 94 (1964).

23 See Bhabha, supra note 3, at 139.

24 Sarah Mahler, *American Dreaming: Immigrant Life on the Margins* 233 (1995).

25 Maxine Margolis, *Little Brazil: An Ethnography of Brazilian Immigrants in New York City* 275 (1994).

26 Kyeyoung Park, *The Korean American Dream: Immigrants and Small Business in New York City* 206 (1997).

27 Hsiang-Shui Chen, *Chinatown No More: Taiwan Immigrants in Contemporary New York* 263 (1992).

28 Roger Sanjek, *The Future of Us All: Race and Neighborhood Politics in New York City* 393 (1998).

29 See Bill Ashcroft, Gareth Griffiths, and Helen Tiffin, *The Empire Writes Back: Theory and Practice in Postcolonial Literatures* (1989).

30 In addition to the ethnographic sources cited elsewhere in this essay, the monographs I draw on in this section include Karen McCarthy Brown, *Mama Lola* (1991); Steven Gregory, *Black Corona* (1998); Philip Kasinitz, *Caribbean New York* (1992); Michel Laguerre, *American Odyssey* (1984); Moshe Shokeid, *Children of Circumstances* (1988); Bonnie Urciuoli, *Exposing Prejudice* (1996).

   For further discussion of the impact of neoliberalism and globalization on the social life of New York City, see Janet Abu-Lughod, *New York, Chicago, Los Angeles: America's Global Cities* (1999); Gregory, supra; Sanjek, supra note 28; Steven Gregory, "The Changing Significance of Race and Class in an African-American Community," 19 *Am. Ethnologist* 255 (1992). See generally Scott Lash and John Urry, *Economies of Signs and Space* (1994) (especially Part III). But see Abu-Lughod, supra, at 399 (discussing the risks of overgeneralization, given the extent to which globalization affects cities in ways that appear to be specific to their situations).

31 Drawing on Deleuze and Guattari's question, "How does it work?" Jameson distinguishes between questions of meaning and questions of narrative technology. Fredric Jameson, *The Political Unconscious* 22 (1987) (quoting Gilles Deleuze and Felix Guattari, *Anti-Oedipus* 109 (1977)).

32 Hannah Arendt, *The Human Condition* 200 (1998).

33 Nadine Gordimer, "The Essential Gesture," in *The Essential Gesture: Writing, Politics, and Places* 285 (Stephen Clingham ed., 1989).

34 Phyllis P. Chock, "The Landscape of Enchantment: Redaction in a Theory of Ethnicity," 4 *Cultural Anthropology* 163 (1989).

35 See Ashcroft, Griffths, and Tiffin, supra note 29; Firdous Azim, *The Colonial Rise of the Novel* (1993); Jacqueline Kaye and Abdelhamid Zoubir, *The Ambiguous Compromise: Language, Literature, and National Identity in Algeria and Morocco* (1990).

36 Georg Lukács, *History and Class Consciousness: Studies in Marxist Dialectics* 19 (Rodney Livingstone trans., Merlin Press, 1971). I have borrowed this phrase from Lukács, referring to Marx. Lukács's reference here is to politics, not fiction. The phrase is Lukács's evocation of dialectic, from an experiential standpoint. Most of Lukács's writing concerns novels, and his views on dialectic and history were central to his positions on literary realism. His phrase offers a deft rendering of fluid states of consciousness—by definition elusive for ethnographers; cf. 1 Jean Comaroff and John L. Comaroff, *Of Revelation and Revolution: Christianity, Colonialism, and Consciousness* 27–32 (1991). I draw on his imagery—but not his implication in the argument as a whole that history is unidirectional. For discussion of dialectic and history in ethnographic terms, see 2 Jean Comaroff and John L. Comaroff, *Of Revelation and Revolution: The Dialectics of Modernity on a South African Frontier* 28–29 (1997).

37 E. Valentine Daniel, *Charred Lullabies: Chapters in an Anthropology of Violence* (1996).

38 Walker, *Secret of Joy*, supra note 9, at 281.

39 Morrison, *Jazz*, supra note 9, at 22–23.

40 Frantz Fanon, *Black Skin, White Masks* (Charles Lam Markmann trans., Grove Press 1967) (1952).

41 W. E. B. Du Bois, *The Souls of Black Folk* (Vintage 1990) (1903).

42 To anticipate the next sections of this essay, it is significant that Ashcroft, Griffths and Tiffin, supra note 29, at 185–86, are referring to postcolonial novels when they write: "The central problematic of [postcolonial] studies of writing is *absence* . . . the message 'event' occupies the apparent social fissure between the acts of writing and reading, the discursive space in which writer and readers as social actors never meet."

43 See Bhabha, supra note 3, at 190–91, for Bhabha's differentiation of Arendt's concept of agency, which he considers a repetitive mimesis "reified in the liberal vision of togetherness," from his suggestion that agency is contingent and temporal: "The process of reinscription and negotiation—the insertion or intervention of something that takes on new meaning—happens in the temporal break in-between the sign, deprived of subjectivity, in the realm of the intersubjective. Through this time-lag—the temporal break in representa-

tion—emerges the process of agency both as a historical development and as the narrative agency of historical discourse." Id. at 191. I am suggesting that the ethnography "works" with an Arendtian notion of agency and that the fiction works by suspending the liberal vision of togetherness in favor of a more specific and personal experience of identification.

44 See Toni Morrison, *Playing in the Dark: Whiteness and the Literary Imagination*, at xi–xiii (1992).

45 Morrison, *Jazz*, supra note 9, at 229.

46 *Civil Rights Act: Hearings on S. 2104 before the Comm. on Labor and Human Resources*, 101st Cong. 1 (1990) (statement of Sen. Edward M. Kennedy (Mass.), Chair, Senate Comm. on Labor and Human Resources).

47 See President's Message to the Senate Returning without Approval the Civil Rights Act of 1990, 26 Weekly Comp. Pres. Doc. 1632 (Oct. 22, 1990) (vetoing S. 2104).

48 42 U.S.C. §§ 12,1010–12,213 (Supp. V 1993).

49 *Americans with Disabilities Act: Hearing before the Comm. on Small Business*, 101st Cong. 29 (1989) [hereafter *Hearings on Americans with Disabilities Act*].

50 *Discrimination against Cancer Victims and the Handicapped: Hearings before the House Subcomm. on Employment Opportunities*, 100th Cong., 3 (1987) [hereafter *Hearings on Discrimination*] (statement of Rep. John Moakley (Mass.)) (emphasis added). Congressional documents regarding testimony on the Americans with Disabilities Act are reproduced and compiled in Bernard D. Reams Jr., Peter J. McGovern and Jon S. Schultz, *Disability Law in the United States: A Legislative History of the Americans with Disabilities Act of 1990*, Public Law 101–336 (1992), a six-volume documentary history of the Act. I cite them as separate government documents, since the pagination in Reams, McGovern and Schultz is not consecutive (it instead reproduces the pagination of the originals).

51 *Americans with Disabilities Act: Joint Hearing on S. 2345 before the Subcomm. on the Handicapped of the Comm. of Labor and Human Resources*, 100th Cong. 8 (1988) (statement of Sen. Thomas Harkin (Iowa)).

52 Id. at 20. (statement of Sen. James Jeffords (Vt.)).

53 Id. at 17 (statement of Sen. Edward M. Kennedy (Mass.)).

54 Id. at 27 (statement of Sandra Parrino, chairperson of the Nat'l Council on the Handi-capped).

55 Id. at 36 (statement of Rep. Tony Coelho (Cal.)).

56 Id. at 4 (statement of Rev. Jesse Jackson, president, National Rainbow Coalition).

57 *Hearings on Americans with Disabilities Act*, supra note 49, at 15 (testimony of Rep. Donald Payne (N.J.), Member, Cong. Black Caucus) ("We must again place America on the right side of history with the passage of this omnibus civil rights statute.").

58 *Hearings on Discrimination*, supra note 50, at 5 (statement of Rep. Matthew Martinez (Cal.)).

59 Id. (statement of Rep. Moakley).

60 Id. at 13 (statement of Rep. Moakley).

61 *Hearings on Americans with Disabilities Act*, supra note 49, at 29 (statement of Rep. John LaFalce (N.Y.), chair, House Comm. on Small Business).

62 Id. at 42 (statement of Kenneth Lewis, representing Nat'l Fed'n of Indep. Bus.).

63 Id. (statement of Les Frieden, professor of rehabiliation at Baylor College).

64 Id. (statement of Rep. James Olin (Va.)).

65 Id.

66 Id. at 42–43 (statement of Joseph Dragonette, U.S. Chamber of Commerce).

67 Id. at 43 (statement of David Pinkus) (emphasis added).

68 Id. at 55 (statement of Rep. LaFalce).

69 Id. at 59–60 (statements of Rep. Olin and James Turner).

70 See Abu-Lughod, supra note 30; Gregory, *Black Corona*, supra note 30; Sanjek, supra note 28; Roger Rouse, "Thinking through Transnationalism: Notes on the Cultural Politics of Class Relations in the Contemporary United States," 7 *Pub. Culture* 353 (1995).

71 Claude Lévi-Strauss, "New York in 1941," in *The View from Afar* 258 (Joachim Neugroschel and Phoebe Hoss trans., 1985) (1977).

72 Id. at 261.

73 See Phyllis P. Chock, "The Irony of Stereotypes: Towards an Anthropology of Eccentricity," 1 *Cultural Anthropology* 347 (1991); Bonnie Urciuoli, "Acceptable Difference: The Cultural Evolution of the Model Ethnic American Citizen," in *Ethnography and Democracy: Constructing Identity in Multicultural Liberal States* 178 (Carol Greenhouse ed., 1998).

74 See Elizabeth Mertz, "The Perfidy of Gaze and the Pain of Uncertainty: Anthropological Theory and the Search for Closure," in *Ethnography in Unstable Places* (Carol J. Greenhouse et al. eds., 2002); see also Urciuoli, supra note 73; Hervé Varenne, "Diversity as an American Cultural Category," in *Ethnography and Democracy*, supra note 73, at 27.

75 See Faye Ginsburg, *Contested Lives: The Abortion Debate in the American Community* (1989); Micaela di Leonardo, *Exotics at Home: Anthropologies, Others, American Modernity* (1998); Homi Bhabha, "Anxiety in the Midst of Difference," 21 *Pol. and Legal Anthropology Rev.* 123 (1998).

76 See Paul Gilroy, *The Black Atlantic: Modernity and Double Consciousness* (1993); Kathleen Stewart, *A Space on the Side of the Road: Cultural Poetics in an "Other" America* (1996).

77 See, e.g., Jean Baudrillard, *America* 15 (Chris Turner trans., Verso 1988).

78 See, e.g., Houston Baker, *Black Studies, Rap and the Academy* (1993).

79 See, e.g., Paul Hockenos, *Free to Hate* (1993); Catherine McNicol Stock, *Rural Radicals: Righteous Rage in the American Grain* (1996).

80 See, e.g., Brown, supra note 30.

81 See, e.g., Felix Guattari, *Chaosophy* 80 (S. Lotringer ed., 1995).

82 See, e.g., Bourgois, supra note 15.

83 See, e.g., Carol J. Greenhouse, *Praying for Justice: Faith, Hope and Community in an American Town* (1986).

84 *See* Slavoj Žižek, " 'I Hear You with My Eyes': or The Invisible Master," in *Gaze and Voice as Love Objects* 90 (Renata Salecl and Slavoj Žižek eds., 1996).

85 See Singh, supra note 7.

86 Lowe, supra note 6, at 19.

87 Cf. Brah, supra note 5.

88 Nicholas B. Dirks, "In Near Ruins: Cultural Theory at the End of the Century," in *In Near Ruins: Cultural Theory at the End of the Century* 1, 15 (Nicholas B. Dirks ed., 1998).

Rules of Law, Laws of Science

Wai Chee Dimock

I s there an analogy between the operations of science and the operations of law? Can the former serve as a heuristic ally for the latter? And what difference does it make to cultural studies to ponder the relation between these two? In what follows, I address these questions by focusing on two related concepts, "rules" and "law-abidingness." This focus is, in part, a response to legal realism,[1] to its well-known arguments against "rules of law." Legal realism, seeing itself as an empirical practice, was not convinced that there could be any set of rules, formalized on the grounds of logic, that would have a clear determinative power on the course of legal action or, more narrowly, on the outcome of litigated cases. The decisions made inside the courtroom—the mental processes of judges and juries—are supposedly guided by rules. Realists argued that they are actually guided by a combination of factors, some social and some idiosyncratic, harnessed to no set protocol. They are not subject to the generalizability and predictability that legal rules presuppose.

That very presupposition, realists said, creates a gap, a vexing lack of correspondence, between the language of the law and the world it purports to describe. As a formal system, law operates as a propositional universe made up of highly technical terms—estoppel, surety, laches, due process, and others—accompanied by a set of rules governing their operation. Law is essentially definitional in this sense: it comes into being through the specialized meanings of words. The logical relations between these specialized meanings give it an internal order, a way to classify cases into actionable categories. These categories, because they are definitionally derived, are answerable only to their internal logic, not to the specific features of actual disputes. They capture those specific features only imperfectly, sometimes not at all. They are integral and unassailable, but hollowly so. In the emphatic words of Karl Llewellyn, "Legal rules mean, of themselves, next to nothing. They are verbal formulae, partly conveying a wished-for direction and ideal. But they are, to law students, empty."[2] Felix Cohen was even more blunt. Jurisprudence, as the decisional rules between linguistic entities, "is a special branch of the science of transcendental nonsense."[3]

Of course, as the realists were the first to remind us, transcendental nonsense can wield enormous power in the world. What gives it this power is, in part, a popular conception of law, honoring it for the very thing that makes it nonsensical to the realists. Law, popularly understood, is an adjudicative vehicle generalized and preexisting, a whole cloth already in place in advance of any application to specific cases. Jerome Frank summarized this view as follows:

> Law is a complete body of rules existing from time immemorial and unchangeable except to the limited extent that legislatures have changed the rules by enacted statutes. Legislatures are expressly empowered thus to change the law. But the judges are not to make or change the law but to apply it. The law, ready-made, pre-exists the judicial decisions.[4]

Law, in the minds of most laymen and most lawyers, enjoys a sequential privilege. It is anterior to what it adjudicates. All its necessary provisions are either already there or deducible from what is there. Its logical sweep—its extendability to new contexts as inferences from what is preexisting—means that it can be counted on to cover any potential case that might arise. By virtue of its antecedence, then, law carries within itself a projective guarantee. Its rules can be projected into the future and can be preserved in a continually generalizable (and thus continually reusable) form, not dependent on and not limited to one specific context of application.

Langdell's Legal Science

This popular view of law was certainly irritating to the realists. But a more immediate and more powerful irritant went by the name of the "case method," a pedagogy that, Karl Llewellyn said, was "blind, inept, factory-ridden, wasteful, defective and empty."[5] This offending pedagogy was the brainchild of Christopher Columbus Langdell. Langdell was named the first dean of the Harvard Law School in 1870; he taught his first case-method class that fall.[6] This was soon adopted by law schools nationwide; it became a "classical orthodoxy," dominating legal education for almost a century.[7] In promoting the case method, Langdell had one special goal in mind. Law was to be made into a science—a logical enterprise, a combination of induction and deduction—laying claim to just that generalizability and predictability popularly attributed to it. Like science, law was to proceed, inductively, from observable phenomena to fundamental principles, and back again, deductively now, from these fundamental principles to more observable phenomena.[8] The compilation of cases was not an idle undertaking. It was to be an exercise in logic, based on the assumption that, once these cases were amassed, once they were classified according to the proper legal categories, broad underlying doctrines would be revealed, applicable to all disputes in existence and *in potentia*. Langdell himself was explicit on this point: "Law, considered as a science, consists of certain principles or doctrines. To have such a mastery of these as to be able to apply them with constant facility and certainty to the ever-tangled skein of human affairs, is what constitutes a true lawyer. . . . The growth [of these doctrines] is to be traced in the main through a series of cases; and much the shortest and best, if not the only, way of mastering the doctrine effectively is by studying the cases in which it is embodied."[9]

The study of case law was similar to the collecting of scientific data. In both endeavors, the exercise was meaningful only because the data could be extended by induction and deduction, which is to say, they could be used to uncover something more basic, a conceptual foundation predictive of any individual instance. Sir Frederick Pollock, professor of law at Oxford and an admirer of Langdell's, made this claim even more forcefully.[10] In an essay with a self-explanatory title, *The Science of Case-Law*, Pollock wrote:

> The ultimate object of natural science is to predict events—to say with approximate accuracy what will happen under given conditions. Every special department of science occupies itself with predicting events of a particular kind. . . . The object of legal science, as we understand it, is likewise to predict events. The particular kind of events it seeks to predict are the decisions of courts of justice.[11]

The predictive claim of case law clearly orients it toward the future, but actually this claim is based on a symmetrical claim about past decisions as well: decisions that can be generalized and whose generalizations will hold for all cases to come. At the heart of case law is thus the principle of stare decisis—literally, to stand by things decided—the principle that subjects all new cases to the logical consistency elaborated by precedents. In theory, precedents comprise all past decisions; in practice, what this means is an almost exclusive reliance on appellate opinions, since legal reasoning is the central feature of the upper courts, which rule on the legal merit of lower-court judgments, rather than of the trial courts, which are charged with fact-finding.[12] These appellate opinions provided case law with its raw data as well as its pedagogic method. Armed with these common law precedents, and extending these scientifically with an inductive and deductive logic, "rules of law" would indeed carry a broad power to generalize and predict.

Langdell and his colleagues were not the first to hanker after the logical sweep of a legal "science." Others had also gestured in this direction: Francis Bacon, William Blackstone, the earl of Mansfield, and Joseph Story, to name just a few.[13] Still, no one had been quite as determined. And the impetus for it did not seem to have stemmed from the practice of law itself. As Robert Gordon points out, law in the late nineteenth century benefited from its own inconsistencies. The day-to-day work of the lawyer was tied to the different statutes of different jurisdictions and consisted mostly of mundane things: drafting of charters, leases, mortgages, bond indentures. In such cases, "lawyers were most likely to use litigation as a tactic for harassment or delay, the aim being to avoid any resolution on the merits of the case. Toward that end, the unscientific, haphazard, and heterogeneous nature of unreformed state law and procedure was a positive advantage."[14] Langdell's legal science was not much in demand in the law office. Its ascendancy had more to do with academic politics, with a growing professionalism that was reshaping the structure and aims of American higher education.[15] Langdell saw himself as a much needed reformer, saving legal education from an ossified pedagogy and putting it on a surer and sounder foundation. In a speech given in 1886, on the 250th anniversary of the founding of Harvard College, he explained what this reform meant to law and to its institutional home, the university:

> [It] was indispensable to establish at least two things: first, that law is a science; secondly, that all the available materials of that science are contained in printed books. If law be not a science, a university will best consult its own dignity in declining to teach it. If it be not a science, it is a species of handicraft, and may best be learned by serving an apprenticeship to one who practices it. If it be a science, it will scarcely be disputed that it is one of the greatest and most difficult of sciences, and that it needs all the light that the most enlightened seat of learning can throw upon it. . . . If printed books are the ultimate sources of all legal knowledge; if every student who would obtain any mastery of law as a science must resort to these

ultimate sources. . . . then a university, and a university alone, can furnish every possible facility for teaching and learning law.[16]

What was at stake, in claiming law as a science, was nothing less than the identity of the legal profession: what sort of profession it was going to be, where its training was to be done, how its membership was to be reproduced. As Langdell saw it, there were two alternatives. Either law was to be a craft, reproduced through an apprentice system; or it was to be a branch of learning, in which case it could only be reproduced through books and reproduced at places where books were abundantly collected. Law, Langdell insisted, was the province of the university. It must be organized as an academic discipline; its practitioners must be formally trained, as scientists were. And so "the library is the proper workshop of professors and students alike; it is to us all that the laboratories of the university are to the chemists and physicists, all that the museum of natural history is to the zoologists, all that the botanical garden is to the botanist."[17]

The birth of the modern law school began with an emphatic nod to science as a disciplinary model. At its most ambitious, this legal science called for a sweeping overhaul of the entire edifice of law, a thoroughgoing systematization. This would culminate in 1923 in the founding of the American Law Institute, made up of law professors and prominent members of the bench and bar, to embark on a massive undertaking, a "Restatement of the Law." The Restatement project, at heart a taxonomic dream, was a direct response to a problem that was the bane of stare decisis, namely, the staggering volume and conflicting nature of precedents.[18] As the institute said,

> In the United States, each of the forty-eight states has its own system of courts making law every day. In addition, there are the federal courts. Decisions of these courts are the precedents for future cases. . . . A lawyer working on a case must not only find, read and digest the cases, past and present, of all the courts in his state, but where the proposition he wants to urge is without firm precedent there, he must research the law of all other states and the federal courts. Even after all this work, he may not find a clear-cut authority.[19]

Law was sorely unscientific at the beginning of the twentieth century; the American Law Institute was to rectify that. Its goal was to reconcile as many cases as possible, ironing out contradictions and getting rid of hopeless anomalies, so that case law would indeed be generalizable and would express "as nearly as possible the rules which courts will apply today. These rules govern not only situations which have already arisen in specific cases, but by analogy all rules which would apply in situations which may arise for the first time."[20]

But the generalization of case law had, in some sense, already been taking place for almost half a century. From the 1870s on, as Morton Horwitz points out, "functional categories useful to practicing lawyers" in contract and torts were done away with, replaced by "general concepts that submerged the concrete particularity of the previous organizing schemes."[21] Different branches of contract law, for instance, were reclassified under such broad headings as "offer and acceptance" and "consideration."[22] In torts, the concept of "negligence" was taken from its hitherto narrow meaning—as the failure to perform a specific duty imposed by statute or contract—and broadened instead into a comprehensive rule: the logical antecedent to "fault" and the limiting condition for liability. In this way, negligence and fault were shown to be the foundation of tort law, underwriting the entire field and descriptive of all its actions. This newly minted foundation radically raised the standard of proof for the reward of damages. Common carriers—railroads—were no longer held liable for injuries regardless of fault, as they had once been under strict liability. Instead, a new prerequisite came into play—a demonstration of "negligence"—narrowing the scope of recoverable injuries and, in the same measure, broadening the scope of legal reasoning. Cases such as *Brown v. Collins* and *Losee v. Buchanan* showed how this worked.[23] Torts was indeed a branch of law with an unusual degree of conceptual order. As such, it was the highpoint of legal science, the showcase of its logic.[24] And, by and large, legal science did not venture much beyond torts and other areas of private law.[25] Some, however, have seen it as a shaping force on public law as well, tracing the laissez-faire constitutionalism of the *Lochner* era also to its conceptual universe.[26]

Laboratory versus Library

And yet, for all its rhetoric, the exact connection between this legal "science" and the natural sciences remains an open question. Langdell's scientific knowledge seems to have been quite perfunctory, oblivious not only to the historical challenge of science but also to the new developments taking place in the very century in which he was writing. Forgetting that the rise of modern science had begun with an explicit repudiation of book-learning, a repudiation of a scholastic tradition based on exegesis and syllogism, Langdell saw no tension at all between the laboratory and the library. He turned a blind eye to the long-standing battle between knowledge acquired through empirical observation and knowledge acquired through "printed books." Galileo's *Dialogue on the Great World Systems,* after all, was as much a swipe at Aristotle as it was an astronomical treatise. Aristotle had a champion here: a character not surprisingly named Simplicius. For Simplicius, the ancient philosopher "was the first, only, and admirable explainer of the syllogistic forms of demonstration, of refutation, of the manner of discovering sophisms and paralogisms, and, in short, of all the parts of logic."[27] Another character, Salviatus, is not so sure. It makes no sense, he says, to "be so strictly wedded to every expression of Aristotle as to hold it heresy to disagree with him in anything."[28] Galileo himself was certainly not wedded in this way. Nor was he wedded to the Bible, devout Christian though he was. As he explained to the Grand Duchess Christine:

> In discussions of physical problems we ought to begin not from the authority of scriptural passages, but from sense-experiences and necessary demonstrations. . . . It is necessary for the Bible, in order to be accommodated to the understanding of every man, to speak many things which appear to differ from the absolute truth so far as the bare meaning of the words is concerned. But Nature, on the other hand, is inexorable and immutable; she never transgresses the laws imposed upon her, or cares a whit whether her abstruse reasons and methods of operation are understandable to men. For that reason it appears that nothing physical which sense-experience sets before our eyes, or which necessary demonstrations prove to us, ought to be called in question (much less condemned) upon the testimony of biblical passages.[29]

The Bible is semantically ambiguous, Galileo said. To have a mass appeal, its words have to mean different things to different people. It is fork-tongued by necessity. This is not the case with nature, which, indifferent to its human audience, is much more straightforward, its nonverbal evidence much more trustworthy than the deceptive statements from the Bible. No one is to be condemned for reasoning from that nonverbal evidence rather than from sacred words.

This letter to the Grand Duchess Christine, written in 1615, was to prove prophetic. Eighteen years later, Galileo was indeed condemned because he had reasoned from the nonverbal evidence of nature rather than from the sacred words of the Bible. On January 20, 1633, under the threat of transportation under chains, Galileo was summoned before the Inquisition in Rome and, after three appearances, convicted of heresy at the age of sixty-nine. Kneeling, he was made to renounce his belief in the Copernican theory, in the earth's motion around the sun. "I abjure, curse, and detest the said errors and heresies."[30] That experience probably did little to strengthen his faith in the truth of sacred words. But, even before this fateful episode, words in general had never been a compelling medium of persuasion to Galileo. His astronomical observations were based not on texts, but on a different "book" altogether:

> Philosophy is written in that great book which ever lies before our eyes—I mean the universe—but we cannot understand it if we do not first learn the language and grasp the symbols in which it is written. This book is written in the mathematical language, and the symbols are triangles, circles, and other geometrical figures, without whose help it is impossible to comprehend a single word of it.[31]

At its most extreme, Galileo's observational science saw itself as a rejection of *all* verbal knowledge. He rejected law and the humanities for just that reason: these text-based disciplines, "wherein there is neither truth nor falsehood," are almost as fork-tongued as the Bible itself.[32] The "book" of nature is the only one that is not fork-tongued. It is such a book as will send written books to their graves, for it has no use for words at all. Its language is mathematics.

Galileo, of course, was not always so stringent, as his own prolific career as a writer demonstrated. Still, for early modern science, being "observational" almost always carried some degree of animus against bookishness, against the tyranny of text-based learning. It was in that spirit that the Royal Society of London, in 1663, chose as its motto this declaration of independence: "Nullius in Verba" (nothing in words).[33] Scientific inquiry would henceforth be conducted in a medium less treacherous and less futile than human language. And nothing better illustrated that treachery and that futility than syllogisms. The Royal Society gave these a wide berth. Its program (as stated by Robert Hooke) was a deliberate departure from text-based subjects: "To improve the knowledge of naturall things, and all useful Arts, Manufactures, Mechanick practises, Engines and Inventions by Experiments—not meddling with Divinity, Metaphysics, Moralls, Politicks, Grammar, Rhetoric or Logick."[34]

Logic, constitutively dependent on language, had the same status as theology or metaphysics as far as the Royal Society was concerned.[35] Any knowledge derived from it is propositionally derivative, parasitic on preassigned verbal entities. Such knowledge comes into being only by fiat, only by an arbitrary act of naming. Logic is thus conventional rather than natural. As such, its sweep is indeed infinite: it can generate a formally complete universe, a universe of self-defined and self-validating terms. But that only made it all the more suspect to experimental scientists of the seventeenth century. That suspicion was amply confirmed by later developments in mathematics. Early in the nineteenth century, a few decades before Langdell was writing, the discovery of several non-

Euclidean geometries—by Karl Friedrich Gauss, Janos Bolyai, Nikolai Loba-chevsky, and Bernhard Riemann—made it clear that logic, as a formal system of reasoning based on propositional derivation, was not in itself an adequate vehi-cle of knowledge.[36] The fact that space could be described by several systems of propositions, all logically consistent within themselves, meant that logical con-sistency was not a sufficient criterion of empirical truth. There is nothing wrong with the axioms of Euclid on the grounds of logic; they just don't always happen to describe the properties of physical space. Under some operative con-ditions, that space is better described by the axioms of other geometries, not Euclidean but just as logically consistent. Each system of formal logic, in short, is only *one* candidate among others that may yield a plausible description of a particular physical event. Its candidacy sometimes comes to nothing. A crucial scientific development of the nineteenth century was thus the unforeseen shakiness of logic, its diminished referential claim. As Morris Kline says, "Non-Euclidean geometry was the reef on which the logic of Euclidean geometry foundered."[37] Out of that foundering would come Einstein's relativity in the twentieth century.[38]

Law and Logic

All of this was lost on Langdell. His twin advocacy—of learning and of logic—was vulnerable to critique on a number of fronts, vulnerable, in fact, to the very charge of not being scientific. Oliver Wendell Holmes sounded the alarm in 1800 when, in his review of Langdell's *Summary of the Law of Contracts*, he made this pointed (and now celebrated) remark: "The life of the law has not been logic; it has been experience."[39] Fifteen years later—at a dinner in honor of Langdell, no less—Holmes tempered his critique only slightly. "The law, so far as it depends on learning," he said, is "the government of the living by the dead." "An ideal system of law should draw its postulates and its legislative justifica-tion from science," he went on, but (lest this be taken as an unmixed tribute to Langdell) he quickly added, "As it is now, we rely upon tradition . . . as our only warrant for rules which we enforce with as much confidence as if they embod-ied revealed wisdom."[40]

Others, more conversant with science than either Langdell or, for that mat-ter, Holmes, went further. Roscoe Pound—who wrote a doctoral dissertation on botany at the University of Nebraska while practicing law in that state,[41] before moving on to his better known career, as law professor and then dean of the Harvard Law School—was able to draw on this unusual background to chide his predecessor. "But what do we mean by the word 'scientific'? What is scientific law? What constitutes science in the administration of justice?" Thus Pound began and quickly noted that a wholesale equation of science with logic was no longer tenable: "We no longer hold anything scientific merely because it exhibits a rigid scheme of deductions from *a priori* conceptions. . . . The idea of science as a system of deductions has become obsolete."[42] He then pointed to biology: "Linnaeus, for instance, lays down a proposition, *omne vivum ex ovo*, and from this fundamental conception deduces a theory of homologies between animal and vegetable organs. He deemed no study of the organisms and the organs themselves necessary to reach or to sustain these conclusions. Yet, today, study of the organisms themselves has overthrown his fundamental proposition."[43] This is what empiricism means, Pound said. And "the revolution which has taken place in other sciences in this regard must take place and is taking place in jurisprudence also."[44] Jurisprudence, in other words, must become "scientific" in the following sense:

> [I]t must be judged by the result it achieves, not by the niceties of its internal structure; it must be valued by the extent to which it meets its end, not by the beauty of its logical processes or the strictness with which its rules proceed from the dogmas it takes for its foundation.[45]

Pound was, of course, speaking more as a lawyer than as a scientist. Still, it was no small help that he was able to point to a conception of science more up-to-date and more rigorous than Langdell's. For Langdell, logical consistency was what made law scientific: this alone was enough; it was a necessary and sufficient criterion. For Pound, it was not enough. A body of law can be logically impeccable and legally unacceptable. It becomes acceptable only if it has something else to show: some achieved result, some progress toward the end it proposes. This consequentialist criterion puts the burden of proof outside law itself, external to anything formalizable on its own terms. It also removes from law any self-testing mechanism, any integral procedure for verification or even falsification.[46] Whether law can still be called "scientific" is an interesting question, but it was not one Pound pursued. Instead, from a consequentialist standpoint (and the standpoint of an ex-botanist), he now proceeded to give an empirical account of what happened when law was aligned too closely with one particular conception of science, when logic was deemed its sole arbiter.

Pound cited the "scientific" affirmation of the liberty of contract in *Lochner* and *Adair*;[47] he also cited a much wider range of judicial failings:

> its inadequacy to deal with employers' liability; the failure of the theory of "general jurisprudence" of the Supreme Court of the United States to give

us a uniform commercial law; the failure of American courts, with centuries of discussion before them, to work out a reasonable or certain law of future interests in land; the breakdown of the common law in the matter of discrimination by public service companies because of inability to make procedure enforce its doctrines and rules; its breakdown in the attempt to adjust water rights in our newer states, where there was opportunity for free development; its inability to hold promoters to their duty and to protect the interests of those who invest in corporate enterprises against mismanagement and breach of trust; its failure to work out a scheme of responsibility that will hold legal entities, or those who hide behind their skirts, to their duty to the public.[48]

All of these happened when law was modeled on an impoverished notion of science. Modeled in this way, a "scientific jurisprudence becomes a mechanical jurisprudence."[49] "Principles were no longer resorted to in order to make rules fit cases. The rules were at hand in a fixed and final form, and cases were to be fitted to the rules. The classical jurisprudence of principles had developed, by the very weight of its authority, a jurisprudence of rules; and it is the nature of rules to operate mechanically."[50]

More at home in science than Langdell, Pound also had a keener sense of what might go wrong when science was known superficially, known only as a label, when its alleged rules of operation were touted as absolute rules in another quarter. Being "mechanical" is sometimes a good thing in science: it furnishes a kind of impersonal guarantee, the guarantee that certain outcomes will always follow from certain experimental conditions, irrespective of who is doing the experiment, where or when it is being done. Generalizability and predictability are the virtues of a "mechanical" science. These virtues do not carry over undiminished into another discipline. A "mechanical" jurisprudence, Pound argued, has the defects of its virtues. Generalizability and predictability are here purchased at the cost of stripping each case of its particulars to fit it into the preassigned categories of the law, boxing individual circumstances into the law's generalized technical language. Formal order is the pride of this language, but also its hazard: for the more formal the language, the cleaner its taxonomic categories, the less likely it is to capture the messy details of each dispute.[51] A "mechanical" jurisprudence is mechanical in the sense that it is automated, unencumbered: well-defined rules applied to well-defined entities. For Pound, that was the problem.

And here, quoting William James, Pound suggested that a logic-based legal "science" is actually not far from something that has no pretensions to being science at all—namely, a primitive nominalism, a magical belief in the power of words and formulae to solve problems and restore order.[52] A legal language answerable only to its own logic is the latest installment of this magical belief: "Current decisions and discussions are full of such solving words: estoppel, malice, privity, implied intention of the testator, vested and contingent—when we arrive at these we are assumed to be at the end of our juristic search. Like Habib in the Arabian Nights, we wave aloft our scimitar and pronounce the talismanic word."[53] Pound was, of course, not one of the legal realists; he was their best-known critic, sharply responded to as such by Karl Llewellyn.[54] Still, as Llewellyn himself later acknowledged, "half of the commonplace equipment" of the realist jurisprudence had actually been outlined by Pound, who had contributed "more than any other individual (unless perhaps John Dewey) to making legal thought in this country result-minded, cause-minded, and process-minded."[55] Pound's critique of "mechanical jurisprudence," for instance, would be repeated and amplified by Jerome Frank.[56] Likewise, his critique of the "talismanic" language of law would be a spur to Felix Cohen's polemics against "transcendental nonsense," against "legal magic and word-jugglery."[57]

A rejection of mechanical jurisprudence—with Cohen as with Pound—hardly meant a rejection of science itself.[58] Quite the contrary. In Cohen's mind, mechanical jurisprudence was entirely distinct from science, and he, for one, was eager to claim the latter as his sole and exclusive ally, not admitting his opponents into the fold. And so in his hands (and in the hands of other polemicists such as Jerome Frank), the Langdellian model suddenly became portrayed as a retrograde, quasi-religious faith, a latter-day scholasticism that the realists, as empirical lawyers, must do their best to demolish.[59] The critique of logic, rules of law, stare decisis—the typical realist agenda—turned out to be fueled by this burning question: "How are we going to substitute a realistic, rational, scientific account of legal happenings for the classical theological jurisprudence of concepts?"[60]

Cohen might well have heeded Pound here. There is always the danger, Pound had cautioned, that law might become "too scientific,"[61] pushing too far its analogy to a discipline whose domain of inquiry is after all quite different. And the worst way of being too scientific is to push the analogy to a term that is itself no more than a label: a term hardened into a convenient clarity, hardened into a unified whole at just those points where its dissonances are most explosive and most interesting. A blanket invocation of science—offered both by Langdell and by some of his realist critics—coarsens what is invoked as well as those who invoke it. As Pound showed by his contrary example, it is more helpful to explore shades and gradations: the extent to which science might be a good analogy for law, and the extent to which it might not. Science, invoked in this consciously qualified way, becomes a sounding board, a heuristic companion. It brings into relief what is formalizable in law and what is not, what falls inside and outside the scope of logic. What exactly is the relation between law and its decisional rules? How far can these rules be generalized from precedents, and how far can they be extended to cases in the distant future? Is law a social "science," as some of the realists claimed,[62] and what does that word mean in any case? Where does this "science" stand among the natural sciences? Does it have anything to say in return to the scientists?

Law-Abidingness

I will address these questions briefly by focusing on one concept pertinent to both science and jurisprudence: law-abidingness. In picking this focus, I hope to suggest three intersecting but ultimately diverging lines of inquiry. First, as will become clear, law-abidingness is a concept that falls with uneven weight across the sciences, for "laws of science" in fact mean very different things in physics and biology. The concept can thus serve as a critical wedge, an axis of differentiation, breaking down the apparent unity of a too-handy label. In highlighting the disagreements among scientists, it highlights as well the heuristic value of a contested definition of science.[63] Second, while law-abidingness is not a word prominently featured in the realists' vocabulary, it is nonetheless an issue implicitly raised by their critique of rules of law. Realists imagined the world to be law-abiding, but only up to a certain point. The world is not so law-abiding that rules can cover all judicial action; it is not so law-abiding that an ironclad forecast can be made of what judges and juries will do. This seems to me a very powerful argument. And it is one that can be transposed, mapped, and investigated on a different analytic register. Rather than dwelling on the unpredictability of courtroom decision and its pressures on legal rules, I want to shift the frame to the unpredictability of technological change and its pressures on existing bodies of law. To address law-abidingness in this transposed context is to ask whether law is diachronically binding, whether its jurisdiction is a jurisdiction over time.

Finally, in bringing forth the diachronic as a challenge to the conceptual order of law, I hope to issue a challenge as well to cultural studies, complicating and broadening its focus on the institutional entanglements of cultural forms. Cultural studies, as it is currently practiced, is overwhelmingly synchronic both in its subject matter and in its methodology. Institutional entanglements are here assumed to be contemporaneous, to operate within the same slice of time. This slice of time is further assumed to be an adequate sample, adequate in its descriptive and explanatory power. A diachronic approach unsettles these assumptions. It highlights not only the crucial fact of change across time but also the unevenness of that change: emerging phenomena not emerging at the same rate or even on the same plane, changing the dynamics of the cultural fabric at any given moment, and assigning a new functional meaning even to terms that might look the same. The natural sciences highlight the diachronic. Both in their debates over the degree of determination ascribable to sequence (a debate central to the history of the universe in astrophysics and to the role of chance in evolutionary biology) and, more directly experienced by us, in their ability to foster rapid technological change, the sciences give us a world in which time is a major player. In both respects, they are a vital part of cultural studies, their importance long overlooked.[64]

Without further ado, then, I proceed to the sciences, to see how the concept of law-abidingness holds up. "Laws of science" is a time-honored concept, idiomatic in its usage. Rudolf Carnap gives a classic definition: "If a certain regularity is observed at all times and all places, without exception, then the regularity is expressed in the form of a 'universal law.' An example from daily life is 'All ice is cold.' This statement asserts that any piece of ice—at any place in the universe, at any time, past, present, or future—is (or was, or will be) cold."[65] Universal laws are propositions whose domain of validity is unlimited: their binding power extends to any point in space, any point in time. While Carnap calls these propositions laws of "science," they are in fact almost exclusively laws of physics. As such, they are mathematical laws, with properties perhaps not immediately discernible in the example of ice.

Richard Feynman offers a more standard example, one most physicists would agree to be a law:

> The Law of Gravitation is that two bodies exert a force upon each other which varies inversely as the square of the distance between them, and varies directly as the product of their masses. Mathematically we can write that great law down in the formula:
>
> $$F = G\,(m_1 m_2)/R^2$$
>
> some kind of a constant multiplied by the product of the masses, divided by the square of the distance. Now if I add the remark that a body reacts to a force by accelerating, or by changing its velocity every second to an extent

inversely as its mass, or that it changes its velocity more if the mass is lower, inversely as the mass, then I have said everything about the Law of Gravitation that needs to be said. Everything else is a mathematical consequence of those two things.[66]

Even though gravity started out as an empirical observation, to be stated as a law, it must take the form of a generalization, a description not in terms of the individual features of the objects but in terms of two abstract attributes: distance and mass. And because these attributes are expressed in that least ambiguous of languages—mathematics—the binding power of this generalization is indeed spectacular. Everything that needs to be said is already there, and "everything else is a mathematical consequence." The Law of Gravitation is complete. The world it describes is law-abiding to the extreme because under a given operative condition there is just one script, featuring the same sequence of events and coming out exactly the same way. It is a script that can be repeated over and over again, a script that can be predicted down to the smallest detail. And it is a script that changes not at all over time. As Feynman says, "But the most impressive fact is that gravity is simple. It is simple to state the principles completely and not have left any vagueness for anybody to change the ideas of the law."[67] This law is here for good. Its reign began before Newton discovered it in the seventeenth century, and it will endure till the end of time.[68]

Feynman's laws have diachronic binding powers no man-made laws can match. This is not a trivial insight. In fact, the heuristic value of physics is just this: it is not a good analogy.[69] Its "laws" dramatize a semantic usage so exacting as to be out of reach for everyone but a physicist. Jurisprudence can never yield the same kind of law-abidingness that gravity does. To be functional, then, the word "laws" cannot have the same definition everywhere; it must mean different things to practitioners of different disciplines. These different meanings do not create an impassable gulf between law and the sciences as a whole, for, in differing from physics, law is actually in good scientific company.

Another branch of science—biology—is on record as differing from physics in just this way. Ernst Mayr, a pivotal figure in modern evolutionary biology, is nothing if not explicit here. "Since the Scientific Revolution," Mayr says, "the philosophy of science has been characterized by an almost exclusive reliance on logic, mathematics, and the laws of physics."[70] Biology does not come under this mantle. Its unique contribution, in fact, "is the deemphasis of laws. In most classical philosophies of science, explanation consists in connecting phenomena with laws. Although laws are also encountered in biology, particularly in physiological and developmental processes, most regularities encountered in the living world lack the universality of the laws of physics. Consequently biologists nowadays make use of the word *law* only rarely."[71]

Laws are necessary to the constitution of physics as a discipline; without their ability to generalize and to predict, physics would not be physics. For most biologists, this is not true.[72] In this discipline, laws are local, occasional, and good for the most part, but they are rarely blessed with the power to clinch the case once and for all. Mayr mentions many reasons for the limited scope of laws in his discipline. These include the centrality of chance in evolution, the non-derivability of a discrete cause from any given effect, the absence of any genetic rules to govern the ordering of phenotypes, and the emergence of unforeseeable functions and properties at every level of aggregation. All of these make predictions and generalizations difficult.[73]

Even a mantra that might look like a law in molecular biology—that "DNA makes proteins"—turns out to be less than what it appears, as Richard Lewontin argues:

> Not *all* the information about protein structure is stored in the DNA sequence, because the folding of polypeptides into proteins is not completely specified by their amino acid sequences. . . . We do not, in fact, know what the rules of protein folding are, so no one has ever succeeded in writing a computer program that will take the sequence of amino acids in a polypeptide and predict the folding of the molecule. Even programs that attempt very crude characterizations of the folding of regions of proteins into major structural classes like alpha-helices and beta-sheets are not more than about 75 percent accurate.[74]

The folding of proteins does not follow a law laid down by DNA sequences, because there are numerous other intervening forces: the environment as both cause and effect; the complex molecular interactions within the organism itself; and, finally, strictly random processes, the "developmental noise" of the organism. Inveterate messiness is the result. Wrestling with that fact, Lewontin comes up with this analogy: "In the United States, which is broken up into separate state governments with different laws, it is often impossible to say what law will hold without knowing in which state the question has arisen. When asked a question, an American lawyer will reply, 'It depends on the jurisdiction.' So too, in biology, it depends on the jurisdiction."[75]

For Lewontin, law sheds light on biology. The obverse is no less true. In both disciplines, laws come with brackets, with qualifiers. In both disciplines, predictions and generalizations go only so far because contextual variables are too numerous and too random to be fully formalizable. This fact alone suggests that if there is indeed a "legal science," it might not take the form envisioned by Langdell.

Law across Time

But biology is not just a heuristic companion for jurisprudence; it is also a technology, an agent of change that encroaches on existing bodies of law, changing the functional meaning of its terms and changing its conceptual order in the process. The recent completion of the Human Genome Project is a case in point. This scientific breakthrough rewrites the ground rules for medicine, putting genetic information and high-tech procedures at its front and center. In doing so, it also multiplies the conundrum of "intellectual property," putting conflicting interpretations on this term, and putting pressure as well on the jurisdictional boundary between the courts and the legislature. What exactly is a "patent," and what exactly is "patentable"? When does information come under the rule of an ownership claim? And who is to determine its scope and legitimacy? Should these questions be litigated in court, or should they be the subject of a public policy debate, resulting in legislative action?

The newfangled technique of gene therapy had brought these questions to a head even before the Human Genome Project was completed. In September 1990, a team at the National Institutes of Health (NIH) used this highly experimental technique for the first time on a human being, four-year-old Ashanthi DeSilva. DeSilva, along with another child, had suffered from a lethal genetic disorder: their bodies failed to produce an enzyme called adenosine deaminase, or ADA, which the body needs in order to produce disease-fighting white blood cells. Since the disorder involves the mutation of only a single gene, it is an especially good target for gene therapy. The medical team, headed by the renowned W. French Anderson, used an *ex vivo* technique: they took from DeSilva some white blood cells called T cells, multiplied these outside the body, then mixed them with a therapeutic virus, a virus disarmed and injected with a normal ADA gene. This normal ADA gene was transferred by the virus to the T cells, which were then returned to the body, spreading the cure. And a cure it was. By all accounts, the technique was a stunning success. Thanks to it, both children are now living near-normal lives. Meanwhile, Anderson and two other members of his team filed for and received a U.S. patent on every kind of human *ex vivo* gene therapy.[76]

Anderson's scientific colleagues reacted with "deep disbelief."[77] The breadth of the patent meant that an entire category of medical procedures was now under its control. As one researcher said, "This is analogous to giving someone a patent for heart transplants."[78] Even though NIH holds the patent, the administration of the patent—facilitated by the Bayh-Dole Act (1980)[79]—was granted to a private company, Genetic Therapy Inc. (GTI), which had jointly funded the research and whose scientific board Anderson chaired. The company was granted an exclusive licensing right, giving it the power to "pick and choose winners in a very young field," since anyone commercializing an *ex vivo* gene therapy in the United States would have to buy a sublicense from the company.[80] Nor was this all. Within three months of the gene therapy patent, GTI was sold for $295 million to the Swiss pharmaceutical giant Sandoz, which in turn merged with its rival, Ciba-Geigy, in a $63 billion merger to form a new conglomerate called Novartis. As a result, the licensing right to the *ex vivo* gene therapy patent is now in the hands of a multinational corporation of truly breathtaking proportions: the world's largest agrochemical company, second-largest seed company, third-largest pharmaceutical company, and fourth-largest veterinary medicine company.[81]

The trajectory of this patent could never have been foreseen by the framers of the Constitution. Under Article I, Section 8, of that document, the framers instructed Congress to "promote the progress of science and the useful arts, by securing for limited times to authors and inventors the exclusive right to their respective writings and discoveries."[82] Congress responded with two landmark statutes: the patent act and the copyright act, the former of which was signed by George Washington on April 10, 1790. Even then, not everyone believed in patents. Jefferson, an active inventor (and one of the three members on the Board of Patent Commissioners), never filed for one. Neither did Benjamin Franklin or Joseph Henry, the inventor of the first electric motor, who saw patents as a roadblock to free inquiry, a low tactic to which no "true man of science" would stoop.[83] Early patents were, in any case, quite different from their latter-day counterparts. In the late eighteenth century, patentability was firmly grounded in tangible objects. Applicants for patents were required to submit physical models of their inventions, along with verbal and graphic descriptions.[84] This practice was discontinued in 1869, and, in the century that followed, patents were granted increasingly not to specific devices but to broad areas of actionable knowledge such as medical procedures, the chemical composition of drugs, and programming techniques for software applications.[85]

The word "patent" remains the same, but it is clearly not what it used to be. The changing meaning of that word—not to mention its changing contexts of usage—amply affirms what Galileo had suspected long ago: that law is a linguistic artifact, dependent on words and haunted by that dependency. Such an artifact is susceptible to time; it can easily be altered out of recognition. As words change their meaning, so too do laws whose wording might remain superficially the same. To enforce the letter of the law is paradoxically to depart from its original meaning, changing its scope and its mode of operation, getting it tangled up in complications entirely unforeseen. In this way, jurisprudence is plagued by all the hazards and all the treacheries of text-based knowledge. "Nullius in Verba" is an ideal it can never attain, never even pretend to champion.

The dream of a "legal science"—the dream of Langdell, as of his realist critics—must be seen in this light. Science as an analogy for law works only up to a point. It ceases to work at just that point where the sciences have succeeded in securing for themselves a domain of inquiry and a body of knowledge arguably not text-based. Jurisprudence will look in vain here for a parallel understanding of the temporal vicissitudes of language. It is at this point, at the limits of science as analogy, that we must look elsewhere, to another heuristic ally no less important, though important for different reasons. The humanities have little to offer in the way of rules. Neither prediction nor generalization is their strong suit. Still, as a repository of words transmitted across time, and interpreted and reinterpreted across time, the humanities do have something to say about what it means to be diachronically predicated, a predication not unlike Benjamin Cardozo's vision of jurisprudence:

> We may think the law is the same if we refuse to change the formulas. The identity is verbal only. The formula has no longer the same correspondence with reality. Translated into conduct, it means something other than it did. Law defines a relation not always between fixed points, but often, indeed oftenest, between points of varying position. The acts and situations to be regulated have a motion of their own. There is change whether we will it or not.[86]

Notes

1 Legal realism is an umbrella term, with loosely defined membership. Karl Llewellyn supplies a good working list: W. Bingham, C. E. Clark, W. W. Cook, A. L. Corbin, W. O. Douglas, J. Francis, J. Frank, L. Green, J. C. Hutcheson, S. Klaus, K. N. Llewellyn, E. G. Lorenzen, U. Moore, H. Oliphant, E. W. Patterson, T. R. Powell, M. Radin, W. A. Sturges, L. A. Tulin, H. E. Yntema. See Karl Llewellyn, "Some Realism about Realism—Responding to Dean Pound," 44 *Harv. L. Rev.* 1222, 1257–59 (1931).

2 Karl Llewellyn, "On What Is Wrong with So-Called Legal Education," 35 *Colum. L. Rev.* 651, 669 (1935).

3 Felix Cohen, "Transcendental Nonsense and the Functional Approach," 35 *Colum. L. Rev.* 809, 821 (1935).

4 Jerome Frank, *Law and the Modern Mind* 35 (Anchor Books 1963) (1930).

5 Llewellyn, supra note 2, at 653; see also Jerome Frank, "Why Not a Clinical Lawyers-School?" 81 *U. Pa. L. Rev.* 903 (1933). Frank portrayed Langdell as a bizarre character with

> an obsessive and almost exclusive interest in books. . . . The lawyer-client relation, the numerous non-rational factors involved in persuasion of a judge at a trial, the face-to-face appeals to the emotions of juries, the elements that go to make up what is loosely known as the "atmosphere" of a case—everything that is undisclosed in judicial opinion—was virtually unknown (and was therefore meaningless) to Langdell. . . . The so-called case system (the "Harvard system" which some university law schools adopted and by which some of them are still largely dominated) was the expression of the strange character of a cloistered, retiring bookish man.

Id. at 907. Contemporary observers saw a direct connection as well between the realists' critique of rules and the pedagogy of the case method. See, for instance, John Dickinson, "Legal Rules: Their Function in the Process of Decision," 79 *U. Pa. L. Rev.* 833 (1931). Perhaps there was a degree of institutional rivalry as well. Legal realism was associated mostly with two law schools: Columbia and Yale. See also Laura Kalman, *Legal Realism at Yale: 1927–1960,* at 67–144 (1986); William Twining, *Karl Llewellyn and the Realist Movement* (1973).

6 Charles Warren, *History of the Harvard Law School,* 359, 363, 372–73 (1908).

7 Thomas C. Grey, "Langdell's Orthodoxy," *U. Pitt. L. Rev.,* Fall 1983, at 1. For the spread of the Langdellian model beyond Harvard, see Robert Stevens, "Two Cheers for 1870: The American Law School," in *Law in American History* 405 (Donald Fleming and Bernard Bailyn eds., 1971), expanded into his *Law School: Legal Education in America from the 1850s to the 1980s* (1983). Bruce Ackerman sees three generations of dissent from the classical orthodoxy: first, Holmes and Thayer at the end of the nineteenth century; then, Brandeis, Frankfurter, and Pound in the early twentieth; and, finally, the legal realists in the late 1920s and 1930s. Ackerman sees the demise of the Langdellian model in the rise of the "Legal Process School," including figures such as Lon Fuller, Paul Freund, Henry Hart, Herbert Wechsler, Alexander Bickel, and Harry Wellington. See Bruce Ackerman, "Jerome Frank's Law and the Modern Mind," 103 *Daedalus* 119 (1974) (book review).

8 For a lucid analysis of the interlocking relation between induction and deduction, not just in Langdell but most of all in John Stuart Mill's *System of Logic* (1843), see Grey, supra note 7, at 19. For an account of the uses of induction and deduction in earlier American legal thought, see Perry Miller, *The Life of the Mind in America: From the Revolution to the Civil War* 156–64 (1965). For a critique of induction by a philosopher often cited by legal realists, see John Dewey, "Logical Method and Law," 10 *Cornell L. Rev.* 17 (1924). For critiques by realists, see, among others, Walter Wheeler Cook, "Scientific Method and the Law," 13 *A.B.A. J.* 303–9 (1927).

9 Christopher Columbus Langdell, preface to *Cases on the Law of Contracts,* at ix (2d ed. 1879).

10 In the 1870s and 1880s, there were close ties between the law faculty at Oxford and the American Langdellian school. See F. H. Lawson, *The Oxford Law School, 1850–1965,* at 69–85 (1968).

11 Frederick Pollock, "The Science of Case-Law," in *Essays in Jurisprudence and Ethics* 237, 238 (1882).

12 The reliance on the Langdellian model in appellate opinions is now a commonplace. Legal realists remarked on this practice from the very outset. See, e.g., Frank, supra note 4, at xxvii–xxix; Frank, supra note 5, at 910–11.

13 Miller, supra note 8, at 156–87. William LaPiana, in particular, emphasizes the continuity between Langdell's legal science and the legal science of Story. See William LaPiana, *Logic and Experience: The Origin of Modern American Legal Education* (1994). For earlier entanglements between law and science, see Barbara J. Shapiro, "Law and Science in Seventeenth Century England," 21 *Stan. L. Rev.* 727 (1969).

14 Robert W. Gordon, "Legal Thought and Legal Practice in the Age of American Enterprise, 1870-1920," in *Professions and Professional Ideologies in America* 70 (Gerald L. Geison ed., 1983).

15 Anthony Chase, in fact, traces the pedagogic reforms at the Harvard Law School less to Langdell than to Charles Eliot, president of Harvard. See Anthony Chase, "The Birth of the Modern Law School," 23 *Am. J. Legal Hist.* 329 (1979).

16 Christopher Columbus Langdell, "Record for the Commemoration on the Two Hundred and Fiftieth Anniversary of the Founding of Harvard College" (1887), quoted in Arthur E. Sutherland, *The Law at Harvard* 175 (1967).

17 Id.

18 Grant Gilmore sees this as the roots of legal realism as well. See Grant Gilmore, "Legal Realism: Its Cause and Cure," 70 *Yale L.J.* 1037, 1041–42 (1961).

19 Herbert F. Goodrich, "The Story of the American Law Institute," *Wash. U.L.Q.*, June 1951, at 283, 286.

20 Id. at 220.

21 Morton Horwitz, *The Transformation of American Law, 1870–1960: The Crisis of Legal Orthodoxy* 13 (1992).

22 Id.

23 Brown v. Collins, 53 N.H. 442 (1873); Losee v. Buchanan, 51 N.Y. 476 (1873). For the rise of the "negligence" and "fault" principles, see G. Edward White, *Tort Law in America* 12–19 (1985).

24 It should be pointed out, however, that "legal science" is an elastic term, with a changing membership. Oliver Wendell Holmes, better known for his dissent in Lochner v. New York, 198 U.S. 45 (1905), turned out to be one of the most influential spokesmen for legal science in his championing of "negligence" in torts. See Oliver Wendell Holmes, "A Theory of Torts," 7 *Am. Law Rev.* 652 (1873), reprinted in 44 *Harv. L. Rev.* 773 (1931).

25 The overwhelming emphasis of legal science was on the private law of tort, contract, property, and commercial law. Public law, including constitutional law, was deemed hopelessly politicized and outside the scope of scientific study. The topics chosen for "restatement" by the American Law Institute were themselves revealing. The series included "Restatements" of the following: Agency (1923–33), Conflict of Law (1923–34), Contracts (1923–32), Judgments (1940–42), Property (1927–44), Restitution (1923–37), Security (1936), Torts (1923–39), and Trusts (1927–35). See Goodrich, supra note 19, at 288–89.

26 Duncan Kennedy sees "classical legal thought" as a legal "consciousness" that encom-

passed laissez-faire constitutionalism. See Duncan Kennedy, "Toward a Historical Under-standing of Legal Consciousness: The Case of Legal Thought in America, 1850–1940," 3 *Res. L. and Soc.* 3 (1980). Grey cautions against an automatic connection. See Grey, supra note 7, at 34–35.

27 Galileo Galilei, *Dialogue on the Great World Systems* 42 (Thomas Salusbury trans., rev. by Giorgio de Santillana, Univ. of Chi. Press, 1953) (1631).

28 Id. at 53.

29 Galileo Galilei, "Letter to Madame Christine of Lorraine, Grand Duchess of Tuscany" (1615), in *Discoveries and Opinions of Galileo* 182, 182–83 (Stillman Drake ed., 1957).

30 Raymond J. Seeger, *Galileo Galilei, His Life and His Works* 32 (1966).

31 Galileo Galilei, *The Controversy on the Comets of 1618*, at 183–84 (Stillman Drake and C. D. O'Malley eds., 1960).

32 Galileo, supra note 27, at 63. "If this of which we dispute were some point of law, or other part of the studies called the humanities, wherein there is neither truth nor falsehood, we might give sufficient credit to the acuteness of wit, readiness of answers, and the greater accomplishments of writers and hope that he who is most proficient in these will make his reason more probable and plausible. But the conclusions of Natural Science are true and necessary." Id.

33 The motto was adopted from Horace, *Epistles*, bk. 1, ch. 1, at 13–14: "Ac ne forte roges, quo me duce, quo lare tuter, / Nullius addictus iurare in verba magistri." See Sir Henry Lyons, F.R.S., *The Royal Society, 1660–1940*, at 39 (1944).

34 Lyons, supra note 33, at 41.

35 Of course, the degree of language-dependency is an open question. For an interesting contri-bution to this debate, see Noam Chomsky, *Aspects of the Theory of Syntax* (1965). In equating syntax with the cognitive substrate of mental events, Chomsky in effect argues for an extremely close relation between logic and language.

36 For the rise of non-Euclidean geometries, see Bas C. van Fraassen, *An Introduction to the Philosophy of Time and Space* 117–33 (1985). For a more technical account, see Lawrence Sklar, *Space, Time, and Spacetime* 13–54 (1974). To be fair to Langdell, I should point out that not everyone in the nineteenth century saw the discovery of non-Euclidean geometries as a decoupling of the physical from the logical. As late as 1883, Arthur Cayley, in his presidential address to the British Association for the Advancement of Science, could still assert that Euclid's parallel axiom "does not need demonstration, but is part of our notion of space—of the physical space of our experience." See Morris Kline, *Mathematics: The Loss of Certainty* 95 (1980).

37 Kline, supra note 36, at 103.

38 The discovery of non-Euclidean geometries was especially important to Einstein. See Al-bert Einstein, "Geometry and Experience," in *Ideas and Opinions* 232 (1954), and his dis-cussion of Euclidean and non-Euclidean continua in *Relativity: The Special and General Theory*, 92–104 (Robert W. Lawson trans., 1961). For a critique of a different logical formal-ism—Kant's—by the Vienna Circle, a critique that also draws on non-Euclidean geometry and Einstein, see Rudolf Carnap, "Kant's Synthetic A Priori," in *An Introduction to the Philosophy of Science* 177 (Martin Gardner ed., 1995).

39 Oliver Wendell Holmes, "Review of Langdell's Summary of the Law of Contracts," 14

Amer. L. Rev. 233 (1880). This sentence was then incorporated into the opening paragraph of *The Common Law*. See Oliver Wendell Holmes, *The Common Law* 1 (1881).

40 Oliver Wendell Holmes, "Learning and Science, Speech at a Dinner of the Harvard Law School Association in Honor of Professor C. C. Langdell (June 25, 1895)," in *The Mind and Faith of Justice Holmes: His Speeches, Essays, Letters, and Judicial Opinions* 34–35 (Max Lerner ed., 1943).

41 Pound's doctoral dissertation on botany at the University of Nebraska was eventually published, in revised form, as Roscoe Pound and Frederic E. Clements, *Phytogeography of Nebraska* (1898). Arthur Sutherland, discussing Pound's better known work, *Outlines of Lectures on Jurisprudence* (1898), comments: "One interested in Pound's intellectual tendencies does well to consider the nature of this book. It suggests his *Phytogeography of Nebraska*; it is a book of scientific ordering, of minutely detailed nomenclatural terms. Here is a botanist explaining the taxonomy and nomenclature of justice." See Arthur Sutherland, *The Law at Harvard: A History of Ideas and Men, 1817–1967*, at 237 (1967).

42 Roscoe Pound, "Mechanical Jurisprudence," 8 *Colum. L. Rev.* 605, 605, 608 (1908).

43 Id. at 609.

44 Id. at 608.

45 Id. at 605.

46 I take the word from Karl Popper, who argues that scientific testability is based not on the broad criterion of verifiability but on the much more limited criterion of falsifiability. See Karl Popper, *The Logic of Scientific Discovery* 78–92 (1992).

47 Lochner v. New York, 198 U.S. 45 (1905); Adair v. United States, 208 U.S. 161 (1908).

48 Pound, supra note 42, at 614.

49 Id.

50 Id. at 607.

51 The realists' call for more minute classifications is a response to the unfairness perpetrated when legal categories are overly broad. Karl Llewellyn writes of "the worthwhileness of grouping cases and legal situations into narrower categories than has been the practice in the past. This is connected with the distrust of verbally simple rules—which so often cover dissimilar and non-simple fact situations." See Llewellyn, supra note 1, at 1237.

52 The passage by James quoted by Pound is from Lecture 2, "What Pragmatism Means," in *Pragmatism* (1907):

> Metaphysics has usually followed a very primitive kind of quest. You know how men have always hankered after unlawful magic, and you know what a great part in magic *words* have always played. If you have his name, or the formula of incantation that binds him, you can control the spirit, genie, afrite, or whatever the power may be. . . . So the universe has always appeared to the natural mind as a kind of enigma of which the key must be sought in the shape of some illuminating or power-bringing word or name. That word names the universe's principle, and to possess it is after a fashion to possess the universe itself. "God," "Matter," "Reason," "the Absolute," "energy," are so many solving names. You can rest when you have them. You are at the end of your metaphysical quest.

> Id. at 52.

53 Pound, supra note 42, at 612.

54 Compare Roscoe Pound, "The Call for a Realist Jurisprudence," 44 *Harv. L. Rev.* 697–711 (1931), with Karl Llewellyn, supra note 1, at 1222–64. For a more detailed account of Pound's rejection of legal realism, see Kalman, supra note 5, at 45–66.

55 Karl Llewellyn, "Roscoe Pound," in *Jurisprudence: Realism in Theory and Practice* 496, 501 (1962). For a discussion of Pound and legal realism, see Wilfred Rumble, *American Legal Realism* (1968), and G. Edward White, "From Sociological Jurisprudence to Realism: Jurisprudence and Social Change in Early Twentieth-Century America," 58 *Va. L. Rev.* 999–1028 (1972).

56 See Jerome Frank, "Mechanistic Law; Rules; Discretion; the Ideal Judge," in *Law and the Modern Mind,* supra note 4, at 127.

57 Felix Cohen, supra note 3, at 821.

58 Several other realists were also science enthusiasts—especially Walter Wheeler Cook. As an undergraduate at Columbia, Cook studied mathematics and physics. After graduation, he took an instructorship in mathematics and, a year later, headed off to Germany for a two-year fellowship in physics. After returning to the United States, he was still hired as an assistant in Columbia's Department of Mathematics, even though he was simultaneously enrolled both in the Law School and in the School of Political Science. See John Henry Schlegel, *American Legal Realism and Empirical Social Science* 28 (1995). For a thoroughgoing attempt to invoke physics as a model for law, see Walter Wheeler Cook, supra note 8, at 303.

59 For Jerome Frank's critique of the Langdellian orthodoxy as scholasticism, see Frank, supra note 4, at 62–74.

60 Cohen, supra note 3, at 821.

61 Pound, supra note 42, at 606.

62 This is not my view, but see John Henry Schlegel, "American Legal Realism and Empirical Social Science: From the Yale Experience," 28 *Buff. L. Rev.* 459 (1980), expanded into his *American Legal Realism and Empirical Social Science* (1995).

63 See, e.g., *The Disunity of Science* (Peter Galison and David J. Stump eds., 1996).

64 An important exception here is Fred Inglis, *Cultural Studies* (1993). Inglis argues that cultural studies, "in its anti-scientific dialectic, will still have to incorporate the scientific canons of method. . . . While the human sciences cannot of their nature make much play with laboratory conditions of proof, or at least of falsifiability, it is now surely reasonable to speak of experiential and historical proof." Inglis calls for "a level of competence on our part at least going as far as the first year of university study in, say, statistics and one of the life sciences." Id. at 111–12.

65 Rudolf Carnap, "The Value of Laws: Explanation and Prediction," in *An Introduction to the Philosophy of Science* 3 (Martin Gardner ed., 1995).

66 Richard Feynman, *The Character of Physical Law* 14–15 (1995).

67 Id. at 33.

68 I do not want to discuss quantum mechanics here, but I do want to point out that the so-called indeterminacy attributed to quantum mechanics is actually not an absolute statement about indeterminacy, and certainly not a statement about change across time. Instead, it is a statement about the relative distribution of indeterminacy between two well-defined terms, velocity and spatial location: the more precise we are about one, the less

precise we are about the other. See 3 Niels Bohr, "Quantum Physics and Philosophy—Causality and Complementarity," in *The Philosophical Writings of Niels Bohr: Essays 1958–1962 on Atomic Physics and Knowledge* 1–7 (1987). An interesting recent challenge to the diachronic invariance of physical laws is Lee Smolin's argument that physical laws might have "evolved" and are different now from what they used to be at the beginning of time. See Lee Smolin, *Life of the Cosmos* (1997).

69 I do not mean to suggest that physics is not a good analogy *tout court,* only that its conception of "law-abidingness" is more stringent than can be upheld in any other discipline. For an attempt to connect physics, law, and literature within a different configuration, see my "Rethinking Space, Rethinking Rights: Literature, Law, Science," 10 *Yale J.L. and Human.* 487 (1998).

70 Ernst Mayr, "Preface" to *Toward a New Philosophy of Biology,* at v (1988).

71 Id. at vi.

72 I should point out, however, that there is an important minority opinion directly challenging the mainstream represented by Mayr. Rupert Riedl argues vigorously for a law-abiding, predictable order in biology, one that can be captured by induction. See Rupert Riedl, "A Systems-Analytical Approach to Macro-Evolutionary Phenomena," 52 *Q. Rev. of Biology* 351 (1977). Recent work in mathematical population genetics supports Riedl, making predictions and generalizations much more central to biology, since there appears to be a mathematical correlation between the complexity of an organism and the degree of freedom open to its developmental pathways. See Günter Wagner, "Complexity Matters," 279 *Science* 1158 (1998).

73 See generally Mayr, supra note 70, at 1–66.

74 Richard Lewontin, *The Triple Helix: Gene, Organism, and Environment* 73–74 (2000).

75 Id. at 87–88.

76 See Seth Shulman, *Owning the Future* 43–54 (1999); Helen Gavaghan, "NIH Wins Patent on Basic Technique Covering All Ex Vivo Gene Therapy," *Nature,* Mar. 30, 1995, at 393.

77 Gavaghan, supra note 76, at 393.

78 Id.

79 The Bayh-Dole Act (1980) gave private institutions ownership of inventions by publicly funded researchers. For the legislative history, see Linda Marsa, *Prescription for Profits* 96 (1997).

80 Gavaghan, supra note 76, at 393.

81 Shulman, supra note 76, at 48–49.

82 U.S. Const. art. I, § 8.

83 Cathleen Schurr, "Two Hundred Years of Patents and Copyrights," *Am. Hist. Illustrated,* July–Aug. 1990, at 60, 63.

84 Id.

85 For an argument against patents in software, see, for instance, Simson L. Garfinkel et al., "Why Patents Are Bad for Software," in *High Noon on the Electronic Frontier* 35 (Peter Ludlow ed., 1996).

86 Benjamin Cardozo, *The Paradoxes of Legal Science* 11 (Greenwood Press, 1970) (1928).

Law, Therapy, Culture
Peter Brooks

I s a cultural study of the law possible? Of course it is. Law is part of culture, and its discourse and social rituals can be studied in the manner of any other social practice. Cultural studies need to include the law, since law is a prime site in the creation of social enactments and rituals. As Guyora Binder and Robert Weisberg recently have claimed, "[L]aw is both the means by which we continuously refashion society and one of the media in which we represent and critique what we have fashioned."[1] But questions remain: What will be the status of this cultural study of the law? Will there be any reciprocal relation of cultural study to legal study? If Paul Kahn worries that cultural critique of the law tends to be recuperated to a reformist project within the law, I think there is equal cause to fear that study of the law as cultural discourse and project will stand outside the law—and outside legal education and training—as something, no doubt full of interest for itself, that nonetheless impinges very little on the law.[2] Thus far, there is little indication that the movement generally known as "law and literature" has made any difference to the practice of the law. While it may provide law students with some interesting truffles in their education, it remains marginal, an exotic specialty of the academy rather than anything the litigator or the opinion-writer has to think about.

There are good reasons for this. The law is resolutely hermetic, by which I do not mean simply that its procedures and its language are arcane and effectively policed against intrusions from the vulgar and the language of daily life— though they are that. I mean that it is premised on the understanding that it can get on with its task only by a gesture of exclusion, which is at once a gesture of formalization. As Ferdinand de Saussure constituted modern linguistics by excluding anything other than the internal relations of the system, language, so the law as system excludes—must exclude—that which does not meet its internal criteria of the legal.[3] Furthermore, the gesture of exclusion is matched by one of domestication. What it takes from other discourses it tames and subdues, so that concepts, motives, and words from the world outside become legal terms of art, obediently defined by their internal reference within the legal arena.

There would be many illustrations one could give of this simultaneous movement of exclusion and domestication. I have for some time been working on confessions, on the law's insistence on a standard of "voluntariness" for confessions, on the test that a confession be the product of a "free and rational will." In fact, study of the situations in which confessional speech is produced from criminal suspects suggests that the actors in question are often far from "free and rational" beings who "voluntarily" assume their confessional discourses.[4] Criminal suspects, warned of their rights and invited to make "knowing waivers" of them, appear in legal opinions as Enlightenment figures, with Dostoyevsky nowhere in sight. The fictions of the actors in criminal procedure promoted by the law are remarkable. I shall return to this question, but first I want to consider another domain in which the law has at times displayed a remarkable hubris in excluding and domesticating a large, complex, and troubling body of human knowledge absolutely central to the decisions it must render. My treatment of a contentious and vexing issue here will have to be all too summary and unnuanced.

What I have in mind is the encounter of the law with psychotherapy in the so-called recovered memory cases. The question generally at issue in those cases is whether memories from deep in the past, usually from childhood, that have not come forward to speak their claim to redress for years or decades—and in fact often claim to have been blocked, repressed, foreclosed from memory during that time—can be allowed into adjudication, which often requires tolling the statute of limitations when the case involves a civil suit. How does the law deal with psychotherapeutic truth, which even in its pop versions implies a vast and murky lore of psychoanalysis, from Freud onward, and a number of narratives about how the past may be retrieved in the present? Psychoanalysis clearly challenges the law's basic construction of human subjects as autonomous moral agents; if admitted within the law, it would subvert adjudication.[5] But in the recovered memory cases, the law is compelled to adjudicate (or to face its incapacity to adjudicate) in the messy arena of claims to psychological truth. What concerns me here is not the reality of "recovered memory" itself as a concept, and not the questions of policy about how to treat claims of past abuse, but rather what we observe in the law's gestures when faced with the concept and the claim. These gestures, I believe, include at once an overt, announced exclusion and a more surreptitious inclusion in a domesticated form.

Take as a first example the opinion of the court in *Franklin v. Duncan*,[6] where the U.S. District Court for the Northern District of California overturned the conviction of George Franklin on a habeas appeal. Franklin had been found guilty by the trial court of murdering eight-year-old Susan Nason on the accusation of his daughter (and Susan Nason's schoolmate), Eileen Franklin-Lipsker, brought twenty years later.[7] The court asserts that "reliance by the jury on 'recovered memory' testimony does not, in and of itself, violate the Constitution."[8] In the court's logic, "By definition, trials are based on memories of the past."[9] The issue is the credibility of memories, which the jury must decide. "This case, then, may be described as a 'recovered memory' case, but in reality it is a 'memory' case like all the others."[10] Franklin-Lipsker's testimony—really the sole matter of the trial, since no other kind of evidence was available—simply needs to be tested "by the time-honored procedures of the adversary system."[11] The court continues: "Admissibility of the memory is but the first step; it does not establish that the memory is worthy of belief. In this regard, mental health experts will undoubtedly, as they must, continue their debate on whether or not the 'recovered memory' phenomenon exists, but they can never establish whether or not the asserted memory is true. That must be a function of the trial process."[12] This seems commonsensical enough: Let the jury decide, as it always must, on the reality and credibility of the "memories" testified to at trial.

But note that in order to rule in this manner, the court must assign the "mental health experts'" debate (on whether the phenomenon to be adjudicated really exists) to a sphere outside the law, while reassuringly admitting into the courtroom a pussycat version of that tigerish phenomenon. Do not be misled by the heated debates of those mental health professionals. It is a memory case like any other. There was in *Franklin* considerable evidence that the memory was not in fact a memory at all in our usual sense of the term. Rather, the evidence suggested that it was a mental image fabricated through the reading of old newspaper reports of the murder and elevated to the status of memory through psychotherapy. (Indeed, George Franklin's conviction was overturned in part because the trial judge had refused to allow introduction of this "public domain" evidence.) Can a memory be tested in court when it is not a memory? Furthermore, the trial court and the appeals court failed to examine both the process by which this "memory" of the murder returned, in psychotherapy, and the many discussions, from Freud onward, about the nature of "psychic truth" or "narrative truth" versus "historical truth" or "material truth."

There is by now a large literature in cultural studies on memory, trauma, dissociation, and repression, which tends to suggest that traumatic experience paradoxically cannot be reclaimed except by way of its loss from memory: it is not subject to narrative reconstruction. In regard to incest—most often the crime alleged in recovered memory cases—it is often hard to know the relations among memory, event, desire, and phantasy, making it difficult to assign causal and narrative precedence. As Judith Butler states the point: "Is [incest] an event that *precedes* a memory? Is it a memory that retroactively posits an event? Is it a wish that takes the form of a memory?" Butler continues:

> Insofar as incest takes traumatic form, it can be precisely that which is not recoverable as a remembered or narratable event, at which point the claim on historical veracity is not secured through establishing the event-structure of incest. On the contrary, when and where incest is *not* figurable as an event, that is where its very unfigurability testifies to its traumatic character. This would, of course, be "testimony" difficult to prove in a court of law, which labors under standards that determine the empirical status of an event. Trauma, on the contrary, takes its toll on empiricism as well.[13]

Nearly all psychoanalytically derived "truth" takes a toll on empiricism, which is why it must be radically excluded by the law. Nonetheless, the law deals in psychoanalytic concepts when they have been sufficiently domesticated to appear to be empirically debatable propositions.

None of the recovered memory cases that I have looked at delves very deeply into how the memories are recovered in the psychotherapeutic process. *Tyson v. Tyson*,[14] in which the Supreme Court of Washington ruled against tolling the statute of limitations to allow Nancy Tyson to bring charges of childhood sexual abuse against her father—a case whose opinion and dissent are both frequently cited—touches on the question. The dissent lost the battle but won the war, since Washington, and then some thirty other states, legislatively tolled the statute of limitations in such cases. The dissenting opinion argues that a "triggering event" often is necessary "to arouse a plaintiff's suspicions regarding a defendant's potential liability."[15] It then cites as precedent an insurance case in which the insured plaintiff was unaware during the entire statutory period that his insurance policy had been wrongfully canceled—until his boat sank, his fishing gear was lost, and he tried to recover. "Similarly," the dissent continues, a "triggering event, such as psychotherapy, is often necessary to help bring these survivors to an awareness of their abusers' potential liability."[16] To anyone familiar with the return of memory and the status of memory in psychotherapy, the fishing-gear insurance cancellation precedent seems a fairly hopeless domestication of a complex and problematic process, its designation as a "triggering event" introducing a naive empiricism.[17]

Since the law must speak with authority—must make a decision—it claims authority where it is doubtful that any exists. It excludes the indecisive complexities produced by the outside authorities and simultaneously creates through a kind of legal *bricolage* its own tamed, usable version of those complexities. In *Johnson v. Johnson*,[18] for instance, a federal district court in Illinois standardized a distinction between "Type 1 Plaintiffs" and "Type 2 Plaintiffs." Type 1 have more or less continuous memories of abuse, though they are not aware of its effects until they become adults, an awareness usually triggered by psychotherapy; Type 2 have a complete loss of memory of abuse until something—often therapy—triggers its return. Type 2 plaintiffs are far more likely to prevail in court than Type 1 because they can make a better case that statutes of limitations should be tolled for them. One can see the logic of this solution. But it is a logic exclusively within the law—within the logic of the statute of limitations and its rationale—which appears to have little to do with the relative claims of the two kinds of memory—and their relative claims to truth—in the world outside the law.

Using a version of Richard Posner's argument against moral philosophy, one could say that psychoanalysis decides nothing and that therefore the law should stick with a rough-and-ready pragmatism that excludes theory.[19] This much, one could say, is merely inevitable if the law is going to get on with its job. One cannot expect judges to cite Judith Butler. More problematic is the somewhat debonair manner in which the law then co-opts what it has excluded in domesticated versions, which reinterpret the excluded theories in ways that may make one uneasy. I note, for instance, that in a much discussed New Hampshire case, *State v. Walters,* the court decided it would admit lay testimony on the claim of recovered memories (recovered, in this case, in dreams, prompted by psychotherapy), while excluding expert testimony "because experts have not offered any data either supporting or refuting any theory of how or whether a 'lost' memory might be recovered."[20] Again, the court's logic is clear enough, but it is a clarity that works by way of exclusion and domestication: Let us have no confusing expert testimony from a field fraught with controversy, but let us rely only on the common sense of lay testimony.

I am aware that in choosing the example of recovered memory litigation I am treading on a minefield. I do not want to be construed as claiming either that childhood sexual abuse is not a terrible reality or that there should be no recourse for it at law—though one at times feels with these cases that the only solution would be Montaigne's proposal in the case of the alleged impostor Martin Guerre: Send the litigants away, with orders to reappear before the court one hundred years later.[21] Rather, this example may indicate that law tends to resolve the natural doubt and distress in the face of so explosive and uncertain a concept as "recovered memory" by pulling up the drawbridge and retreating into an Axel's castle of self-referential certainty. This tendency may be particularly marked when the law has to deal with complex issues of human agency, motivation, and behavior in actors brought within the sphere of criminal procedure, since the need to assign guilt and punishment makes short shrift of all that we know—from the great novelists as well as from psychoanalysis— about these murky depths. If the law has been able to absorb certain principles of economics, for instance, its reaction to more problematic and unsettling forms of cultural knowledge is instinctively protective, self-defensive.

Let me now return to the issue of confessions in the law. I want to suggest how a psychologically subtle situation is handled by a "commonsense" analysis that obscures more than it clarifies, in opinions that seem to beg for literary and cultural analysis while their rhetoric seems blinded to this possibility. *Oregon v. Elstad*[22] is one of those cases in which the Supreme Court retrenched the protections afforded by *Miranda v. Arizona*[23] and admitted as "voluntary" certain confessions that had not been preceded by proper "warnings." Police arrived at the home where eighteen-year-old Michael Elstad, suspected in the burglary of a neighbor's house, lived with his parents. While Officer McAllister took Mrs. Elstad into the kitchen, where he explained that he had a warrant for her son's arrest, Officer Burke began to question Michael Elstad, who admitted that he was at the burglary scene. Transported to the sheriff's headquarters an hour later, Elstad was given his Miranda warnings and made a full statement of his involvement in the burglary. At trial, Elstad's attorney moved to suppress both his initial admission and his signed confession, on the grounds that the original, unwarned admission "let the cat out of the bag" and tainted the subsequent confession as "fruit of the poisonous tree." The judge excluded Elstad's earlier unwarned statement but allowed the subsequent confession since any "taint" had been dissipated prior to the written confession.[24] Elstad was convicted. The Oregon Court of Appeals reversed the decision, arguing that the initial unwarned statement had "coercive impact" because "in a defendant's mind it has sealed his fate" and that the "cat was sufficiently out of the bag to exert a coercive impact on [respondent's] later admissions."[25] The U.S. Supreme Court then reversed the appellate court's decision and reinstated Elstad's conviction in a 6–3 decision, with a majority opinion written by Justice O'Connor and dissents by Justice Brennan (joined by Justice Marshall) and Justice Stevens.[26]

"The arguments advanced in favor of suppression of respondent's written confession," writes O'Connor, "rely heavily on metaphor."[27] The "tainted fruit of the poisonous tree" metaphor comes from a Fourth Amendment case, *Wong Sun v. United States*,[28] and has had a long life in debates about whether illegally seized evidence can ever be used at trial or must be excluded because the method by which it was obtained permanently taints it as evidence.[29] O'Connor argues that when there is a sufficient break between an illegally obtained confession and a legally obtained one, the second confession is judged "sufficiently an act of free will to purge the primary taint."[30] Her response to the "taint" metaphor is to find language in which the taint is judged to be purged by an act of free will (which may simply compound the metaphorical problem).

The "cat is out of the bag" metaphor comes from *United States v. Bayer*—a case from long before *Miranda*—where Justice Robert Jackson stated, "[After] an accused has once let the cat out of the bag by confessing, no matter what the inducement, he is never thereafter free of the psychological and practical disadvantages of having confessed. He can never get the cat back in the bag. The secret is out for good. In such a sense, a later confession always may be looked upon as a fruit of the first."[31]

In *Elstad*, O'Connor finds that the Oregon Court of Appeals has "identified a subtle form of lingering compulsion" (like a poison lingering in one's bloodstream?) in the "psychological impact of the suspect's conviction that he has let the cat out of the bag and, in so doing, has sealed his own fate"[32] (the open bag now equals the sealed fate). In her view, "[E]ndowing the psychological effects of voluntary unwarned admissions with constitutional implications would, practically speaking, disable the police from obtaining the suspect's informed cooperation even when the official coercion proscribed by the Fifth Amendment played no part in either his warned or unwarned confessions."[33] She continues: "This Court has never held that the psychological impact of voluntary disclosure of a guilty secret qualifies as state compulsion or compromises the voluntariness of a subsequent informed waiver."[34] O'Connor assumes that Elstad's original unwarned admission was voluntary—though *Miranda* doctrine would presume it was not—and then suggests that the link between the earlier and the later confession is merely a matter of psychology, a guilty secret that will out. As such, it is a matter the Court refuses to address. O'Connor goes on: "[T]he causal connection between any psychological disadvantage created by his admission and his ultimate decision to cooperate is speculative and attenuated at best. It is difficult to tell with certainty what motivates a suspect to speak."[35] Having thus disposed of the darker reaches of psychological motivation, she implicitly reestablishes the law's traditional language of the will: "We hold today that a suspect who has once responded to unwarned yet uncoercive questioning is not thereby disabled from waiving his rights and confessing after he has been given the requisite Miranda warnings."[36] In other words, the suspect's volition is still intact, his will is not overborne—he still can choose to put that cat back in the bag. If he does speak to the police, this must indicate that he has freely chosen to waive his rights to counsel and to silence, and therefore his confession is free and knowing.

"Taken out of context, each of these metaphors can be misleading,"[37] O'Connor writes of the "tainted fruit" and the "cat out of the bag." Yet the metaphors of *Elstad*, as my quotations should suggest, keep proliferating. Replying in a footnote to Brennan's fierce dissent in the case, O'Connor rebuts the relevance of the many cases he cites against her conclusion: "Finally, many of the decisions Justice Brennan claims require that the 'taint' be 'dissipated' simply recite the stock 'cat' and 'tree' metaphors but go on to find the second confession voluntary without identifying any break in the stream of events beyond the simple administration of a careful and thorough warning."[38]

Unpacking the metaphors of this sentence would be an thankless enterprise: they range from dissipating taints through stock cats and trees (where "stock" is perhaps a metaphor of metaphor, or a metaphor reduced to cliché) to streams broken by the administration of warnings. The metaphors of *Elstad* proliferate no doubt precisely because it *is* difficult to tell exactly what motivates a suspect to speak. And the Court's admixture of legal doctrine and "commonsense" psychology applied to motivation seems to produce an imagistic texture of dubious clarity.

Brennan in dissent accuses the Court of "marble-palace psychoanalysis," which "demonstrates a startling unawareness of the realities of police interrogation."[39] Turning to the question of motivation, he cites Justice Benjamin Cardozo: "The springs of conduct are subtle and varied. . . . One who meddles with them must not insist upon too nice a measure of proof that the spring which he released was effective to the exclusion of all others."[40] This sounds to me like a clock spring (or the spring of some wind-up object, such as an automaton), but a moment later Brennan cites a standard interrogation manual on the importance of securing the initial admission from a suspect: "For some psychological reason which does not have to concern us at this point 'the dam finally breaks as a result of the first leak' with regards to the tough subject. . . . Any structure is only as strong as its weakest component, and total collapse can be anticipated when the weakest part begins to sag."[41]

Here we are in a watery world (were those springs really wellsprings?), one evoked again in the next paragraph, which quotes another interrogation manual to the effect that the first admission is the "breakthrough" and the "beachhead."[42] Later, Brennan objects that O'Connor's approach is "completely at odds with established dissipation analysis," which sounds vaguely like a chemical procedure. He claims that "today's opinion marks an evisceration of the established fruit of the poisonous tree doctrine."[43] The process of evisceration of the doctrine seems, by taint, to take place on established fruit and on the poisonous tree where it hangs in a curiously vivid image.[44]

The metaphorical layering and figurative incoherence of the Court's language undermine its confident assertions about Elstad's agency. The importance of the issue joined in this case does not produce a correspondingly authoritative rhetoric. Rather, the question of what prompts a confession elicits a confused, imagistic language in which an everyday psychology traversed by legal dogma yields unconvincing and dubiously analytic pronouncements. It is indeed difficult to tell what motivates anyone to confess, and in the end the Court's split over Michael Elstad's confession has little to do with legal interpretation; it has much more to do with ideology, primitive psychology, and differing senses of how we want those accused of crime to behave. The metaphors of the case expose the Court's uncertainties about how we describe the motives and uses of confessional discourse—a discourse that rarely seems to be wholly "voluntary" but seems instead a product of abjection, dependency, and attempted propitiation.

Solemnly debating the meanings and implications of cats out of the bag and tainted psychological fruit, the Court calls on metaphors found in other Court opinions—which themselves derive from a kind of homespun, aphoristic, popular psychology—and treats them as though they were good currency in the analysis of the suspect's lived experience and thus helpful in determining whether or not his rights have been violated. The Court does not ask whether these metaphors are in fact of much use in determining psychological motivation. One might think it would seek help from professional literature on the subject, in search of a more coherent picture of human motivation. But the Court relies instead on "common sense" and its own peculiar vernacular because to do otherwise would be dangerously to breach the enclosure of the law, to let it be infiltrated by an unsettling (and perhaps equally inconclusive) language from another domain. Whatever the doctrinal wisdom of the *Elstad* decision, the Court's opinions appear to offer a fairly stunning performance in rhetorical self-blinding.

Those who would place legal discourse in dialogue with other cultural discourses need, I think, to be aware of the law's capacity both to exclude and to admit a tamed and domesticated version of the disputed theory clamoring outside its castle walls. The problem of the "voluntary" confession in general, and the recovered memory cases in particular, may offer an allegory of the problem I tried to define at the outset of these remarks: the imperviousness of the law to its recontextualization within cultural studies. Yes, a cultural study of the law is possible. And it may be useful and illuminating. But given what the law, as a practice and an exercise of the power to adjudicate, is and needs to do, will cultural studies—or *can* it—make any difference to the law? Whether it *should* make a difference is open to debate, but that may be a debate that only takes place at academic conferences.

Notes

1   Guyora Binder and Robert Weisberg, "Symposium: The Critical Use of History: Cultural Criticism of the Law," 49 *Stan. L. Rev.* 1149, 1219 (1997).

2   See Paul W. Kahn, *The Cultural Study of Law: Reconstructing Legal Scholarship* (1999).

3   My argument here has affinities with that advanced by Stanley Fish. See Stanley Fish, "The Law Wishes to Have a Formal Existence," in *There's No Such Thing as Free Speech* 141, 156 (1994) (noting that "the law is continually creating and recreating itself out of the very materials and forces it is obliged, by its very desire to *be* law, to push away"). But see Jane B. Baron, "Law, Literature, and the Problems of Interdisciplinarity," 108 *Yale L.J.* 1059, 1061 (arguing that "[l]aw-and-literature scholarship has not questioned what the category 'law' consists of and has thus tended inadvertently to reinforce the notion of law as autonomous"). Baron's provocative challenge needs to be taken up in an argument about the practice of the law as social instrument.

4   For further discussion of these issues, see Peter Brooks, *Troubling Confessions: Speaking Guilt in Law and Literature* (2000).

5   For an extreme form of this subversion, see Freud's argument that criminals commit crimes in order to satisfy a powerful, preexisting, unconscious sense of guilt and a need for punishment. Guilt precedes crime, and the desire for punishment motivates the commission of crime. This neatly undoes the usual premises of criminal justice. See 14 Sigmund Freud, "Criminals from a Sense of Guilt," in *The Standard Edition of the Complete Psychological Works of Sigmund Freud* 332 (James Strachey ed., 1957).

6   884 F. Supp. 1435 (N.D. Cal. 1995).

7   Id. at 1438.

8   Id.

9   Id.

10   Id.

11   Id.

12   Id.

13   Judith Butler, "Quandaries of the Incest Taboo," in *Whose Freud?: The Place of Psycho-analysis in Contemporary Culture* 39, 40–41 (Peter Brooks and Alex Woloch eds., 2000).

14   727 P.2d 226 (Wash. 1986).

15   Id. at 236 (Pearson, J., dissenting).

16   Id.

17   The literature on repression, resistance, and the retrieval of memory in psychoanalysis is, of course, immense. For an interesting account, see 23 Sigmund Freud, "Constructions in Analysis," in *The Standard Edition of the Complete Psychological Works of Sigmund Freud* 257 (James Strachey ed., 1964); see also Donald Spence, *Narrative Truth and Historical Truth* (1982).

18   701 F. Supp. 1363 (N.D. Ill. 1988).

19   See Richard A. Posner, *The Problematics of Moral and Legal Theory* (1999).

20   Daniel P. Brown et al., *Memory, Trauma Treatment, and the Law* 605 (1998) (quoting State v. Walters, Nos. 93-S-2111–2112 (Superior Court, Hillsborough, S.D.N.H., 1995) (rev'd 698 A.2d 1244 (N.H. 1997)).

21   See Michel de Montaigne, "Des Boyteux," in *Essais,* bk. 3, essay 11, at 1156 (Albert Thibaudet ed., 1961).

22   470 U.S. 298 (1985).

23   384 U.S. 436 (1966).

24   470 U.S. at 302.

25   State v. Elstad, 658 P.2d 552, 555 (Or. App. 1983), quoted in 470 U.S. at 303.

26   470 U.S. at 298.

27   Id. at 303.

28   371 U.S. 471 (1963).

29   Although O'Connor cites to *Wong Sun,* the "taint" and "fruit of the poisonous tree" language appears to originate in Nardone v. United States, 308 U.S. 338, 341 (1939).

30   371 U.S. at 487–88.

31   United States v. Bayer, 331 U.S. 532, 540 (1947).

32   470 U.S. at 311.

33   Id.

34   Id. at 312.

35   Id. at 314.

36   Id. at 318.

37   Id. at 304.

38   Id. at 314.

39   Id. at 324 (Brennan, J., dissenting).

40   Id. at 327 (Brennan, J., dissenting) (quoting Harrison v. United States, 392 U.S. 219, 224–25 (1968) (quoting Di Cicco v. Schweizer, 221 N.Y. 431, 438 (1917))).

41 Id. at 328 (Brennan, J., dissenting) (quoting A. Aubry and R. Caputo, *Criminal Interrogation* 291 (3d ed. 1980)).

42 Id. (quoting R. Royal and S. Schutt, *The Gentle Art of Interviewing and Interrogation: A Professional Manual and Guide* 143 (1976)).

43 Id. at 346 (Brennan, J., dissenting).

44 Somewhere in the background of the "tainted fruit of the poisonous tree" arguments lurks a Miltonic echo: "Of Man's first disobedience, and the fruit / Of that forbidden tree whose mortal taste / Brought death into the World, and all our woe." John Milton, *Paradise Lost*, bk. 1, lines 1–3 (Northrop Frye ed., Holt, Rinehart and Winston 1960) (1667). In *Paradise Lost*, the fruit is poisonous in its effects because the tree is forbidden, not because the tree is poisonous. The "exclusionary rule" derived from the Fourth Amendment may claim, by analogy, that the "fruits" of an illegal search are poisonous because the search was forbidden. But the rhetoric of the Court tends to make the tree itself poisonous, thus setting up a slightly skewed—or tainted?—original metaphor from which it then derives its other metaphorical strings.

A Ghost in the House of Justice:
Death and the Language of the Law
Shoshana Felman

A witness faints on the stand during the Eichmann trial. This essay will
explore the meaning of this unexpected legal moment and will ask: Is the
witness's collapse relevant—and if so, in what sense—to the legal framework of
the trial? How does this courtroom event affect the trial's definition of legal
meaning in the wake of the Holocaust? Under what circumstances and in what
ways can the legal default of a witness constitute a legal testimony in its own
right?

I will present, first, Hannah Arendt's reading of this episode, and will later
contrast her reading with my own interpretation of this courtroom scene. Still
later, I will analyze the judges' reference to this scene.

These different and successive analytical and textual vantage points will be
systematically and commonly subordinated to the following three overriding
theoretical inquiries:

1. What is the role of human fallibility in trials?

2. Can moments of disruption of convention and of discourse—moments of
unpredictability that take the legal institution by surprise—nevertheless contribute to the formulation of a legal meaning?

3. How can such moments shed light on (what I set out to highlight as) the
key structural *relation between law and trauma*? What tools does the law
have—and what are the law's limits—in adjudicating massive death and in articulating legal meaning out of massive trauma?

Part One: Death and the Language of the Law

I

Two Visions of Historic Trials

In the postwar trials that attempted to judge history and to resolve the horrors of administrative massacre in the wake of the unprecedented trauma of the Second World War, two antithetical legal visions of historic trial have emerged: that of the Nuremberg trials in 1945 and that of the Eichmann trial in 1961. The difference between these two paradigms of historic trial derived from their divergent evidentiary approach: the Nuremberg prosecution made a decision to shun witnesses and base the case against the Nazi leaders exclusively on documents, whereas the prosecution in the Eichmann trial chose to rely extensively on witnesses as well as on documents to substantiate its case. While both prosecutors similarly used the trial to establish what in Nietzsche's term can be called a "monumental [legal] history,"[1] Nuremberg was a monumental documentary case, whereas the Eichmann trial was a monumental testimonial case (despite its equally substantial use of documents). In 1954, the chief prosecutor and the architect of the Nuremberg trials, Justice Robert Jackson, retrospectively explained the grounds for his choice of proof:

> The prosecution early was confronted with two vital decisions. . . . One was whether chiefly to rely upon living witnesses or upon documents for proof of the case. The decision . . . was to use and rest on documentary evidence to prove every point possible. The argument against this was that documents are dull, the press would not report them, the trial would become wearisome and would not get across to the people. There was much truth in this position, I must admit. But it seemed to me that witnesses, many of them persecuted and hostile to the Nazis, would always be chargeable with bias, faulty recollection, and even perjury. The documents could not be accused of partiality, forgetfulness, or invention, and would make the sounder foundation, not only for the immediate guidance of the tribunal, but for the ultimate verdict of history. The result was that the tribunal declared, in its judgment, "The case, therefore, against the defendants rests in a large measure on documents of their own making."[2]

The documentary approach matched the bureaucracy of the Nazi regime and was particularly suitable to the exposure of the monstrous bureaucratic nature of the crime and of its alibis. The testimonial approach was necessary for the full disclosure of the thought-defying magnitude of the offense against the victims, and it was particularly suitable to the valorization of the victims' narrative perspective.

The reason he decided to add living witnesses to documents, the Israeli prosecutor Gideon Hausner explained, was that the Nuremberg trials had *failed to transmit*,[3] or to impress on human memory and "on the hearts of men," the knowledge and the shock of what had happened. The Eichmann trial sought, in contrast, not only to establish facts but to transmit (transmit truth as event and as the shock of an *encounter* with events, transmit history as an experience). The tool of law was used not only as a tool of *proof* of unimaginable facts but, above all, as a compelling *medium of transmission*—as an effective tool of national and international *communication* of these thought-defying facts. In comparing thus the evidentiary approach of Nuremberg to his own legal choices, the Israeli prosecutor wrote:

> There is an obvious advantage in written proof; whatever it has to convey is there in black and white. . . . Nor can a document be . . . broken down in cross-examination. It speaks in a steady voice; it may not cry out, but neither can it be silenced. . . .
>
> This was the course adopted at the Nuremberg trials. . . . It was . . . efficient. . . . But it was also one of the reasons why the proceedings there failed to reach the hearts of men.
>
> In order merely to secure a conviction, it was obviously enough to let the archives speak. . . . But I knew we needed more than a conviction; we needed a living record of a gigantic human and national disaster. . . .
>
> In any criminal proceedings the proof of guilt and the imposition of a penalty, though all-important, are not the exclusive objects. Every trial also . . . tells a story. . . . Our perceptions and our senses are geared to limited experiences. . . . We stop perceiving living creatures behind the mounting totals of victims; they turn into incomprehensible statistics.
>
> It was beyond human powers to present the calamity in a way that would do justice to six million tragedies. The only way to concretize it was to call surviving witnesses, as many as the framework of the trial would allow, and to ask each of them to tell a tiny fragment of what he had seen

and experienced. . . . Put together, the various narratives of different people would be concrete enough to be apprehended. In this way I hoped to super-impose on a phantom a dimension of reality.[4]

Because of the differences in their evidentiary approach, the Nuremberg trials made a more solid contribution to international law, in setting up a binding legal precedent of crimes against humanity; the Eichmann trial made a greater impact on collective memory. The two trials dramatize the difference between human and nonhuman evidence. Jackson desires to exclude human vulnerability both from the process of the law and from the exercise of judgment. He thus protects the courtroom from the death it talks about. Because Jackson wants his legal evidence to be literally invulnerable, he has to give preference to nonhuman and nonliving evidence. "The documents could not be accused of partiality, forgetfulness, or invention." "[W]itnesses," on the other hand, "many of them persecuted," "would always be chargeable with bias, faulty recollection, and even perjury."[5]

In choosing, on the contrary, to include as evidence the previously excluded, fragile testimony of the persecuted, the Eichmann trial quite specifically gives legal space to the potential legal failings and shortcomings Jackson fears. It consciously *embraces* the vulnerability, the legal fallibility, and the fragility of the human witness. Paradoxically, it is precisely the witness's fragility that is called upon to testify and to bear witness.[6]

An Oath to the Dead (A Pseudonym)

Nowhere was this fragile essence of the human testimony more dramatically exemplified and more acutely tested than when, in one of the most breathtaking moments of the trial, a witness fainted on the stand.

He was called to testify because he was a crucially relevant eyewitness: he had met Eichmann in Auschwitz.[7] But he collapsed before he could narrate this factual encounter. His testimony thus amounted to a legal failure, the kind of legal failure Jackson feared. And yet this legal moment of surprise, captured on videotape,[8] has left an indelible mark on the trial and has impressed itself on visual and historical memory. This courtroom scene has since been broadcast many times on radio and television. Despite the repetition, the power of this legally compelling moment does not wane, and its force of astonishment does not diminish and does not fade. It has remained a literally unforgettable key moment of the trial, a signal or a symbol of a constantly replayed and yet ungrasped, ungraspable kernel of collective memory.[9] I propose to try to probe here the significance of this mysteriously material kernel.

Who was this witness? He happened to be a writer. He was known under the pseudonym Ka-Tsetnik, or K-Zetnik.[10] He saw himself as a messenger of the dead, a bearer of historical meaning he had the duty to preserve and to transmit. K-Zetnik is a slang word meaning a concentration camp inmate, one identified not by name but by the number the Nazis tattooed on each inmate's arm. "I must carry this name," K-Zetnik testified during the Eichmann trial, "as long as the world will not awaken after the crucifying of the nation . . . as humanity has risen after the crucifixion of one man."[11] K-Zetnik had published, prior to the Eichmann trial, several books that were translated into many languages and that had gained celebrity on both sides of the Atlantic. Describing human existence in extermination camps, they were all published as the successive volumes of what the author calls "the Chronicle of a Jewish Family in the Twentieth Century." The name K-Zetnik was selected almost automatically. The author began writing soon after he was liberated from Auschwitz, in a British army hospital in Italy. He had asked the Israeli soldier who was taking care of him to bring him pen and paper. He had made an oath to the dead, he said, to be their voice and to chronicle their story; since he felt his days were numbered, he had to hurry up; his writing was from the beginning racing against death. For two and a half weeks he hardly got up, writing in one fit his first book. He asked the soldier who was taking care of him to transfer the finished manuscript to Israel. Reading the title "Salamandra" on the first page, the soldier whispered: "You forgot to write the name of the author." "The name of the author?" the surviving writer cried out in reply: "They who went to the crematories wrote this book; write their name: Ka-Tsetnik."[12] Thus the soldier added in his handwriting the name that soon was to acquire world fame.

II

Testimony

"What is your full name?" asked the presiding judge.[13]

"Yehiel Dinoor,"[14] answered the witness. The prosecutor then proceeded. "What is the reason that you took the pen name K-Zetnik, Mr. Dinoor?"

"It is not a pen name," the witness (now seated) began answering. "I do not regard myself as a writer who writes literature. This is a chronicle from the planet of Auschwitz. I was there for about two years. Time there was different from what it is here on earth. Every split second ran on a different cycle of time. And the inhabitants of that planet had no names. They had neither parents nor children. They did not dress as we dress here. They were not born there nor did anyone give birth. Even their breathing was regulated by the laws of another nature. They did not live, nor did they die, in accordance with the laws of this world. Their names were the numbers, 'K-Zetnik so and so. . . .' They left me, they kept leaving me, left . . . for close to two years they left me and always left me behind. . . . I see them, they are watching me, I see them—"

At this point, the prosecutor gently interrupted: "Mr. Dinoor, could I perhaps put a few questions to you if you will consent?"

But Dinoor continued speaking in a hollow and tense voice, oblivious to the courtroom setting, as a man plunged in hallucination or in a hypnotic trance. "I see them. . . . I saw them standing in the line. . . ."

Thereupon the presiding judge matter-of-factly intervened: "Mr. Dinoor, please, please listen to Mr. Hausner; wait a minute, now you listen to me!"

The haggard witness vacantly got up and without a warning collapsed into a faint, slumping to the floor beside the witness stand.

Policemen ran toward Dinoor to lift his collapsed body, to support him and to carry him out of the courtroom.[15] The flabbergasted audience remained motionless, staring in disbelief. "Quiet, quiet, quiet!" ordered the presiding judge: "I am asking for silence." A woman's cry was heard from the direction of the audience. A woman wearing sunglasses was coming from the audience toward the unconscious human body held by the policemen, saying she was the witness's wife. "You may approach," the bench conceded. "I do not believe that we can go on." The witness was still limp and lifeless, plunged in a deep coma. "We shall take a recess now," declared the presiding judge. "Beth Hamishpat"—["the House of Justice"]—shouted the usher, as the audience rose to its feet and the three judges in their black robes were going out. An ambulance was called and rushed the witness to the hospital, where he spent two weeks between life and death in a paralytic stroke. In time, he would recover.[16]

The Legal versus the Poetical

The poet Haim Gouri who covered the trial wrote:

> What happened here was the inevitable. [K-Zetnik's] desperate attempt to transgress the legal channel and to return to the planet of the ashes in

order to bring it to us was too terrifying an experience for him. He broke down. Others spoke here for days and days, and told us each his story from the bottom up. . . . He tried to depart from the quintessential generalization, tried to define, like a meteor, the essence of that world. He tried to find the shortest way between the two planets among which his life had passed. . . .

Or maybe he caught a glimpse of Eichmann all of a sudden and his soul was short-circuited into darkness, all the lights going out. . . .

In a way he had said everything. Whatever he was going to say later was, it turns out, superfluous detail.[17]

This empathetic description, which took the testimony on its terms and which, examining it from the vantage point of its own metaphors, poetically reflected back the shock and the emotion of the audience, was a poet's coverage of a fellow poet's testimony. The legal coverage of this episode that Hannah Arendt sent to the *New Yorker* and later published in her famous *Eichmann in Jerusalem* was much harsher and much less forgiving.

Arendt disputed fundamentally the way in which the prosecution framed the trial by narratively focusing it on the victims. The state sought to narrate a unique legal story that had *never before been told* and that had failed to be articulated by the Nuremberg trials. To do so, it sought to reconstruct the facts of the Nazi war against the Jews from the victims' point of view and to establish, for the first time in legal history, a "monumental history" not of the victors but of the victims. But Arendt argued that the trial should be focused on the criminal, not on the victim; she wanted it to be a cosmopolitan trial, rather than a Jewish nationalist one; she wanted it to tell the story of totalitarianism and of totalitarian crimes against humanity, rather than the story of the Jewish tragedy and of the crime against the Jewish people. She thus felt impelled to fight Jewish self-centeredness on every point (and on every legal point) and systematically to deconstruct and to decenter the prosecution's monumentalizing victim narrative. In her role as legal reporter for the *New Yorker*, Arendt finds a stage for exercising her ironic talents not only to dispute the story of the prosecution but also to narrate a contrapuntal legal narrative and to become in turn an ironic or a *contrapuntal prosecutor*—a prosecutor or (in Nietzsche's terms) a critical historian of the monumental trial.[18]

When she was first confronted with the Nazi crimes during the Nuremberg trials, Arendt believed the magnitude of the phenomenon and the abyss it opened in perception could not be apprehended by the law, except by rupturing its legal framework. She thus wrote in 1946 to Karl Jaspers, her ex-teacher and the continued German friend and interlocutor whom she refound at the end of the war, and through whose sole agency she has now reconnected with her own disrupted German youth:

> Your definition of Nazi policy as a crime ("criminal guilt")[19] strikes me as questionable. The Nazi crimes, it seems to me, *explode the limits of the law*; and that is precisely what constitutes their monstrousness. For these crimes, no punishment is severe enough. . . . That is, this guilt, in contrast to all criminal guilt, oversteps and shatters any and all legal systems. That is the reason why the Nazis in Nuremberg are so smug. . . . And just as inhuman as their guilt is the innocence of the victims. Human beings simply can't be as innocent as they all were in the face of the gas chambers (the most repulsive usurer was as innocent as a newborn child because no crime deserves such a punishment). We are simply not equipped to deal, on a human, political level, with a guilt that is beyond crime and an innocence that is beyond goodness or virtue. This is *the abyss* that opened up before us as early as 1933 . . . and into which we have finally stumbled. I don't know how we will ever get out of it, for the Germans are burdened now with . . . hundreds of thousands of people who cannot be adequately punished within the legal system; and we Jews are burdened with millions of innocents, by reason of which every Jew alive today can see himself as innocence personified.[20]

Jaspers does not agree with Arendt. Her attitude, he says, is *too poetical.* But poetry, he emphasizes, is a much more inadequate, a much less sober tool of apprehension than the law. Poetry by definition is misguided because, by its very nature, it is made to *miss the banality* of the phenomenon. And the banality, in Jaspers's eyes, is the constitutive feature of the Nazi horror, a feature that should not be mystified or mythified.

> You say that what the Nazis did cannot be comprehended as "crime"—I'm not altogether comfortable with your view, because a guilt that goes beyond all criminal guilt inevitably takes on a streak of "greatness"—of satanic greatness—which is, for me, as inappropriate for the Nazis as all the talk about the "demonic" element in Hitler. . . . It seems to me that *we have to see these things in their total banality*, in their prosaic triviality, because that's what truly characterizes them. . . . I regard any hint of myth and legend with horror. . . . Your view is appealing—especially as contrasted with what I see as the false inhuman innocence of the victims. But all this would have to be expressed differently. . . . The way you express it, *you've*

almost taken the path of poetry. And a Shakespeare would never be able to give adequate form to this material—his instinctive aesthetic sense would lead to falsification of it. . . . There is no idea and no essence here. Nazi crime is properly a subject for psychology and sociology, for psychopathology and jurisprudence only.[21]

From its inception, the future concept of the "banality of evil" emerges as a concept that defines itself by its methodological invalidation of the "path of poetry," against which it sets up the purposely reductive terminology of "jurisprudence only" and the sobering path of the law (and of the social sciences). "I found what you say about my thoughts on 'beyond crime and innocence' half convincing," Arendt replies at first ambivalently; but she concedes: "We have to combat all impulses to mythologize the horrible."[22]

When the Eichmann trial is announced fifteen years later, Jaspers and Arendt switch positions. Jaspers maintains that Israel should not try Eichmann because Eichmann's guilt—the subject of the trial—is "larger than law."[23] Arendt insists that only law can deal with it: "We have no tools to hand except legal ones," she says.[24] By now, the tool of law is in her hands, par excellence, *a tool of apprehension of banality*, a tool specifically of *demythologization* and of deliberate sobering reduction. And if the perpetrator must be banalized and demythologized to be understood in its proper light, so must the victim. No longer can the victim's innocence be allowed to burst the legal frame or to explode the tool of law. No longer can the victim be spared the banality of innocence.

III

Arendt's Contrapuntal Tale

Arendt reserves some of her harshest language and some of her fiercest irony in *Eichmann in Jerusalem* for the description of K-Zetnik's unsuccessful court appearance. Indeed, nowhere is Arendt's role as contrapuntal, critical historian of the trial more clearly and more blatantly expressed than in her narration of this episode. Arendt views K-Zetnik's failure on the stand as symptomatic of the general misfire of the trial. She blames this general misfire on the misdirections and the blunders of the prosecution, whose witness has symbolically defaulted through its own fault.

Generally, Arendt makes three objections to the prosecution's choice of witnesses:

1. Contrary to legal rules of evidence, the witnesses are not selected for their relevance to Eichmann's acts but for the purposes of the depiction of a larger picture of the Nazi persecution of the Jews. "This case," writes Arendt disapprovingly, "was built on what the Jews had suffered, not on what Eichmann had done."[25] This depiction by the victims of the persecution they had suffered and their reconstruction of the global history of their victimization is irrelevant in Arendt's eyes. K-Zetnik as a witness seems to Arendt to exemplify the witnesses' irrelevance.

2. Contrary to Arendt's judgment and to her taste, the prosecution prefers witnesses of prominence. It has a predilection, in particular, for famous writers such as K-Zetnik and Abba Kovner. The former's testimony was a fiasco. The latter, Arendt caustically notes, "had not so much testified as addressed an audience with the ease of someone who is used to speaking in public and resents interruptions from the floor."[26] In Arendt's eyes, a witness's fame is a corrupting element of the judicial process. The writer's professional articulateness compromises the truth of the testimony in turning testimonies into speeches. Such is K-Zetnik's case.

3. The prosecution's choice of witnesses is guided, Arendt charges, by theatrical considerations. The witnesses are called for the sensational effects provided by their "tales of horror."[27] K-Zetnik's breakdown is an accidental yet consistent illustration of this logic that transforms testimony into a theatrical event that parasitizes the trial.

Arendt writes:

> At no time is there anything theatrical in the conduct of the judges. . . . [J]udge Landau . . . is doing his best, his very best to prevent this trial from becoming a show trial under the influence of the prosecutor's love of showmanship. Among the reasons he cannot always succeed is the simple fact that the proceedings happen on a stage before an audience, with the usher's marvelous shout at the beginning of each session producing the effect of the rising curtain. Whoever planned this auditorium . . . had a theater in mind. . . . [C]learly, this courtroom is not a bad place for the show trial David Ben Gurion, Prime Minister of Israel, had in mind when he decided to have Eichmann kidnapped in Argentina and brought to the district court of Jerusalem to stand trial for his role in "the final solution to the Jewish question." . . .
>
> Yet no matter how consistently the judges shunned the limelight, there they were, seated at the top of the raised platform, facing the audience as from the stage in a play. . . . [T]he audience was supposed to represent the

whole world. . . . [T]hey were to watch a spectacle as sensational as the Nuremberg Trials, only this time "the tragedy of Jewry as a whole was to be the central concern." . . .

It was precisely the play aspect of the trial that collapsed under the weight of the hair-raising atrocities. . . .

Thus, the trial never became a play, but the show trial Ben Gurion had had in mind . . . did take place.[28]

Most of the witnesses, Arendt narrates, were Israeli citizens who "had been picked from hundreds and hundreds of applicants."[29] But Arendt is suspicious of witnesses who volunteer. She is allergic to the narcissism she keeps spying both in the legal actors (the chief prosecutor in particular) and in the witnesses whom she suspects of seeking or being complacent with the elements of spectacle that parasitize and compromise the trial. K-Zetnik is for her a case in point. The narrative of his collapse becomes, in Arendt's hands, not an emotional account of human testimonial pathos but a didactic tale that illustrates ironically what accidents can happen when a witness is, quite paradoxically, too eager to appear. It is thus with her most sarcastic, most undercutting, and funniest style that Arendt will approach this testimony.

How much wiser it would have been to resist these pressures altogether . . . and to seek out those who had not volunteered! As though to prove the point, the prosecution called upon a writer, well known on both sides of the Atlantic under the name K-Zetnik . . . as the author of several books on Auschwitz which dealt with brothels, homosexuals, and other "human interest stories." He started off, as he had done at many of his public appearances, with an explanation of his adopted name. . . . He continued with a little excursion into astrology: the star "influencing our fate in the same way as the star of ashes at Auschwitz is there facing our planet, radiating toward our planet." And when he had arrived at "the unnatural power above Nature" which had sustained him thus far, and now, for the first time, paused to catch his breath, even Mr. Hausner felt that something had to be done about this "testimony," and, very timidly, very politely, interrupted: "Could I perhaps put a few questions to you if you will consent?" Whereupon the presiding judge saw his chance as well: "Mr. Dinoor, *please, please* listen to Mr. Hausner and to me." In response, the disappointed witness, probably deeply wounded, fainted and answered no more questions.[30]

"[E]ven Mr. Hausner felt that something had to be done about this 'testimony.'" For Arendt, this is a "testimony" only in quotation marks. It is an aberration of a testimony. Arendt's derision is, however, not directed personally at K-Zetnik but derives from an impersonal black-humorous perception of the ludicrous, hilarious way in which the courtroom as a whole could be mistaken, at this legally surprising moment, for a theater of the absurd. The buffoonery comes from the situation, not from the people. The farcical or comic element derives from the discrepancy and from the total incommensurability between the two dimensions that the testimony inadvertently brings into dialogue: the natural and the supernatural, the rationality and discipline of courtroom protocols and the irruption of irrationality through a delirious rambling or what Arendt calls an "astrological excursion" (the witness's voyage into "other planets").[31] I would argue differently than Arendt that the courtroom in its very legal essence here flirts with madness and with nonsense. For some, this courtroom drama and the suffering it unfolds both in the past and in the present of the courtroom constitute a tragedy, a shock. For Arendt, this is a comedy. Pain is translated into laughter. If this is theater, sometimes potentially sublime or tragic, it is a Brechtian theater. Keeping her distance is crucial for Arendt. The ludicrous example of K-Zetnik's fainting and his default as a witness illustrates, for Arendt, not the proximity uncannily revealed between madness and reason, not the profound pathos of a cognitive abyss abruptly opened up inside the courtroom and materialized in the unconscious body of the witness, but the folly of the prosecution in both its disrespect for legal relevance and in its narcissistic and misguided predilection for witnesses of prominence. This double folly of the prosecution gets both its poetic justice and its comic punishment when its own witness faints out of the witness stand and inadvertently becomes an inert, hostile witness who "answers no more questions."[32]

Evidentiary Misunderstandings

Looking at the facts, Arendt's fierce irony ironically is based on two erroneous assumptions:

1. Contrary to what Arendt presumes, Dinoor did not volunteer to share his "tale of horror" on the witness stand but instead was an involuntary and reluctant witness. As a writer, he had always shunned public appearances as a matter of principle. Consequently, he had at first refused to testify. The chief prosecutor pressured Dinoor to obtain his reluctant consent to appear before the court.

2. Among the trial's testimonies, Arendt depicts K-Zetnik's as the testimony that is self-evidently the most crazily remote from facts.[33] She thus regards this testimony as the most grotesque and hyperbolic illustration of "the

right of the witnesses to be irrelevant,"[34] and she presumes it could not possibly bear any legal relevance to Eichmann's case. What Arendt does not know and does not suspect is that Dinoor was one of the very few survivors known to have actually met Eichmann at Auschwitz.[35] Had he been able to complete his testimony, he would have turned out to be a material eyewitness.

Yet what K-Zetnik wants is not to prove but to transmit. The language of the lawyer and that of the artist meet across the witness stand only to concretize within the trial their misunderstanding and their *missed encounter*.[36]

"When the prosecutor invited me to come and testify at the Eichmann trial," writes K-Zetnik more than twenty years after the trial,

> I begged him to release me of this testimony. The prosecutor then said to me: Mr. Dinoor, this is a trial whose protocol must put on record testimony proving that there was a place named Auschwitz and what happened there. The mere sound of these words made me sick to my stomach, and I said: Sir, describing Auschwitz is beyond me! Hearing me, his staff eyed me with suspicion. You, the man who wrote these books, you expect us to believe you can't explain to the judges what Auschwitz was? I fell silent. How could I tell them that I am consumed by the search for the word that will express the look in the eyes of those who headed toward the crematorium, when they passed me with their gaze inside my eyes? The prosecutor was not convinced, and I appeared at the Eichmann trial. Then came the judge's first question about Auschwitz and no sooner did I squeeze out a few miserable sentences than I dropped to the floor and was hospitalized half paralyzed and disfigured in my face.[37]

Trauma and the Language of the Law

" 'Mr. Dinoor,' " goes Arendt's contrapuntal narrative, " 'please, please listen to Mr. Hausner and to me.' In response, the disappointed witness, probably deeply wounded, fainted and answered no more questions."[38]

There follows Arendt's serious commentary on her own sarcastic and laughingly didactic tale: "This, to be sure, was an exception, but if it was an exception that proved the rule of normality, it did not prove the rule of simplicity or of ability to tell a story, let alone of the rare capacity for distinguishing between things that had happened to the storyteller more than sixteen, and sometimes twenty, years ago, and what he had read and heard and imagined in the meantime."[39] For these very reasons, Nuremberg at the war's end excluded living witnesses and limited the evidence to documents, opting for a case of legal invulnerability that only the nonhuman and nonliving paper evidence could guarantee. "The documents," said Jackson, "could not be accused of partiality, forgetfulness, or invention. . . . Witnesses," on the other hand, "many of them persecuted and hostile to the Nazis, would always be chargeable with bias, faulty recollection, and even perjury."[40] In a similar vein, Arendt disqualifies K-Zetnik as a witness because his testimony fails to meet legal criteria and fails to be contained by the authority of the restrictive safeguards of the legal rules. In Jackson's spirit, out of concern for the law as representative of culture and as the arbiter of truth in history, Arendt excludes K-Zetnik's discourse because it stands for the *contamination between facts and fiction*—for the confusion and the interpenetration between law and literature—that the law in principle cannot accept and has to resolutely, rigidly rule out.

By legal standards, K-Zetnik represents for Arendt a communicative failure. I will argue here that Arendt in her turn represents, in more than one sense, in her stance toward K-Zetnik, *the limits of the law* in its encounter with the phenomenon of *trauma*.[41]

I would like now to contrast Arendt's interpretation of K-Zetnik's legal failure with my own reading of this courtroom scene.

IV

Intrusions

What Arendt's irony illuminates is how the law is used as a straightjacket to tame history as madness.

Arendt's sarcastically positivistic vision of K-Zetnik's failure makes a positivistic recourse to a summarily explanatory psychological vocabulary, through which the legal vision overrides (and Arendt condescendingly dismisses) the witness's (narcissistic) subjectivity. "In response, the disappointed witness, probably deeply wounded, fainted and answered no more questions."[42]

Against this simplifying psychological vocabulary, I will propose to use a psychoanalytic one informed by jurisprudential trauma theory.[43] I will combine thereby a psychoanalytic with a philosophical and legal reading of this courtroom scene.

Out of the witness stand falls, in my vision, not a "disappointed witness," but a terrified one. The witness is not "deeply wounded"; he is *retraumatized*. The trial reenacts the trauma.

I have argued elsewhere that the law is, so to speak, professionally blind to its constitutive and structural relation to both private and collective cultural trauma, and that its "forms of judicial blindness" take shape wherever the structure of the trauma unwittingly takes over the structure of a trial and wherever the legal institution, unawares, triggers a legal repetition of the trauma that it puts on trial or attempts to cure.[44] In K-Zetnik's case, this happens punctually.

When the judge admonishes Dinoor from the authoritarian position of the bench, coercing him into a legal mode of discourse and demanding his cooperation as a witness, K-Zetnik undergoes severe traumatic shock in re-experiencing the same terror and panic that dumbfounded him each time when, as an inmate, he was suddenly confronted by the inexorable Nazi authorities of Auschwitz. The judge's words are heard not as an utterance originating from the present of the courtroom situation but rather as a censure uttered from within "the other planet," as an intrusive threat articulated right out of the violence of the traumatic scene that is replaying in K-Zetnik's mind.[45] The call to order by the judge urging the witness to obey—strictly to answer questions and to follow legal rules—impacts the witness *physically* as an invasive call to order by an ss officer. Once more, the imposition of a heartless and unbending rule of order violently robs him of his words and, in reducing him to silence, once more threatens to annihilate him, to erase his essence as a *human* witness. Panicked, K-Zetnik loses consciousness.[46] He will later write about his unrelenting Auschwitz nightmares:

> In a trembling I lift my eyes to see the face of God in its letters, and see in front of me the face of an ss man.[47]

> I grow terrified. . . . The rules here are invisible. . . . No telling what's permitted and what's prohibited.[48]

> I was seized by fear and trembling. I am crying of dread. I want to hide my face and not be seen. But there is no escape from Auschwitz. There is no hiding place in Auschwitz.[49]

Between Life and Death: Frontier Evidence

Prior to his fainting spell, at the point where the prosecutor interrupts him, K-Zetnik tries to define Auschwitz by re-envisaging the terrifying moment of Selection, of repeated weekly separation between inmates chosen for an imminent extermination and inmates arbitrarily selected for life. This moment is ungraspable, the witness tries to say: "And the inhabitants of that planet had no names. They had neither parents nor children. . . . They did not live, nor did they

die, in accordance with the laws of this world. Their names were the numbers.
... They left me, they kept leaving me, left ... for close to two years they left me
and always left me behind ... I see them, they are watching me, I see them ..."[50]

What K-Zetnik keeps reliving of the death camp is the moment of departure, the last gaze of the departed, the exchange of looks between the dying and
the living at the very moment in which life and death are separating but are still
tied up together and can for the last time see each other eye to eye.

"Even those who were there don't know Auschwitz," writes K-Zetnik in a
later memoir:

> Not even someone who was there for two long years as I was. For
> Auschwitz is another planet, whereas we humankind, occupants of the
> planet Earth, we have no key to decipher the code-name Auschwitz. How
> could I dare defile the look in the eyes of those who head toward the cre-
> matorium? They passed me, they knew where they were going, and I knew
> where they were going. Their eyes are looking at me and my eyes are look-
> ing at them, the eyes of the going in the eyes of the remaining, under silent
> skies above the silent earth. Only that look in the eyes and the last silence.
> . . .
>
> For two years they passed me and their look was inside my eyes.[51]

A Community of Death, or Giving Voice to What Cannot Be Said

In constantly reliving through the moment of departure the repeated separation
between life and death, what K-Zetnik testifies to is, however, not the separation or the difference between life and death but on the contrary their interpenetration, their ultimate resemblance. On the witness stand, he keeps reliving his connection to the dead, his bond to the exterminated. His loyalty to
them is symbolized by his adopted name K-Zetnik, with which he signs, he
says, the stories that in fact are theirs:

> Since then this name testifies on all my books. . . .
> I am a man! . . . A man who wants to live!
> "You have forgotten to write your name on the manuscript. . . ."
> "The nameless, they themselves! The anonymous! Write their name:
> K-Zetnik."[52]

> How could I explain that it was not me who wrote the book; they who
> went to the crematorium as anonymous, they wrote the book! They, the

anonymous narrators. . . . For two years they passed before me on their way to the crematorium and left me behind.[53]

> All of them are now buried in me and continue to live in me. I made an oath to them to be their voice, and when I got out of Auschwitz they went with me, they and the silent blocks, and the silent crematorium, and the silent horizons, and the mountain of ashes.[54]

In a way K-Zetnik on the witness stand is not alone. He is accompanied by those who left him but who live within him. "I made an oath to them to be their voice." The writer K-Zetnik therefore could symbolically be viewed as the most central witness to the trial's announced project to *give voice to the six million dead.* K-Zetnik's testimony and his literary project pick up on the prosecutor's legal project.

> When I stand before you, Judges of Israel, in this court [the prosecutor said in his opening address] I do not stand alone. With me . . . stand six million prosecutors. But alas, they cannot rise to level the finger of accusation in the direction of the glass dock and cry out *J'accuse* against the man who sits there. For their ashes are piled in the hills of Auschwitz. . . . Their blood cries to Heaven, but their voice cannot be heard. Thus it falls to me to be their mouthpiece and to deliver the awesome indictment in their name.[55]

Between Two Names

Because he is in turn speaking for the dead, K-Zetnik must remain, like them, anonymous and nameless. He must testify, that is, under the name K-Zetnik.[56] His memory of Auschwitz is the oblivion of his name. But, in a court of law, a witness cannot remain nameless and cannot testify anonymously. A witness is accountable precisely to his legal, given name.

"*Mr. Dinoor*, please, please listen to Mr. Hausner and to me,"[57] says the presiding judge impatiently, putting an end to the account that the witness gives of his adopted name.

K-Zetnik faints because he cannot be interpellated at this moment by his legal name, Dinoor: the dead still claim him as *their* witness, as K-Zetnik who belongs to them and is still one of them. The court reclaims him as *its* witness, as Dinoor. He cannot bridge the gap between the two names and the two claims. He plunges into the abyss between the different planets. On the frontier between the living and the dead, between the present and the past, he falls as though he were himself a corpse.

V

Unmastered Past

Having no interest in sociopsychological or psychoanalytical phenomena, Arendt has neither a profound insight into nor an interest in trauma. She has an interest, however, in its *legal remedy*—in the trial as a means to *overcome* and to subdue a traumatic past. But K-Zetnik does not seize his legal chance to overcome the trauma on the witness stand. He is, rather, once more overcome by it. What is worse, he makes a spectacle of his scandalous collapse within the legal forum. K-Zetnik thus defeats the purpose of the law, which is precisely to *translate the trauma into consciousness.* He loses consciousness and loses his self-mastery, whereas the purpose of the law is on the contrary to get under control and to regain a conscious mastery over the traumatic nightmare of a history whose impact, as Arendt recognizes in her nonpathetic, understated style, continues to have repercussions in the world's consciousness and thus remains with all of us precisely as the world's—Israel's as well as Germany's—"unmastered past."[58]

At the heart of the "unmastered past," the trial tries to master an abyss.[59]

Trials and Abysses

K-Zetnik's loss of consciousness materializes in the courtroom what the trial cannot master: at once an abyss of trauma and an epistemological abyss, a cognitive rupture that Arendt, unrelatedly, will theorize and underscore in her political and philosophical account of the Nazi genocide.[60] Arendt in turn experienced this epistemological abyss when the news of Auschwitz reached her for the first time as a shock that could not be assimilated. "What was decisive," Arendt confides to Günter Gaus in a German radio interview in 1964,

> was the day we learnt about Auschwitz. That was in 1943. And at first we didn't believe it . . . because militarily it was unnecessary and uncalled for. My husband . . . said don't be gullible, don't take these stories at face value. They can't go that far! And then a half-year later we believed it after all, because we had the proof. That was the real shock. Before that we said: Well one has enemies. That is entirely natural. Why shouldn't a people have enemies? But this was different. *It was really as if an abyss had opened.*[61]

But despite the shock, despite the cognitive rupture and the epistemological gap in history and in historical perception, Arendt's life consists in crossing the abyss and overstepping it, beyond the rupture it has left. It later seems to Arendt, as she says to Günter Gaus, that "there should be a basis for communication precisely in the abyss of Auschwitz."[62] The law provides a forum and a language for such communication.

I would argue that the Eichmann trial is, for Arendt, quite precisely what she calls "the basis for communication" in and over the abyss of Auschwitz. But K-Zetnik's plunge into a coma interrupts the process of communication painstakingly established by the law. K-Zetnik has remained too close to the reality and to the shock of the event, perhaps too close for Arendt's comfort. He is still a captive of the planet of the ashes. He is still *in* the Holocaust, still on the brink of the abyss, which he unwittingly reopens in the courtroom when the law has barely started to construct its legal bridge.

The law requires that the witness should be able to narrate a story in the past, to recount an event in the past tense. K-Zetnik is unable to regard the Holocaust as past event but must relive it in the present, through the infinite traumatic repetition of a past that is not past, that has no closure and from which no distance can be taken.

Law, on the contrary, requires and provides distance from the Holocaust. Its inquiry and judgment are contingent on a separation between past and present. Law requires and brings closure and totalization of the evidence and of its meaning. This is why K-Zetnik's testimony, which defies at once legal reduction and legal closure, must remain unrealized, unfinished.

Part Two: Evidence in Law and Evidence in Art

VI

Between Law and Art

In 1964, a leading avant-garde literary critic in America, Susan Sontag, in a discussion of a German literary work about the role played by the pope during the Holocaust, surprisingly and quite provocatively argued that the Eichmann trial was "the most interesting and moving work of art of the past ten years."[63]

We live in a time in which tragedy is not an art form but a form of history. Dramatists no longer write tragedies. But we do have works of art (not always recognized as such) that attempt to resolve the great historical tragedies of our time. If then the supreme tragic event of modern times is the murder of six million Jews, the most interesting and moving work of art of the past ten years is the trial of Adolf Eichmann in Jerusalem in 1961.[64]

I do not believe, for my part, that the Eichmann trial—or any trial—can be reduced to, or subsumed in, the performance or the drama of a work of art. There is at least one crucial difference between an event of law and an event of art, no matter how dramatic they both are: *a work of art cannot sentence to death.* A trial, unlike art, is grounded in the sanctioned legal violence it has the power (and sometimes the duty) to enact.[65]

While it cannot be accepted at face value, Sontag's paradoxical remark about the Eichmann trial is nevertheless illuminating, not as a comment about trials but as an observation about art's relation to (juridical) reality. While the Eichmann trial can under no circumstances be regarded as a work of art, works of art have come today to imitate, to replicate, or to mimic the legal structures of the Eichmann trial.

The strongest and most eloquent example of this trend (which reached its climax decades after Sontag's article) can be seen in the film *Shoah* by Claude Lanzmann, a work of art made of reality whose legal, testimonial format is informed (and perhaps inspired) by the Eichmann trial[66] and of which it could indeed be said, in Sontag's words, that it is "the most interesting and moving work of art of the past years."[67]

I speak here of *Shoah* as *emblematic* of art after the Holocaust and as *paradigmatic* of the work of art of our times. I argue that the Eichmann trial is the complementary event (the legal correlative) of the contemporary process of art's invasion by the structures of the trial and of its transformation into testimony, a process by which writers like K-Zetnik (like Elie Wiesel, Paul Celan, Albert Camus, and others) have precisely vowed to make of art itself a witness, to present, that is, historical and legal evidence by means of art. What, then, is the difference between law and art when both are underwritten by the legal process and when both vow to pursue reality? "Reality," says Arendt, "is different from, and more than, the totality of facts and events, which anyhow is unascertainable. Who says what is . . . always tells a story."[68] In Arendt's words, I argue that *law's story* focuses on ascertaining *the totality of facts* and events. *Art's story* focuses on *what is different from,* and *more than,* that totality. I argue that the breakdown of the witness in the Eichmann trial was (unwittingly) at once part of the totality of facts and part of what was different from, and more than, that totality. In that sense, it was inadvertently *law's story* and *art's story* at the same time. "The truth" says Lanzmann, "kills the possibility of fiction."[69] In the same way that art is today transpierced, invaded by the language and the structures of the trial, the Eichmann trial—through K-Zetnik's court appearance—was transpierced, invaded by the artist's language, by the artist's testimony and by the artist's astonishing collapse.

The artist's language cannot relegate traumatic suffering to the past. "The worst moral and artistic crime that can be committed in producing a work dedicated to the Holocaust," says Lanzmann, "is to consider the Holocaust as past. *Either the Holocaust is legend or it is present: in no case is it a memory.* A film devoted to the Holocaust . . . can only be an investigation into the present of the Holocaust or at least into a past whose scars are still so freshly and vividly inscribed in certain places and in the consciences of some people that it reveals itself in a *hallucinated timelessness.*"[70] In a similar way, K-Zetnik does not treat the Holocaust as past but lives it as a present that endlessly repeats itself in a hallucinated timelessness. The hallucinated timelessness—the time of traumatic repetition and the time of art—is the precise time of K-Zetnik's legal testimony. But legal temporality cannot admit, cannot include, cannot acknowledge timelessness except as rupture of the legal frame. K-Zetnik's court appearance marks, thus, an invasion of the trial and of legal temporality by the endless, timeless temporality of art.

Law is a language of abbreviation, of limitation and totalization. Art is a language of infinity and of the irreducibility of fragments, a language of embodiment, of incarnation and of embodied incantation or of endless rhythmic *repetition.* Because it is by definition a discipline of limits, law distances the Holocaust; art brings it closer. The function of the judgment in the Eichmann trial was paradoxically to *totalize* and *distance* the event: the *trial made a past out of the Holocaust.*[71] And yet, within the courtroom, in the figure of K-Zetnik, the Holocaust returned as a ghost or as an incarnated, living present.

K-Zetnik's discourse in the trial has remained unfinished and, like art, interminable. In the courtroom, its lapse into interminability—into unconsciousness and silence—was paradoxically a physical reminder of the real, a physical reminder of a bodily reality that fractured the totality of facts sought by the law. But the testimonial power of this real presence, of this irreducible bodily presence of the witness, lay precisely in the pathos—in the crying power —of its legal muteness.

"But what can I do when I'm struck mute?" K-Zetnik will write almost thirty years after the Eichmann trial, in trying to explain at once the legal failure of his testimony and the very principle of interminability and inexhaustibility of his continued testimonial art:

But what can I do when I'm struck mute? I have neither word nor name for it all. Genesis says: "And Adam gave names . . ." When God finished creating the earth and everything upon it, Adam was asked to give names to all that God had created. Till 1942 there was no Auschwitz in existence. For Auschwitz there is no name other than Auschwitz. My heart will be ripped to pieces if I say, "In Auschwitz they burned people alive!" Or "In Auschwitz people died of starvation." But that is not Auschwitz. People have died of starvation before, and people did burn alive before. But that is not Auschwitz. What, then, is Auschwitz? I have no words to express it; I don't have a name for it. Auschwitz is a primal phenomenon. I don't have the key to unlock it. But don't the tears of the mute speak his anguish? And don't his screams cry his distress? Don't his bulging eyes reveal the horror? I am that mute.[72]

Muteness in a courtroom is normally negative or void, devoid of legal meaning. Muteness in art, however, can be fraught with meaning. It is *out of its muteness* that K-Zetnik's writing in this passage *speaks*. It is out of its silence that his testimonial art derives its literary power. *Art is* what makes silence speak.

I would argue that it was precisely through K-Zetnik's *legal muteness* that the trial inadvertently *gave silence a transmitting power* and—although not by intention—managed to transmit the legal meaning of collective trauma with the incremental power of a work of art. Once the trial gave transmissibility to silence, other silences became, within the trial, fraught with meaning.[73] At the limit of what could be legally grasped, something of the order of K-Zetnik's mute cry—something of the order of the speechlessness and of the interminability of art—was present in the courtroom as a silent shadow of the trial or as a negative of the proceedings. It was present in the interstices of the law as a ghost inside the house of justice. The poet Haim Gouri noted in his coverage of the trial: "With an unmatched force, the court has managed to restrain the crushing power of the cry that burst out, now as if for the first time, and to transmit it partially into a language of facts and numbers and dates, while letting the remainder of that cry float over the trial like a ghost."[74]

VII

The Judgment

Unlike K-Zetnik's testimony, the Eichmann trial did have closure. For his crimes against the Jewish people, his war crimes and his crimes against humanity, the judges sentenced Eichmann to "the greatest penalty known to the law."[75] The judgment totalized a statement of the evidence. Like Arendt, the judges underscored the fact that their authority for doing justice (and of making justice seen) was contingent on the *force of limitation* of the law. "The Judgment in the Eichmann case," Arendt reports for once approvingly, "could not have been clearer":

> All attempts to widen the range of the trial had to be resisted, because the court "could not allow itself to be enticed into provinces which are outside its sphere. . . . The judicial process [wrote the judges] has ways of its own, which are laid down by law, and which do not change, whatever the subject of the trial may be." The court, moreover, could not overstep these limits without ending "in complete failure." Not only does it not have at its disposal "the tools required for the investigation of general questions, *it speaks with an authority whose very weight depends upon its limitation.*"[76]

And yet, even the judges felt the need to point to the fact that there was something in the trial that went beyond their jurisdiction and beyond the jurisdiction of the law. Thus they wrote:

> If these be the sufferings of the individual, then the sum total of the suffering of the millions—about a third of the Jewish people, tortured and slaughtered—is certainly beyond human understanding, and who are we to try to give it adequate expression? This is a task for the great writers and poets. *Perhaps it is symbolic that even the author who himself went through the hell named Auschwitz, could not stand the ordeal in the witness box and collapsed.*[77]

What the judges say is not simply that law and art are two modes of transmission of the Holocaust, two languages in which to translate the incomprehensible into some sort of sense, two modes of coping with collective trauma and of crossing the abyss of a mad and nightmarish history.

The judges recognize that even in the legal mode, within the language of the trial, the collapse of the writer and his breakdown as a witness were endowed with meaning. They further recognize that when the artist lapsed into unconsciousness, a dimension of infinitude and interminability registered itself within the trial *as what was uncontainable by its containment,* as what remained untotalizable precisely by and in the law's totalization, within the very legal text of the totalization that constitutes their judgment.

The judgment in the Eichmann trial takes note of the fact that, in the meeting point between law and art with which the courtroom was unwittingly confronted through K-Zetnik's testimony, *the law has dialogued with its own limits* and has touched upon a boundary of meaning in which sense and senselessness, meaning and madness seriously, historically commingled and could not be told apart. The court acknowledges, however, that this surprising legal moment that unsettled legal norms and threw the courtroom into disarray was a profoundly meaningful and not senseless moment of the trial.

Part Three: Traumatic Narratives and Legal Frames

VIII

Story and Anti-Story: Between Justice and the Impossibility of Telling

I want now to return to Arendt's story, but to return to it differently: to listen not just to her statement but to her utterance; to seek to understand not only her juridical critique but her own inadvertent testimony as a writer. I propose to show how Arendt's legal narrative in *Eichmann in Jerusalem* unwittingly encapsulates not only the reporter's critical account but also the thinker's own (erased) artistic testimony and the writer's own traumatic narrative.[78]

Like the judges, Arendt views K-Zetnik's fainting as a symbol.[79] But while for the judges, the writer's collapse encapsulates—within the trial and beyond it—the *collapse of language* in the face of uncontainable and unintelligible suffering, for Arendt, the writer's collapse encapsulates the *legal failure* of the trial. While for the judges, the collapse is a dramatization of *a failure of expression*, for Arendt, the collapse is a dramatization of *a failure of narration.*

"This," says Arendt, "to be sure, was an exception, but if it was an exception that proved the rule of normality, it *did not prove the rule* of simplicity or *of ability to tell a story.*"[80] As an exception that confirms the rule of normality, that is, as a symbol of the legal abnormality of the trial as a whole, Arendt faults K-Zetnik for his *inability to tell a story,* and thus to testify coherently. "Who says what is . . . always tells a story, and in this story the particular facts lose their contingency and acquire some humanly comprehensible meaning," Arendt will write in "Truth and Politics,"[81] doubtless remembering unconsciously the unforgettable essay called "The Storyteller"[82] written by her dead friend Walter Benjamin, whose name she will in 1968—five years after the Eichmann book—redeem from anonymity and namelessness by publishing his work in the United States, but whose lost friendship she will silently mourn all her life as an intimate grievance, a wordless wound, a personal price that she in turn has secretly paid to the Holocaust.[83] I hear a reference to "The Storyteller" in the conclusion of Arendt's account of K-Zetnik's testimony: "[I]t did not prove the rule of simplicity or of *ability to tell a story*."[84] There are several other references in *Eichmann in Jerusalem* to storytelling and to "The Storyteller."[85] While Benjamin's name is never mentioned and his text is never cited in the book, Benjaminian words and formulations unwittingly pervade its pages like stylistic echoes that form an impassioned philosophical *subtext* under and through the irony, the wryness, and the dryness of the legalistic text. At stake in this subtext is a relation between death and writing, an intimately personal relation that the writing "I" cannot possess or formulate directly but can relate to indirectly through Benjamin's reflection on the relation between death and storytelling. Benjamin's memory and presence—the presence of his death and of his text—unwittingly yet hauntingly, persistently inform Arendt's style and permeate her writing and her utterance. "Death," wrote Benjamin precisely in his essay, "is the sanction of everything that the storyteller has to tell. He has borrowed his authority from death."[86]

Has Arendt in her turn borrowed her authority as storyteller of the trial from a legacy of death of which she does not speak and cannot speak? I will suggest indeed that, through its understated but repeated reference to the storyteller, *Eichmann in Jerusalem* is also Arendt's book of mourning.[87] It is, in other words, a book—an unarticulated statement—on the *relation between grief and justice*, as well as on the counterparts of grief and justice in narrative and storytelling. "It is perfectly true," Arendt will write in "Truth and Politics," "that 'all sorrows can be borne if you put them into a story or tell a story about them.' "[88] Both the Eichmann trial and Arendt's critical rehearsal of it are preoccupied—albeit in different styles—with the translation of grief into justice. Both are therefore mirror images of the translation of grief into grievance as what underlies precisely the capacity and the significance of saying "I accuse," of crying out *J'accuse* in the name of those who can no longer say it.[89]

Eichmann in Jerusalem, I would suggest, is inhabited by Arendt's mourned and unmourned ghosts. Benjamin is one of those. (Another ghost, I would suggest, is Heidegger, but I will not dwell here on his ghostly significance in *Eichmann in Jerusalem*.)[90]

In all language, Benjamin argued, there is a lament that mutes it out.[91] "In all mourning there is an inclination to speechlessness, which is infinitely more than the disinclination or the inability to communicate."[92] Benjamin's unmentioned name and subterranean presence as an inadvertent and complex subtext of *Eichmann in Jerusalem* is linked, I argue, both to Arendt's testimony in this book and to her silence, a silence which in turn is linked not just to her discretion but to her speechlessness, that is, to her own *inability to tell a story.* There is, in other words, a crucial story Arendt does not tell and cannot tell, which underlies the story of the trial she does tell.[93]

"Familiar though his name may be to us," wrote Benjamin, "the storyteller in his living immediacy is by no means a present force. He has already become something remote from us and something which is getting even more distant. . . . Less and less frequently do we encounter people with the ability to tell a tale properly. . . . It is as if something that seemed inalienable to us . . . were taken from us: the ability to exchange experiences."[94]

Benjamin intuitively knew that the inability to tell a story was related to the essence of traumatic experience.[95] Specifically, he linked this inability to tell to the collective, massive trauma of the war. "Was it not noticeable at the end of the war that men returned from the battlefield grown silent—not richer, but poorer in communicable experience?"[96]

Benjamin spoke of the First World War.[97] K-Zetnik's testimony at the Eichmann trial showed how people returned even more tongue-tied—even poorer in communicable experience, grown even more silent—from the death camps and from the traumatic nightmare of the Second World War. "When I got out of Auschwitz," writes K-Zetnik, "they went with me, they and the silent blocks, and the silent crematorium, and the silent horizons, and the mountain of ashes."[98]

I would argue differently from Arendt (and with hindsight she could not possess) that (unpredictably, unwittingly) it was the *inadvertent legal essence* and legal innovation and uniqueness of the Eichmann trial, and not its testimonial accident, to voice the muteness generated by the Holocaust and to *articulate the difficulty of articulation* of the catastrophic story, the difficulty of articulation and the tragic unnarratability of the ungraspable disaster and of its immeasurably devastating, unintelligible trauma. The impossibility of telling is not external to this story: it is the story's heart.[99] The trial shows how the inherent inability to tell the story is itself an integral part of the history and of the story of the Holocaust. The function of the trial thus becomes precisely to articulate the impossibility of telling through the legal process and to convert it into legal meaning.[100]

My conception of the trial is, then, fundamentally different from that of Arendt. Logically speaking, it is, however, Arendt's text that has helped me to read the trial differently from her. It is precisely Arendt's own surprised insistence on "how difficult it was to tell the story"[101] and her own *excessive* utterance—her own haunted allusions to Benjamin and to "The Storyteller"—that have contributed to the shaping of my own perspective. All along, I have been reading Arendt's text to understand what was unique (peculiar) in the trial and to gain an insight into what was happening in the courtroom through the magnifying lens of Arendt's sharp and critically insightful eyes. In this essay, I have suggested that besides the criticism there is also an unspoken element of grief in Arendt's text, that a relation between grief and justice indirectly and unconsciously informs Arendt's utterance, and that it is precisely this excessiveness of Arendt's utterance over her statement that gives her book authority and gives her text a literary depth, an existential density and a political and legal-philosophical charisma that go beyond the conscious terms of her spoken argument.

I wish now to draw out this unspoken potential of Arendt's text and to pursue it further in my own (quite different) way. In the remainder of my argument, I will go farther than Arendt does in drawing on the haunting relevance of Benjamin to *Eichmann in Jerusalem* and, more generally, in using Benjamin's reflection to highlight important aspects of the trial. Although I will, from this point on, use Benjamin to read the trial differently from Arendt (to argue with and argue *beyond* Arendt), my different understanding and my different proposition, to the extent that they rely in turn on Benjamin's authority and on his haunting presence, will also paradoxically be speaking *with* Arendt's text and *from her storyteller's silence*: from the unconscious pathos of her own excessive and yet silenced, *muted,* self-erased, and self-transcendent utterance.

IX

The Dramatic

In the wake of Benjamin, I argue therefore that the testimonial muteness underlying (and exceeding) Arendt's legal story reenacts, ironically enough, the literary muteness of K-Zetnik's story, and that K-Zetnik's *legal muteness*—his inability to tell a story in the trial—is part of the impossibility of telling at the trial's heart. Indeed, K-Zetnik's discourse prior to his fainting strives to *thematize* precisely the impossibility of telling, both in its use of the figure of "the other planet,"[102] testifying to the utter foreignness of Auschwitz and trying to convey the astronomical scale of distance separating its ungraspability and unnarratability from the narration in the courtroom in Jerusalem, and in its effort to narrate the scene of the extermination as a repeated scene of parting and of silence, a primal scene of silence whose sole meaning wordlessly resides in the exchange of looks between the living and the dying: between the not-yet-dead and the not-yet-surviving who remain behind for no other purpose than to tell and to retell the story that cannot be told.

But K-Zetnik's testimony does not simply tell *about* the impossibility of telling: it dramatizes it—*enacts it*—through its own lapse into coma and its own collapse into a silence. "It was the most *dramatic* moment of the trial," writes Tom Segev, "one of the most dramatic moments in the country's history."[103]

For Arendt, as a critical legal observer and as a conscious representative of the traditional conception of the law, however,[104] *the dramatic* as such is by definition *immaterial* and extraneous to the trial. Arendt's view follows the classical axioms of jurisprudential thought. The process of the law, says Justice Oliver Wendell Holmes in one of the most authoritative statements of Anglo-Saxon jurisprudence in the twentieth century, "is one, from a lawyer's statement of the case, eliminating as it does all the dramatic elements . . . and retaining only the facts of legal import, up to the final analyses and abstract universals of theoretic jurisprudence."[105] This precisely is what Arendt tries to do, in discarding the dramatic and in theorizing in her legal proposition about the Eichmann trial the "abstract universal" of a new crime and of a new criminal without *mens rea*—without motive. "The banality of evil" is, in fact, strictly a "theoretical jurisprudential" concept: an *antiseptic* legal concept that is formed by the strict *reduction of the drama* that has given rise to its conceptual necessity. "If a man goes into law," says Holmes, "it pays to be a master of it, and to be a master of it means to look straight through all the dramatic incidents."[106]

Arendt therefore unambiguously discards the dramatic in the trial and denies it legal meaning. I would argue here, in contrast, that the dramatic *can be* legally significant. I submit that in the Eichmann trial (as the passing comment of the judges has in fact conceded) the dramatic *was* indeed endowed with *legal meaning*, meaning that the classical jurisprudential, legalistic view was programmed to miss and that Arendt consequently overlooked.

"As Hannah Arendt and others have pointed out," writes Susan Sontag:

[T]he juridical basis of the Eichmann trial, the relevance of all the evidence presented and the legitimacy of certain procedures are open to question on strictly legal grounds. . . .

But the truth is that the Eichmann trial did not, and could not, have conformed to legal standards only. . . . The function of the trial was rather that of the tragic drama: above and beyond judgement and punishment, catharsis. . . .

[T]he problem with the Eichmann trial was not its deficient legality, but *the contradiction between its juridical form and its dramatic function.*[107]

Arendt herself acknowledged in the epilogue of *Eichmann in Jerusalem* that, as the saying goes, "justice must not only be done but must be seen to be done."[108] The legal function of the court, in other words, is in its very *moral essence,* a *dramatic* function: not only that of "doing justice" but that of "*making justice seen*" in a larger moral and historically unique sense.[109] It was through the perspective of this larger cultural and *historic visibility* the trial gave dramatically, historically to justice that the Eichmann trial was (I would propose) *jurisprudentially dramatic.*

In a different context, Walter Benjamin in turn defines the dramatic: "The mystery is, on the dramatic level, that moment in which it juts out of the domain of language proper to it into a higher one unattainable for it. *Therefore, this moment cannot be expressed in words but is expressible solely in representation*: it is the 'dramatic' in the strictest sense."[110] Law in principle *rules out* what cannot be disclosed in words. In contrast, the dramatic, Benjamin says, is a beyond of words. It is a physical gesture by which language points to a meaning it cannot articulate.

Such is K-Zetnik's fall beside the witness stand. It makes a corpse out of the living witness who has sworn to remain anonymous and undifferentiated from the dead.

I argue that the witness's body has become within the trial what Pierre Nora would call "*a site of memory.*"[111] In opposition to the trial's effort to create a conscious, totalizing memory and a totalizing historical consciousness, the site of memory is an unintegratable, residual unconscious site that cannot be translated into legal consciousness and into legal idiom. This site materializes in the courtroom the memory of death both as a physical reality and as a limit of consciousness in history.

On this legal site, the witness testifies through his unconscious body. Suddenly, the testimony is invaded by the body. The speaking body has become a dying body. The dying body testifies dramatically and wordlessly beyond the cognitive and the discursive limits of the witness's speech.

The body's testimony thus creates a new dimension in the trial, a *physical legal dimension* that dramatically expands what can be grasped as legal meaning. I argue that this new dimension in its turn transforms and dramatically reshapes not just the legal process of the Eichmann trial but the conception and the very frameworks of perception of the law as such.

How is it that the body can unconsciously transform the parameters of law as such? The witness's fainting—the body's dramatic collapse in the midst of the witness's verbal testimony—could strikingly exemplify *within the structure of the trial* what Walter Benjamin calls "the expressionless":

> The life undulating in it [Benjamin writes, and I would specify: the life undulating in the trial] must appear petrified and as if spellbound in a single moment. . . . What . . . spellbinds the movement and interrupts the harmony is the expressionless. . . . *Just as interruption by the commanding word is able to bring the truth out of the evasions . . . precisely at the point where it interrupts, the expressionless compels the trembling harmony to stop.* . . . For it shatters whatever still survives of the legacy of chaos . . . the false, errant totality, the absolute totality. Only the expressionless completes the work [completes the trial], by shattering it into a thing of shards, into a fragment of the true world, into the torso of a symbol.[112]

To borrow Benjamin's inspired terms to describe the trial, I would argue that K-Zetnik's fainting and his petrified body stand for the "expressionless"— *das Ausdruckslose*—that suddenly irrupts into the language of the law and *interrupts* the trial. In Benjamin's terms, I would argue that K-Zetnik's collapse can be defined as "the caesura" of the trial:[113] a moment of petrification that interrupts and ruptures the articulations of the law and yet grounds them by shattering their false totality into "a fragment of the true world"; a sudden *"counter-rhythmic rupture"* in which (as Benjamin put it) "every expression simultaneously comes to a standstill, in order to give free reign to an expressionless power."[114]

The fainting that cuts through the witness's speech and petrifies his body interrupts the legal process and creates a moment that is legally traumatic not just for the witness but chiefly for the court and for the audience of the trial. I argue in effect that, in the rupture of the witness's lapse into a coma, it is the law itself that for a moment loses consciousness. But it is through this breakdown of the legal framework that history emerges in the courtroom and, in the legal body of the witness, exhibits its own inadvertently dramatic (nondiscursive) rules of evidence. It is precisely through this breach of consciousness of law that history unwittingly and mutely, yet quite resonantly, memorably *speaks*.[115]

And it is for these moments in which history as injury dramatically, traumatically has spoken—these moments that combined the legal, the dramatic, and the legally traumatic, yet whose eloquence and legal meaning could not be translated into legal idiom—that the Eichmann trial is remembered. It is precisely through these moments that the Eichmann trial has impressed itself on memory, as a remarkable legal event in which the law itself was shattered into a new level of perception and into a new historical and legal consciousness.

Part Four: Conclusion

This essay has dealt with a legal moment that took the legal institution by surprise and stupefied at once the judges and the audience of the trial. In their written opinion, the judges marked the unique evidentiary position of this moment in the trial. They thought it was significant that it was a literary writer who collapsed and that it was an artist's testimony that the trial exploded. Indeed, law has exploded here the literary framework. In turn, the conflation of the writer's literary testimony with the law has brought about a parallel explosion of the legal framework. Both the legal and the literary frameworks came apart as a result of their encounter in the trial. I argue that this breakdown—this caesura—was legally significant although (and because) it was legally traumatic.

This moment in which the human witness, flabbergasting both the audience and the judges, plunges into the abyss between the different planets—and falls as though he were himself a corpse—is internal to the trial. I argue that it is a moment *inside law*, although its power comes from its interruption of the law, its interruption of discourse by what Walter Benjamin called "the expressionless." The expressionless, I argue, grounds both the legal meaning of the trial and its inadvertent literary and dramatic power.

For the purpose of transmission of the Holocaust, literature and art do not suffice. And yet, a trial is equally insufficient. I believe that only the *encounter between law and art* can adequately testify to the abyssal meaning of the trauma.

It is remarkable that such an encounter between trauma, law, and art happens inside a trial. Inside the trial, *in the drama of the missed encounter* between K-Zetnik and the legal actors (judge and prosecutor), there is a unique confrontation between literature and law as two vocabularies of remembrance. The clash between these two dimensions and these two vocabularies brings about a breakdown of the legal framework through the physical collapse of the witness. Yet, through this inadvertent breakdown of the legal framework, history uncannily and powerfully speaks. "Everything," said Benjamin, "about history that, from the very beginning, has been untimely, sorrowful, unsuccessful, is expressed in a face,[116] or rather in a death's head."[117]

This death's head emerges in the trial as history is uncannily transmitted through K-Zetnik's fainting and through his endlessly reverberating courtroom silence.

In borrowing the words of Lanzmann, I will therefore argue that what Arendt calls the *failures*[118] of the trial were *necessary failures*.[119] I argue that the Eichmann trial dramatically articulated legal meaning that no legal categories could apprehend precisely through its failures. I further argue that it is in general a feature of pathbreaking trials to speak through the explosion of the legal framework, to legally say something (or show something) that is not containable precisely by the concepts and the logic of the legal. Moments of rupture of the legal framework can be—as they were, I argue, in the Eichmann trial—moments of legal and conceptual breakthrough. Moments of institutional collapse and of "caesura" of the legal discourse—such as during K-Zetnik's fainting —can be moments in which both art and history unwittingly speak in and through the legal tool.[120]

I offer this as food for thought: great trials are perhaps specifically those trials whose very failures have their own necessity and their own literary, cultural, and jurisprudential *speaking power*.

Notes

1   Friedrich Nietzsche, *The Use and Abuse of History for Life* 12–17 (Adrian Collins trans., Liberal Arts Press 1957) (1949).

2   Robert Jackson, introduction to Whitney Harris, *Tyranny on Trial: The Evidence at Nuremberg*, at xxix, xxxv–xxxvi (1954).

3   "Novelist Rebecca West, covering the first 'historic' Nuremberg trial for the *New Yorker*, found it insufferably tedious," writes Mark Osiel, *Mass Atrocity, Collective Memory, and the Law* 91 (2000) (referring to Rebecca West, "Extraordinary Exile," *New Yorker*, Sept. 7, 1946, at 34). "This reaction was not uncommon," Osiel continues: "As one reporter notes: 'It was the largest crime in history and it promised the greatest courtroom spectacle. [But] ... [w]hat ensued was an excruciatingly long and complex trial that failed to mesmerize a distracted world. Its mass of evidence created boredom, mixed occasionally with an abject horror before which ordinary justice seemed helpless." Id. at 91 (quoting Alex Ross, "Watching for a Judgment of Real Evil," *N.Y. Times*, Nov. 12, 1995, § 2 at 37).

4   Gideon Hausner, *Justice in Jerusalem* 291–92 (1968).

5   Jackson, supra note 2, at xxxv–xxxvi.

6   In a short text called "The Witness," Borges writes: "Deeds which populate the dimensions of space and which reach their end when someone dies may cause us wonderment, but one thing, or an infinite number of things, dies in every final agony, unless there is a universal

memory. . . . What will die with me when I die, what pathetic and fragile form will the world lose?" Jorge Luis Borges, "The Witness," in *Labyrinths: Selected Stories and Other Writings* 243, 243 (1962).

It is because humans, unlike documents, do not endure that the Eichmann trial calls on each witness to narrate the singular story that will die when he or she dies. Transience is inscribed within this legal process as the witness's death is, from the start, implicitly inscribed within each testimony. While documents—unlike the living witnesses—exclude death as a possibility inherent in the evidence, and while the Nuremberg trials claim authority precisely in the act of sheltering the courtroom from the death it talks about, in the Eichmann trial, on the contrary, "death is the sanction of everything the storyteller has to tell. He has borrowed his authority from death." Walter Benjamin, "The Storyteller," in *Illuminations: Essays and Reflections* 83, 94 (Hannah Arendt ed., 1968).

7   Attested to by the chief prosecutor's widow in *The Trial of Adolf Eichmann*, a PBS documentary home video (B3470) (coproduced by ABC News Productions and Great Projects Film Company 1997).

8   The Eichmann trial was the first trial televised in its entirety. The complete trial footage is kept in the archives of the state of Israel.

9   "Our memory," writes Valéry, "repeats to us the discourse that we have not understood. Repetition is responding to incomprehension. It signifies to us that the act of language has not been accomplished." Paul Valéry, "Commentaires de *Charmes*," in 1 *Oeuvres* 1507, 1510 (1957) (author's translation).

10   The writer published the English translation of his works under the pseudonym Ka-Tsetnik 135633. An alternative orthography of the author's name, the one used in the trial's English transcripts and in Hannah Arendt, *Eichmann in Jerusalem* (1964), is K-Zetnik (since the name is modeled on the German letters KZ, pronounced "ka-tzet," from *Konzentrationslager*, "concentration camp"). The latter orthography is the one I will hereafter use.

11   Criminal Case 40/61 (Jerusalem), Attorney General v. Eichmann (1961). English translation of the trial transcripts in 3 *The Trial of Adolf Eichmann: Record of Proceedings in the District Court of Jerusalem*, Session No. 68 (June 7, 1961), Jerusalem 1963, at 1237 [hereafter 3 *Proceedings*]. I use here the modified English version quoted in Arendt, supra note 10, at 224.

12   K-Zetnik, *Tzofan: Edma* 32 (Hakibbutz Hameuchad Publishing House Ltd. 1987), translated in Ka-Tsetnik 135633, *Shivitti: A Vision* 16 (Eliyah Nike De-Nur and Lisa Hermann trans., Harper and Row 1989).

13   The narrative that follows is a literal transcription of the trial footage (session of K-Zetnik's testimony), as seen in *The Trial of Adolf Eichmann*, supra note 7. *See also* 3 *Proceedings*, supra note 11, at 1237.

14   Yehiel Dinoor was forty-five years old at the time of the trial. Born in Poland as Yehiel Feiner, he changed his legal name to the Hebrew name Dinoor, meaning "a residue from the fire." Tom Segev, *The Seventh Million: The Israelis and the Holocaust* 4 (Haim Watzman trans., Hill and Wang 1993) (1991). The name Dinoor is spelled alternatively as Dinur (in the trial's English transcripts, see 3 *Proceedings*, supra note 11, at 1237, as De-nur (in the English translation of K-Zetnik, *Shivitti*, supra note 12, and consequently, in the English version of Segev, *The Seventh Million*, supra), or as Dinoor (in Arendt, *Eichmann in Jeru-*

salem, supra note 10). I am following Arendt's orthography because it best corresponds to the Hebrew pronunciation of the name.

15 "All Israel held its breath," Tom Segev will remember thirty years later. "It was the most dramatic moment of the trial, one of the most dramatic moments in the country's history." Segev, supra note 14, at 4.

16 Author's transcription of archival footage as seen in *The Trial of Adolf Eichmann, supra* note 7; see also 3 *Proceedings, supra* note 11, at 1237.

17 Haim Gouri, *Facing the Glass Cage: The Jerusalem Trial* 124 (1962) (author's translation).

18 See Nietzsche, supra note 1. On the difference between the "monumental" and the "critical" versions of the Eichmann trial, see Shoshana Felman, "Theaters of Justice: Arendt in Jerusalem, the Eichmann Trial and the Redefinition of Legal Meaning in the Wake of the Holocaust," chapter 3, *The Judicial Unconscious: Trials and Traumas in the Twentieth Century* (2002).

19 Karl Jaspers, *The Question of German Guilt* (E. B. Ashton trans., Capricorn Books 1961) (1947).

20 Letter from Hannah Arendt to Karl Jaspers (Aug. 18, 1946), in *Correspondence: 1926–1969*, at 54 (Lotte Kohler and Hans Saner eds., Robert and Rita Kimber trans., 1992) (emphasis added).

21 Letter from Arendt to Jaspers (Oct. 19, 1946), in *Correspondence, supra* note 20, at 62.

22 Letter from Arendt to Jaspers (Dec. 17, 1946), in *Correspondence, supra* note 20, at 68.

23 Letter from Arendt to Jaspers (Dec. 16, 1960), in *Correspondence, supra* note 20, at 413.

24 Letter from Arendt to Jaspers (Dec. 23, 1960), in *Correspondence, supra* note 20, at 417.

25 Arendt, supra note 10, at 6.

26 Id. at 230.

27 Id. at 223. Cf. id. at 8 ("As witness followed witness and horror was piled upon horror, [the audience] sat there and listened in public to stories they would hardly have been able to endure in private.").

28 Id. at 4–9.

29 Id. at 223.

30 Id. at 223–24.

31 Id.

32 Id. at 224.

33 Arendt refers to the common sense of the situation. But, as Robert Ferguson notes, "common sense, as anthropologists have begun to show, is basically *a culturally constructed use of experience to claim self-evidence; it is neither more nor less than 'an authoritative story'* made out of the familiar." Robert Ferguson, "Untold Stories in the Law," in *Law's Stories: Narrative and Rhetoric in the Law* 87 (Peter Brooks and Paul Gewirtz eds., 1996) (emphasis added) (referring to Clifford Geertz, "Common Sense as a Cultural System," in Geertz, *Local Knowledge: Further Essays in Interpretive Anthropology,* 73 (1983)).

34 Arendt, supra note 10, at 225.

35 In the *The Trial of Adolph Eichmann, supra* note 7, Hausner's wife corroborates this fact, explaining why her husband chose to call K-Zetnik despite the reluctance of the writer.

36 I analyze this *missed encounter* and this *professional misunderstanding* for different purposes than simply to contrast (as does, for instance, Mark Osiel) *disciplinary differences.* Osiel writes:

It is this confessedly subjective experience—irrelevant to criminal law—that oral historians have only recently sought to explore. In this respect, scholars have perceived the need to overcome what they perceive as a 'legal' concern with the factual accuracy of personal testimony in order to apprehend its historical significance. That is, these scholars try to grasp the meaning of the period's most traumatic events through the continuing memory of those who lived through its trauma. One such scholar writes:

"Testimonies are often labeled as "subjective" or "biased" in the legal proceedings concerning war crimes. The lawyers of war criminals have asked the most impertinent questions of people trying to find words for a shattered memory that did not fit into any language. . . . They demand precise statements of facts. . . . A lawyer's case is after all merely another kind of story. . . .

"It is not the task of oral historians to give the kind of evidence required in a court of law. . . . [Some historians attempt to uncover] the ways in which suffering is remembered and influences all other memory. . . . One is dealing with an effort to create a new kind of history that cannot be used as legal evidence since it explicitly records subjective experience."

Selma Leydersdorff, "A Shattered Silence: The Life Stories of Survivors of the Jewish Proletariat at Amsterdam," in *Memory and Totalitarianism* 145, 147–48 (Luisa Passerini ed., 1992), quoted and surveyed in Osiel, supra note 3, at 103–4.

My own interest is not in contrasting the historical recording of trauma with that of the law, but on the contrary in exploring and in analyzing ways in which collective trauma is apprehended (and misapprehended) by the law, as well as ways in which the very *limits of the law* in its encounter (or its *missed encounter*) with the phenomenon of trauma *reveal* precisely cultural aspects of its traumatic meaning.

37 Ka-Tsetnik, supra note 12, at 32 (translation modified by author according to Hebrew original, supra note 12, at 50).

38 Arendt, supra note 10, at 224.

39 Id.

40 Jackson, supra note 2, at xxxv–xxxvi.

41 On the relation between trauma and the law, see Shoshana Felman, "Forms of Judicial Blindness: Traumatic Narratives and Legal Repetitions," in *Memory, History and the Law* 25 (Austin Sarat and Thomas R. Kearns eds., 1999), and chapter 2 in Shoshana Felman, *The Juridical Unconscious: Trials and Traumas in the Twentieth Century* (2002).

42 Arendt, supra note 10, at 224.

43 For my own "jurisprudential trauma theory," see Felman, "Forms of Judicial Blindness," supra note 41. For trauma theory in general and its importance in the humanities, see, e.g., Bessel A. Van der Kolk and Onno Van der Hart, "The Intrusive Past: The Flexibility of Memory and the Engraving of Trauma," in *Trauma: Explorations in Memory* 158 (Cathy Caruth ed., 1995); Cathy Caruth, *Unclaimed Experience: Trauma, Narrative and History* (1996).

44 See Felman, "Forms of Judicial Blindness," supra note 41, at 25–93.

45 On the phenomenon of intrusive memory and of traumatic repetition prevalent in the aftermath of trauma, see for instance, Van der Kolk and Van der Hart, supra note 43.

46 This terrified collapse is at the same time an improbable act of resistance, a gesture of defiance of the court and of its ruling.

47 Ka-Tsetnik, supra note 12, at 9 (translation modified by author according to Hebrew original, supra note 12, at 24). I will use this literary, autobiographical narrative written subsequently by K-Zetnik to describe his psychiatric therapy from his recurrent Auschwitz nightmares, to retrospectively illuminate the drama of the courtroom scene.

48 Id. at 95 (translation modified by author according to Hebrew original, supra note 12, at 107).

49 Id. at 40 (translation modified by author according to Hebrew original, supra note 12, at 57). Compare: "But I have no choice. I am unable to answer questions. In general I cannot sustain interrogation. This is a trauma whose origin is in the torture cellar of the Gestapo in Katowice." Id. at 20.

50 3 Proceedings, supra note 11, at 1237.

51 Id. at x–xi (translation modified by author according to Hebrew original, supra note 12, at 8–9).

52 Id. at 16 (translation modified by author according to Hebrew original, supra note 12, at 32).

53 Id. at x–xi (translation modified by author according to Hebrew original, supra note 12, at 33).

54 Id. at 18 (translation modified by author according to Hebrew original, supra note 12, at 34).

55 Criminal Case 40/61 (Jerusalem), Attorney General v. Eichmann, translated in 1 *The Trial of Adolph Eichmann: Record of Proceedings in the District Court of Jerusalem*, Session No. 6, Apr. 17, 1967, Jerusalem 1962, at 62 [hereafter 1 *Proceedings*], quoted in Hausner, supra note 4, at 323–24; Arendt, supra note 10, at 260.

56 Under this name with which he signs his literary work and that materializes his oath to the dead, Dinoor continues not just to remember those who left him but also, as a writer, to give literary voice to their last look and to their final silence.

57 *The Trial of Adolph Eichmann*, supra note 7 (author's literal transcription) (emphasis added).

58 "It now appeared," writes Arendt,

> that the era of the Hitler regime, with its gigantic, unprecedented crimes, *constituted an "unmastered past"* not only for the German people or the Jews all over the world, but for the rest of the world, which had not forgotten this great catastrophe in the heart of Europe either, and had also been unable to come to terms with it. Moreover—and this was perhaps less expected—general moral questions, with all their intricacies and modern complexities, which I would never have suspected would haunt men's minds today and weigh heavily on their hearts, stood suddenly in the foreground of public concern.

Arendt, supra note 10, at 283 (emphasis added).

59 On the relation between trials and historical and cultural abysses, see Felman, supra note 41, at 69–83.

60 This abyss, this epistemological rupture, is what the Eichmann trial and its "monumental history" (at once the prosecution's case and the text of the judgment) precisely fails to perceive in Arendt's eyes. "I have insisted," Arendt writes,

> on . . . how little Israel, and the Jewish people in general, was prepared to recognize, in the crimes that Eichmann was accused of, an unprecedented crime. . . . In the eyes of the Jews, thinking exclusively in terms of their own history, the catastrophe that had befallen them under Hitler, in which a third of the people perished, appeared not as the most recent of crimes, the unprecedented crime of genocide, but on the contrary, as the

oldest crime they knew and remembered. This misunderstanding . . . is actually at the root of all the failures and the shortcomings of the Jerusalem trial. *None of the participants ever arrived at a clear understanding of the actual horror of Auschwitz, which is of a different nature from all the atrocities of the past. . . .* Politically and legally . . . these were "crimes" different not only in degree of seriousness but in essence. Arendt, supra note 10, at 267.

Compare Arendt's insistence in her 1946 letter to Jaspers on the abyss that, henceforth inhabiting both guilt and innocence, explodes the tool of law in bursting open all legal frameworks: "The Nazi crimes, it seems to me, *explode the limits of the law.* . . . [T]his guilt, in contrast to all criminal guilt, oversteps and *shatters any and all legal systems.* That is the reason why the Nazis in Nuremberg are so smug. . . . [A]nd just as inhuman as their guilt is the innocence of the victims. . . . *This is the abyss that opened up* before us as early as 1933 . . . and into which we have finally stumbled. I don't know how we will ever get out of it." Letter from Arendt to Jaspers, supra note 20 (emphasis added).

61 Hannah Arendt, " 'What Remains?' The Language Remains: A Conversation with Günter Gaus," in *Essays in Understanding, 1930–1954,* at 13–14, (Jerome Kohn ed., 1994).

62 Id. at 14.

63 Susan Sontag, "Reflections on *The Deputy,*" in *The Storm over* The Deputy 18 (Eric Bentley ed., 1964). This comment was, of course, an utterly astonishing remark whose value lay in the surprise that it reserved, in its unsettling power with respect to any simple-minded or reductive legalistic understanding of the trial. Provocatively, Sontag argued that there was a dimension in the trial that was excessive to its legal definition. She called this dimension "art" because she felt the trial left an impact on the audience that was, in its strength and depth, comparable to the expressive power of a work of art. The trial moved her and existentially and philosophically engaged her. Sontag insisted therefore that the trial had a *literary meaning* in addition to its *legal meaning,* and that this extralegal meaning was somehow utterly important for a full grasp of what was at stake in this event of law. The value of Sontag's interpretation lies, in my eyes, not in its axiomatic categorization of the trial as a work of art (a categorization I cannot accept), but in the power of this unexpected categorization to destabilize the category of the legal and to open it for further thought and for a larger cultural interrogation.

64 Id. at 118–19. Art, says Sontag, no longer stands in opposition to reality: while twentieth-century reality becomes more and more hallucinated, more and more divorced from what we used to call reality, art moves closer to reality than it ever was before and mixes in with its jurisprudential gestures. Art no longer is a statement: it is an intervention in a conflict, an action, a commitment, an engagement. It is *politicized* and *de-aestheticized.* A "work of art" no longer is aesthetics: it is politics. See id.

65 See Robert Cover, "Violence and the Word," in *Narrative, Violence and the Law: The Essays of Robert Cover* 203 (Martha Minow et al. eds., 1995).

66 *Shoah* borrows some of its main witnesses from the Eichmann trial. The most striking example is that of Simon Srebnik, whose extraordinary testimony was first heard during the proceedings of the Eichmann trial. Compare Session No. 66, in 3 *Proceedings,* supra note 11, at 1197–1201, with *Shoah*'s extraordinarily moving opening scene, in Claude Lanzmann, *Shoah: The Complete Text of the Film* (1985).

67 Like the Eichmann trial, Lanzmann's film puts in evidence before the audience a fact-

finding process whose goal is—like that of the legal process—to elicit truth and to prohibit its evasions. Lanzmann borrows his procedures—his techniques of cross-examination and of detailed, concrete interrogation—from the legal model of a trial. Like the Eichmann trial, *Shoah* hears testimonies in a multiplicity of languages and uses an interpreter to simultaneously translate them into the language of its legal process. And, like the Eichmann trial, the film wishes not only to *prove* but to *transmit*. " 'My problem,' Lanzmann says, 'was to transmit. To do that one cannot allow oneself to be overwhelmed with emotion. You must remain detached. . . . I tried rather to reach people through their intelligence.' " Shoshana Felman, "The Return of the Voice," in Shoshana Felman and Dori Laub, *Testimony: Crises of Witnessing in History, Psychoanalysis and Literature* 204, 239 (1992) (quoting Claude Lanzmann) (citation omitted). For a more elaborate study of the film *Shoah*, see id.

68 Arendt, "Truth and Politics," in *Between Past and Future* 227, 261 (Penguin Books 1993) (1961).

69 Deborah Jerome, "Resurrecting Horror: The Man behind *Shoah*," *Record*, Oct. 25, 1985 (interviewing Claude Lanzmann).

70 Claude Lanzmann, "From the Holocaust to 'Holocaust,' " in *Dissent*, Spring 1981, at 194 (emphasis added).

71 On the historicizing role of the judges and more generally on the relation between law and history, see the remarkable analysis of Michal Shaked, "Hahistoriah Beveit Hamishpat Uveit Hamishpat Bahistoria: Piskei Hadin Bemishpat Kastner Vehanarrativim Shel Hazikaron" [History in court and the court in history: the opinions in the Kastner trial and the narratives of memory], 20 *Alpaim* 36 (2000).

72 Ka-Tsetnik, supra note 12, at 31–32 (translation modified by author according to K-Zetnik, supra note 12, at 49).

73 See Arendt, supra note 10, at 231 ("During the few minutes it took Kovner to tell of the help that had come from a German sergeant, a hush settled over the courtroom; it was as though the crowd had spontaneously decided to observe the usual two minutes of silence in honor of the man named Anton Schmidt.").

There were moments in which even the prosecutors were overcome by silence and, for a minute, could not go on. On these inadvertent moments of silence, compare the retrospective testimony of Justice Gabriel Bach, at the time assistant prosecutor in the Eichmann trial, in the documentary film *The Trial of Adolf Eichmann*, supra note 7, with Hausner, supra note 4, at 324–25:

The story of the extermination in Poland followed, and the wholesale killings by the *Einsatzgruppen*. . . . There, I knew, words could not describe the mass shooting of close to a million and four hundred thousand people before open pits. I cut short the address and read, instead, a lullaby composed at the time in the Wilno ghetto. . . . When I finished reading there was silence for a moment. I simply could not go on. Fortunately it was almost 6 p.m., about time for the adjournment of the session. The presiding judge must have realized my predicament; he asked whether this was a convenient place to stop. I nodded thankfully.

74 Gouri, supra note 17, at 244.

75 Reading of the Judgment of the District Court, 5 *The Trial of Adolf Eichmann: Record of Proceedings in the District Court of Jerusalem*, Session No. 121 (Dec. 15, 1961), Jerusalem 1964, at 2218 [hereafter 5 *Proceedings*].

76 Arendt, supra note 10, at 253–54 (emphasis added). "Hence," Arendt concludes, "to the question most commonly asked about the Eichmann trial: What good does it do? there is but one possible answer: It will do justice." Id. at 254.

77 5 *Proceedings*, supra note 75, at 2146 (emphasis added).

78 In her own turn, Arendt narrates not only the totality of facts, but also what is different from, and more than, that totality. Arendt's encounter with the Eichmann trial in turn partakes not only of law's story but also (mutely, indirectly) of art's story, or more precisely of the way in which law's story in the trial is transpierced, pervaded by the writer's testimony.

79 "Perhaps it is symbolic," said the judges, "that even the author who himself went through the hell named Auschwitz, could not stand the ordeal in the witness box and collapsed." 5 *Proceedings*, supra note 75, at 2146; see supra text accompanying note 77.

80 Arendt, supra note 10, at 224.

81 "The telling of factual truth comprehends much more than the daily information supplied by journalists. . . . Reality is different from, and more than, the totality of facts and events, which, anyhow, is unascertainable. Who says what is . . . always tells a story, and in this story the particular facts lose their contingency and acquire some humanly comprehensible meaning." Arendt, supra note 68, at 261.

82 Benjamin, supra note 6.

83 The German-Jewish writer Walter Benjamin (1892–1940) was a friend of Arendt's during their exile years in Paris. She admired his works and wanted to help him emigrate to the United States, but he committed suicide during his illegal and aborted escape from France in 1940. In 1942, when she first learns about the existence of the Nazi death camps, Arendt writes "a poem for her dead friend, a farewell and a greeting," titled simply "W.B.:" "[D]istant voices, sadnesses nearby / Those are the voices and these the dead / whom we have sent as messengers ahead, to lead us into slumber." Quoted in Elizabeth Young-Bruehl, *Hannah Arendt: For Love of the World* 162–63 (1982).

The last time Walter Benjamin saw Hannah Arendt in Marseille, he entrusted to her care a collection of manuscripts he hoped she could deliver to the United States. After his death, Arendt travels to the cemetery of Port Bou on the Franco-Spanish border only to discover that her dead friend who was buried there does not even have an individual, *named* grave. In a letter to Gershom Scholem written on October 21, 1940 (less than a month after Benjamin's death), Arendt describes the shock of her realization that in this cemetery, "the most fantastic . . . and beautiful spot" she has ever "seen in [her] life," there is nothing left to bear witness to Benjamin's life and death: "[His grave] was not to be found, his name was not written anywhere." Quoted in Gershom Scholem, *Walter Benjamin: The Story of a Friendship* 226 (Harry Zohn trans., Jewish Publication Soc'y of Am. 1981) (1975).

In 1968, Arendt redeems Benjamin from namelessness in publishing his manuscripts in the United States. In her introduction to Benjamin's work, Arendt narrates (and mourns) her friend's absurd, untimely, and tragically ironic (needless) suicide:

On September 26, 1940, Walter Benjamin, who was about to emigrate to America, took his life at the Franco-Spanish border. There were various reasons for this . . . nothing drew him to America, where, as he used to say, people would probably find no other use for him than to . . . exhibit him as "the last European." But the immediate occasion for Benjamin's suicide was an uncommon stroke of bad luck. Through the armistice agreement between

A Ghost in the House of Justice / 297

Vichy France and the Third Reich, refugees from Hitler's Germany . . . were in danger of being shipped back to Germany. . . . [T]o save this category of refugees . . . the United States had distributed a certain number of emergency visas through its consulates in unoccupied Europe. Thanks to the efforts of the Institute in New York, Benjamin was among the first to receive such a visa in Marseilles. Also, he quickly obtained a Spanish transit visa to enable him to get to Lisbon and board a ship there. However, he did not have a French exit visa . . . which the French government, eager to please the Gestapo, invariably denied the German refugees. In general this presented no great difficulty, since a relatively short and none too arduous road to be covered by foot over the mountains to Port Bou was well known and was not guarded by the French border police. Still, for Benjamin apparently suffering from cardiac condition . . . even the shortest walk was a great exertion, and he must have arrived in a state of serious exhaustion. The small group of refugees that he had joined reached the Spanish border town only to learn that Spain had closed the border that same day and that the border officials did not honor visas made out in Marseilles. The refugees were supposed to return to France the next day. During the night Benjamin took his life, whereupon the border officials, upon whom this suicide had made an impression, allowed his companions to proceed to Portugal. A few weeks later the embargo on visas was lifted again. One day earlier Benjamin would have got through without any trouble; one day later the people in Marseilles would have known that for the time being it was impossible to pass through Spain. Only on that particular day was the catastrophe possible.

Arendt, introduction to *Illuminations*, supra note 6, at 5–18. See also Arendt's letter of May 30, 1946, to Gertrude Jaspers, the Jewish wife of the German philosopher; the letter evokes another mutual dead acquaintance and the two correspondents' shared personal relation to the Jewish problem:

Or perhaps he was just tired and didn't want to move on again, didn't want to face a totally alien world, a totally alien language, and the inevitable poverty, which so often, particularly at first, comes close to total destitution. This exhaustion, which often went along with the reluctance to make a big fuss, to summon so much concentration for the sake of this little bit of life, that was surely the biggest danger we all faced. And it was the death of our best friend in Paris, Walter Benjamin, who committed suicide in October 1940 on the Spanish border with an American visa in his pocket. This atmosphere of sauve qui peut at the time was dreadful, and suicide was the only noble gesture, if you even cared enough to want to perish nobly. . . . What you wrote about *"our" problem* moved me very much . . . and today that means *our dead*.

Letter from Arendt to Gertrude Jaspers (May 30, 1946), in *Correspondence*, supra note 20, at 40–41 (emphasis added).

84   Arendt, supra note 10, at 224.

85   There is another witness who, in contrast to K-Zetnik, did prove able to tell a story. His name is Zyndel Grynszpan, and the story he narrates is that of his forced deportation, at the beginning of the war, from Germany to Poland. He is in Arendt's eyes the ideal storyteller— the ideal witness—although no other witness in the trial can live up to his example. His plainly factual and chronologically coherent narrative stands in contrast to the disjointed account of K-Zetnik. *"Now he had come to tell his story,"* Arendt writes, "carefully answer-

ing questions put to him by the prosecutor; *he spoke clearly and firmly, without embroidery, using a minimum of words."* Id. at 228 (emphasis added). Compare Benjamin's similar stylistic preference in "The Storyteller": "There is nothing that commends a story to memory more effectively than the *chaste compactness* that precludes psychological analysis. And the more natural the process by which the storyteller forgoes psychological shading, the greater becomes the story's claim to a place in the memory of the listener, the more completely is it integrated into his own experience, the greater will be his inclination to repeat it to someone else." Benjamin, supra note 6, at 91.

Arendt indeed repeats verbatim Grynszpan's testimony and does not paraphrase or summarize it, as she did with K-Zetnik's discourse. Arendt is so remarkably and deeply moved by Grynszpan's testimony that she steps out of her boundaries and (for a moment) pleads against her own legal objection to the victim's story and against her own puristic, legalistic emphasis on strict legal relevance:

> This story took no more than perhaps ten minutes to tell, and when it was over—the senseless, needless destruction of twenty-seven years in less than twenty-four hours—one thought foolishly: *Everyone, everyone should have his day in court.* Only to find out, in the endless sessions that followed, *how difficult it was to tell the story,* that—at least outside the transforming realm of poetry—it needed a purity of soul, an unmirrored, unreflected innocence of heart and mind that *only the righteous* possess. No one either before or after was to equal the shining honesty of Zindel Grynszpan.

Arendt, supra note 10, at 229–30 (emphasis added). The reason Arendt is so overwhelmed with emotion, I would suggest, is that her own traumatic story of *the loss of Germany* is unwittingly, unconsciously reflected back to her from Grynszpan's modest story. This narrative of a forceful removal across national borders is also Benjamin's story (the cause of his death).

What is significant for my point here, however, is that Arendt describes Grynszpan in *Benjamin's literal words.* The apotheosis of Arendt's uncharacteristic pathos in this passage is a literal stylistic echo, a literal rhetorical and verbal reminiscence of Benjamin's concluding sentence in "The Storyteller." Benjamin writes in his signature phrase: "The storyteller is the figure in which *the righteous man* encounters himself." Benjamin, supra note 6, at 109 (emphasis added). Similarly, resonantly, Grynszpan is described as having "a purity of soul" that *"only the righteous possess."* Arendt, supra note 10, at 229.

Another reference to "The Storyteller" makes itself evident at the beginning of the book. In the first chapter, in one of her rare moments of self-inclusion, Arendt situates herself as part of the audience of the trial whose task it is *"to face the storyteller:"* "[The audience] was filled with *"survivors,"* with middle-aged and elderly people, immigrants from Europe, like myself, *who knew by heart all there was to know,* and who were in no mood to learn any lessons. . . . [A]s witness followed witness and horror was piled on horror, *they sat there and listened in public to stories* they would hardly have been able to endure in private, when they would have had *to face the storyteller."* Id. at 8 (emphasis added). Arendt here places herself significantly among the *survivors,* those who inadvertently *share with those who took the stand the knowledge* of how difficult it is to tell the story of survival (to testify at once to life and to the death—the dying—the survival has entailed). The expression "to face the storyteller" (in which Arendt as a listener and as a survivor also faces herself) is reminiscent again of Benjamin's "Storyteller," in which *the listener be-comes a storyteller* in her turn. "For storytelling is always the art of repeating stories," writes Benjamin. "The more self-forgetful a listener is, the more deeply is what he listens to impressed upon his memory. . . . [The listener] listens to the tales in such a way that the gift of retelling them comes to him all by itself." Benjamin, supra note 6, at 91. It is as though Arendt facing Eichmann in Jerusalem and judging the trial at the level of her statement were also at the same time, at the level of her utterance, listening to the whisper of Benjamin's voice reciting, as it were, "The Storyteller" from his deathbed (like the original narrator in his essay):

> It is . . . characteristic that *not only a man's knowledge or wisdom*, but *above all his real life*—and this is the stuff that stories are made of—*first assumes transmissible form at the moment of his death*. Just as a sequence of images is set in motion inside a man as his life comes to an end, unfolding the views of himself under which he has encountered himself without being aware of it—suddenly in his expressions and looks the unforgettable emerges and imparts to everything that concerned him that authority which even the poorest wretch in dying possesses for the living around him. This authority is at the very source of the story.
>
> Id. at 94 (emphasis added).

86   Benjamin, supra note 6, at 94.

87   See Arendt, supra note 10, at 6 ("Justice . . . demands seclusion, it permits sorrow rather than anger.").

88   Arendt, supra note 68, at 262. Arendt borrows this sentence from Isak Dinesen, "who not only was one of the great storytellers of all times but also—and she was almost unique in this respect—knew what she was doing." Id.

89   Cf. Prosecutor's Opening Statement, in 1 *Proceedings*, supra note 55. For an in-depth inter-pretation of this statement, see Felman, supra note 18.

90   I am arguing that Benjamin and Heidegger are the two *absent addressees* of *Eichmann in Jerusalem* (symbolically, the German-Jewish casualty and the compromised German phi-losopher: a lost friendship and a lost love).

91   "Even where there is only a rustling of plants," Benjamin writes lyrically, "there is always a lament. Because she is mute, nature mourns . . . [and] the sadness of nature makes her mute." 1 Walter Benjamin, "On Language as Such and on the Language of Man," in Selected Writings, 1913–1923, at 73 (Marcus Bollock and Michael W. Jennings eds., Edmund Jeph-cott trans., 1996).

92   Id.

93   This speechless story is a story of mourning and of the inability to mourn: the story of a trauma and of the trauma's silencing and willful disavowal. In the middle of the writing of *Eichmann in Jerusalem*, Arendt also had a violent car accident in which she almost died: another brutal inner rupture, another intimate relation to death which similarly, equally was silenced and has left no visible mark on the tight argument of the book. Arendt tells Jaspers about this near-fatal accident: "It seemed to me that for a moment I had my life in my hands. I was quite calm: death seemed to me natural, in no way a tragedy or, somehow, out of the order of things. But, at the same time, I said to myself: if it is possible to do so *decently*, I would really like, still, to stay in this world." Quoted in Young-Bruehl, supra note 83, at 335 (emphasis added).

94   Benjamin, supra note 6, at 83.

95   "It is only for convenience that we speak of . . . '*traumatic memory*,'" writes the psychiatrist Pierre Janet. "*The subject is often incapable of making the necessary narrative which we call memory regarding the event; and yet he remains confronted by a difficult situation in which he has not been able to play a satisfactory part.*" Quoted in Van der Kolk and Van der Hart, supra note 43, at 160 (emphasis added).

96   Benjamin, supra note 6, at 84.

97   On Benjamin's relation to the First World War and on the role of silence and of trauma in his work, see chapter 1 in Felman, *The Juridical Unconscious*, supra note 41.

98   Ka-Tsetnik, supra note 12, at 18 (translation modified by author according to Hebrew original, supra note 12, at 34).

99   The importance of the story element in trials is by now a commonplace in legal scholarship. What is less well known is that, to the extent that trauma is what cannot be narrated (Benjamin, Janet), it also incorporates the paradoxical story of an inherent resistance to storytelling. Every trauma thus includes not only a traumatic story but also a *negative story element*, an *anti-story*. I argue that the Eichmann trial is an unprecedented legal event that articulates at once a monumental *legal story* and a collective, monumental *anti-story*, the unanticipated story of the impossibility of telling.

      On the theory of trauma as incapacity for narration, see, e.g., Van der Kolk and Van der Hart, supra note 43; Caruth, supra note 43. For general discussions of the relation between law and narrative, see, e.g., Derrick Bell, *And We Are Not Saved: The Elusive Quest for Racial Justice* (1987); *Critical Race Theory: The Cutting Edge* (Richard Delgado ed., 1995); *Critical Race Theory: The Key Writings That Formed the Movement* (Kimberlé Crenshaw et al. eds., 1995); *Law's Stories: Narrative and Rhetoric in the Law* (Peter Brooks and Paul Gewirtz eds., 1996); *Narrative and the Legal Discourse: A Reader in Storytelling and the Law* (David Ray Papke ed., 1991); *Narrative, Violence and the Law: The Essays of Robert Cover* (Martha Minow et al. eds., 1995); Robin West, *Narrative, Authority, and Law* (1993); Patricia Williams, *The Alchemy of Race and Rights: Diary of a Law Professor* (1991); Kathryn Abrams, "Hearing the Call of Stories," 79 *Cal. L. Rev.* 971 (1991); Richard Delgado, "Storytelling for Oppositionists and Others: A Plea for Narrative," 87 *Mich. L. Rev.* 2411 (1989); James R. Elkins, "On the Emergence of Narrative Jurisprudence: The Humanistic Perspective Finds A New Path," 9 *Legal Stud. F.* 123 (1985); James R. Elkins, "The Quest for Meaning: Narrative Accounts of Legal Education," *J. Legal Educ.* 577 (1988); Daniel A. Farber and Suzanna Sherry, "Telling Stories Out of School: An Essay on Legal Narratives," 45 *Stan. L. Rev.* 807 (1993); Felman, supra note 41; Mari Matsuda, "Looking to the Bottom: Critical Legal Studies and Reparations," 22 *Harv. C.R.-C.L. L. Rev.* 323 (1987); Austin Sarat, "Narrative Strategy and Death Penalty Advocacy," 31 *Harv. C.R.-C.L. L. Rev.* 353 (1996); Richard Sherwin, "Law Frames: Historical Truth and Narrative Necessity in a Criminal Case," 47 *Stan. L. Rev.* 39 (1994).

100 Because the unanticipated force of the event of the impossibility of telling caught everyone off guard and must have been surprising even to the trial's architects and to its legal actors, Arendt treats it as a symptom of their oversight and of their failure. I see it as a proof of the success of their conception beyond their grasp.

      In the same way that K-Zetnik's fainting could not be foreseen and was not planned, the legal narrative of the impossibility of telling could not be planned. It had to happen. It was the human and the legal meaning of what happened. *But no one could articulate this meaning at the time.* It was the unanticipated essence of the event, not part of the trial's stated ideology. It is only now in retrospect that this significance comes into view and can be recognized and formulated.

101 Arendt, supra note 10, at 229.

102 Id. at 223–24.

103 Segev, supra note 14, at 4 (emphasis added).

104 I now return from the "subtext" of *Eichmann in Jerusalem* to Arendt's conscious and explicit *text*: the conscious critical report she gives as a legal historian of the trial.

105 Oliver Wendell Holmes, "The Path of the Law," address delivered at the dedication of the new hall of the Boston University School of Law (Jan. 8, 1897), reprinted in 110 *Harv. L. Rev.* 991 (1997).

106 Id. at 1006. "When we study law," Holmes asserts, "we are not studying a mystery." Id. at 991. Eichmann's banality, Arendt insists, and the banality of Nazism as a whole, is not a mystery. Its essence is its shallowness, its hollow lack of depth. And this, says Arendt , is why "it is in the nature of this case that we have no tools to hand except legal ones, with which we have to pass sentence on something that cannot even be adequately represented either in legal terms or in political terms." Letter from Arendt to Jaspers (Dec. 23, 1960), in *Correspondence*, supra note 20, at 417. The tool is purposely, revealingly reductive: "When we study law we are not studying a mystery."

107 Sontag, supra note 63, at 118–19 (emphasis added).

108 Arendt, supra note 10, at 277.

109 In this sense, the Eichmann trial did fulfill its function, even in Arendt's critical eyes. "Those who are convinced that justice, and nothing else, is the end of law will be inclined to condone the kidnapping act, though not because of precedents." Id. at 264–65. "This last of the Successor trials will no more, and perhaps even less than its predecessors, serve as a valid precedent for future trials of such crimes. This might be of little import in view of the fact that its main purpose—to prosecute and to defend, to judge and to punish Adolph Eichmann—was achieved." Id. at 272–73.

110 1 Walter Benjamin, "Goethe's Elective Affinities," in *Selected Writings*, supra note 91, at 297, 355 (emphasis added).

111 Pierre Nora, "Between Memory and History: *Les Lieux de Mémoire*," in 26 *Representations* 7 (Mark Roudebush trans., 1989).

112 Benjamin, supra note 110, at 340.

113 Benjamin (using Hölderlin's terms) speaks of "the caesura of the work." Id. at 354, 340–41.

114 "Thereby, in the rhythmic sequence of the representations . . . there becomes necessary what in poetic meter is called the caesura . . . the counter-rhythmic rupture . . . that caesura in which, along with harmony, every expression simultaneously comes to a standstill, in order to give free reign to an expressionless power." Id. at 340–41.

115 It is as though, summoned to court, history acquired power of speech in amplifying and in making audible K-Zetnik's own repeated yet repeatedly mute cry. He writes: "That mute cry was again trying to break loose, as it had every time death confronted me at Auschwitz; and, as always when I looked death in the eye, so now too the mute scream got no further than my clenched teeth that closed upon it and locked it inside me. Indeed that was the

essence of that cry: it was never realized, never exposed to the outside air. It remained a strangled flame inside me." Ka-Tsetnik, supra note 12, at 1–2 (translation modified by author according to Hebrew original, supra note 12, at 18).

116 Compare the strikingly resonant statements of the French philosopher Emmanuel Levinas:

> The relation to the face is all at once the relation to the absolutely weak—what is absolutely exposed, what is naked and what is deprived . . . and at the same time . . . the face is also the "Thou shall not kill." . . . It is the fact that I cannot let the other die alone, it is as though there were [from the face] an appeal to me. . . . For me, he is above all the one for which I am responsible. . . . *It is always from the face, from my responsibility for the other, that justice emerges.*

Emmanuel Levinas, "Philosophie, Justice, Amour," in *Entre Nous: Essai sur le Penser à L'autre* 114–15 (1991) (author's translation) (emphasis added).

117 Walter Benjamin, *The Origin of German Tragic Drama* 166 (John Osborne trans.,1985) (1966).

118 Arendt writes:

> And indeed, before we come to any conclusion about the success or *failure* of the Jerusalem court, we must stress the judges' firm belief that they had no right to become legislators, that they had to conduct their business within the limits of Israeli law, on the one hand, and of accepted legal opinion, on the other. It must be admitted furthermore that *their failures* were neither in kind nor in degree greater than the failures of the Nuremberg Trials or the Successor Trials in other European countries. On the contrary, part of *the failure of the Jerusalem court* was due to its all too eager adherence to the Nuremberg precedent.

Arendt, supra note 10, at 274 (emphasis added).

119 Asked what was his concept of the Holocaust, Lanzmann answered: "I had no concept. I had obsessions, which is different. . . . The obsession of the cold. . . . The obsession of the first time. . . . The obsession of the last moments, the waiting, the fear. *Shoah* is a film full of fear. . . . You cannot do such a film theoretically. *Every theoretical attempt was a failure, but these failures were necessary.* . . . You build such a film in your head, in your heart, in your belly, in your guts, everywhere." Interview with Claude Lanzmann at Yale University, New Haven, Conn. (May 5, 1986) (film and transcript available at Fortunoff Video-Archive for Holocaust Testimonies at Yale) (transcription at 22–23) (emphasis added).

120 The present essay constitutes the fourth chapter of my book *The Juridical Unconscious: Trials and Traumas in the Twentieth Century* (Harvard Univ. Press 2002).

Lacan and Voting Rights

Anthony Paul Farley

> . . . Black body swinging in the southern breeze,
> Strange fruit hanging from the poplar trees.
> —Billie Holiday, "Strange Fruit"

White majorities rarely elect black representatives.[1] The black image in the white mind is not representative of white representational desires. Whites *see* themselves as whites. Whites *represent* themselves as whites. Peering into the dark mirror of the Other, peering into the mirror of the dark Other, standing opposite the mirror, whites *see* themselves as white, whites *see* themselves *represented* as white, whites *represent* themselves as white. The mirror is both for and before the look. Enter the Other: a dark, two-dimensional figure that seems, paradoxically, to possess an infinite depth. So stands the mirror image known as the "black" Other. Whites look deep into the mirror—the place of the black—to see themselves as sufficient unto themselves, as absolute beginnings, as coherent parts of a whole, as Leviathan. This essay is a look at this look and a discussion of the ways in which this look is written into law, specifically, voting rights.

Our yearning for rights is nothing other than the expression of our wounds.[2] Rights talk is the language of the wound. Rights are the words our wounds speak. We are political animals, according to Aristotle. Our wounds are politics. We are wounded animals, and when our wounds speak we become human. We are our wounds.

Leviathan

Our wounds speak of rituals of scarification that are codified as law and made into memories of future behavior. Our wounds, then, are the beginning of the social order. We become a social order, a body politic, a Leviathan, in and through memories of pain, memories of fragmentation, memories of underdevelopment. The social order, the body politic, Leviathan, is a collective work composed of the various scars written on our bodies by painful operations of law. And our bodies are, therefore, our collective works. Our bodies are the collective art we have made of ourselves. Each of us finds our place and function in the social order, the body politic, Leviathan, literally cut into our flesh.

One of the deepest cuts of the twentieth and now the twenty-first century is caused by the *colorline*. The wound it opens is *race*. The scar left in its wake is *race relations*. The *colorline* cuts so deeply into our bodies that our psyches must literally be pulled to pieces for us to see its operations clearly. The wound called *race* causes such pain that its reality overwhelms all else. The scar called *race relations* marks and masks our inability to imagine or grow healthy flesh over the wound opened by the colorline. *Race relations* serves as the tough, leathery substitute for the full recovery of undifferentiated flesh, for the full healing of the *wound*, for the end of the *colorline*.

In the imagination of the white Overmind, the body politic is held together in a form known as Leviathan. The Leviathan's organs are us. We are held together as a body politic by our mutual fear of and desire for the ordered liberty that is Leviathan. This fearful desire, a remembrance of pain, is sometimes expressed as a contract: a social contract. We are said to have engaged in a war of all against all until each of us surrendered her autonomy to the superior catholic hand of Leviathan. Until that moment in which we all *chose* to surrender that which we were *made* to surrender, we are said to have led lives that were "solitary, poore, nasty, brutish, and short":

> Whatsoever therefore is consequent to a time of Warre, where every man is Enemy to every man; the same is consequent to the time, wherein men live without other security, than what their own strength, and their own invention shall furnish them withall. In such condition, there is no place for Industry; because the fruit thereof is uncertain: and consequently no Culture of the Earth; no Navigation, nor use of the commodities that may be imported by Sea; no commodious Building; no Instruments of moving, and removing such things as require much force; no Knowledge of the face of the Earth; no account of Time; no Arts; no Letters; no Society; and which is

worst of all, continuall feare, and danger of violent death; And the life of man, solitary, poore, nasty, brutish, and short.³

We do not remember these past lives. Our past lives are said to have occurred in the nontime before the social contract. Leviathan is eternal. In the twentieth century and now in the twenty-first, Leviathan is white. In thinking of Leviathan and of the way we become ourselves in and through it and of the way it forms our connection not just to ourselves but to each other, we are thinking thoughts that take us to the deepest depths of our humanity. We are plunging deep into the mirror.

Whiteness is a peculiar thing, and to divine its deep meaning is no easy feat. The whiteness of our corporate body is produced by its mirror: those "beings of an inferior order altogether unfit to associate with the white race."⁴ Voting is the way that Leviathan binds itself together as a coherent being. Voting is the way that this colorlined society binds itself together in a vast white skin. Leviathan is white; to be white is to exclude blacks from the drama of becoming Leviathan. The central drama of Leviathan is, in the imagination of the white Overmind, the vote. To exclude blacks from the body politic, from becoming Leviathan, it is necessary to prevent blacks from exercising a meaningful vote.

The rituals of exclusion that together formed our notion of the "right" to vote are well known. Lillian Smith observed:

> The race issue was used, roughly, in this fashion: One politician outsmarted his rival by slapping the poll tax on his state's law books. His opponent retaliated by bloc-voting the Negroes. This led to fresh retaliation. The first one who could, put further restrictions on voting by setting up "literacy tests" (which could be passed by most whites, through the quickly enacted "grandfather clause," which exempted an illiterate from the test if his grandfather had voted). So it went, each building power for himself and his machine by reducing the number of people who could vote—and doing it in any way he could. But politicians, powerful as they are, cannot write poll-tax laws and grandfather clauses on a state's books—not in a democracy. The people must put them there. To persuade them to do so, fears must first be aroused. So the demagogues got busy. They drilled with their electric lies deep into our memories, stirring up the unhappy past, telling ghost stories about "race dangers," seasoning their barbecue speeches with obscene innuendoes about "mongrelizing," about "your sister marrying a Negro," and sadistic phrases: rivers of blood . . . troops with bayonets . . . invasion of the home. Then what happened? More lynchings—naturally. For the mentally unstable (white and colored) were aroused by

such speeches and did violent, foolish things, hardly knowing why they did them. Immediately after a lynching, more segregation statutes were put on lawbooks to "control racial violence." Signs went over doors, over drinking fountains; public buildings were often out of bounds to Negroes. Jim Crow travel cars were set up—hooked onto trains going South at Washington, D.C. Eating together in restaurants and in trains in the South was banned.[5]

Smith's observation was mirrored in the shattered bodies of black would-be voters. Robert Toatley, a former slave, reported the consequences of attempting to enter the white body politic: "Night rider come by and drop something at your door and say, 'I'll just leave you something for dinner.' Then ride off in a gallop. When you open the sack, what you reckon in there? One time it was six nigger heads that was left at the door. Was it at my house door? Oh, no! It was at the door of a nigger too active in politics."[6]

Let us look at the bodies that are ruined in order to produce the mirror image upon which the white body politic relies for its vision of itself, its body, and its future possibilities. It may be enlightening for us to follow the *colorline* all the way down to the *wounds* it caused and causes and then to the *scars* that those wounds have been rationalized into being. Let us read the *scars* as signs, as meanings, as terms of art in the social contract, as the codification of fear and desire, as the flesh and bone and blood of Leviathan.

The Mirror

These are the images of castration, mutilation, dismemberment, dislocation, evisceration, devouring, bursting open of the body. . . . One has only to listen to children aged between two and five playing, alone or together, to know that pulling off the head and ripping open of the belly are themes that occur spontaneously to their imagination, and that this is corroborated by the experience of the doll torn to pieces.—Jacques Lacan, "The Mirror Stage as Formative of the Function of the I . . ."

And everybody started screaming again. And I looked and I saw the troopers charging us again and some of them were swinging their arms and throwing canisters of tear gas. And beyond them I saw the horsemen starting their charge toward us. I was terrified. What happened then is something I'll never forget as long as I live. Never. In fact, I still dream about it sometimes. I saw those horsemen coming toward me and they had those awful masks on; they rode right through the cloud of tear gas. Some of them had clubs, others had ropes or whips, which they swung about them like they were driving cattle. . . . I don't know if I was screaming or not, but everyone else was.—Sheyann Webb, in *Selma, Lord, Selma*

Lacan argued that the infant sees in its reflection an imagined future coherence, a coherence that is not yet. The infant—fragmented—sees in the mirror an image of a wholeness, an integrity that it does not possess. The infant comes to exist as an individual through the disjunction between its actual fragmentation and the imagined unified self it sees in the mirror. There is a necessary moment of fiction in the creation of the self. This stage, called the mirror stage by Lacan, is not really a stage because it is never really over.[7]

The infant is dependent upon others to provide it with a mirror, just as the adult it will later become is dependent on others to provide a mirror image. Drucilla Cornell argues that the law serves as a lifelong mirror: "[T]he state and the legal system should themselves be understood as symbolic Others that confirm and constitute who is established as a person."[8] The law gives us a reflection of a coherence that we do not truly possess: "It is only through the mirroring process that the infant comes to have an identity. The body's coherence depends on the future anteriority of the projection, in that what has yet to be, is imagined as already given. The infant, then, does not recognize a self that is already 'there' in the mirror. Instead, the self is constituted in and through the mirroring process as other to its reality of bodily disorganization, and by having itself mirrored by others as a whole."[9] We imagine ourselves as actually possessing the qualities we see reflected in the mirror of the law: "Our 'bodies' are never really our own. The idea that we own our bodies is a fantasy that imagines as completed that which always remains in the future. Therefore, to protect 'ourselves' from threats to our bodily integrity, we have to protect the future into which we project our unity and have our bodily integrity respected by others."[10]

The future ("we have to protect the future into which we project our unity"), when it comes to black voting rights, resembles the past. Black voting rights have been imagined as intimately connected to the protection from threats to bodily integrity. The dismemberment of the black body politic provides the white body politic with a mirror of its white unity and protection for its white future. In 1965, the year that the Voting Rights Act was passed, nine-year-old Sheyann Webb, on the eve of her decision to fully participate in the Selma Movement, understood the connection between bodily integrity, self-ownership, and the vote: "I kept thinking about the words Hosea Williams had said about if you can't vote, then you're a slave."[11]

Justice Sandra Day O'Connor, writing for the Court in *Shaw v. Reno*, upheld a challenge by white voters to the plan under which North Carolina sent black representatives to Congress for the first time since Reconstruction.[12] At issue in *Shaw v. Reno* was a North Carolina reapportionment plan creating two majority-black voting districts for the House of Representatives. As Justice O'Connor's opinion notes, one voting district had "been compared to a 'Rorschach ink-blot test and a bug splattered on a windshield.'"[13] The other voting district, Justice O'Connor's opinion informs us, was "even more unusually shaped . . . [being] approximately 160 miles long, . . . for much of its length no wider than the I-85 corridor, . . . [and moving] in snake-like fashion through tobacco country, financial centers, and manufacturing areas 'until it gobbles in enough enclaves of black neighborhoods.'"[14] The voting districts in question had been created in response to the objection of the attorney general of the United States, under the Voting Rights Act of 1965, to the dilution of black votes that would have occurred under a previous plan providing for only one majority-black congressional district in the state of North Carolina.

The first image of the opinion, that of the "Rorschach inkblot test," invites an examination of its second image, that of the "snake." The snake is a doubly interesting way to interpret the district's shape. The snake evokes images of the Temptation and the Fall as well as images of the *phallus.* The "Temptation" for Justice O'Connor seems to be the forbidden fruit of race consciousness. However, one can turn her opinion's "Rorschach ink-blot test" on her opinion's own image and wonder whether the strange fruit, the black body swaying from southern trees, is not the temptation before which she herself has fallen. Lynching was and remains a classic American way of severing black political connections. Both the voting registrar and the lyncher's rope appear to be part and parcel of the same process of white-over-black. It appears as though Justice O'Connor has partaken of the strange fruit. And, as she herself admits, "reapportionment is one area in which appearances do matter."[15] We are, therefore, not entirely out of line in seeing whether we can mark traces of the colorline in the *Shaw v. Reno* voting rights decision.

Justice O'Connor writes: "A reapportionment plan that includes in one district individuals who belong to the same race, but who are otherwise separated by geographical and political boundaries, and who may have little in common with one another but the color of their skin, bears an uncomfortable resemblance to political apartheid."[16] For Justice O'Connor, such connections are "bizarre."[17] Worse yet, they serve to reinforce "the perception that members of the same racial group—regardless of their age, education, economic status, or the community in which they live—think alike, share the same political interests, and will prefer the same candidates at the polls."[18]

Residents of the "bizarre" voting district could have nothing in common with each other, according to Justice O'Connor. For Justice O'Connor, "race" means skin color: "Racial classifications of any sort pose the risk of lasting harm to our society. They reinforce the belief, held by too many for too much of our history, that individuals should be judged by the color of their skin."[19] When Justice O'Connor writes of "our history," she cuts away the entire dreadful history of white-over-black in the United States, in an opinion which is both historically suspect and logically unsound.[20]

Fragments

Imagine that there was a ritual of exclusion centered on the consumption of your body. Imagine a communion in remembrance of your exclusion from the body politic. Imagine it was your blood they drank and your body they ate as they imagined themselves freed by their feast from sin and mortality. Imagine that when you tried to register to vote—to enter the body politic—they gathered together as one flesh, one spirit, one witness, one whiteness, and then pulled your flesh to pieces while setting you ablaze. Imagine that they used their ecstasy in your pain as a way of remembering their right to exclude you from being, to exclude you from the body politic, to exclude you from Leviathan. Imagine that they used the Gothic horror of what you suffered as a sign and a warning to others of the rightness of the ritual, the whiteness of the ritual. Imagine that your fragmentation was the mirror of Leviathan's future completion. To imagine all this is to see that this is the blood-stained gate, this is the birth of a nation, this is democracy in America.

Judicial opinions matter only to the extent that they are carved into our bodies. Voting—choosing our terms of endearment to each other and to Leviathan—is, in the imagination of the liberal Overmind, an important ritual of birthing the body politic. The colorline appears in the birth of a nation as an umbilical cord. C. Vann Woodward observed: "Thomas P. Bailey, a Southern educator, [writes]: '[D]isen-franchisement of the negroes has been concomitant with the growth of political and social solidarity among the whites.' The more white men sharply recognize their kinship with their fellow whites, and the more democracy in every sense of the term spreads among them, the more the negro is compelled to 'keep his place'—a place that is gradually narrowing in the north as well as in the south."[21]

The law both creates and is created by the myriad lines that cut and bind the social. These lines cut our bodies into different patterns, meanings, histories, destinies, and products. These cuts, these wounds, are feelings we have in and about our flesh, not just abstractions in our minds. These feelings are instructed, educated, and intensified according to patterns laid out in our flesh and our legal texts. White-over-black is an *orientation* toward a peculiar institutionalized form of s/m: the colorline. Justice O'Connor's thoughts regarding district voting lines are not just thoughts; they are feelings of the flesh. Feelings long denied do not lose their hold over the body and its thoughts. Such feelings, moreover, are experienced in the body of the justice as much as in the bodies of those on whom her fantasies are imposed through law.

Lacan made this observation: "A train arrives at a station. A little boy and a little girl, brother and sister, are seated in a compartment face to face next to the window through which the buildings along the station platform can be seen passing as the train pulls to a stop. 'Look,' says the brother, 'we're at Ladies!'; 'Idiot!' replies his sister, 'Can't you see we're at Gentlemen?'"[22]

This arrival at one's destiny takes place in the nontime before one is. One's destiny has always already left the station. The system of white-over-black that is Leviathan anticipates our arrival just as certainly and as surely as the system marked "Ladies" and "Gentlemen" described by Lacan.

Tell Me How Long the Train's Been Gone

In "Going to Meet the Man," James Baldwin wrote of the persistence of memory in a way that sheds light on Justice O'Connor and the fin de siècle of voting rights:

> "What's the matter?" she asked.
> "I don't know," he said, trying to laugh, "I guess I'm tired."[23]

The man, impotent, has lost his erotic connection to his wife; "[e]xcitement filled him like a toothache, but it refused to enter his flesh."[24] The empty space between them is filled with talk of black voting rights protests:

> "Go to sleep," she said, gently, "you got a hard day tomorrow."
> "Yeah," he said, and rolled over on his side, facing her, one hand still on one breast. "Goddamn the niggers. The black stinking coons. You'd think they'd learn. Wouldn't you think they'd learn? I mean, *wouldn't* you?"[25]

The specter of a black connection to the body politic has severed the man's own erotic connection to his wife in ways he has hidden from himself. More terrible still, the idea of black solidarity—of a black unity of political interests— has undone their marital connection. The man, a sheriff, has been hard at work denying the possibility of connection:

"There was this nigger today," he said; and stopped; his voice sounded peculiar. He touched Grace. "You awake?" he asked. . . . "What a funny time," he said, "to be thinking about a thing like that—you listening?" She mumbled something again. He rolled on his back. "This nigger's one of the ringleaders. . . . Well, [we] really had to whip that nigger's ass today." He looked over at Grace; he could not tell whether she was listening or not; and he was afraid to ask again. "They had this line you know, to register"—he laughed, but she did not—"and they wouldn't stay where Big Jim C. wanted them, no, they had to start blocking traffic all around the court house so couldn't nothing or nobody get through . . . and they wouldn't move and they just kept up the singing."[26]

The blacks are all connected together in the struggle for the vote—in the struggle to join the body politic as equal citizens and live the bourgeois legality promised by the Fifteenth Amendment. They are in a state of grace as they wed themselves to piercing the colorline. Their struggle for the franchise—their line—undoes all manner of white connections ("blocking traffic all around the court house"). Their singing ("they just kept up the singing") eludes the man's understanding as he lies in bed with Grace, his wife. Somehow, the man understands his inability to enter a state of grace as intimately connected to the Sorrow Songs and to the black bodies that have become as one in this new ceremony called civil rights:

"They were still singing and I was supposed to make them stop. Well I couldn't make them stop for me but I knew he could make them stop. He was lying on the ground jerking and moaning, they had threw him in a cell by himself, and blood was coming out his ears from where Big Jim C. and his boys had whipped him. Wouldn't you think they'd learn? I put the prod to him and he jerked some more and he kind of screamed—but he didn't have much voice left."[27]

The man, still lying in bed with Grace, recalls the way he had conducted the torture ritual ("I put the prod to him"), but the singing does not stop (even though "he didn't have much voice left"). Whether these are the Hosannas that greeted Christ and maddened the Romans, or the Trumpets with which Joshua fought the battle of Jericho, it is a joyful noise. Their singing enfeebles the whiteness all around:

" 'You are all going to stop your singing,' I said to him, 'and you are going to stop coming to the courthouse and disrupting traffic and molesting the people and keeping us from our duties and keeping doctors from getting to sick white women and getting all them northerners in this town to give our town a bad name—!' "[28]

The man's body does his thinking for him as he tries to rescue his white world from the singing: "His foot leapt out, he had not known it was going to, and caught the boy flush on the jaw."[29] The boy is knocked into darkness. Raising himself up from the pit of unconsciousness, he replies:

> "White man," said the boy, from the floor, behind him.
> He stopped. For some reason, he grabbed his privates.
> "You remember Old Julia?"[30]

"Old Julia" was the "boy's" grandmother. In one of the myriad microaggressions that make up the colorline, the man is forced to recall that he had years earlier refused to address "Old Julia" by her proper name.[31] The ritual being acted out over voting rights and black connectedness had been acted out years earlier between the two antagonists:

> The boy said from the floor, with his mouth full of blood, and one eye, barely open, glaring like the eye of a cat in the dark, "My grandmother's name was Mrs. Julia Blossom. *Mrs.* Julia Blossom. . . . And those kids ain't going to stop singing. We going to keep on singing until every one of you miserable white mothers go stark raving out of your minds." Then he closed the one eye; he spat blood; his head fell back on the floor.[32]

The man remembered the encounter and the inexplicable defiance of a boy, then less than ten years old:

> "Old Julia home?" . . .
> "Don't no Old Julia live here" . . .
> "This is her house. I know her. She's lived here for years." . . .
> "You might know a Old Julia someplace else, white man. But don't nobody by that name live here."

Everything went awry that afternoon under the boy's gaze. The object—the black body—was looking back. The object was looking back in anger and thereby refashioning itself as a person, as a subject. The man—the white man—felt his world take a surrealistic turn:

> The sun beat down on them both, still and silent; he had the feeling that he had been caught up in a nightmare, a nightmare dreamed by a child; perhaps

one of those nightmares he himself had dreamed as a child. It had that feeling—everything familiar, without undergoing any other change, had been subtly and hideously displaced: the trees, the sun, the patches of grass in the yard, the leaning porch and the very weary steps and the cardboard in the windows and the black hole in the door which looked like a cave, and the eyes of the pickaninny, all, all were charged with malevolence. *White man.*[33]

The impotent man is still in bed with hand on his wife's breast as he recalls this moment. He is in bed with his hand on Grace's breast, *and* he is standing in a cell over the broken body of his rebellious prisoner for black solidarity, *and* he is standing in the sun as he recalls his encounter with that same rebellious prisoner as a "pickaninny" turned dangerous by thoughts of black solidarity. Time has lost its meaning and its grip; he is here, there, and everywhere. The memory within the memory disturbs him because his encounter with the black boy, too, had ended with exclusion from his desired goal:

> The boy said nothing.
> "Well," he said, "tell her I passed by and I'll pass by next week." He started to go; he stopped. "You want some chewing gum?"
> The boy got down from the swing and started for the house. He said, "I don't want nothing you got, white man." He walked into the house and closed the door behind him.[34]

The man, trembling "with what he believed was rage," begins the torture of his prisoner with a vengeance.[35] The man's erection, as he "howled" over the boy's unconscious body, surprises him.[36]

The singing does not stop.[37] The man—his hand still on the breast of his wife Grace—recalls the singing of an earlier time, a time spent with his father and a time not spent with his boyhood friend Otis: "He had a black friend, his age, eight, who lived nearby. His name was Otis. They wrestled together in the dirt. Now the thought of Otis made him sick."[38]

"*I stepped in the river at Jordan.*" The "line came flying up at him with melody and beat."[39] The man's father had said, "I guess they singing for him."[40] "Him" referred to the young person who was the communion meal of their family picnic: "You won't ever forget *this* picnic—!"[41] We recall through the eyes of this child who later chooses to be the man: "By this time there were three cars piled behind the first one, with everyone looking excited and shining, and Jesse noticed that they were carrying food. It was like a Fourth of July picnic."[42] The man's name, we find out, is Jesse. Baldwin, himself the son of a preacher, names his protagonist after the father of King David:

> What did he do? Jesse wondered. . . . He was seated on his father's shoulders, but his father was far away. There were . . . friends of his father's, raising and lowering the chain; everyone indiscriminately responsible for the fire. . . .
>
> He turned his head a little and saw the field of faces. He watched his mother's face. Her eyes were very bright, her mouth was open: she was more beautiful than he had ever seen her, and more strange. He began to feel a joy he had never felt before. He watched the hanging, gleaming body, the most beautiful and terrible object he had ever seen till then. One of his father's friends . . . held a knife: and Jesse wished he had been that man. It was a long, bright knife and the sun seemed to catch it, to play with it, to caress it—it was brighter than the fire. And a wave of laughter swept through the crowd. . . . The man with the knife walked toward the crowd, smiling slightly; as though this were a signal. . . . Then the man with the knife walked up to the hanging body. He turned and smiled again. . . . The man with the knife took the nigger's privates in his hand, one hand, still smiling, as though he were weighing them. . . . Then the dying man's eyes looked straight into Jesse's eyes—it could not have been as long as a second, but it seemed longer than a year. Then Jesse screamed, and the crowd screamed as the knife flashed, first up, then down, cutting the dreadful thing away, and the blood came roaring down. Then the crowd rushed forward, tearing at the body with their hands, with knives, with rocks, with stones, howling and cursing. . . . Someone stepped forward and drenched the body with kerosene. Where the man had been, a great sheet of flame appeared. Jesse's father lowered him to the ground.
>
> "Well, I told you," said his father, "you wasn't never going to forget *this* picnic." . . . At that moment Jesse loved his father more than he had ever loved him. He felt that his father had revealed to him a great secret which would be the key to his life forever.[43]

Afterward, the man's father says, "[T]hey'll come and get him by and by. I reckon we better get over there and get some of that food before it's all gone."[44] The ritual humiliation of the lynching was a form of communion ("you wasn't never going to forget *this* picnic"). The entire *ensemble,* the American way of life, was connected to the ritual. The family feelings binding husband and wife, parent and child, neighbor and neighbor, were all connected to the "long, bright knife." The knife is a mirror: the black body is alone, no longer attached to anything or anyone: "[A]nd this is what is hard to explain—you see people like you never saw them before. They shine as bright as a razor. Maybe it's because you see people differently than you saw them before your trouble started."[45] "Trouble means you're alone."[46] Leviathan stirs, its connectedness reestablished by the lynching, by the ritual disintegration of the black body.

The black body's fragmentation mirrors a future coherence for its white other. Indeed, the black body's dismemberment is experienced as an ecstasy of whiteness. The man, on recalling this scene from his childhood, "feels his old nature returned to him." This, in turn, leads him to wake and make love with his wife Grace: " 'Come on, sugar, I'm going to do you like a nigger, just like a nigger, come on sugar, and love me just like you'd love a nigger.' He thought of that morning as he labored and she moaned."[47] In the ecstatic moment of creating the wound, of capturing the *phallus*, of white-over-black, husband and wife and child and memory and forgetting and every white person with every other white person come together as one flesh. "There is a phallic kind of enjoyment in the symbolic operations of a language which stands for, and designates at the same time, another enjoyment, connected to sexual intercourse,"[48] write Lacan scholars Bice Benvenuto and Roger Kennedy, a comment that illuminates both "Going to Meet the Man" and *Shaw v. Reno*. In the case of the colorline, white-over-black is a form of pleasure akin to s/m.[49]

Justice O'Connor's Phallus

The phallus is the privileged signifier of that mark in which the role of the logos is joined with the advent of desire.—Jacques Lacan, "The Signification of the Phallus"

Justice O'Connor's opinion in *Shaw v. Reno* can be read as a celebration of white citizenship and white community akin to the one described in James Baldwin's "Going to Meet the Man." Her opinion can be read by the light of the "long, bright knife." Her white "feminine" voice captures the moment perfectly. Suzanna Sherry suggests that the "thoroughly individualist liberal philosophy" that, in her view, has grounded most contemporary constitutional interpretation would be aided by a return to the "less individualist republican spirit" that animated "the Revolution."[50] Sherry fears that such a project may be a "futile exercise" unless it enlists the services of what she describes as a "feminine jurisprudence": "[M]odern liberalism is a characteristically masculine response to the failure of Jeffersonian republicanism. Because the masculine perspective has been the dominant—and virtually the sole—influence on the legal and political structure, that structure is bound to reflect a more masculine or liberal emphasis on individualism over community. A feminine jurisprudence, instead of rejecting the communitarian and virtue-based framework of Jeffersonian republicanism, might embrace and adapt it for modern society."[51]

For Sherry, Justice O'Connor's "feminine jurisprudence" has embraced and adapted "Jeffersonian republicanism" for our modern society. Thomas Jefferson, we may recall, kept blacks in slavery. Even as he enjoyed the strange fruit of black slavery, he advocated black exclusion from the Republic:

It will probably be asked, Why not retain and incorporate the blacks into the State, and thus save the expense of supplying by importation of white settlers, the vacancies they will leave? . . . To these objections, which are political, may be added others, which are physical and moral. The first difference is that of color. . . . Is it not the foundation of a greater or less share of beauty in the two races? Are not the fine mixtures of red and white, the expressions of every passion by greater or less suffusions of color in the one, preferable to that eternal monotony, which reigns in the countenances, that immovable veil of black which covers the emotions of the other race? Add to these, flowing hair, a more elegant symmetry of form, their own judgment in favor of whites, declared by their preference of them, as uniformly as is the preference of the Oran-ootan for the black woman over those of his own species. The circumstance of superior beauty, is thought worth attention in the propagation of our horses, dogs, and other domestic animals; why not in that name.[52]

In addition to marking blacks as "ugly," Jefferson the slavemaster held blacks to be stupid: "In reason [blacks are] much inferior, as I think one could scarcely be found capable of tracing and comprehending the investigations of Euclid; and that in imagination they are dull, tasteless, and anomalous. . . . Never yet could I find that a black had uttered a thought above the level of plain narration; never saw even an elementary trait of painting or sculpture."[53] Jeffersonian republicanism, from what Sherry could call, in terms consistent with her own language, "the unique perspective of [blacks] in general," was inextricably connected to black slavery. The "connections" between blacks during slavery took the form of chains. These connections were updated when the black codes were translated into segregation, and again when they were translated into neosegregation (as with *Shaw v. Reno*). Sherry concludes: "Finally, recognition of Justice O'Connor's unique perspective, and *the unique perspective of women in general*, might aid us in ameliorating the distortions of an overly individualist liberal paradigm. Insufficient attention to *connection* promotes naked self-interest at the expense of altruism, impoverishes our self-perception, and stunts our capacity for growth. Merely communicating a feminine emphasis on connection may be enlightening: 'Teaching is not always a matter of either arguing or providing evidence. . . . It is sometimes rather a matter of imparting a way of looking at things."[54]

O'Connor's "way of looking at things" like the right to vote looks like the old way of looking at the right to vote. Justice O'Connor's way of looking at things is as old as the colorline and older than the Republic. In *Shaw v. Reno*, Justice O'Connor pays white "feminine" attention to the "connections" by dismembering the black body politic. Justice O'Connor dismembers the black body politic by cutting away the snakelike district ("cutting the dreadful thing away").[55] In so doing, she partakes of the forbidden fruit of Billie Holiday's southern trees.

Sherry joins Justice O'Connor's table. Justice O'Connor's act of "cutting the dreadful thing away" resembles the way in which Sherry, in her celebration of Justice O'Connor's jurisprudence, uses the terms "feminine" and "woman." When Sherry describes "the unique perspective of women in general," she represents a white-over-black perspective as the general perspective of women. What might be described as "the unique perspective of [blacks] in general" is lost through Sherry's act of "cutting the dreadful thing away." Sherry, in possession of the *phallus*, decides what is general and what is not. Sherry states that a "feminine jurisprudence" might pay attention to the "connections" and choose to "embrace" Jeffersonian republicanism. Sherry's "feminine jurisprudence" is white. It is difficult to imagine a black jurisprudence, feminine or masculine, so easily choosing to "embrace" Jeffersonian republicanism. Slavery, the peculiar institution that was the cornerstone of Jefferson's entire world of imagined possibilities, was a perpetual lynching. The attack on memory is itself an act of lynching. Sherry and Justice O'Connor both join the forces of forgetting in the battle against memory.

When we contemplate the spectacle of at least one form of lynching, we can see that race is often attached to gender. We may go further and examine the colorline itself as gendered. When white men and white women banded together as *whites* to unsex the bodies of the black would-be voters they selected for their mutilation rituals, they turned whiteness into a gender of sorts. Whiteness opposes blackness like a gender. The gender called *white* is the one with the *phallus*. Consider the lynching of Claude Neal in this regard: "After taking the nigger to the woods about four miles from Greenwood, they cut off his penis. He was made to eat it. Then they cut off his testicles and made him eat them and say he liked it."[56]

Why did whites so frequently sexually mutilate the black victims of their antivoting registration drives? Perhaps, in cases involving male victims, the penis represented the *phallus*. Perhaps, in cases involving female victims, the *phallus* was represented by the penis. The bearer of the *phallus* is the one in charge. Whites, as bearers of the *phallus*, make themselves a common gender vis-à-vis blacks. This was, as can be seen from the Dionysian revelry of the lynching ritual, a deeply erotic moment, a white wedding, a coming together of scattered white bodies as one flesh, as Leviathan.

In the lynching, blacks are made into an opening. Blacks are made into an opening for whites to enter. And who can resist an opening? The *phallus* is, for whites in colorlined societies, both the symbol of their rightful place above blacks and the instrument of their pleasure-in-being-white. White-over-black is a form of ecstasy. The *phallus* is the key to this opening: "He felt that his father had revealed to him a great secret which would be the key to his life forever."[57] The whites at the lynching of Claude Neal made their victim open his mouth to their now-white *phallus* and "say he liked it." Whites—male and female alike— become as one flesh in this ritual and blacks become the Other flesh. Whiteness is the one, and blackness is its Other. The Other is the one with the lack. The Other is the one with the wound. The "bizarre district" in *Shaw v. Reno* presented a Rorschach nightmare: a snake and a temptation. The *phallus* was torn from the black body politic by Justice O'Connor just as the *phallus* was torn from the black bodies in southern trees.

The *phallus* was shared by Baldwin's white couple in their marital bed. There is no mourning the evisceration of the black body's connections. To the contrary, the "bright shining blade" reflects the whiteness of the erotic experience that takes them until morning. In contemplating the snakelike district that was cut away, recall that Robinson O. Everett of Durham, North Carolina, arguing before the Supreme Court on behalf of the appellants in *Shaw v. Reno*, twice described the district as "political pornography."[58] The past and the scars by which we can trace its passage are not so easily cut away, whatever Justice O'Connor might write. As Baldwin observed: "It is a sentimental error, therefore, to believe that the past is dead; it means nothing to say that it is all forgotten, that the Negro himself has forgotten it. It is not a question of memory. Oedipus did not remember the thongs that bound his feet; nevertheless the marks they left testified to that doom towards which his feet were leading him."[59]

Pastoral Scenes of the Gallant South

Consider James Meredith's description of U.S. Highway 51 in August 1960 in the light of Justice O'Connor's "long bright knife," and the lynching quality of *Shaw v. Reno* becomes clear: The fact that black connectedness, the black body politic, was the essence of Justice O'Connor's problem with so viewing North Carolina's I-85 becomes clear. Obviously, Justice O'Connor could have considered the fact that white supremacy unified the blacks along 1–85 as a community of interest, as a community interested in the eradication of the colorline. Meredith's description of U.S. 51 illustrates a method:

> Highway 51 is code word for the millions of Negroes who have driven north to south and south to north for the past twenty-five years. This was the route taken by us—my wife and six-month-old son and me—into Mississippi . . . I had traveled the road many times and knew practically every hill and curve. . . . It had long been my practice to fill up the gas tank in Memphis, so I would not have to face the "peckerwoods" at a station in Mississippi. One tank of gas would take you to Kosciusko or Jackson where you could go to a Negro-operated station. This time it was more pressing than ever to get gas because I had my wife and son with me, and God only knew what I would do if an incident occurred while I was with my family.[60]

Like Lacan's train station, Highway 51 is a destiny, albeit racial, rather than gendered:

> I pulled into a station that I had used for quite a few years on this route, because they did not have segregated toilets for "White Ladies," "White Men," and "Colored." Thinking that the practice would be the same as before, I didn't go through the customary ritual used when a Negro pulls into a gas station in the South and is not sure about the discrimination practices. Since some of the white folks there are a little more human, or just plain smarter, than the crackers and rednecks, they mark the facilities for whites as just "Ladies" and "Men" and put the Negro toilet in the back where you cannot see it. The Negro will ask the attendant, "Do you have a bathroom?" (although he is looking right at the big signs that read "Ladies" and "Men"). If the attendant says, "Yes, right there," then the Negro says, "Fill it up, and check everything." If the answer is, "Yeah, go round the back," then the Negro drives away and looks for another station. I pulled up, spoke to the man, and told him to "fill it up." Then my wife left to go to the bathroom. When she reached the toilet, the sign read "White Ladies

ONLY." Upon asking the attendant about the restrooms, we were told that the "Colored" was in the back. . . . It was filthy, nasty, and stinking. The toilet wouldn't flush and there was no toilet paper or water to wash one's hands. . . . This was the much talked-about progress I had been making since the 1954 Supreme Court decision that said "separate but equal" was no longer the law of the land.[61]

Meredith connects the personal and the political as he presents his phenomenology of U.S. 51:

The first thing you see when you head south on old U.S. 51 from Memphis and Shelby County, Tennessee—the home of the Cotton Queens and the famous or infamous "Crump political machine" and the place where the Negro blues originated—is a big flashy sign: WELCOME TO MISSISSIPPI. This sign arouses mixed emotions in the thousands of Negroes who pass it. For many it is a joke; for others it recalls the days gone by, their work in the cotton fields in Mississippi, their migration to the North, their jobs in the warplants during the forties and in the factories of today.

For me, it is indeed a sign of frustration. Always, without fail, regardless of the number of times I enter Mississippi, it creates within me feelings that are felt at no other time. There is the feeling of joy. Joy because I have once again lived to enter the land of my fathers, the land of my birth, the only land in which I feel at home. It also inspires a feeling of hope because where there is life there is also a hope, a chance. At the same time, there is a feeling of sadness. Sadness because I am immediately aware of the special subhuman role that I must play, because I am a Negro, or die.[62]

All along the way Meredith notes the political ties—local governments, businesses, police and police practices, entertainment centers, and places of integration—that bound black Mississippians to each other and to the land all along the asphalt.[63] What emerges is a portrait of an irregularly shaped space—U.S. 51 seems rather like I-85—that connects the black body politic. Indeed, the white community of interests surrounding U.S. 51 was also quite recognizable to James Meredith, and to the entire world. It was, therefore, entirely unsurprising when his 1966 "March against Fear"—an attempt to walk the length of Mississippi on U.S. 51—was greeted by buckshot that sent him north to the hospital.[64]

The black body is smashed into fragments, and the broken bits form the mirror that casts an ideal reflection back on those who wish to see themselves as white. This is an old, old idea: "Negro districts are never able to elect Negro representatives because their districts comprise the center of pies in which the largest portions of each ward slice are white."[65]

Conclusion: Doctrine as Culture Study

Here is a strange and bitter crop.—Billie Holiday, "Strange Fruit"

Cultural studies as a field of knowledge may be characterized by the habit or tendency to listen to as many stories as possible. The stories to which one listens when doing cultural studies are those stories that people tell themselves and each other about what they think they are doing. This collection of essays is filled with such stories. Cultural studies, then, is less a specific field of knowledge than a postmodern style or symptom. As a style, it is marked by its resistance to disciplinary boundaries such as the one dividing jurisprudence and psychoanalysis. As a symptom, it is marked by a deep skepticism toward grand narratives. Cultural studies has also to do with performance: to be recognized as *doing* cultural studies is to *perform* a routine or set of routines that display one's antidisciplinary tendencies alongside with one's interdisciplinary orientations.

We are always doing cultural studies but are not always open about doing it. Consider the Rorschach inkblot test and the snakelike district in Justice O'Connor's opinion. Consider the use of poetry from a law review article alongside metaphors from the *Wall Street Journal* in Justice O'Connor's opinion. Consider these things, and what emerges is a portrait of Justice O'Connor as a cultural studies jurist. Everyone does cultural studies—albeit some less openly than others.

Legal realism too often stops with social science. Law, the realists argued, was not "science," but "science" was "science." Law, therefore, was indeterminate and, therefore, political. The realists fought formalism because formalism blocked the path to science, and science they too often imagined as existing above or outside politics in a place where it could be made to serve human values. Of course, those values came with choices and indeterminacies and politics, which tipped the scales to one or the other side of the either/or of binary thinking. To *perform* cultural studies is to move in a way that shows that no field of knowledge is "outside" politics.

Legal realism/formalism—each is immanent in the other—is limited by its refusal to contest the politics of the discipline of law. Antidisciplinary approaches—cultural studies, for example—have produced and will continue to produce many interesting, surprising performances. A surprise of great interest is the news that the "mainstream" is no more disciplined than its outside. Indeed, the stories told within the veil of law's discipline can be reread to show the monsters and demons that reside within and provide the magic of apparently logical coherence.

In this essay, I have tried to show, using psychoanalysis, the horror within the voting rights jurisprudence of Justice Sandra Day O'Connor in *Shaw v. Reno*. Her opinion works because of these horrors. The horror is constitutive of the white body politic. The horror shatters—lynches—the black body politic. Leviathan is this perpetual white-over-black along with its perpetual denial. Politics, indeed, is merely the politic term for mutilation performed literally and literarily on black bodies by the "long, bright knife" that is always and everywhere "cutting the dreadful thing away." This essay—this performance—is part of the struggle of memory over forgetting that is cultural analysis.

Notes

Earlier versions of this essay were presented at the University of Toronto and at Yale University. I thank Austin Sarat and Jonathan Simon for their encouragement of this project. I thank my copanelists Shoshana Felman and Nahum Chandler for their excellent contributions and comments. I thank my wife, Maria Grahn-Farley, for her always brilliant comments on legal theory.

The epigraph at the head of this essay is from Billie Holiday, "Strange Fruit," on *Lady Day* (1939–1944) (Commodore Records 1988). This lyric, credited to "Richard Allen," was sung and made known to the world by Billie Holiday. "Richard Allen" was really Abel Meeropol, the adoptive father of the two sons of the Rosenbergs. See David Margolick, *Strange Fruit: The Biography of a Song* 11 (2001).

1 When I write of "whites," I write not of persons, peoples, or of any essential qualities of persons or peoples. When I write of "whites," I write of a form of sadistic pleasure in humiliating blacks, directly or indirectly, through the colorline. When I write of "blacks," I write not of persons, peoples, or of any essential qualities of persons or peoples. When I write of "blacks," in a non-revolutionary situation, I write of a form of masochistic pleasure in being humiliated, directly or indirectly, by the colorline. Both forms of ecstasy, pleasure in producing pain by treating Others as objects and pleasure in suffering the pain of being treated as Other and as object, provide the sense of self-identity and coherence known as "race." See generally Anthony Paul Farley, "The Black Body as Fetish Object," 76 *Or. L. Rev.* 457 (1997) [hereafter Farley, "Black Body"]; Anthony Paul Farley, "s/m and the Colorline," in *Black Men on Race, Gender and Sexuality: A Critical Reader* (Devon Carbado ed., 1999) [hereafter Farley, "s/m"]; Anthony Paul Farley, "The Poetics of Colorlined Space," in *Crossroads, Directions, and a New Critical Race Theory* (Francisco Valdes et al. eds., 2002).

2 I owe this observation about rights to Maria Grahn-Farley, "A Theory of Child Rights," 57 *U. Miami L. Rev.* (forthcoming 2002).

3 Thomas Hobbes, *Leviathan* 186 (C. B. Macpherson ed., Penguin 1985) (1651).

4 Dred Scott v. Sandford, 60 U.S. 393 (1856).

5 Lillian Smith, *Now Is the Time* 42–43 (1955).

6 Interview by W. W. Dixon with Robert Toatley, near White Oak, S.C., in *Before Freedom, When I Can Just Remember: Twenty-seven Oral Histories of Former South Carolina Slaves* 121 (Belinda Hurmence ed., 1989).

7 Jacques Lacan, "The Mirror Stage as Formative of the Function of the I as Revealed in Psychoanalytic Experience," in *Écrits* 1, 11–12 (Alan Sheridan trans., W. W. Norton 1977) (1936). For two useful examples of Lacanian legal theory, see David S. Caudill, *Lacan and the Subject of Law: Toward a Psychoanalytic Critical Legal Theory* (1997); Drucilla Cornell, *The Imaginary Domain: Abortion, Pornography and Sexual Harassment* (1995).

8 Drucilla Cornell, "The Right to Abortion and the Imaginary Domain," in *Human, All Too Human* 220, 227 (Diana Fuss ed., 1996).

9 Id. at 224.

10 Id.

11 Sheyann Webb and Rachel West Nelson, *Selma, Lord, Selma: Girlhood Memories of the Civil-Rights Days* (as told to Frank Sikora) 11 (1980). In the second epigraph at the head of this section of my essay, Sheyann Webb is describing her participation, at age nine, in Bloody Sunday, the march across the Edmund Pettus Bridge from Selma to Montgomery on Mar. 7, 1965. Id., at 96.

12 Shaw v. Reno, 509 U.S. 630 (1993).

13 Id. at 635 (citing Shaw v. Barr, 808 F. Supp. 461, 476 (E.D.N.C. 1992) (Vorhees, C. J., concurring in part and dissenting in part) and quoting Editorial, "Political Pornography—II," *Wall St. J.*, Feb. 4, 1992, at A14).

14 509 U.S. at 635–36.

15 Id. at 647.

16 Id.

17 Id. at 644.

18 Id. at 647.

19 Id. at 657.

20 Jayne Chong-Soon Lee observes: "Justice O'Connor exploits the rhetorical power of unitary definitions of race and an either/or binary framework of biological and social definitions of race. She depends on a biological notion of race to argue that the law should not recognize race. Tautologically, she defines race as skin color in order to prove that the law should not recognize race, since it means nothing more than skin color." Jayne Chong-Soon Lee, "Navigating the Topology of Race," in *Critical Race Theory: The Key Writings That Formed the Movement* 445 (Kimberlé Crenshaw et al. eds., 1995). For an informative critique of identity politics and binary frameworks, see generally Maria Grahn-Farley, "Not for Sale!" 17 *N.Y.L. Sch. J. Hum. Rts.* 271 (2000).

21 C. Vann Woodward, *The Strange Career of Jim Crow* 76 (1964).

22 Jacques Lacan, "The Agency of the Letter in the Unconscious or Reason since Freud," in *Écrits*, supra note 7, at 146, 152.

23 James Baldwin, "Going to Meet the Man," in *Going to Meet the Man*, 198, 198 (1965).

24 Id.

25 Id.

26 Id. at 200–201.

27 Id. at 201.

28 Id. at 201–2.

29 Id. at 202.

30 Id.

31 For a discussion of the way the legal system protects the microaggressions of which the colorline is composed, see generally Peggy Davis, "Law as Microaggression," 98 *Yale L.J.* 1559 (1998).

32 Baldwin, supra note 23, at 202.

33 Id. at 203.

34 Id.

35 Id. at 204.

36 Id.

37 Rachel West recalls her participation, as a nine-year-old girl, in the civil rights movement:
> The people were standing there listening and I heard the sheriff say something to the effect, "You must disperse from the area of the courthouse. This is an unlawful assembly. You're ordered to cease this gathering and disperse." When he finished, he had held the paper down at his side, then placed his hands on his hips, sort of like those pictures you see of General George C. Patton. There wasn't a sound for a few seconds, just the wind blowing. Then from down at the far end, somebody started singing and it caught all along the ranks. *We shall not, we shall not be moved.* "Shut up!" shouted the sheriff, and his voice was surprised and angry. "Stop that now! You niggers cut that out!" *We shall not, we shall not be moved.* I was on the right side of the marchers, on the outside of the ranks, holding hands with an elderly woman and a teenage girl; we did that when we sang to show our unity.

Webb and Nelson, supra note 11, at 39.

38 Baldwin, supra note 23, at 208.

39 Id. at 207.

40 Id. at 208.

41 Id. at 211.

42 Id. at 210.

43 Id. at 215–17.

44 Id. at 218.

45 James Baldwin, *If Beale Street Could Talk* 7 (Delta 2000) (1974).

46 Id. at 8.

47 Baldwin, supra note 23, at 218.

48 Bice Benvenuto and Roger Kennedy, *The Works of Jacques Lacan* 188 (1986).

49 See generally Farley, "Black Body," supra note 2; Farley, "S/M," supra note 1.

50 Suzanna Sherry, "Civic Virtue and the Feminine Voice in Constitutional Adjudication," 72 *Va. L. Rev.* 543, 543 (1986).

51 Id. at 543–44. Sherry turns a colorblind eye to the experiences of the enslaved, the segregated, and the neosegregated. Indeed, she uses the term "feminine" despite the fact that she writes only about the experiences of women who are white. The colorline marks the border of her exploration of the "feminine." This is a serious limit.

52 Thomas Jefferson, "Laws," in *Notes on the State of Virginia,* in *Race and the Enlighten-*

ment: *A Reader* 95, 97–98 (Emmanuel Chukwudi Eze ed., Blackwell Publishers 1997) (1787).

53 Id.

54 Sherry, supra note 53, at 615–16 (citing Richard T. Eldridge, "On Knowing How to Live: Coleridge's 'Frost At Midnight,'" 7 *Phil. and Literature* 213, 227 (1983)) (emphasis added).

55 Baldwin, supra note 25, at 215–17.

56 James R. McGovern, *Anatomy of a Lynching: The Killing of Claude Neal* 80 (1982).

57 Baldwin, supra note 25, at 215–17.

58 Oral argument of Robinson O. Everett on behalf of Appellants in Shaw v. Reno (1993), quoted in 221 *Landmark Briefs and Arguments of the Supreme Court of the United States* 557. See also "Political Pornography—II," supra note 15; Shaw, 509 U.S. 630, 635 (quoting "Political Pornography—II," supra note 15).

59 James Baldwin, "Many Thousands Gone," in *Notes of a Native Son* 24, 29 (Beacon Press 1984) (1955).

60 James Meredith, *Three Years in Mississippi* 3–4 (1966).

61 Id.

62 Id. at 4–5.

63 Id. at 3–22.

64 See John Dittmer, *Local People: The Struggle for Civil Rights in Mississippi* (1994).

65 Stetson Kennedy, *Southern Exposure* 124 (1946).

"Into the Blue": The Image Written on Law

Alison Young

If we trace the space between an idea and its referent, between the move to judge and the act of judgment, a shadow falls within it. Between the opening mouth, the scratching pen, or the blank stare of the judge and the materialization of decision, a shadow is indelibly if illegibly inscribed. This shadow names and marks the always fading subject.

This essay is broken into two parts. In the first part, my concern is with the written texts of law; in the second, it is with the visual texts of culture. The theme of both parts is nevertheless the interpretation of HIV and its relation to the process of judgment, its force as a limit or liminal case in revealing the imaginary order of judgment.

In substance, the essay will concentrate on the reading of cases concerning the judgment of the gay man and, more specifically, the HIV positive gay man before the law. Although my argument focuses on the appearance of the gay man in judgment, its implications might well extend to the suffering that many groups experience as they oscillate between negation and derogation in the legal imagination. The intent of this essay is not to advocate any kind of withdrawal from the legal sphere, any opting-out of legal discourse. Rather, my intent is to find hopefulness in paradox: it is only in the disappearance of images that the compassionate envisioning of the other can take place.[1] And then, in response to the pain and passion of the lover/the other, what might ideally be asked of the judge is compassionate judgment: *judgment with passion,* a connection to law's lost emotional body. And it is in the immaterial judgments of art and cinema that reflections of an ethics of judgment in law might be glimpsed.

To this end, I begin by emphasizing a largely unremarked feature of modern judgment—namely, the legal *recognition* of phantasy as a distinct order of reality. The specific phantasy in question involves a narrative of abuse variously thematized in terms of homosexual sex and HIV infection. This phantasy is set in motion in an attempt to gain exemption from the ordinary responsibilities of legal subjecthood. I explore the judicial response to this move, namely, a narrative of the betrayal of trust between men. My argument in the first half of the essay will be that the modern textuality of law has been occupied by a visual order of representation: to the extent that judgment has not been reduced to the anesthetic product of administration, judgment becomes an aesthetics of appearance that returns law to the horizon of "our" values.

The second part of the essay turns this understanding of judgment on its head. The resources for this task are the artwork of Felix Gonzalez-Torres and the cinema of Derek Jarman. These texts comprehend the judgment of HIV/AIDS as an aesthetics of disappearance. Paradoxically, the visual texts are iconoclastic. As Jarman puts it, our prayer or plea must be to be delivered from image. My gloss on the visual texts of culture draws this iconoclastic process into relation with an ethics of alterity and the materials for reconstructing judgment. And, in the essay's coda, I will make some comments on how this argument might contribute to the much vaunted and much debated conjunction of law and culture, or law and cultural studies, that characterizes contemporary jurisprudence.

HIV and the Legal Aesthetics of Appearance

In *Green v. R*,[2] the accused, Malcolm Green, had been convicted of murdering his friend Don Gillies, the local real estate agent. It was well known, by Green and in the small town in which they lived, that Gillies was gay. One night, Green and Gillies ate dinner and watched television together. They drank a considerable amount of alcohol, and at least one of them used amyl nitrate. Green stayed the night. At some point, Green beat Gillies and killed him by stabbing him with scissors and bashing his head against the bedroom wall. Green tried to clean up the blood; he failed and then called the police.

At the trial, the prosecution argued that Green had killed Gillies pursuant to a premeditated plan to kill and that his defense story was an invention. The defense's claim was that Gillies had made persistent homosexual advances to Green, which had prompted in Green an image of his father beating his mother and sexually assaulting his sisters, causing him to lose self-control and kill Gillies. Convicted of murder, he unsuccessfully appealed against the conviction to the Court of Criminal Appeal of New South Wales, and then successfully appealed to the High Court of Australia. His case was sent back for retrial; at the second trial, Green was acquitted of murder and convicted of manslaughter on the grounds of provocation, receiving a sentence of ten years' imprisonment.

Legal Phantasies

The *Green* case, then, is one of a number of so-called homosexual advance cases: in a series of Australian and North American cases, heterosexually identified male defendants have argued that an alleged homosexual advance provides a basis for the defense of provocation (and sometimes self-defense).[3] This claim has become increasingly common in homicide trials in Australia.[4] Although straightforward claims that the accused killed in direct response to a homosexual advance have been successful, defense lawyers soon realized that an argument based on homosexual advance would be more persuasive if it could be tethered to some additional feature. Use of the homosexual advance defense has become increasingly opportunistic: for example, the defendant in *Parsons v. Galetka* attempted to claim that the victim had made a homosexual advance to him, despite evidence from others that the victim was heterosexual and that no advance had been made.[5] In *Jones v. Johnson* (in the context of a killing motivated by theft), the defendant still tried to claim that a homosexual advance had provoked a homicidal response.[6] In order to raise the chances of succeeding with a claim that a homosexual advance had been made, defense lawyers would link the alleged discomfort of such an advance with the memory of abuse at an earlier age. Thus, in *Bibbee v. Scott*, the defense led psychiatric evidence that after an unwanted homosexual experience as a teenager, any subsequent advance by a gay man would trigger a violent response from Bibbee.[7] In his attempt to raise the homosexual advance defense, one of Matthew Shepard's killers, Aaron McKinney, cited a retrospective trail of traumatic homosexual encounters: forced oral sex with a neighborhood bully at the age of seven, "more trauma" caused by sex at fifteen with his male cousin, and, at twenty, breaking down in tears after accidentally entering a "gay church" and seeing men kissing.[8] The conventional tactic thus asserts that the interconnection of a contemporary homosexual advance and a previous abusive experience causes a homicidal reaction.

However, the case of *Green* is distinctive for its linking of homosexual advance to a *phantasy* of abuse (as opposed to any actual experience of abuse). During police questioning, Green said two crucial things. The first arose soon after he arrived at the police station: "He told the police: 'Yeah, I killed him, but he did worse to me.' When asked why he had done it, the appellant said: 'Because he tried to root me.' "[9] Green thus constructed himself in the now-classic manner as the object of a homosexual advance, wherein the possibility of homosexual anal intercourse is viewed as worse than death. However, later in the interrogation, Green also added the following: "In relation to what had happened this night I tried to take it as a funny joke but in relation to what my father had done to four of my sisters it forced me to open more than I could bear."[10] Green was asked at trial to explain what he meant by this: "Well, it's just that when I tried to push Don away and that and I started hitting him it's just—I saw the image of my father over two of my sisters . . . and they were crying and I just lost it. . . . Because of those thoughts of me father just going through me mind. . . . About [him] sexually assaulting me sisters."[11] In short, the defense that was persuasive for the High Court and for the jury at the retrial comprised two elements: one, a homosexual advance by a male friend; and two, an image of heterosexual and incestuous abuse. As Justice McHugh stated: "The sexual, rather than homosexual, nature of the assault filtered through the memory of what the accused believed his father had done to his sisters, was the trigger that provoked the accused's violent response."[12] In the arguments of the defense, accepted by the majority of the High Court, these two elements are fused so that Gillies's actions become characterized as sexual abuse by a father figure. Only on the basis of the displacement of homosexuality and its replacement with abuse by a father figure does the judiciary bind the objectivity of what has now become "sexual abuse" with a subjective phantasy.

Concerning the image of the abuse that the accused said he experienced, the prosecution argued that it was concocted, or irrelevant. But the reality of this image of abuse was endorsed in the High Court, and endorsed in a distinctive way. All the judges noted that the accused did not witness directly the sexual abuse of his sisters; all noted that whether or not such abuse occurred is immaterial. What was important is that the accused was told of the abuse and told by his mother and sisters. What the accused heard from the lips of others became a visual scene that he played in his head. The accused became, as described by his lawyer and the High Court judges, a person carrying around "mental baggage,"[13] with the image of abuse a burdensome prosthesis. Gillies's sexual overtures—touching Green on the hip as they lay in bed together—animated this prosthesis so that, the defense argued, in killing Gillies, Green was killing the image (of his father). As Justice McHugh (dissenting in the Court of Criminal Appeal) confirms: "He sees the advance through the spectacles of what his father had done to his sisters."[14] The validity of Green's substitution mechanism is affirmed by the High Court's determination to reconstruct the victim as a father figure. As Chief Justice Brennan comments, "The real sting of the provocation could have been found not in the force used by the deceased but in his attempt to violate the sexual integrity of a man who had trusted him as a friend and father figure . . . and in the evoking of the appellant's recollection of the abuse of trust on the part of his father."[15] The victim, then, in his sexual touching of Green, betrayed the trust between friends, between men.

The case of *Green*, then, marks the recognition by law of the visual force of phantasy. More than this, however, it recognizes a visual phantasy that exists through a conversion of *oral* familial stories into the realm of the *visual*.[16] The force of such phantasy cannot be evaluated by reference to an empirical reduction: there is no derivation of the image from the father's behavior as seen by Green (in fact, Green had not seen his father for approximately twelve years). And it cannot be reduced to the symbolic order of law: this is not homophobia per se (although the majority in the High Court and the minority in the Court of Criminal Appeal cannot restrain themselves from commenting on the moral reprehensibility and horror of an amorous homosexual encounter).[17] In short, phantasy emerges here as a space of the imaginary: it is the specular phantasy of law. As Lacan emphasizes, phantasy has a protective quality for the subject; he compares the scene of phantasy to a frozen image on a cinema screen, as if the film had been stopped in order to avoid showing a traumatic scene.[18] Phantasy fixes and immobilizes a threat or trauma, which can then be excluded from representation. The tales told in law become specularized as a visual phantasy that can screen out or guard against the threat embodied by the object of law—here, portrayed as the gay man.

Killing the Image

The following two recent cases show how the law's recognition of the visual phantasy of the gay man as a betrayer of the trust between men can be given additional force through its reconfiguration with HIV. The two cases also show the judiciary actively participating in the defendant's phantasy of the gay man. In *Andrew and Kane*, also involving the murder of a gay man, the phantasy again involves the narrative of abuse and betrayal by the gay man, but it is conjoined with the imagined embodiment of the gay man as a repository of HIV infection. In this case, two sixteen-year-old boys killed a man called Wayne Tonks.[19] They were prosecuted for murder: the jury found Peter Kane guilty of murder and Benjamin Andrew guilty of manslaughter.

At the trial, Andrew argued that, several weeks earlier, he had been forced to have sex with Tonks and that he became increasingly aggrieved over this. Andrew had come into contact with Tonks by finding his name and phone number in a public toilet. Andrew was being teased at school for possibly being gay; he said at trial that he wanted to ask Tonks, whom he did not know, for advice. It turned out that Tonks was a schoolteacher, albeit at a different school and with his identity as a gay man unknown to family and colleagues. Andrew went to Tonks's apartment in the early hours of one morning; they drank alcohol and watched a porn video. Andrew alleged that he was then forced to have anal sex with Tonks. Some time later, he became convinced that he was infected with HIV and obtained an HIV test.[20] Tonks was not HIV positive, and the accused did not test positive. In a state of anxiety about the encounter he had had, Andrew, with his friend Kane, returned to Tonks's apartment equipped with a baseball bat, duct tape, and a plastic bag: they had agreed beforehand that Andrew would verbally abuse Tonks and, if necessary, hit him.[21]

The sentencing judge commented that it was plain that Andrew's aim was "to avenge himself on the victim by inflicting . . . bodily injury serious enough to expunge what . . . was his firm conviction that he had been subjected to vile and degrading conduct wholly unprovoked by, and wholly unwelcome to, him."[22] Together, Andrew and Kane beat Tonks with the baseball bat, bound, gagged, and blindfolded him and left him with the plastic bag fastened over his head, so that he later suffocated. Though Kane was convicted of murder, Andrew was convicted of manslaughter by reason of provocation.

His defense had succeeded in ways similar to those played out in *Green.* In both cases, gay sex is identified with sexual abuse. In both cases, sexual abuse is then hitched to a phantasy—of familial abuse in *Green* and of HIV infection in *Andrew and Kane.* In both cases, the salience of the phantasies is that they are elements in a legal narrative of the betrayal of trust between men (in *Andrew and Kane,* Tonks is judicially constructed as the teacher, the older man, the paternal figure of trust, who should have given advice but who instead exacted anal intercourse). And finally, in both cases, this legal narrative of betrayal produces an antiportrait of the dead, gay man. Where in *Green,* however, this specular image belonged to the defendant and was recognized by the judges, in *Andrew and Kane* the sentencing judge himself participated in the perception of the victim as an embodiment of infective abuse. Judge Sully considered the event described by Andrew and his phantasy of infection as being significant in understanding the "objective criminality" of Andrew.[23]

This objective criminality is measured against an imagined portrait of the dead man. As with many cases of homophobic murder, the judge noted that the dead cannot speak; others speak to the court on their behalf. Judge Sully characterized this "body of material" representing the deceased as "damaging as it inevitably was in its illumination of the character and lifestyle of the dead man."[24] The oral tales told by witnesses were transformed into a judicial image of the identity of the victim. In this conversion, law attaches an intention or desire to the dead. Tonks was described by Judge Sully as having "a clandestine but active homosexual lifestyle" and "a particular attraction towards teen-aged boys and young men. He actively sought out homosexual encounters with such partners, doing so by a number of methods of which one was to solicit, in effect, by leaving appropriate invitations and personal details inscribed on the walls of public toilets."[25] Judge Sully glossed this "lifestyle" as follows:

> It could scarcely be doubted that there are many people—and, more probably than not, a clear majority of people—in contemporary Australian society for whom the kind of lifestyle that the late Mr. Tonks is shown to have followed would be morally reprehensible, physically repellent and socially subversive. All the more reason to emphasize in the strongest and most uncompromising of terms that a person who follows that lifestyle, even if that lifestyle entails the committing of serious criminal offences, does not become on that account an outlaw whose life is simply forfeit to anybody who feels strongly enough to take it in fact. The paramount purpose of the rule of law is to uphold in principle and to shield in practice the absolute and fundamental sanctity of human life: all human life.[26]

A compromise is being effected here, evidenced in the acceptance of the defense of provocation, the leniency recommended by the jury, and the judge's endorsement of leniency in a reduced sentence of six years' imprisonment. The compromise is between the moral principle of the sanctity of all human life (which has no exceptions, which cannot be sacrificed in ideal or in practice) and the subjective legitimacy, for law, of killing those who are its practical exceptions: the abusive and infectious outlaws whose necessary and contradictory inclusion within legal discourse shores up the moral principle of the legal sanctity of life.

Bleeding Wounds

Enthusiastic judicial participation in the phantasy of a gay man as an embodiment of abuse is also found in a civil case involving a discrimination suit brought against the Australian army by a recruit who was discharged when he tested HIV positive. The case begins as *X v. Department of Defence* and becomes *X v. The Commonwealth* in its later stages.[27] X served as a signaler in the Signals Regiment of the Army Reserve for two years, then applied to enlist in the Australian Defence Force (the army proper). He began recruit training in November 1993. Blood was taken from him to screen for HIV: this was military policy for all new recruits.[28] On December 21, the army discovered that X was HIV positive; on

December 24, he was discharged. He complained to the Human Rights and Equal Opportunity Commission that his discharge was unlawful discrimination under the Disability Discrimination Act of 1992 (HIV being categorized as a disability under that statute). The Department of Defence argued that, by virtue of being HIV positive, X could not fulfill an inherent requirement of military employment, namely "deployment as required" in any field of army service, including combat or field training. If X were to be "deployed as required," the army claimed that this would risk the infection of other soldiers (who are assumed to be HIV negative).

The commission agreed that there was a risk, varying in the circumstances of combat or training, "that a soldier may be infected with HIV by another who is HIV positive."[29] This risk did not mean, however, that X was unable to carry out the inherent requirements of his employment and thus the discharge of X had been unlawful discrimination. The Department of Defence promptly appealed the decision to the Federal Court, which dismissed the appeal; the department then appealed to the Full Court of the Federal Court, which set aside the commission's decision, allowing the appeal. X then appealed to the High Court of Australia.

The High Court accepted the army's contention that it was necessary for a soldier "to 'bleed safely' in the sense of not having HIV . . . [as] an inherent requirement of the employment."[30] Although this was discriminatory (meaning that no HIV positive person could be recruited into the army in any capacity), the High Court found that the army's "specialness" did indeed allow it exemption from discrimination law.[31] What makes the army special is the effect of a phantasy shared by the army as the civil defendant and the judges in both the full Federal Court and the High Court.

This shared phantasy centers on the figure of blood, the blood spilled by soldiers in battle and the blood that signifies the transmission of HIV.[32] The army had argued as follows:

> [D]eployment is not available to [X] because in the course of service with the ADF a soldier, whether in training or in combat, may suffer an injury, be it a major or minor one, which may involve the discharge of bodily fluids including blood which may be transferred to the body of another by some form of physical contact . . . rang[ing] from, on the one hand, an urgent blood donation or a major blood spill because of serious injury incurred in combat to, on the other, any accidental contact with even a small blood deposit, e.g. on an obstacle used for training purposes by another who may have even a minor skin lesion.[33]

From the gift of blood to an injured soldier, through the rubbing of blood on equipment, to the flowing of blood out of wounds, the army imagines a spilling pool of infected blood that threatens to engulf it. Although X's preference for deployment was the Signals Unit where he had served before and where the risk of blood flow would be minimal, the army argued that soldiers were required to be deployable in all fields, not simply in some. Medical evidence was admitted, estimating the risk of transmission in the field as "not zero" and "not fanciful."[34] In response to X's suggestion that soldiers could routinely use protective devices such as plastic gloves, the army countered that they would be unlikely to "take appropriate care that such protective equipment was maintained in good order and condition," an ironic claim given the fetishization of care and order commonly associated with other army equipment such as guns, uniforms, and the like.[35]

The army did not want to admit that it should issue protective devices to its personnel because of its self-image as a protective device (a kind of rubber glove or condom for the nation). To concede the need for protection within its own protectiveness would admit that something had got past it, had insinuated itself through its borders. To that extent, then, the HIV positive recruit is to be screened out in much the same way that a rubber glove is thought to prevent HIV, in flowing blood, from getting access to the body within. For the army, the virus constitutes X as the mark of exclusion.

Such a phantasy of flowing viral blood is shared by the judges. In the High Court, Justice Callinan described his view of the army:

> By an Army . . . I mean a class of men set apart from the general mass of the community, trained to particular uses, formed to peculiar notions, governed by peculiar laws, marked by particular distinctions, who live in bodies by themselves, not fixed to any certain spot, nor bound by any settled employment, who neither 'toil nor spin'; whose home is their Regiment; whose sole profession and duty it is to encounter and destroy the enemies of their country wherever they are to be met with.[36]

In the army's successful appeal in the Federal Court, Justice Burchett began his judgment thus:

> This appeal . . . has much to do with blood. Modern warfare may seem less brutally physical than such a struggle as that of Horatius and his companions to hold the bridge, depicted by Lord Macaulay in his *Lays of Ancient Rome*, which cumbered with corpses—"*the narrow way / where, wallowing in a pool of blood, / The bravest Tuscans lay.*" But the big and small wars of the twentieth century, the [defendant] contends, have shown clearly enough that the science of slaughter still inflicts physical wounds, from which soldiers bleed, perhaps copiously. Realistic training exercises,

too, may entail injuries. Bleeding, for today's army, involves a soldier's comrades in dangers unknown to Horatius, or to those American Indian warriors who were accustomed to seal their brotherhood in mutual blood. For the deadly viruses Hepatitis B, Hepatitis C and HIV have become prevalent, which infect through transmission of blood and other bodily fluids.[37]

The army is configured as a fraternal order, entrusted with the safety of the nation, and trusting in each other. That mutual fraternal trust is endangered by the specter of the HIV positive man, whose blood cannot be used as the life-giving transfusion for the injured and whose blood may put at risk his fellow soldiers. His status, as the embodiment of infection, means that he can no longer be part of the fellowship of soldiers; he must be put out of its ranks.[38]

In the judicial discourse, we can read a validation of the military imagination of the HIV positive as an uncontrollable danger to other soldiers, a kind of enemy agent or weapon within the ranks. The army envisages soldiers bleeding on equipment during training, bleeding on the field of battle due to injury, having to give blood transfusions in the field when a fellow soldier has lost blood, or having the partially healing wounds of training or injury come into contact with the flowing blood of another soldier. However, in the military body, it is not simply that blood flows freely. In addition to "safe bleeding," soldiers are required to be "deployed as required," sent anywhere, receiving any orders. X wanted to be contained, he wanted only a semiotic function, to be an army signaler, to stay in one place, sending and receiving signals, transmitting only messages. The army, however, saw him as indiscriminate and peripatetic, moving all over the place, signifying the viral weakening of the military body from within. X is thus figured as indiscriminate in the same way as the victim in *Andrew and Kane*: a man who left his name and phone number on toilet walls inviting sex, "soliciting" as the judge put it, and thus indiscriminate in his seduction of strangers. It does not matter that X did not want indiscriminate military mobility: since HIV infection is part of a catachresis conjoining gay sexuality, risk, and promiscuity, the HIV positive individual is narrated in law as peripatetic, prolific, unfixable, and in perpetual motion, flowing like blood around, under, and through the military shield.

"Into the Blue": The Aesthetics of Disappearance

My reading of these three cases has shown that judgment in legal texts is predicated on an aesthetics of *appearance*—a conversion of writing into a specular image. Moreover, that aesthetics subjects the appearance of gay sex and HIV positivity to the horizon of "our values": the values of the "ordinary" person, of the territorial nation-state, of the living. In reading these three cases, I have sought to show the *carceral* effects of imagination: the image of the gay man conjured in each judgment freezes and frames the victims Gillies, Tonks, and X. And at the same time, the defendants—Green, Andrew, the Australian army— are retrospectively empowered to act in response to that image, to act without the constraints that normally enjoin against killing or against discrimination. My aims in this second part of the essay are to reject law's judgment, through its invocation of appearance (of the *image*), of the gay man or the HIV positive gay man, and to argue instead that we might look toward the aesthetics of *disappearance* achieved in certain cultural texts. These texts—artworks and cinema —help us forestall the closure of community effected by the legal aesthetics of appearance and open the processes of judgment to the proximate others dwelling in law. In the written texts of law, HIV is *made to appear* through a phantasy of abuse (leading to the legitimate annihilation of the personae of infection), while the visual texts of culture approach the representation of HIV through *an image of disappearance,* or disappearing images.

A comparative reading of the legal and cultural texts of HIV allows us to ask what understanding of *judgment* could take account of the suffering and fleshly body. In *Andrew and Kane* and *X,* judgment proceeds from the sense of betrayal imagined in the transmission of HIV. The judge projects anger and vengeance in response to such an imaginary event and makes it an *a priori* condition for any judgment of the gay man. In the cultural texts that this essay will go on to examine, HIV transmission is more than any phantasy; it is bodily reality. In both artworks and cinema, the artists offer an approach to the lover and a means to approach the image as if it were the body of the other, without vengeance or anger. In contrast to the self-righteously violent judgment of law, in these cultural texts can be found a means for the compassionate judgment of the other.

Touch the Body of the Lover

In the art of Felix Gonzalez-Torres, the art object is always about to disappear.[39] His installations are organized around certain formal modalities: some works are *word lists* (seemingly random recitations of personal and public events fixed to particular dates but listed out of chronological order);[40] *billboards* (photographs or word lists produced as billboards and installed at multiple locations around a city);[41] *puzzles* (letters or photographs reprinted as jigsaw puzzles and sealed within plastic bags);[42] *spills* (sweets or candies piled in a corner or spread across the floor);[43] *stacks* (identical sheets of paper, sometimes with an image or words printed on them, forming a solid cube composed of hundreds of separate sheets);[44] and *drapes* (curtains, beads, or strings of light bulbs arranged around doorways, window frames, and walls).[45] In this essay, I will be concentrating on the spills, stacks, and drapes: each of these forms rejects the idea of a static artwork and, indeed, creates the artwork on the basis of its continual movement, always on the verge of vanishing.

Gonzalez-Torres—who died of AIDS in 1996, five years after his lover also died of AIDS—produced many works that deal explicitly with HIV and AIDS: for example, the spectator passes through a doorway draped with blue beads in *Untitled (Chemo)*, and through another doorway laced with red beads in *Untitled (Blood)*. As Spector notes, the works' titles make direct reference to AIDS and its treatment, "but the sheer tactility of these interactive and appealing objects . . . foregrounds the body, *your* body, by the experience of moving through them."[46] The reductivism effected by HIV on the body is foregrounded in *Untitled (21 Days of Bloodwork—Steady Decline)*, a work that shows how the scopic regime of the medical gaze dismembers the corporeal self in favor of an abstracted geometry (the graphs of declining T cells uncannily similar to the cool abstractions of minimalist art). He also participated in AIDS activism, making a billboard work for the Day Without Art in 1990 (*Untitled*).[47] The works on which I wish to dwell, however, approach the subject of AIDS more obliquely, through the vanishing self, the vanishing lover.

In *Untitled (Loverboy)*, a stack of sheets of blue paper is placed on the floor against a white gallery wall.[48] It is the space of the imaginary. Gonzalez-Torres has said of it: "The beautiful blue creates a glow on the wall when it rests on the floor . . . [I]t has a gender connotation; you can't get away from that. But I also meant it as this beautiful blank page onto which you can project anything you want, any image, whatever."[49] The work is a screen onto which images can be projected by the spectator, but its apparent solidity is always already fragmented and its certainties bent by refraction into reflection. Like Gonzalez-Torres's other paper stacks, it exists in a constant state of diminution and replenishment. Designed to reach a certain height, it is described as being made of "endless copies." Visitors to the museum or gallery are invited by the label on the wall to take a sheet or sheets. As the stack reduces, gallery staff periodically add more sheets. As Gonzalez-Torres has stated, "[T]hese stacks are made up of endless copies or mass-produced prints. Yet each piece of paper gathers new meaning, to a certain extent, from its final destination, which depends on the person who takes it."[50] Diminution, dispersal, and replenishment also occur in the spills, with visitors enjoined to help themselves to the sweet candies strewn on the floor or heaped in corners. In *Untitled (Portrait of Ross in L.A.)*, 175 pounds (the body weight of the artist's lover, Ross) of Fruit Flashers candies are piled in a corner of the gallery with visitors enjoined to take one (to eat or to keep). *Untitled (Loverboys)* involves 350 pounds of candies, the combined body weight of the artist and his lover. In *Untitled (Placebo—Landscape for Roni)*, thousands of candies, glinting in their metallic plastic wrappers and evoking the sugar pills of a drug trial, are spread across the museum floor and collected or eaten at random by spectators. These stacks and spills, then, are configured as always in motion and always on the verge of disappearance.

In the blue stack that is *Untitled (Loverboy)* and the candy spill of *Untitled (Portrait of Ross in L.A.)*, Gonzalez-Torres created aporetic works of art that are always fading and always returning. Gonzalez-Torres described his intentions as follows: "I wanted to do a show that would disappear completely. It has a lot to do with disappearance and learning. . . . Freud said that we rehearse our fears in order to lessen them. In a way, this 'letting go' of the work, this refusal to make a static form, a monolithic sculpture, in favour of a disappearing, changing, unstable, and fragile form was an attempt on my part to rehearse my fears of having Ross disappear day by day right in front of my eyes."[51]

In inviting the spectator to remove parts of the artwork, Gonzalez-Torres rehearses the death of the lover and the death of the self that will follow. The selected piece of the artwork that the spectator removes is taken away from the rest permanently, whether it is eaten or placed in a drawer at home or pinned on a wall. The artwork is always diminishing, heading toward nothingness, toward the abyss. And yet, the abyss is always held at bay, always deferred, since fragments of the artwork are transported by spectators into new places.[52] Here, the generosity of the artist is not simply about undercutting the art market's fetishization of acquisition and ownership that operates in a closed circuit of display and ownership; it is also a gift that both invokes the transmission in HIV infection and rewrites it otherwise than as infection. In contrast to the abjection attached to notions of the "exchange of bodily fluids," Gonzalez-Torres invites spectators to take part of the image representing his lover's body into their own bodies, to ingest or to secrete in a pocket or a drawer. As Weintraub comments, "individuals who have taken a sheet of paper from his stacks are 'carriers' " in a metaphorical circuit.[53] It is a gift without price or return, in a circuit that is open and unending. An artwork about HIV transforms the circuit of transmission from the criminalized, abjected, and reviled archetype condensed around HIV infection into a rehearsal of loss *and* an act of giving, a positive positivity.

In the later version of *Lover Boy*, wherein sheer blue fabric is draped across a window, forming a transparent curtain, Gonzalez-Torres evokes the evanescence of the amatory relationship and the mutability of the body of the object of desire. With an opened window behind the curtain, the fabric moves with every breath of air, rarely at rest, an artwork that is never still, always in motion, impossible to fix. The fabric provides a screen onto which desire is projected and interpreted; yet the fabric's sheerness creates a screen that does not attach the gaze of the spectator to the surface of the object: it points to a beyond, an other side, a farther horizon. It veils but does not mask. As with the spills and stacks, it bespeaks loss. And for Gonzalez-Torres, in its selected blue color, whether in stack form or fabric, *Lover Boy* enacts "a memory of a light blue. For me, if a beautiful memory could have a color, that color would be light blue . . . an innocent blue."[54] In the chromatic hues of judgment—where blood colors the law's phantasy of the gay man—here blue is the color of memory, the rehearsal of a loss yet to come, the loss of a lover, the loss of the self.[55] And, like the stacks and spills, *Lover Boy* establishes a relation with the spectator that is prior to vision, operating instead through *touch.* The papers in each stack, the candies spilled on the floor, the curtain moving in the breeze: each exists to touch and be touched by the spectator. As Irigaray comments, "Touch makes it possible to wait, to gather strength, so that the other will return to caress and reshape, from within and without, a flesh that is given back to itself in the gesture of love."[56]

The works project a past experienced through the touch of memory into a future prefigured through evanescence. The mobile artworks of Gonzalez-Torres succeed in precluding the grounds for visual judgment, reinstituting judgment instead as a re-hearing, a past re-membered, and a future imagined, a moving image oscillating on the border of appearance and disappearance. Where the judgments in the cases of legal phantasy of HIV and gay sex turn loss toward the self of law (the self of the army, the self of the accused), these artworks are concerned to respect absolute alterity through an act of compassionate judgment that brings self and other into proximate, tangible relation.

Hear the Voice of the Lover

The liminal moment between appearance and disappearance also structures a film made by Derek Jarman, the British artist, filmmaker, writer, and gardener, who died of AIDS in 1994. The film is titled *Blue,* and it is at once a meditation on color and also a film without a moving image.[57] For seventy-five minutes the screen is filled with cobalt blue, while voices, sounds, and music enact scenes, read poems, toll bells, and provide an aural landscape for that which cannot be seen. *Blue* gives up the glamour and the visual charge of cinema, in much the way that Gonzalez-Torres's artworks eschew expressionism or pictorial figuration. *Blue*'s abstractions, however, are still rooted in narrative: a narrative of pleasure (sunshine on a warm summer day, sex with a good-looking stranger, dancing in nightclubs),[58] of anger (at AIDS activism, at the double bind of AIDS drug trials),[59] of grief (for lost friends already dead from AIDS),[60] of mourning and the contemplation of one's own death. Of the film, Lombardo writes: "With a violent leap, the most bodyless film ever produced projects the human body in its most cruel and unspeakable presence: pain, illness, suffering at the borderline between the physical and the mental, the conscious and the unconscious, life and death."[61] Like the artworks of Gonzalez-Torres, *Blue* is a judgment of death, of the inscription of bodily pain: the pain of radical otherness, of the loss of self and the loss of the other. The object of judgment, in the film like the artworks, is death.

Jarman was losing his sight as a result of cytomegalovirus (CMV).[62] *Blue* allows us to imagine sightlessness and the rehearsal of imminent but still uncertain death. Rehearsal, as with Gonzalez-Torres, becomes the main modality of existence: "The worst of this illness is the uncertainty. / I've played this scenario back and forth each hour of the day for the last six years."[63] Rehearsal and repetition: with every opening succeeded by a moment of closure, as the narrative plays on and out toward its end.[64]

"Blue" is not only the color of the screen that captivates the gaze of the spectator; it also names and marks the site to which the oral speech is destined or transmitted (in a juridical terminology, it is *justice*). And just as Gonzalez-Torres's artworks tend always toward disappearance, *Blue* always moves toward death. The film's key motifs are given a melancholic finality in its closing words:

> Our name will be forgotten
> In time
> No one will remember our work
> Our life will pass like the traces of a cloud
> And be scattered like
> Mist that is chased by the
> Rays of the sun
> For our time is the passing of a shadow
> And our lives will run like
> Sparks through the stubble.
> I place a delphinium, Blue, upon your grave.[65]

In some ways, the film makes literal the difficulties inherent in the struggle to portray the unpresentable that is HIV, the virus that cannot be seen, the illness that for years has no symptoms other than invisible antibodies present in the blood. As Haver evocatively suggests, the struggle to represent the relation of the self to the loss of self occasioned by AIDS "signals what will henceforth be the impossibility of language, communication, and sociality,"[66] an impossibility inscribed as a narrative of melancholia, desire, and mourning. David Wojnarowicz, another artist who died from AIDS, spoke angrily of the pain of being frozen in the image: "Sometimes I come to hate people because they can't see where I am. I've gone empty, completely empty and all they see is the visual form. . . . I'm a xerox of my former self. . . . I am disappearing. I am disappearing but not fast enough."[67]

Blue engages with the paradoxical acceleration of invisibility in the image imposed on marginal groups (often those who have become synonymous with the transmission of HIV): gay men, injecting drug users, whiteness's racial others, prisoners. Jarman's film can thus be understood as an activist intervention, from an artist who for years had been sickened by the endless parade of stereotypes deployed by the British media when depicting gay sexuality and when depicting HIV/AIDS.[68] As Jarman asks in *Blue*, "How are we to be perceived, if we are to be perceived at all? For the most part we are invisible."[69] Jarman is all too aware that visibility can be a projection, an image constructed around a condensation of fearful signifiers.[70] He notes what HIV infection invokes: "All the old taboos of / Blood lines and blood banks / Blue blood and bad blood / Our blood and your blood / I sit here and you sit there," linking social class, racial and sexual segregation, and homophobia in the overcoded signifier of blood that works to effect a paradoxical visual invisibility.[71]

Both intensely figurative (representing blue as sexual desire, sadness, melancholy, serenity, and so on) and also utterly literal in that it presents to us no image other than a blue screen, *Blue* is a cinematic work that rejects *kinesis,* the moving image. It has no personae in the sense of actors or characters, places or scenes. It thus removes the object of the gaze by providing instead a visual object that remains unmoving. *Blue* is thus strangely paradoxical: film is the art of the moving image, while *Blue* is a film whose image does not move. Where Gonzalez-Torres interrupts attachment to the image by setting the artwork in motion, for Jarman attachment to the image is interrupted by the immobile image of blue. While the spectator seeks in vain for *something to look at,* the film insists rather that we *listen* and *re-member,* as Jarman tells us: "In the roaring waters / I hear the voices of dead friends . . . My heart's memory turns towards you / David. Howard. Graham. Terry. Paul."[72] *Blue* detaches the spectator from the screen and attaches the viewer to the voice. In this process, we are re-moved into an audience of voices, into an ethical relation that allows a response to the suffering other.

The Scene of Another Judgment

Jarman's displacement of visual personae is not simply a consequence of filmmaking after the advent of blindness; rather, "In the pandemonium of image / I present you with the universal Blue / Blue an open door to soul / An infinite possibility / Becoming tangible."[73] Caught in the tension between the tyranny of the image ("a prison of the soul")[74] and the desire to make images, Jarman enjoins us: "For accustomed to believing in image, an absolute idea of value, [the] world had forgotten the command of essence: Thou Shalt Not Create Unto Thyself Any Graven Image, although you know the task is to fill the empty page. From the bottom of your heart, pray to be delivered from image."[75]

Thus Jarman uncovers the attachment to the visual order that is entailed when phantasy seizes the imagination. His injunction—"pray to be delivered from image"—substitutes "image" for "evil" in the conventional invocation. A plaintiff before the court was archaically said to "pray" to the court for relief. One of my aims in this essay has been to trace this indelible, if illegible, prayer as the vocation of judgment. As *Green, Andrew and Kane,* and *X* make clear, judgment proceeds by means of a series of configurations, personae, or images of infection that fix and immobilize the subject of HIV and gay sex. The written texts of law reconstruct the event (the "real") of HIV in the order of vision, where judgment is governed by the desire to see and, in "seeing," to have done with HIV.[76] The vision of law remains an aesthetic in which an inscribed image breaks the link between the eye and the pain of the other. The way that the law sees HIV is defensive, self-protective. Goodrich comments: "The constitution, the community of doctrine and of law, had to be defended and indeed would define itself antirrhetically . . . against an outside peopled by strangers, foreigners, . . . and other untouchables. Similarly, there were enemies within the constitution and against whose antiportrait the image of the upstanding legal subject could be projected."[77]

The visual texts of culture expose the writing of law as idolatry. They draw the event closer *to and through* an ethics of alterity, an ethics that confounds the juridical order of vision (a vision of the self, of the State). Their interventions turn our attention away from the image: they bind us to the other through oral and tangible media. With *Blue*, we attend to the voice of the other; with *Lover Boy*, we attend to the body of the other. These aural and corporeal relations point toward the materiality of another scene of judgment.

Coda: Law in the Imaginary Realm of Cultural Studies

Just as the artworks contemplated in this essay signal a trajectory toward an other scene of judgment, so also do they point toward the relation that might ensue in the move from the visual realism of law toward the imaginary realm of cultural studies. The trajectory of this essay has moved from the written texts of law to the visual texts of culture. Such a trajectory re-stages the larger scene of contemporary legal studies in the Anglo-American tradition. In the recent years of this tradition, a shift has taken place that promises to understand law as culture and jurisprudence as cultural studies.[78] The law and literature movement evokes literature as sensitizing the judge, while the interest in hermeneutics binds the process of legal interpretation to the virtue or character of the judge.[79] Where we were once encouraged to be literary, to become social and to "get real," now we are exhorted to "do" cultural studies. What has been at stake in this injunction, and this conjunction, of law and culture?

For my purposes, it is that modern law wants (for) judgment. More specifically, I seek to ask what understanding of judgment could take account of the fragmented, suffering, fleshly body? Gonzalez-Torres's artworks and Jarman's film suggest the elements of a response. As I hope to have made clear, the judgment of HIV takes place on the site of conditions of attachment to (the) law (of the other). If judgment is a matter of memory, incorporation, and hearing, then attention is due to the process of inscription—understood here as the naming and marking of the body. In the written texts of law, the eye of the judge has become disconnected from the pain of law's proximate others.

Nevertheless, it is still possible that the eye of the law could be made to flicker from the mark to the pain of the other in law, for the stilled voice to listen or hear, for the upright hand that holds the rule to waver. Gonzalez-Torres and Jarman remind us that law has not been totally occupied by the modern textuality. There is a site through which judgment can take place, reconstructed around the aural and corporeal scenes of attachment. Gonzalez-Torres re-stages the loss of the other in terms of fleshly touch, as the art object brushes up against and inscribes the other on the body of the spectator. Jarman interrupts the idolatry of modern textuality by reasserting the melancholy claims of speech, as the moving image inscribes the other in the ear of the spectator. The transmission of law in the moment or scene of judgment takes place, as a response to the other, through the corporeal and audible inscription of the pain and passion of the lover. Legal judgment may be dominated by modern textuality and the order of the visual, but the texts of culture show that there are materials (which operate through memory, incorporation, hearing) through which to respond in judgment to the proximate other. Unlike law, which subjects the death and dying of others to the horizon of "our" values—the values and phantasies of the living—cultural studies might subject the legal and the living to the horizon of deathbound subjectivity.[80] What would remain is not the dead letters of law but the materials of voice, touch, and memory. Such is the value of cultural studies to law: the provision of material for a reconstruction of judgment in proximity with the fragmented bodies of law's suffering others.

Notes

I am indebted to Austin Sarat and Jonathan Simon for the opportunity to participate in the symposium "Cultural Studies and the Law: Beyond Legal Realism in Interdisciplinary Legal Scholarship," to the symposium participants for their thoughtful comments, and particularly to Peter Rush, for the "art and part" of his accessorial glosses.

1   For other evocations of ethical or compassionate judgment, see Arthur Glass, "The Compassionate Decision-Maker," in 3 *Law/Text/Culture* 162 (1997); and Peter Goodrich, *Languages of Law* (1990).

2   (1997) 148 *A.L.R.* 659 (High Court).

3   See, e.g., *R v. Pritchard* (1990) 50 *A. Crim. R.* 67; *R v. Stiles* (1990) 50 *A. Crim. R.* 13; *R v. Grmusa* (1990) 50 *A. Crim. R.* 358; *R v. Preston* (1992) 58 *A. Crim. R.* 328; *R v. Whittaker* (1993) 59 *A. Crim. R.* 476. The homosexual advance defense has received much attention, judicial and academic, in Anglo-American jurisdictions. See, e.g., Adrian Howe, " 'More Folk Provoke Their Own Demise': Homophobic Violence and Sexed Excuses—Rejoining the Provocation Law Debate, Courtesy of the Homosexual Advance Defence," 19 *Sydney L. Rev.* 336 (1997); Adrian Howe, "Reforming Provocation (More or Less)," 12 *Austl. Feminist L.J.* 127 (1999); Peter Johnston, " 'More Than Ordinary Men Gone Wrong': Can the Law Know the Gay Subject?," 20 *Melbourne U. L. Rev.* 1152 (1996); Robert B. Mison, "Homophobia in Manslaughter: The Homosexual Advance as Insufficient Provocation," 80 *Cal. L. Rev.* 133 (1992); Leslie J. Moran, *The Homosexual(ity) of Law* (1996). An attempt to establish the homosexual advance defense was made in the trial of Aaron McKinney, one of the two men charged with killing Matthew Shepard in Laramie, Wyoming, in 1998. The trial judge ruled that any evidence as to an alleged homosexual advance could not be introduced because it would point toward the defenses of diminished capacity or temporary insanity, neither of which are available under Wyoming law. See Michael Ellison, "Roofer Beat Gay Student to Death," *Guardian* (United Kingdom), Nov. 4, 1999, at 21; Susan Estrich, " 'Homophobia' Defense Rests," *Denver Post*, Nov. 6, 1999, at B7.

4   For example, between 1993 and 1995 in New South Wales, thirteen murder trials saw the homosexual advance defense invoked. Of those trials, two resulted in acquittals, two in jury verdicts of murder, and three in verdicts of not guilty of murder but guilty of manslaughter; eight resulted in pleas being accepted to a lesser charge such as manslaughter; and one case was dismissed. See Attorney-General's Department (New South Wales), *Review of the "Homosexual Advance Defence"* 10 (1996). Successful attempts to enter evidence about a homosexual advance can be seen in the following cases. For example, one accused said an elderly man invited him for a drink in his house; he accepted. The old man grabbed his buttocks and made an indistinct comment. The accused beat him with a garden gnome and then stabbed him to death. He was found guilty of manslaughter rather than murder and received a three-year sentence of imprisonment. In another case, the defendant, while riding his bike along a cycle path, saw a man in a dress waving his penis and shouting at him. The defendant beat the man to death. He was found not guilty of murder and guilty of manslaughter. See David Marr, *The High Price of Heaven* 60 (1999).

5   57 F. Supp. 2d 1151 (D. Utah 1999).

6   171 F.3d 270 (5th Cir. 1999).

7   No. 98–6445, 1999 WL 1079597, at *1 (10th Cir. Nov. 29, 1999).

8   Ellison, supra note 3, at 21.

9   *Green v. R* (1997) 148 *A.L.R.* 659, 700 (Kirby J.).

10   Id. at 667 (Toohey J.).

11   Id.

12   Id. at 683. With regard to the homosexual advance, the prosecution did not concede that there had been such an advance. At most, there had been amorous or sexual touching by Gillies that the accused could easily have rebuffed. As Justice Kirby remarked in his dissenting opinion in the High Court, "[If] every woman who was the subject of a 'gentle,' 'non-aggressive' although persistent sexual advance . . . could respond with brutal violence rising to an intention to kill or inflict grievous bodily harm on the male importuning her, and then claim provocation after a homicide, the law of provocation would be sorely tested and undesirably extended." Id. at 719.

13   Transcript of application for special leave to appeal to the High Court at supra note 9, *Green v. R* S172/1996 (10 Dec. 1996) (quoting defense counsel and Gunnow J.) (on file with author) [hereafter Green Transcript].

14   Id. at 30.

15   *Green,* 148 *A.L.R.* at 683 (McHugh J.). Justice McHugh also describes Gillies as "a person whom the accused looked up to and trusted." In the Court of Criminal Appeal, Justice Smart commented on "the deceased's betrayal of the relationship of trust, dependency, friendship and the abuse of his hospitality." Id. at 704. In applying for special leave to appeal to the High Court, defense counsel argued: "He said . . . there were flashes of his father over his two sisters, at the time he lost self-control, that he kept hitting him because he felt trapped. The evidence . . . would establish a clear connection between his relationship with the deceased as a father figure and his own sense of betrayal in relation to his relationship with his father." Green Transcript, supra note 13, at 2.

16   But see *R v. Moffa* (1977) 13 *A.L.R.* 225 (High Court) (emphasizing that words must be of a violent or extreme character in order to be provocative); *R v. Tuncay* [1998] 2 *VR* 19 (same).

17 See, e.g., *Green*, 148 *A.L.R.* at 665 (Brennan C. J.) ("Some ordinary men would feel great revulsion at the homosexual advances being persisted with in the circumstances. . . . They would regard it as a serious and gross violation of their body and their person." (quoting Justice Smart (Ct. Crim. App.))).

18 Jacques Lacan, *Le Seminaire: Livre IV: La Relation d'objet, 1956–57*, at 119–20 (Jacques-Alain Miller ed., 1994). On phantasy and the structure of attachment more generally, see J. Laplanche and J-B. Pontalis, "Fantasy and the Origin of Sexuality," in *Formations of Fantasy* 5 (Victor Burgin ed., 1986).

19 See *Benjamin Bruce Andrew and Peter Clive Kane* (S. Ct. N.S.W. 2 July 1999) [1999] NSWSC 647, available at http://www.austlii.edu.au/ [hereafter *Andrew and Kane*].

20 Id. at 11, 15.

21 Id. at 11.

22 Id. at 18–19 (Sully J.).

23 Id. at 7.

24 Id. at 7; see also Green Transcript, supra note 13, and accompanying text.

25 *Andrew and Kane*, supra note 19, at 6–7.

26 Id. at 7. This echoes the comments of Justice Smart in the Court of Criminal Appeal in *Green*, when he describes the "great revulsion" that "some ordinary men" would feel at a homosexual advance. *Green*, 148 *A.L.R.* at 665 (quoted by Brennan C. J.).

27 *X v. Dep't of Def.* (29 June 1995 Hum. Rts. and Equal Opportunity Comm'n) [1995] HREOCA 16; *Commonwealth v. HREOC* (Fed. Ct. 1996) 70 F.C.R. 76 (Cooper J.); *Commonwealth of Australia v. HREOC and Another* (Full Ct. of the Fed. Ct. 1998) 76 F.C.R. 513, and at 13 Jan 1998 [1998] 3 FCA 1; *X v. The Commonwealth* (High Ct. Austl. 2 Dec. 1999) [1999] HCA 63; available at http://www.austlii.edu.au/ and on file with author.

28 "Applicants are to be informed, before entry, that such testing will take place . . . and they are to be given the option to refuse and to withdraw their application. As with newly inducted entrants in whom other potentially serious diseases have been detected, personnel with HIV infection are to be discharged." Australian Defence Force, *Service Policy* cl. 12 (quoted in *X v. Dep't of Def.*, at 5).

29 *X v. Dep't of Def.*, at 8.

30 *X v. The Commonwealth*, at 6.

31 The majority of the High Court found in favor of the army, sending the case back to the commission for further adjudication by a different commissioner. Compare *Green*: in the judgment of the High Court, as also in the argument of defense counsel, the phantasy of paternal abuse is characterized as giving rise to a "special sensitivity to a history of violence and sexual assault within his family." *Green v. R* (1997) 148 *A.L.R.* 659, 682 (McHugh J.).

32 Further on blood, see Shaun McVeigh et al., "A Judgment Dwelling in Law: Violence and the Relations of Legal Thought," in *Law, Violence and the Possibility of Justice* (Austin Sarat ed., 2001).

33 *X v. Dep't of Def.*, at 6.

34 Id. at 8. These calculations of risk are strikingly vague in comparison with the usual epidemiological calibrations that occur in other cases concerning the possibility of HIV transmission. See, e.g., *Mutemeri v. Cheesman* (1998) 100 *A. Crim. R.* 397; *Hall v. Victorian Amateur Football Ass'n*, Administrative Appeals Tribunal of Victoria (1998), unreported.

On the calibration of risk in relation to HIV transmission, see the following: Robert Burns Neveldine, *Bodies at Risk* (1998); Deborah Lupton, *Moral Threats and Dangerous Desires* (1994); Catherine Waldby, *AIDS and the Body Politic* (1996); and Cherry Grimwade, "Reckless Sex: The Discursive Containment of Gender, Sexuality and HIV/AIDS," in *Sexed Crime in the News* (Arian Howe ed., 1998). On risk more generally, see Ulrich Beck, *Risk Society* (1992), and Anthony Giddens, "Risk and Responsibility," 62 *Mod. L. Rev.* 1 (1999).

35 *X v. Dep't of Def.*, at 8.

36 *X v. The Commonwealth*, at 36.

37 *Commonwealth of Australia v. HREOC and Another*, at 5–6.

38 Note that an impassioned dissent is provided in the High Court by Justice Kirby (who also dissented in *Green*, and who is the only "out" gay man on the High Court Bench). He states: "It would be as well . . . if the courts were to avoid the preconceptions that lie hidden, and not so hidden, in tales of . . . soldiers wallowing in blood (however vivid may be the poetic image), or in descriptions of regimental life and soldierly duty in the heyday of the British Empire (however evocative may be the memories)." *X v. The Commonwealth*, at 34. He also notes the persistent difficulty of obtaining legal recognition of discrimination and victimization: "The field of anti-discrimination law is littered with the wounded who appear to present the problem of discrimination which the law was designed to prevent and redress but who, following closer judicial analysis of the legislation, fail to hold on to the relief originally granted to them." Id. at 24.

39 On Gonzalez-Torres's work generally, see Nancy Spector, *Felix Gonzalez-Torres* (1995); Monica Amor, "Felix Gonzalez Torres: Towards a Postmodern Sublimity," 30 *Third Text* 67 (1995); Jan Avgikos, "This Is My Body," 6 *Artforum* 79 (1991); T. J. Demos, "The Aesthetics of Mourning," 184 *Flash Art (Int'l)* 65 (1995); Nancy Princenthal, "Felix Gonzalez-Torres: Multiple Choice," 48 *Art + Text* 40 (1994); Robert Storr, "Setting Traps for the Mind and Heart," 84 *Art in America* 70 (1996); and Simon Watney, "In Purgatory: The Work of Felix Gonzalez-Torres," 39 *Parkett* 38 (1994).

40 See, for example, the work that lists: "People with AIDS Coalition 1985 Police Harassment 1969 Oscar Wilde 1895 Supreme Court 1986 Harvey Milk 1977 March on Washington 1987 Stonewall Rebellion 1969." In another work, the list reads: "Red Canoe 1987 Paris 1985 Blue Flowers 1984 Harry the Dog 1983 Blue Lake 1986 Interferon 1989 Ross 1983." Finally, a third list cites: "Alabama 1964 Safer Sex 1985 Disco Donuts 1979 Cardinal O'Connor 1987 Klaus Barbie 1944 Napalm 1972 Bitberg Cemetery 1985 Walkman 1979 Capetown 1985 Waterproof Mascara 1971 Computer 1981." Reproductions of these and other works by Gonzalez-Torres discussed in this essay can be found in the comprehensive accompaniment to his 1995 Guggenheim retrospective. See Spector, supra note 39.

41 See, e.g., *Untitled (the New Plan)* (a photograph of undulating denim displayed in one location); *Untitled (for Jeff)* (a photograph of a man's hand, displayed in thirty locations); *Untitled (Strange Bird)* (a photograph of distant birds against a cloudy sky, displayed in twenty locations); *Untitled* (a photograph of a rumpled bed, with the imprints of two heads still visible on the pillows, displayed in twenty-four locations). A photograph of this last billboard on location in New York can be seen on the cover of 13 *Yale Journal of Law and the Humanities* (2001), in which this essay originally appeared.

42 See, e.g., *Untitled (Ross and Harry)*; *Untitled (Lover's Letter)*; *Untitled (Klaus Barbie as a Family Man)*; *Untitled (Waldheim to the Pope)*.

43 See, e.g., *Untitled (Portrait of Dad)* (175 pounds of white candies piled into a corner); *Untitled (USA Today)* (a corner pile of red, white, and blue candies); *Untitled (Welcome Back Heroes)* (hundreds of Bazooka bubble gum chews spread across the floor).

44 See, e.g., *Untitled (NRA)* (a stack of sheets of red paper edged in black); *Untitled* (two stacks placed side by side: each sheet in one stack reads "Somewhere better than this place," while each sheet in the other stack reads "Nowhere better than this place"); *Untitled (Death by Gun)* (which reproduces on each of its sheets the names, ages, and faces of the 464 people who were killed by gunshot wounds in the United States in a one-week period).

45 For examples of drapes using lightbulbs, see *Untitled (March 5th)* and *Untitled (Ischia)*; for drapes using beads, see *Untitled (Chemo)* and *Untitled (Blood)*; for fabric drapes, see the various versions of *Untitled (Lover Boy)*.

46 Spector, supra note 39, at 171 (emphasis in original).

47 The full text of the billboard reads: "HEALTH CARE IS A RIGHT. A government by the people, for the people, must provide adequate health care to the people. NO EXCUSES." The billboard was simultaneously displayed in ten locations around New York City.

48 According to Gonzalez-Torres, "Around 1989 everyone was fighting for wall space. So the floor space was free, the floor space was marginal." See the interview with the artist in Tim Rollins, *Felix Gonzalez-Torres* 13 (1993). Note that another version of *Lover Boy* drapes sheer blue fabric as curtains, perhaps because the window space in galleries is also marginal. In his placement of the art object within the gallery, then, Gonzalez-Torres metaphorizes the marginality awarded to the gay man, the racial other, the HIV positive person.

49 Spector, supra note 39, at 62.

50 Rollins, supra note 48, at 23.

51 Id. at 13.

52 Gonzalez-Torres said in this regard: "I wanted people to have my work. The fact that someone could just come in and take my work and carry it with them was very exciting." Id.

53 Linda Weintraub et al., *Art on the Edge and Over* 113 (1996).

54 Rollins, supra note 48, at 15, 17. Note that, for the artist, the color evokes the erotic relation: "Ross and I would spend summers next to a body of blue water or under clear, Canadian skies." Id. at 17.

55 For similarly evanescent artworks evoking the loss of friends to AIDS, see the blurred and indistinct photographs of Bill Jacobson, reproduced in *Bill Jacobson, 1989–1997* (1998), and discussed in Anastasia Aukeman, "Coming Together and Letting Go," 94 *ARTnews* 95 (1995); see also David Wojnarowicz, "Untitled (Hujar Dead)," in *Fever: The Art of David Wojnarowicz* 60 (Amy Scholder ed., 1999).

56 Luce Irigaray, *An Ethics of Sexual Difference* 187 (1993).

57 Derek Jarman, *Blue* (Basilisk Communications 1993) [hereafter Jarman, *Blue*]. See also Derek Jarman, *Chroma* (Overlook Press 1995) (1988) [hereafter Jarman, *Chroma*]; the chapter "Into the Blue" represents the text of the film *Blue*. The text of *Chroma* (1995) is the source for subsequent quotations of lines from the film. The film's image is motivated by Jarman's admiration of Yves Klein, of whom Jarman writes: "The great master of blue—the French painter Yves Klein. No other painter is commanded by blue." Id. at 104. On the film, see Patrizia Lombardo, "Cruellement Bleu," 36 *Critical Q.* 131 (1994); Peter Schwenger, "Derek Jarman and the Colour of the Mind's Eye," 65 *U. Toronto Q.* 419 (1996); Paul Julian Smith, "BLUE and the Outer Limits," 3 *Sight and Sound*, Oct. 1993, at 18.

58 Jarman says, variously: "Lost in the warmth / Of the blue heat haze," Jarman, *Chroma*, supra note 57, at 108; "Kiss me again / Kiss me / Kiss me again / And again / Never enough / Greedy lips / Speedwell eyes / Blue skies," id. at 118; "The smell of him / Dead good looking / In beauty's summer / His blue jeans / Around his ankles / Bliss in my ghostly eye," id. at 124; "Dance in the beams of emerald lasers . . . What a time that was." Id. at 116.

59 On AIDS activism, Jarman states: "I shall not win the battle against the virus—in spite of the slogans like 'Living with AIDS.' The virus was appropriated by the well—so we have to live with AIDS while they spread the quilt for the moths of Ithaca across the wine dark sea." Id. at 110. Jarman's ambivalence about the AIDS Quilt (also known as the Names Project) is also expressed elsewhere: "When the AIDS quilt came to Edinburgh during the film festival I attended out of duty. I could see it was an emotional work, it got the heartstrings. But . . . I shall haunt anyone who ever makes a quilt panel for me." Derek Jarman, *Derek Jarman's Garden* 91 (1995). Of drug trials, he says in *Blue*: "Oral DHPG is consumed by the liver, so they have tweaked a molecule to fool the system. What risk is there? If I had to live forty years blind I might think twice. . . . The pills are the most difficult. . . . I'm taking about thirty a day, a walking chemical laboratory." Jarman, *Chroma*, supra note 57, at 120.

60 Of lost friends, he laments, "The virus rages fierce. I have no friends now who are not dead or dying. Like a blue frost it caught them." Id. at 109.

61 Lombardo, supra note 57, at 133.

62 Note also the artwork of John Dugdale, photographer, who has also lost his sight to AIDS. His blue-washed images are now made with the help of assistants; they can be seen in John Dugdale, *Lengthening Shadows before Nightfall* (1995).

63 Jarman, *Chroma*, supra note 57, at 109.

64 To that extent, *Blue* has a perfectly circular, or perhaps spiraling, structure. The opening lines of *Blue* evoke an awakening to vision: "You say to the boy open your eyes / When he opens his eyes and sees the light / You make him cry out. Saying / O Blue come forth / O Blue arise / O Blue ascend / O Blue come in." "Blue" is marked as the space of subjectivity and relationality: "Blue of my heart / Blue of my dreams / Slow blue love / Of delphinium days." Jarman, *Blue*, supra note 57, at 107–8. In *Blue*'s closing poem, having moved through details of illness, treatment, and decline, the final line rewrites "blue" as the space of subjectivity, relationality, *and death*: "I place a delphinium, Blue, upon your grave." Id. at 124.

65 Id. at 123–24.

66 William Haver, *The Body of This Death* 124 (1996).

67 David Wojnarowicz, *Untitled* (1992).

68 See the account in Tony Peake, *Derek Jarman* (1999), especially chapter 27; and in James Cary Parkes, "Et in Arcadia . . . Homo: Sexuality and the Gay Sensibility in the Art of Derek Jarman," in *Derek Jarman: A Portrait* 137 (1996) (catalog accompanying the Jarman retrospective at the Barbican Art Gallery, London).

69 Jarman, *Chroma*, supra note 57, at 113. See also the discussion of visibility, nationality, and queer politics in the "cinema of AIDS" (including Jarman's *Blue*) in Smith, supra note 57.

70 As Burns Neveldine writes, "[O]nly an accumulation, an overaccumulation, of representations will make AIDS, and the bodies of persons with AIDS, radically *visible* and therefore *viable*: granted life, authorized to be written and read, allowed to mingle, or condemned to

wither away, or condemned *for* withering away." Burns Neveldine, supra note 34, at 150. For more on the metaphorization of HIV/AIDS and its consequences, see, for example, Susan Sontag, *AIDS and Its Metaphors* (1991); Waldby, supra note 34; Simon Watney, *Policing Desire* (1989); and Alison Young, *Imagining Crime* (1996).

71 Jarman, *Chroma*, supra note 57, at 121.

72 Id. at 108.

73 Id. at 112.

74 Id. at 115.

75 Id. at 114–15.

76 The Aristotelian account of the will to knowledge as a desire to see constructs the juridical moment of metaphysics as the pronunciation of judgments on the correctness of the world. Minkinnen notes the aporetic and agonizing nature of this will or desire when remarking that "[j]ustice constitutes the desired object (*to orekton*) of a 'first philosophy' of law, but in the judgments of correctness that a mortal man is capable of, such justice is forever delayed. . . . For the ownmost essence of things, that is, justice in itself, or the future that will come to be, is a matter fit only for infinite gods." Panu Minkinnen, *Thinking without Desire: A First Philosophy of Law* 47 (1999).

77 Peter Goodrich, "The Continuance of the Antirrhetic," 4 *Cardozo Stud. L. and Literature* 207 (1992).

78 As examples within this shift, see *Law, Culture and the Questions of Feminism* (Nina Puren and Alison Young eds., 2000); *Law in the Domains of Culture* (Austin Sarat and Thomas R. Kearns eds., 1998); and Richard Sherwin, *When Law Goes Pop* (2000).

79 On the law and literature conjunction generally and from very varying perspectives, see the following: Martha Nussbaum, *Poetic Justice: The Literary Imagination and Public Life* (1995); Richard Posner, *Law and Literature: A Misunderstood Relation* (1988); Richard Weisberg, *Poethics and Other Strategies of Law and Literature* (1992); John Fischer, "Reading Literature/Reading Law: Is There a Literary Jurisprudence?" 72 *Tex. L. Rev.* 135 (1993); Judith Resnik, "Changing the Topic," 7 *Austl. Feminist L.J.* 95 (1996); and Richard Weisberg, "The Law-Literature Enterprise," 1 *Yale J.L. and Human.* 1 (1988). For a critique of the exhortation in law and literature debates for the judge to "get literary," see Jonathan Morrow, "Soft Times: The 'Literary Imagination' as Poetic Injustice," 10 *Austl. Feminist L.J.* 35 (1998). The invocation of literary texts by the majoritarian judges in the Federal Court and High Court decisions in *X v. The Commonwealth* would seem to support Morrow's contention that literature has no necessarily humanizing effect on the personality of the judge.

80 I have explored the implications of this argument for a contemporary jurisprudence of judgment in McVeigh et al., supra note 32, at 122–29.

Contributors

Paul Schiff Berman is a professor at the University of Connecticut School of Law.

Peter Brooks is Tripp Professor of Humanities and director of the Whitney Humanities Center at Yale University.

Wai Chee Dimock is a professor of English and American studies at Yale University.

Anthony Paul Farley is a professor of law at the Boston College School of Law.

Shoshana Felman is Thomas Donnelley Professor of French and Comparative Literature at Yale University.

Carol J. Greenhouse is a professor of anthropology at Princeton University.

Paul W. Kahn is Robert Winner Professor of Law and Humanities at Yale Law School.

Naomi Mezey is an associate professor at Georgetown University Law Center.

Toby Miller is an associate professor of cinema studies at New York University.

Austin Sarat is William Nelson Cromwell Professor of Jurisprudence and Political Science at Amherst College.

Jonathan Simon is a professor of law at the University of Miami School of Law.

Alison Young is a professor of criminology at the University of Melbourne.

Index

Library of Congress Cataloging-in-Publication Data
Cultural analysis, cultural studies, and the law : moving beyond legal
realism / edited by Austin Sarat and Jonathan Simon.
Includes index.
ISBN 0-8223-3107-1 (cloth : alk. paper)
ISBN 0-8223-3143-8 (pbk. : alk. paper)
1. Culture and law. 2. Sociological jurisprudence. I. Sarat, Austin.
II. Simon, Jonathan, 1959–
K487.C8C85 2003   340'.115—dc21   2002156642